Perspectives in Immigrant and Minority Education

Edited by
Ronald J. Samuda
Queen's University
Kingston, Canada

and

Sandra L. Woods
Florida International University
Miami, U.S.A.

"This book was developed pursuant to a Teacher Corps grant awarded to The School Board of Dade County, Florida and Florida International University for and on behalf of the Florida Board of Regents."

UNIVERSITY
PRESS OF
AMERICA

LANHAM • NEW YORK • LONDON

DEDICATION

To William L. Smith

Formerly Director, Teacher Corps, Dr. Smith is Director of Overseas Program, U.S. Office of Education, Washington, D.C. This spring, Secretary of Education, Dr. Terrell Bell, nominated Dr. Smith for the Presidential Rank Award of Distinguished Senior Executive. On October 14, 1981, President Ronald Reagan conferred on Dr. Smith the rank of Distinguished Executive at a ceremony in the Rose Garden of the White House. Dr. Smith, who was one of 25 Federal employees to receive this distinction, has noted that the Teacher Corps, forerunner of the Center for Urban and Minority Education (CUME), has the greatest potential for providing school districts, communities, colleges and universities with a demonstration of how to effectively bring about institutional change in the area of personnel development. Each one of the Teacher Corps experiences in all 50 states, the District of Columbia, Puerto Rico and in most of our island territories, embodies a commitment to the strengthening of opportunities for children from low-income families.

The project presented or reported herein was performed pursuant to a Teacher Corps grant to Florida International University and Dade County Schools from the United States Office of Education. The points of view expressed in this book are those of the authors and do not necessarily reflect the position or policy of the U.S. Office of Education and no official endorsement by the U.S. Office of Education should be inferred.

CONTENTS

PART IV PROGRAMS AND CURRICULUM STRATEGIES

CONTRIBUTORS

James A. Banks
H. Prentice Baptiste, Jr.
Milton Blount, Jr.
John W. Berry
Joann Coates-Gibson
John G. Corbett
Ray Chodzinski
Guarione M. Diaz
James Dowis
Steven Fain
Carol A. Fineman
Erwin Flaxman
Shelley Goldman
Olga M. Garay
Deborah Goldstein
Delia C. Garcia
Asa Grant Hilliard III
Allan B. Henkin
M. Ahmed Ijaz
I. Helene Ijaz
Sharon Kossack

Wallace E. Lambert
Magaly Rodriguez Mossman
George S. Morrison
Anthony Maingot
Liem Thanh Nguyen
Ralph Robinett
Sylvia H. Rothfarb
Ronald J. Samuda
John F. Stack, Jr.
James T. Stein
Donald M. Taylor
Jethro W. Toomer
Horace Jerome Traylor
Adolph A. Thompson
Sylvia M. Unzueta
Aaron Wolfgang
Frank B. Wilderson, Jr.

In Consultation with

Stanley Wilson
Irwin S. Loibman
Adolph A. Thompson
Tee S. Greer

Carlos M. Alvarez
Zuzel F. Suarez
Edwina Hoffman
Joseph DeChurch

PREFACE

By Gregory B. Wolfe

Florida has become America's leading living laboratory for examining and experiencing the problems associated with the assimilation of new immigrants. The University is proud to participate as a 'laboratory technician' and counselor in helping public and private agencies to come to grips with the delivery system requirements in education as well as social services that serve refugees humanely and professionally. We are also grateful for the opportunity to get closer to and more deeply involved in resolving some of the concerns of refugees as a social group and helping hasten their membership into our community life.

The University has been a beneficiary of the new wave of immigration that Florida, and especially the Miami region, has experienced in recent years. The ranks of the student body and faculty have surely been strengthened by it. Our departments in arts and sciences and the professions have gained wisdom and immensely important research opportunities as a result of the immigrant populations' arrival. In light of recent determinations made by the U.S. Supreme Court, we are perhaps readier now than some other institutions to deal with the new responsibilities that are developing for all educational and social agencies concerned with helping refugees, especially younger ones, to become good Americans.

This monograph is an example of how the faculty are responding to new opportunities for service that have been generated by refugees in Southeast Florida. It deals with the crucially vital matter of how non-English speaking ethnic minorities and their teachers communicate in an environment that promotes learning and which advances prospects for its applications. I am confident that it will contribute to increased understanding of the immigrant and minority communities and to the more effective service of our educational system to them.

PART ONE
OVERVIEW AND PERSPECTIVES

OVERVIEW AND PERSPECTIVES

This is the first of a set of publications which represent the tangible products of a series of invitational symposia and conferences, held at Florida International University over the past year and a half. In June, 1981, the first invitational seminar occurred under the auspices of The Center for Urban and Minority Education. The context of the seminar series flowed from a realization of the Manifesto of the Center of May 26, 1981, written by the joint Editors of this Monograph.

The Center for Urban and Minority Education (CUME) was officially unveiled at a meeting of the University's Institute for Technical Assistance on April 22, 1981, as a key factor in working toward the solution of immigrant and ethnic minority educational problems. Although the program for CUME grew out of the thrust and pattern of activities originally associated with the Teacher Corps, expanding from the original notion of the latter to become institutionalized as a joint organization linked to both the University's School of Education and the Dade County School Board, the conceptual notion of the center encompasses a larger and greatly expanded role which is more than service to the school systems and community of the Inner-City. The primary goal of the center is to establish an integrative agency at the University to initiate, foster, and implement cooperative endeavors related to urban and minority education. The center sets out, as its essential purpose, to inaugurate and coordinate a three-fold focus in terms of: Research and Publication; Community/Technical Service; and Teacher Training Programs at the preservice, inservice, and graduate levels of intellectual activity.

The contributors to this Monograph participated in an invitational Seminar, *The Comparative Acculturation of Ethnic Minority Immigrants,* June 18-19, 1981, and in a Conference, *The Education of Ethnic Minority Immigrants: Perspectives on the Programs and Strategies,* December 13-16, 1981. The Conference was jointly sponsored by CUME and the South Atlantic Bilingual Education Service Center.

Many of the papers submitted to the first invitational seminar and the subsequent conference were concerned with theoretical matters. The papers which are published as Volume I of the book have set the tone by elucidating the *philosophical and historical bases of multiculturalism and immigrant and minority education* within the context of recent patterns of settlement in the United States, and by charting *perspectives on the ethnic background and patterns of immigration.* On the whole, the papers which are to be published as Volume II will be severely practical: *Counseling, Testing, and Placement;* and *Programs and Curriculum Strategies.* The general issue, however, is the same.

Multiculturalism is a complex issue. A case in point was a national contest recently staged by the *National Association of Bilingual Education* to ascertain the thinking of students on the theme: *What does bilingual education matter to me?* The First-Prize Winner, a ten-year old girl fourth grader, wrote:

> Bilingual education is the only and the best way to learn. I belong to a Spanish-speaking family. I was very afraid when I attended an American school for the first time. I thought nobody would understand me, that I would never be able to learn because I knew no English. I was greatly surprised when my first school-mistress took me by the hand and addressed me in Spanish. I felt at home for I did not feel afraid, and I began to love my school. I am still asking myself: What would I have done if the school were not bilingual? And to you who are reading these words, I ask: What would you do if you were in a place where you did not know the name for anything, what you had to do, or how to behave? I am very certain that you would run away screaming because you would feel absurd and silly. If these words do not convince you, try using any language you do not understand and see what happens. From my experience I can say that bilingual education has meant everything in my life, since my wish is to return to school each day to receive the education necessary for living in two worlds: English and Spanish.*

Within the context of recent patterns of settlement in the United States, educationalists who teach their students to teach, feel that their methods are not wholly adequate. They may teach psychology, but do they enable the teachers-to-be to *understand* their pupils? This matter of 'understanding' as distinct from knowing about multiculturalism was discussed at the first invitational seminar and subsequent conference. There are those of us who believe that the best way to accommodate an immigrant is to hasten their assimilation into the host culture by emphasizing the acquisition of the language and folkways of the host country, regardless of their own heritage.

On the other hand, there are those of us who believe that the encouragement of native and ethnic heritage provides a more viable alternative to the methodology of the 'melting pot'. This dichotomy has been publicized in more recent years and has been made more visible by the massive influx of Third World immigrants to the industrialized countries of the world. Our intention is to provide a vehicle for the various philosophical perspectives so as to enlighten us, not only in terms of the various theoretical stances, but also to give expression to the programs, strategies, and methods which might enhance and augment the education of immigrant and minority individuals who now comprise a significant proportion of the students in South Florida.

*Letter contributed to Correo, *El Miami Herald* by Eva O. Somoza, Coordinadora, Proyecto de Demostracion para las Escuelas Bilingues, Condado de Dade, May 23, 1982.

Now, the educational practitioner must, to do his/her job properly, be trained to develop as sensitive a sounding board as possible in himself/herself by means of which s/he can sense the bewilderment, the hostilities, the anxieties of his/her clients, so that s/he can say: I have felt just like that myself — I understand how it feels. That is why the educationalists, who are anxious to improve the understanding of their students, call in the social workers to help them. This is not the whole story, of course. The educationalists help one another; the social workers may gain from contemplating the problems of the educationalists. The main purpose of such a conference, as emerges from these papers, is to consider methods whereby students entering the teaching profession should achieve insight into the problems of their pupils and clients.

It is, however, futile to consider how to help preservice and inservice teachers to gain insight into other people unless we ourselves understand the problems which the former are facing. An eminent historian, Professor Gilbert Highet, has noted that some of his counterparts have written important books on individual cultures but have made the mistake of treating those cultures in isolation as though each of them were composed only of people interacting with one another and with the physical environment: although, in fact, surrounding ideas and neighboring peoples are a powerful active part of the environment of many civilizations. Highet has suggested that one of the chief relationships between human groups is, in the broadest sense, *educational:* that the history of the world could also be written as a history of *the movement of ideas* from one group of human beings to another. To see whether or not this point of view helps to comprehend more of the destinies of humanity, Adolph Thompson's paper, *The Movement of Ideas from One Group of People to Another: As Dynamic for Collective Enterprise,* reviews evidence which demonstrates that although the history of contacts between civilizations deals principally with contacts involving violence or disruption — so much so that it occasionally views interacting civilizations as assailant and victim — it does bring out the importance of peaceful and educative relationships between different cultures, and sketches certain laws of cultural radiation which explain these relationships in terms of the 'migration of ideas'. The implications of these findings for improving history teaching and learning in the schools are considered.

A different aspect of the predicament of preservice and inservice teachers is given us by Professor Anthony Maingot, who discusses *Relative Power and Strategic Ethnicity in Miami.* Students — and everyone else for that matter — are entangled in the social networks in which we interact. One type of network is concerned with power relations. Professor Maingot pays special attention to these, implying that outmigration of non-Hispanic Whites, combined with the phenomenal growth of the Latin sector, virtually guarantees the trend toward Hispanization of Dade County, Florida. This is conditional on acceptance, and acceptance is conditional on understanding. Mere unintelligible 'forcework' arouses resentment. Is it an advantage or a disadvantage to employ new strategies and materials for the teacher-learner setting in the area to assure a program of bilingual education to assist children of limited English proficiency to improve their English language skills? Rules there must be — barriers to freedom — but if acceptance is to be achieved, the need for such barriers must be made plain, and there should be none for which there is no good reason. In educational (and other) institutions this may call for a drastic revision o. .ae regulations. The attitude of mind of the authority, then, should be tempered by insight into the point of view of those called upon to obey. Experience of such principles of insight, this time into the structure of institutions rather than into the structure of persons, would pave the way toward an improvement of the power network in which the students themselves will hold authoritative status. Maingot's paper has determined what are the key factors to be taken into account in analyzing 'immigration assimilation' and 'acculturation', and has explained the difference between 'strategic acculturation' and 'strategic ethnicity' in Miami.

So much for what one might call the 'raw material'. What is to be done to make it adequate for the tasks that lie ahead? Professor Asa Grant Hilliard III discusses *The Immigrant and the Pedagog*. He expands the theme which has already been indicated: The attempt to understand or to explain either individual or group behavior without reference to information on history and culture is an empirical fallacy and will generate certain error. ... If we had a theory of culture in education, we would be forced to extend our view from a restriction of attention to students to a look at both teachers' and students' cultural dynamics. One of the most interesting contributions made by Dr. Hillard is his attempt to define 'culture pattern', 'cultural quotients', 'cultural concepts', and 'the personality of a given culture' — the simultaneous mixture of feeling and intellectual understanding which must be aimed at.

All this naturally raises the question of selection. What is the rationale and the best way for the American society to help salvage minority languages and cultures and to help develop a new generation of children who could be happy to be both American *and* Hispanic, Haitian or whatever? "It would be inappropriate", says Professors Lambert and Taylor's paper, *Language in the Education of Ethnic Minority Immigrants: Issues, Problems and Methods*, "to let language considerations play the dominant role when there are policy decisions to be made about education for children from immigrant families, even in the case where the immigrant youngster has a home language different from that of the school and of the home nation. ... While keeping the aims of education in the center focus and then taking into consideration the language competencies and weaknesses of ethnic immigrant pupils, policy makers must adjust their perspective to include the host nation peers of the immigrant youngsters. The English-speaking white and black mainstream students are not passive onlookers to the struggles of ethnic immigrants — indeed, their reactions determine the ultimate success or failure of the struggles".

Professor John W. Berry, after defining what the concept 'acculturation' comprehends, went on to observe that: "Our only concern is in the implementation of language-enriched educational programs because the implementation requires that policy-makers be sensitive to the psychological and the social realities of language for all groups in the society — the ethnic immigrant, the mainstream white English-speaking and the mainstream black English-speaking".

In discussing *Shared Problems of Culturally Distinct Peoples Seeking a Place in the Educational Process,* Professor Frank B. Wilderson, Jr. points to the need for counselors to be made aware that most colleges and universities today are beginning to show some responsiveness to the social and cultural needs of Hispanic, Native American and Black students, many of whom are intimidated by the initial college experience and fail to take advantage of those services available to them.

The American system of education is the logical outcome of absorbing into a coherent society people with differing backgrounds but inspired in the main with a determination to be more free in their new home than they were in the old. The influx of Haitian immigrants to South Florida has made for many social, educational, economic and political problems. The Haitian scene is surveyed by Professor Sandra L. Woods and Adolph Thompson in their *Haitian Immigrants in South Florida: Economic, Social and Cultural Issues and Problems.* The paper addresses the vast range of problems faced by an atypical group undergoing acculturation to a new society. This contribution makes profitable and instructive reading for everyone who needs to be prepared to fit in with the regime of the inner-city school in which s/he works by being given insight into comparative structural relations in the respective public school systems in Haiti and the United States. One gathered from the way this topic was debated in some of the discussion groups that this is a very real problem.

The problem presented by the contrast between theory and practice in immigrant and minority education is also touched on by Professors Stack and Corbett in three assumptions about 'crystalization of ethnicity' and 'ethnic conflict' on which the thesis of their paper *The Ethnic Polarization of Miami* is based. Can their analogy of an 'American Beirut' be used to strengthen the teacher learning setting in South Florida?

Guarione M. Diaz's paper *Dade Cuban Immigrants: Integration Patterns and Special Education Needs* points to available data which indicate: Usage of English is related to a higher level of education (in the United States); even among Cuban college graduates, Spanish is spoken more in Miami than in other cities, with large Cuban populations (e.g. Union City); although the Cuban community is making a substantial contribution to Dade County's economic development, the majority of Cubans in the labor force are employed by businesses not owned by other Cubans; by and large, Cuban workers are integrated with the area's work force; whatever entrepreneurship Miami Cubans have shown is in keeping with prescribed goals and values of the host society and thus a positive sign of social integration; and yet the development of ghetto economy which precludes the usage of English to obtain goods, services, and/or employment, acts as a deterrent to integration with the society at large. The implications of the paper raise a number of questions: In the light of the aforegoing, compare the values of Miami and Union City. How do these relate to the different modes of life in each? Is there a relation (however indirect) between environment and values in this comparison? Could you therefore say that environment determines values in immigrant and minority education?

Returning to the notion of 'polarization', Silvia M. Unzueta's paper *The Mariel Exodus: An Unfolding Experience* narrates the untoward events in the inter-relation between the Cuban 'entrants', called Marielitos, and the community life of Dade County, Florida. It concludes that these events, and what has been perceived as inadequate leadership on behalf of Cuban-Americans, have helped to polarize residents of the area to the point that dialogue at present is more difficult to achieve. The implications of the paper have to do with the qualities of leadership best suited to youth, and to improving communication among both Cuban-Americans and Mariel Cubans, and other ethnic cultural groups in the area. After considering their *An Investigation into the Economic, Social and Cultural Patterns of West Indians, Russian Jews, and Indo-Chinese Immigrants in South Florida,* it appears to Professors Shelley Goldman and Stephen Fain that there is much to learn from observing these groups in this moment in time and in this place. Immigration in Miami usually brings visions of Cubans and Haitains to mind. These groups are newsworthy and the media seem to make it clear that each of these groups is experiencing difficulty. ... On the other hand, their efforts have convinced the authors that social progress is being made more effectively by Russian, Vietnamese, and Jamaican immigrants. These groups seem to share something with the European immigrants of one hundred years ago. They are conservative and they are not 'in tune' with a good deal of mainstream culture. They are building on their pasts to create a new future for themselves and their children. Their dream is the American dream and they want to dream it as Americans. The paper appears to support a suggestion that social progress may depend more on the way a thing is done than on what is done.

Given that the intent of Vietnamese to maintain major home characteristics has important implications for educational programs designed to serve these populations, general themes in terms of family patterns and quality of parental involvement emerge in the aforementioned paper by Goldman and Fain and in the paper *Perceived Sociocultural Change among Indochinese Refugees: Implications for Education* by Liem Thanh Nguyen and Alan B. Henkin.

The number of books on the philosophy and practice of multiculturalism does not yet strain the capacity of libraries to house them. Most of this experimentation in educational practice has gone on, as it were, in the periphery. Nowadays, the problems of immigrant and minority education are becoming matters of widespread concern. There is general interest as well as professional interest in such matters as multilingualism. This concern is, we think, an aspect of that increasing social awareness which pervades our age, and finds expression in the rise to prominence in Universities and Colleges of anthropology, sociology and social psychology. It may be somewhat fanciful to suggest that societies, as they become more closely knit, develop a kind of introspective interest in themselves; yet that is what it looks like.

Education we have had for generations; now we — not just a few specialists — ask what it is for. We are told something about meeting the needs of children. We — and not just a few specialists — ask whether these needs are met. We are aware of difficult children, behavior difficulties and the like within the context of recent patterns of settlement in the United States. The pressure of life may, some say, be responsible for an increase in maladjustment, and proof of this is proliferating. What is certain is that more people are asking what is being done about it.

Most of those who attended the seminar series were specialists, and one was aware of the considerable ferment among those professionally engaged in handling people. In our view, this 'ferment' is the sensitive conscious experience of a more widespread 'ferment' in our society. Social workers are engaged in 'handling people'. That, we all know, but so are teachers. *That* was not so obvious. It is, we suggest, a sign of the times that this is taken seriously. If it is taken seriously, what more natural than that social workers, teachers, school administrators, and the trainers of all three categories should come together? This inter-disciplinary collaboration was taken for granted at these conferences and the four parties got down to practical considerations.

Those responsible for these conferences would not wish to make excessive claims, but we do not think it excessive to suggest that they may be the vanguard of a general movement. They are expressing in their actions that concern felt by our society about its immigrant and minority individuals, which is such a striking feature of our times.

THE MOVEMENT OF IDEAS FROM ONE GROUP OF PEOPLE TO ANOTHER: AS DYNAMIC FOR COLLECTIVE ENTERPRISE

By Adolph A. Thompson
Former Jamaican Ambassador
to the Republic of Haiti,
and the Dominican Republic.

PREAMBLE

My assignment is to take a close look at some of the things we know about education for multicultural understanding under conditions of social flux as a basis for re-examination of our practices, in restructuring history teaching and learning situations in the education of ethnic minority immigrants.

According to the late Alfred North Whitehead: "The problem is not how to produce great men but how to produce great societies." A society in flux, in order to escape destruction, must develop the kind of educational structure that will facilitate continuous re-adjustment on the part of its members to changing social patterns. This entails a continued modification of the educational offering for the immature members of society, our children, to an extent that up to now we have not found necessary. Much more than this, however, it entails the adoption of the concept of the multicultural learning society. Simply stated, a multicultural learning society is an educative society which offers its members the opportunity, the facilities, and the incentive to take part in multicultural learning experiences throughout life.

In a sense America has always been moving in the direction of the multicultural learning society. Two significant instances of this movement of ideas from one group of people to another as dynamic for collective enterprise are the Rhodes Scholars and the Fulbright Alumni. In 1981, past recipients of Fulbright scholarships have been riding to the rescue of the prestigious award and other cultural exchange programs facing President Ronald Reagan's budget axe, and making some progress in convincing Congress. Fulbright alumni and other scholars argue that the exchange programs are a good way to educate future foreign leaders about America. Named for former Senator J. William Fulbright, the scholarships have brought about 85,000 students from other countries to the United States since World War II, and have sent about 45,000 Americans abroad to study.

The Arkansas Democrat, who was chairman of the Senate Foreign Relations Committee for many years, says the program gives foreign students, many of whom become leaders, an understanding of America. And he once testified that he doubts the late President Lyndon Johnson would have escalated the Vietnam War had Johnson been a Fulbright alumnus and known more about Asia. "If he had lived in Asia for a year under this program, he would not have engaged in that conflict, I believe", Fulbright told the House Committee three years ago. "This can apply to anybody in a powerful position. I think it's one of the reasons there is so much sympathy and understanding abroad for this country."

In his day, Senator Fulbright had been a Rhodes Scholar. Thirty-two American college students, including an 18-year-old concert pianist, a starting guard on the Army football team, and a former Miami Herald intern, have been selected as 1981 Rhodes Scholars. The winners, who will receive two years of study at Oxford University, include five students from Princeton, three from Yale, and two from the Air Force Academy. The 20 men and 12 women were chosen according to criteria established in 1902 by Cecil John Rhodes, a British diamond and gold magnate and African colonialist, who sought to unite the English-speaking world with scholarships for students who excelled in intellect, character, leadership and physical vigor. Besides the 32 Americans, another 40 Rhodes Scholars will be chosen this year from 16 other countries. All winners are given full tuition and fees for two years of study in any academic field at any of the Oxford colleges plus a living stipend of about $7,000 per year.

Changing the character or the trends of a national education system is a difficult task, involving as it does the traditions, habits, and values of an immense number of people. Still there are some things we can do. Instructional improvement in history teaching and learning in the schools is not the least important of them. Only if history is taught as a way of thinking about men and events — thinking grounded in multicultural knowledge — can it achieve its purposes, one of which is to enable students to face the problems of their own day with a long historical perspective.

The study of human societies has traditionally been divided into two school "subjects" — history which deals with man's story in time, and geography which deals with his contemporary environment and way of life in space. It may be that this distinction is an artificial one; it may be also that the comparatively new studies of sociology and anthropology could be profitably studied at the school level. Anthropology has deep roots in the past, but it took its modern line just over a century ago. It was E. B. Tylor who formulated for the English-speaking world the concept of culture. The opening sentence of his *Primitive Society,* written in 1871, defines the term: "Culture or Civilization, taken in its wider ethnographic sense, is that complex whole which includes knowledge, belief, art, morals, law, custom and any other capabilities and habits acquired by man as a member of society." This definition set the stage for the modern science of anthropology. Though Tylor's definition may have been superseded, it is worthwhile pausing to examine it. Four major elements remain important; (1) it includes the *whole range* of human behavior, not merely some selected aspects; (2) it takes cognizance of the fact that culture refers to *learned* behavior, not a part of man's biological equipment; (3) it recognizes that cultural behavior is *shared by a community,* and is not the peculiar behavior of individuals; and (4) it recognizes that cultural elements from a *unity,* a "complex whole." The history of anthropology as a science may be seen in the development of the concept *Culture.*

The cultural understanding of man has provided the basis for a new way of looking at the behavior of our neighbors and of ourselves. This new way of seeing human behavior has, in turn, causes us to reexamine many of our laws and institutions. There are, after all, three basic ways that we may explain the differences between one people and another. The first way is theological. That is, we may believe in the sons of Shem and the sons of Ham, or that God has created the saved and the damned, or any number of fundamentally theological presumptions which are a part of our cultural heritage. The second way is biological. With the development of the natural sciences, which coincided with the early accumulation of knowledge of human diversity, these variations were increasingly explained in biological terms. Broadly speaking, the diverse human ways of life were like so many different species, each with its own complicated pattern of life. Thus, most human behavior was thought to be "instinctive." In this context, the word *race* was loosely used, so that the French or the Jews or the Hottentots were races, with the sometimes tacit, sometimes overt assumption that Nature, rather than God, had placed each man in his station. Clearly this was the basic intellectual and scientific position during the second half — the Darwinian half — of the nineteenth century. The third way, the anthropological way, of looking at human diversity is to see it fundamentally as a product of culture — that is, as the historically derived lifeways shared by a people and learned by each child as he grows up. Fundamentally, this cultural understanding asserts that the traits of behavior which differentiate one people from another are a product of a process of learning and experience rather than of the process of genetic inheritance. By extension, it asserts that much, though by no means all, of the differences between individuals are also a product of their experience rather than their biological heritage. It elevates learning and reduces instinct as important to understanding differences among men.

Other scholarly disciplines have contributed to both the factual knowledge and the theoretical sophistication of a cultural approach to human behavior; notably history, psychology, and sociology. But the point of view is essentially anthropological, precisely because it is the anthropologist's central concern to deal with the behavioral characteristics of groups. In developing this cultural way of looking at man, anthropology had an advantage over history and sociology because it took direct account of the biological aspects of human nature and could therefore deal directly with the problem of nature versus nurture. Again, anthropology had an advantage over sociology and psychology, because it dealt with peoples of diverse traditions, and was thus freed from the presuppositions of our own culture, and the limitations of a single set of traditions. No science follows a lone course, but while other disciplines have made significant and important contributions to the understanding of culture, it has been anthropology that has taken the central role in the philosophical revolution that has placed culture as the key to understanding human behavior.

The cultural understanding of human diversity now dominates our scientific understanding. Theological and racial explanations are still found among the lay public, and occasionally appear in more scholarly circles. Not only most anthropologists but also intellectuals of other disciplines see human diversity in cultural terms. What is still more important, so do the intellectual leaders of the world at large. We have come to formulate policies in cultural terms, and therefore it behooves us to understand what that means — particularly since there is a tendency in some quarters to overemphasize the cultural factor and to assert too great a malleability of the human animal.

INTRODUCTION

It is possible to see at least three different purposes in the teaching of history. We may think of it as a study pursued purely for its own sake, considering that no one is fully educated who does not know what has happened in the past. The danger of this approach, which is often used to justify a superficial course stretching from the Stone Age to Winston Churchill, is that because of its superficiality the series of historical "events" which are learnt have no real interest for the pupil and are soon forgotten. The famous parody *1066 And All That* illustrates the final result of such a course. Nor can any practicable limits be set to the range of such teaching. If the educated person ought to know in this sense the history of his own country, why not that of Europe, of Russia, of the British Commonwealth, or of America? J. L. Dobson, writing in the *Durham Research Review* (September, 1957) said of this kind of history teaching: "But there is little doubt that the primitive teaching of history in schools before 1870 — history as something to be memorized, without being understood — left the subject with a reputation for dullness and incomprehensibility which has not yet been shaken off entirely. Perhaps of all studies history is the one in which it is easiest to fall under the spell of conventional techniques, so that creative thought and understanding drop out of the picture."

Another approach sees in history a study which, if pursued with understanding and therefore necessarily in a fairly limited field, will help to develop the pupil's capacity for interpreting and even judging human motives. This is clearly the kind of history teaching to which Montaigne was referring when he said, "Do not so much imprint on the pupil's memory the date of the ruin of Carthage as the manners of Hannibal and Scipio; not so much whee

Marcellus died as why it was unworthy of his duty that he died there. Do not teach him so much the narrative part as the business of History", and again, "We only toil and labor to stuff the memory and in the meantime leave the conscience and the understanding unfurnished and void." Finally, there are those who believe that an important purpose of history teaching is to develop in the pupil some understanding not of historical events as they are interrelated, but of the historian's art or technique. We study history, they say, not merely to understand how people and circumstances have interacted in the past and so learn to judge more accurately how they are interacting in the present, but to understand how the historian recreates the past for us.

There is something to be said for all these points of view. Even the first is justified to some extent by the fact that the other two are impossible unless the pupil holds in his mind some framework of historical facts against which he can begin to make judgments. What is neither possible nor desirable is that this framework should cover the whole of history or that the whole of it should be retained in the memory. All three purposes can be fulfilled at almost all levels of history teaching — quite young children can, in a local history project, learn something of the art of the historian — but Dobson is surely right in emphasizing the special danger, in history teaching and the planning of history syllabuses, of an excessive attention to the first.

This paper describes an approach to history which is relatively new. The history of nations and civilizations is usually written in political or economic terms. But within recent years anthropologists, sociologists, and historians have become more deeply interested in the influence of ideas upon human affairs, and have interpreted many important events as results of the movement of fertilizing and challenging thoughts from one group, nation, or civilization to another. The aim of the paper is to outline this conception and give some significant examples to justify it. It suggests that we might do well to think of nations, and tribes, and social groups, and even races, not only as political and social rivals, and not only as economic competitors or collaborators, but also as *pupils and teachers;* that one of the chief relationships between human groups is, in the broadest sense, *educational;* and that if the history of the world were written as a history of *the movement of ideas* from one group of human beings to another, it would illuminate many areas of the past which are now misunderstood and also — although this is not strictly the duty of the historian — give many of us a much needed confidence in the reason and the future of mankind.

POLITICS AND SOCIETY

In comparatively recent history there is one remarkable series of events which is best understood as being educational rather than political or economic. A nation of 30,000,000 people deliberately put itself to school, and in a few years learned how to practice innumerable techniques and manage innumerable ideas it had never touched before. This was Japan.

In 1868 the emperor of Japan publicly took an oath, the Charter Oath, to change and reform the empire. This was clearly an announcement of the policy of an important party among his ministers. The final clause of the oath was this: *Knowledge shall be sought for throughout the world.* From thenceforward it was, and has remained, the permanent policy of the Japanese to learn as much as possible from other nations. This is all the more remarkable because the Japanese are proud people, who dislike putting themselves in a dependent position such as that of pupil to teacher, and they had for many generations distrusted and hated foreigners. But they have a strong will, and once they had determined on this policy they carried it through. Those who determined on it were few in number, but they were surely makers of history. One of them was Hirobumi Ito. While still a very young man, he persuaded his feudal lord, Choshu, to abandon the traditional bows and arrows for rifles and artillery. Soon after that, with his lord's encouragement, he and four others committed a crime for which the penalty was death: they went abroad. They spent a year in London, studying. On their return, they became leaders of the progressive party in Japan. In 1882 Ito was commissioned to prepare a Constitution for his country, which until then had had none and had lived in a sort of medieval anarchy with civil wars mitigated by dictatorship. Taking a large staff, Ito went through the countries of Europe, interviewing distinguished people and studying the working of various systems of constitutional government. Seven years later, in 1889, after many discussions and preliminary legislative acts, the new constitution of Japan was promulgated by the emperor. It was modeled on the constitution of Bavaria. The emperor's speech was heard by scores of noblemen and officials. All of them wore European official dress — with one lonely exception, Prince Shimadzu of Satsuma. With his hair dressed in the old style, he appeared in the beautiful medieval costume which all Japanese gentlemen had worn for centuries and had now, in less than a lifetime, dropped. History moves faster through education than through warfare.

Within the same generation other equally revolutionary changes were made in Japan, all by learning from abroad. The old feudal system was abolished, and the old degrees of rank were forgotten: a powerful new hierarchy of princes, marquesses, counts, viscounts, and barons was created on the European model. In 1871 the Chinese calendar, so cumbersome and inaccurate was abandoned, and the Western calendar officially adopted. Until then, Japanese money had been rather like the money of medieval Europe: in 1868 there were four kinds of gold coins, two kinds of silver coins as well as bars and globes of silver, six types of cash, and 1600 different currencies of paper money. This reflected the old division of the country into quasi-independent clan territories. It also allowed the first foreign businessman who got into Japan to drain away almost all the gold in the country. But in 1872 the Bank of Japan was established, and in a few years the currency was stable. The Bank of Japan was modeled on the Bank of Belgium.

In the same way, the Japanese built up their navy and their army. First, they sent a mission to Europe to study the organization and training of contemporary defense forces. Then they returned and established the groundwork: central dockyards, arsenals, training schools, a universal draft law, and so on. Then they engaged foreign instructors — a British naval mission for the fleet and a Prussian military mission (headed by General Meckel) for the army. Only a few years later, the navy was efficient enough to destroy the Chinese fleet, and the army of peasants and factory workers overthrew a powerful force of rebellious clansmen in a dangerous civil war. The subsequent history of the Japanese army and navy we know.

The Japanese did not merely go abroad to learn. Under the Charter Oath they brought in no less than 5000 men and women teachers from abroad, including 1200 Americans. (They were first called *yatoi,* 'hired aliens,' and later, when they justified themselves, *o yatoi,* 'honorable hired aliens.') W. E. Griffis, who was one of them, recalled how strange it was to teach young men who were longing for knowledge and who eagerly received all the instruction he could give them, and then walk home along streets that were still in the Middle Ages, passing (it might well be) the corpse of a poor man on whom a samurai had tested a new backswing of his powerful sword. In a panegyric on his colleagues, Griffis cries: "Noble are the records of Pumpelly in mining, of Brunton in lighthouse engineering ... of Knipping in meteorology ... of Milne in initiating the science of seismology, of Lyman in revealing true geology, of Baeltz and Scriba in anatomy, physiology, and ethnology."

Of course, it would be a misrepresentation to suggest that all this learning came to Japan with lightning rapidity and utterly without preparation. As early as 1741 the Shogun Yoshimune had ordered two scholars to learn Dutch (the Dutch being then the only Europeans allowed to visit Japan); and in 1771 a Japanese physician, Sugita, got hold of a German-Dutch manual of anatomy, tested its truth by watching a dead body being dissected, and then had it translated and published. Western painting, geography, and astronomy were beginning to be studied about the same time. But all this was, proportionately, only preparation for the great educational revolution of the 1860's and succeeding decades.

The whole story is astonishing. It is even more astonishing to realize that it happened not once in the history of Japan but twice. Far back in the Dark Ages, Japanese had apparently been a Mongolian tribe which (like the "Indians" of America) drifted eastward in search of a home. They found it in the islands, which they conquered and cultivated. As they grew in numbers and security, they determined to become civilized. They were on the fringe of the highly civilized Chinese empire; and in A.D. 645 they adopted much of its civilization without becoming its vassals. From China they learned, and introduced into their own society, a centralized bureaucracy; Buddhism as a higher religion; writing, based on Chinese script; the principles of their fine arts, which are really Chinese art simplified; and many other appurtenances of civilization. And how it has happened a third time. The United States, after defeating Japan militarily and truncating its power economically, occupied the country for a number of years. And which was the most important act, the one which will have most powerful effects in the future? Military conquest, or economic mastery? Or will it prove to have been the process of education that took place during those years?

There, then, is one example of the movement of ideas from one group to another, and of the enormous historical effects which this movement can have. Of course, this way of looking at history raises special problems of its own. For instance, we should like to know how the transference of ideas into the minds of the Japanese was made; why it was initiated, what motives drove men like Ito and Sugita; who were the leaders in the movement, and what was their relation to the rest of the country. We shoudl also like to understand the differentiae: for instance, why did the learning process work out so differently in Japan and in its neighboring country, China? We must think over these questions as we go on.

There are many more examples of this movement of ideas as an important historical force. The story of Turkey is another.

When the Turks entered modern history in the Middle Ages, they were a small group of nomads moving westward out of central Asia. Full of vigor and energy, they drove in upon the eastern Roman empire, attacked it doggedly for generations, and ultimately took it over. Like the Japanese, they remained a medieval nation until almost within living memory, and they have retained some medieval traits today. But after the Ottoman empire was lost in 1918, the Turks — or rather the governing group of the Turks — determined to learn from European nations and to convert Turkey into a modern, Westernized people. Within ten short years, between 1925 and 1934, Roman letters were introduced (no books were printed in Arabic script after 1928); universities and schools were reorganized and enlarged; the metric system of measurement was introduced; polygamy was abolished, and women were given the vote; a new civil coce of law was adopted, modeled on Swiss law; English (rather than Arabic, Persian, or French) was made the second language; the old titles, such as pasha, were dropped; the fez of the Middle East was abolished and the hat substituted (similarly the wearing of European dress is official in Japan for nearly all important functions).

The enormous results of these two enterprises, in Japan and Turkey, can be measured by comparing these nations with other potentially powerful groups in the Middle and Far East. Suppose that the densely populated isle of Java, or the rich land of Burma, had been educated in the same way as the Japanese educated themselves; or suppose that the swarming millions of Egyptians had determined to learn from the West in the same way as the Turks: who can doubt that the history of the world would have been radically different — especially in the last sixty and the coming twenty years?

From an earlier period there is a similar but even more important case of history being made by education. This is the process which began in ancient Rome about 250 B.C.

Like the Turks and the Japanese, the Romans first appear in history as a simple people, brave, conservative, uneducated, peripheral, and rather unpromising. They were peasants clustered about a few little towns in a fertile plain, mixed (if the legends are true) with outlaws and masterless men, and dominated for a time by the brilliant and sinister Etruscans, a far more highly civilized race; one might have expected them to remain rooted in their fields for many centuries while history swept over their heads like the changing seasons. But some obscure and almost unanalyzable drive propelled them outward: they grew and grew, they learned and adapted, until they became the conquerors and defenders of the civilized world. Now, the Romans had many merits which fitted them to be governors. They believed in law, not in arbitrary will. They believed in self-discipline rather than self-expression. They drew no color line. They were fine technologists — road-builders and engineers and town planners: it was really the Romans, with their enormous irrigation systems, who transformed the Western Mediterranean land region from jungles and deserts into a rich country of orchards and vineyards and prosperous fields, keeping it so for five hundred years. Even if they had done no more than abolish savagery, organize production and commerce, and establish a world-wide rule of law, they would have been remembered as the makers of a material civilization.

The Romans knew, however, that civilization was much more than material wealth. They determined to introduce meaning into their culture, to give themselves more than what they could eat and drink and play with. In the second century they conquered Greece; and almost at once they became its prisoners.

To express this in our own terms, the Romans became the willing pupils of Greece. Like the Japanese in the nineteenth century, they brought in tutors from abroad: Greek experts to lecture to them, Greek scientists to improve their knowledge and practice of the sciences, Greek philosophers to live with them. Many of the greatest Romans had Greek thinkers living permanently in their homes, in order to keep up their intellectual standards by constant discussion of lofty and difficult subjects. For instance, the younger Cato, the republican opponent of Caesar, the man whom we think of as a stern traditional Roman, was in fact a thinker trained by the Stoic philosopher Athenodoru Cordylio, who lived in his home. Roman homes were decorated by Greek artists. Their literature was formed on Greek models, with the exception of a very few literary types, such as satire; and the proudest boast of a Roman author was that he had, in his own language, equaled one of the Greek masters.

The result of this was not, as we might expect, to create a culture that was a mere copy of Greece. By tradition, by social structure, by education, the Romans differed profoundly from the Greeks. They knew that they were relatively stupid, so they learned from Greece; they felt that they were insensitive to art, so they got Gree artists to make their lives beautiful; but they were not ashamed of their own qualities — moral sense, patriotism, responsibility, and a consciousness of time that the eternally youthful Greeks never possessed. They knew their language was less flexible and more limited in range than Greek; but they were not ashamed of its power and energy and its somber music. Therefore they wrote poems, plays, speeches, philosophical dialogues, and histories which no Greek could have composed, and yet which were clearly modeled on Greek types.

In fact, the Romans contributed to a civilization that had two phases, two complementary aspects, harmonizing like treble and bass in a great instrument. The Greeks produced philosophers; the Romans produced statesmen, who had learned from the Greeks to be philosophers too, and therefore greater statesmen. The Greeks developed oratory; the Romans put ethical and social content into it. The Greeks worked out exquisite lyric meters and filled them with delicate feeling. The Romans took over the form, deepened the feeling, and added profounder thought. Before the rise of Rome it is possible to talk of Greek culture; but from 250 B.C. or so it is really better to speak of the Greco-Roman civilization, to which both belonged, in which one had been master and the other pupil, and in which finally both were friendly rivals and challenging collaborators.

The Roman Empire. The very phrase sounds as though we were writing history exclusively in military and political terms, to which an economic explanation might be added. But such descriptions are inadequate. It would be more revealing to consider the whole complex as an educational process. Of course it can be portrayed as a series of bloody conquests and vain rebellions, with the eagles of the legions turned to vultures above the bleeding bodies of myriads of unhappy tribesmen; and it can certainly be described as a tremendous racket, into which economic exploitation and waste ran wild and wrecked a whole society. But there was something else in it, and that something else was the aspect of more permanent value: its will and its ability to educate. It is for their educational value that we still study the classics of Greece and Rome; and it is for their power to educate that we admire the Romans. We are their pupils.

For it was Rome who civilized and taught the barbarians who were the ancestors of the Spaniards, the Gauls, the British, the Balkan peoples, the Roumanians, and the North Africans. Rome found them scattered tribes living in the early Iron Age, illiterate and poor. In a few generations she taught them agriculture, trade, architecture, and industry; in a few more she taught them law, philosophy, literature, and religion. Perhaps these people could scarcely have assimilated Greek civilization directly, even if they had had the opportunity: it was too intense, too difficult, too highly developed. But as it passed through the coarser mind of Rome, it became comprehensible and acceptable to the recently civilized savages. Also, Rome added much that was her own: notably the sense of law; and an un-Greek seriousness about religion.

For surely the greatest lesson taught through Rome was Christianity. Like so much else in that civilization it began in the Middle East, and in its early days was Greek-speaking; then it was translated into Latin and transformed into something Roman. Both the Greek and the Roman elements can be traced in Christianity, as well, of course, as the original Hebrew foundation; but most of *our* Christianity reminds one of Rome.

We have looked at three cases in which history was made by education: Japan; Turkey; and the civilization of Greece and Rome, which flowed into our ancestors' minds, which indeed is still educating us. Surely it is scarcely possible to understand any nation, or any group, through its *own* history alone; surely we must always inquire, "Who were its most powerful teachers and what did it learn from them?" Take one further example, the impact of Africans on the New World. The survival and creativity of West Africans in the New World is perhaps one of the greatest accomplishments of a captive people in the history of mankind. These achievements are all the more remarkable given the circumstances under which the Africans were brought to the New World: they were captured and torn away from their native lands; they were subjected to industrial slavery; and once emancipated had to bear the obloquy and the prejudice of domineering whites. Because of these circumstances much of the African's contribution to New World cultures and societies will never be known or acknowledged, for fear that this would enhance his status — something that his masters and detractors wished to avoid. Dubois certainly had this in mind when he said: "... the American Negro is and has been a distinct asset to this country and has brought a contribution without which America could not have been; and ... perhaps the essence of our so-called Negro problem is the failure to recognize this fact and to continue to act as though the Negro was what we once imagined and wanted to imagine him — a representative of a subhuman species fitted only for subordination."

Indeed, the African's gifts to the New World have been largely denigrated; and when his genius has forced recognition, his creations have been pre-empted and used for profit by the dominant groups. The history of the African in the New World is a history of striving for recognition; of being frustrated in the quest; but of persisting against great odds. At long last it appears as if the genius of the New World African is being permitted to flower, and his contribution to the World is being recognized — not because they were absent, but because he, and the continent from whence he came are being freed from European domination.

A number of scholars and publicists have attributed the resilience of Africans in the New World to a "childlike nature" which made it possible for them to adjust easily to the most unsatisfactory social situation. In contrast to the American Indians, who preferred extinction to slavery, the Africans allegedly accepted their lot and even happily. The African was held to have survived because he was the "most docile and modifiable" of all races. He was believed never to have evolved a civilization of his own, with the result that he readily took the tone and color of his social environment, assimilating to the dominant culture with little resistance.

Herskovits believed that the African's resilience was due to a deep-seated tradition in Africa, especially in West Africa. He said that in this area it was common for both conquerors and conquered to take over one another's gods. Moreover, the West Africans deemed it more advantageous to give way to a point of view against which they could not prevail, than to persist in their attitude, however firmly they might hold an opinion. Thus the African reacted to his captivity and sojourn in the New World with a great deal of pragmaticism. He recognized the power of the whites and "unconsciously" identified with and adapted the culture of those who possessed power and wealth.

The problem with the above hypotheses is that, when not downright derogatory, they are completely inadequate to explain the complex reaction of the African to the captivity, enslavement, and oppression over the past five hundred years. It is a moot point whether the Negro African is the most adaptable member of the human family. The fact remains that his biocultural adaptation to West Africa did not stand him in good stead when Europeans with a more complex socio-cultural system appeared on the coast, seized or bought his people, shipped them away, and subsequently conquered and colonized his societies. Thus, adaptability *qua* adaptability is a two-way street: some kinds of adaptations make for viability; others do not. Moreover, to say that the African in the new world adapted, and in adapting, survived, is to deny him that foresight, creativity, and intelligence that was so characteristic of him during many centuries of a rather difficult existence. What indeed the history of the West African in the New World shows is that despite an economic system that reduced him to chattel slavery; despite the continued denial of his humanity and his rights to life, liberty, and the pursuit of happiness; and despite the claim that he "invented and created nothing," he was an important factor in the development of the New World, and his embattled descendants continue to influence its evolution.

Without the African, the European would have had difficulty exploring, conquering, and developing the New World. Eric Williams once said: "The Western World is in danger of forgetting today what the Negro has contributed to Western Civilization. The American continent would have had to pay a high price for the luxury of remaining a white man's country." According to some tradition Africans accompanied Columbus on the first voyages of discovery of the New World, and the captain of one of his ships, the Pinta, was "pietro Alonzo, el Negro." It is a fact that Nuflo de Olano, an AFrican, and about thirty black slaves journeyed with Balboa to the Pacific Ocean in 1513, and built a ship for him. Cortes took Negroes with him for the Conquest of Mexico in 1519, and in 1526, Pizzaro took both Mulattoes and Negroes with him to conquer Peru. When, during the course of this expedition, Almagro, the co-commander with Pizzaro, was wounded in the right eye by a dart, and was pressed upon by the Indians, "he would have been left for dead if he had not been rescued by a Negro slave of his." In 1527, Negroes accompanied Aylion on his expedition northward from the Florida Peninsula to found a settlement, San Miguel, near what the English who came later were to call Jamestown. They also accompanied Narvaez on his ill-fated expedition to the southwestern part of what became the United States in 1526, and when he died, served his successor, Cabeza de Vaca in 1527. One of the Africans, Estevanico or Estevanillo, who took part in those two expeditions, was later (1539) to carve a name for himself in the annals of exploration of the American Southwest by first reaching the fabled "Seven Cities of the Zuni." There were few places either in North or South America where Africans did not go with the Spanish explorers. When several centuries later, in 1909, Commodore Perry's expedition finally reached the North Pole, Matthew A. Henson, an Afro-American, was with him.

Africans not only heoped the Spaniards explore the New World, they helped them conquer it. Africans fought with Francisco de Montejo in Honduras in 1539 and one who had learned the local language was sent to burn the Indian villages. And in 1534 in Peru, about thirty Africans were part of a military force of some seventy persons who fought the local inhabitants. In the course of these battles, Africans also lost their lives.

The New World colonists' need for labor was the primary reason for Atlantic slave trade. The shortage of manageable labor in the New World quickly became apparent to Columbus, and profiting from his earlier experience with the slave trading off the African coast, he looked to that source for labor. However, it was Columbus' replacement, Nicholas de Ovando, who first authorized to take African slaves to the New World.

In 1501 Ferdinand and Isabella informed him that "No Jews, Moors, or new converts wre to go to the Indies, or to be permitted to remain there; but Negro slaves born in the power of Christians were to be allowed to pass to the Indies, and the officers of the royal revenue were to receive the money to be paid for their permits." These slaves reached Santo Domingo on April 15, 1502, but significantly, they revolted against their assignment. Ovando wrote the Crown and "solicited that no Negro slaves should be sent to Hispaniola, for they fled amongst the Indians and taught them bad customs, and never could be captured." However, despairing of the shortage and quality of labor, and putting wealth before the fear of the influence of African slaves on the Indian population, Ovando soon appealed to the Spanish crown for additional African slaves.

The Spaniards, and almost all the Europeans who wished to develop the New World, wanted African labor. Firstly, the Africans were held to be quite strong; and, secondly, they were considered a cheap bargain. Thus less than one hundred years after Columbus' voyage the Africans were becoming what Bergenroth was to call the "strength of the Western World."

The Portuguese competitors of the Spaniards in the New World quite early recognized the need for African labor. According to Arthur Ramos: "Negro labor made possible in large measure the creation of a Brazilian civilization. It was the slave who toiled in the cane fields, picked the coffee berry, and extracted precious metals from the mines."

The English, who challenged Spanish and Portuguese monopoly of New World territories, also appreciated the importance of African labor. Even before they made serious attempts to colonize the New World, John Hawkins and other English freebooters were already participating in the lucrative slave trade. It was not until 1619 that some of the English settlers in America were to procure slaves, and this they did, not from English freebooters, but from the Dutch. Some of the farming colonies in the southern part of English America felt they had to have slaves, and slaves were eagerly sought in South Carolina. In contrast, others like Georgia and the New England colonies disliked the use of slave labor. Oglethorpe of Georgia attempted to ban both rum and the slave traffic "refusing to suffer slavery (which is against the Gospel as well as the fundamental law of England) to be authorized under our authority." Nevertheless, in Georgia, as in New England, Virginia, New Jersey, Delaware and other colonies, many of the inhabitants were in favor of slavery. Africans were brought across colonial boundaries and enslaved for life. And later, African slavery, made more profitable by King Cotton, was to be one of the factors in the Civil War.

African labor was deemed necessary for the development of the British Islands in the Caribbean. Eric Williams stated: "It was the Negro, without whom the islands would have remained uncultivated and might as well have been at the bottom of the sea, who made these islands into the prizes of war and diplomacy, coveted by the statesmen of all nations ... Between 1640 and 1667, when sugar was introduced, the wealth of Barbados increased forty times. All the European wars between 1660 and 1815 were fought for the possession of these valuable Caribbean islands and for the privilege of supplying the "tons" of labor needed by the sugar plantation. Between 1760 and 1813 St. Lucia changed hands seven times."

However, one important consequence of the introduction of sugar and African labor in the West Indies was that white colonists were driven out. The white population in Barbados declined until it is now only five per cent of the total. Whites in Antigua and Nevis were also pushed out by sugar and slaves. Many of these small farmers and artisans moved from island to island and finally ended up in the United States, where some of their descendants may have signed the American Declaration of Independence. At least one of the revolutionaries, Alexander Hamilton, was born in Nevis.

The French, who seized Guadeloupe and Martinique from the Spaniards in 1635 and occupied the western third of Hispaniola in 1697, first tried to colonize these islands with indentured servants, and a few African slaves. Both the indentured servants and the Africans proved inadequate for the task, and the French formed trading companies primarily to supply their colonies with slaves. Even in the frozen wastes of Canada, the resident French colonists asked for African labor. African captives were imported to Canada by the French; others were brought in by the British who migrated to Canada with their slaves.

When the Dutch took over Surinam from the British by treaty in 1674 they found a colony already inhabited by English planters from the West Indies and Jewish planters from both england and Portugal (by way of Brazil). These people had brought African labor into the territory when sugar, "the 'money-making' industry was introduced into Surinam." From 1674 to 1807 the Dutch introduced some 300,000 slaves into Surinam. According to Johnstons, "the Dutch were hard taskmasters; as slaveholders disliked perhaps more than the British or the British Americans."

A number of Northern European countries: the Duchy of Courland, brandenburgh, Sweden, and Denmark attempted to establish plantations in the New World, but only the Danes succeeded in doing so. Between 1666 and 1733 the Danes acquired the islands of St. Thomas, St. Croix, and St. John either by annexation or by purchase and started to introduce Africans from Ghana (Gold Coast) in 1680. The Danes were often hard taskmasters and attempted to get as much slaves and profit as they could. For example, "Sugar cultivation covered every square mile of utilizable soil on St. Croix, and the slave population of this island in 1792 must have risen to sixty thousand."

The first Africans sent to the New World were taken from Spain, and must have come originally from the general area between Senegal and Sierra Leone. However, once the New World was really opened up for colonization and plantations the primary areas of procurement shifted southward. Baohen states that during the height of the traffic most of the slaves were exported from "the region between modern Ghana and the Cameroons, hence the coastline became known as the Slave Coast."

Africans lost their dominant demographic position in the New World because of large-scale white migration and through absorption by the dominant European groups. Even in the United States where miscegenation was illegal or tabooed, the African population's percentage declined through absorption and through massive white immigration. Thus whereas in 1790 the 757,203 persons of African descent made up 19.3 per cent of the population, the 22.6 million persons of African descent in 1970 represented only about 11 per cent of the population. The economic impact of Africans in the New World was far more impressive and important than the demographic impact. As Dubois once pointed out: "The primary reason for the presence of the African in America was, of course, his labor." As we saw above, the early European colonists did not believe that the New World could be developed without African labor, and the people of Africa, especially the West Africans, were imported to be the "hewers of wood and the drawers of water." There was no kind of work in the New World that the African did not perform.

Coming historically after mining, but superseding it as the main economic activity of the Africans in the New World, was of course, agriculture. Africans were used as farmers almost everywhere that commercial crops were grown. Tobacco, like sugar, equally became one of the New World's gifts to the Old, thanks in large part to the industry of the African. Ortis states: "It was the Negroes of Hispaniola who quietly came to esteem the qualities of tobacco and not only copied from the Indians the habits of smoking it, but were the first to cultivate it on their owners' plantations. They said it 'took away their weariness' to use Oviedo's words. But the Spaniards still looked askance at it. 'Negro stuff' ... but by the middle of the sixteenth century in Havana, where each year the Spanish fleets assembled and set out across the ocean in convoy, tobacco had already become an article of trade, and it was the Negroes who carried on the business. The whites realized that they were missing a good venture, and the authorities issued ordinances forbidding the Negroes to go on selling tobacco to the fleets. The Negro could no longer sell or cultivate tobacco except for his own use; the Negro could not be a merchant. From then on, the cultivation and trade in tobacco was the economic privilege of the white man."

Thus, here in the economic sphere, as it was later to be true in most areas of life, the dominant Europeans were to ensure that they profitted from every contribution the African made to the development of the New World.

The African bore the brunt of the economic development of Haiti, but the white man profited from its riches. Harry Johnston declared: "Perhaps nowhere in America was existence made more delightful for the White man; and this small territory of ten or eleven thousand square miles produced during the eighteenth century more sugar, coffee, chocolate, indigo, timber dye-woods, drugs, and spices than all the rest of the West Indies put together."

There is a wide consensus that African labor contributed immensely to the development of Brazil, Ramos states. "It was the slave who toiled in the cane fields, picked the coffee berry and extracted precious metals from the mines." Tannenbaum tells us that "in Brazil the Negro was so much the laborer that no one else seemed to labor at all, and until very recently (c. 1940) it was considered unseemly even to carry a small parcel in the city of Rio." Mawe said, after his trip to Brazil, that the Negro seemed to be the most intelligent person he met because every occupation, skilled and unskilled, was in the Negro's hands. Harry Johnston concurs, and with his usual patronage, declared: "The irrepressible Negro and Negroid — you may dislike their physiognomy, call them fop, gorilla, and other disagreeable names, but they always come up smiling and bear little malice — enters all careers, serves in all trades, professions and employments in Brazil, from humblest to nearly the highest, from the scavenger and sewage collector to the priesthood, college professorships, party-leadership, even perhaps to the presidential throne."

The rhetoric aside, we find that in addition to working as miners in Minas Geraes, the Africans, especially the Mandingoes from West Africa, were successful cattle-breeders in the Matto Grasso. The Africans taught the

Portuguese "many useful practices in connection with the breeding and keeping of cattle," and "even imparted those gifts to his hybrids with the Amerindians and with the white man." Africans had almost exclusive monopoly of blacksmith's work in Matto Grasso, and made all sorts of implements for the whites and Amerindians among whom they lived.

The economic impact of Africans on the United States was quite substantial. Dubois was substantially correct when he declared: "The Negro worked as farmhand and peasant proprietor, as laborer, artisan and inventor, and as servant in the house, and without him, America as we know it, would have been impossible." This was especially true in the South, but even in the northern states which were largely settled by colonists, Africans comprised 25 per cent of the labor force in 1790, and did a great deal of work. Their role in the production of the great export crops can be gauged from the following data: "In 1619, 20,000 pounds of tobacco went from Virginia to England. Just before the Revolutionary War, 100 million pounds a year were being sent, and at the beginning of the twentieth century, 800 million pounds were raised in the United States alone. The cotton crop rose correspondingly. England, the chief customer at first, consumed 13,000 bales in 1781, 572,000 in 1820, 871,000 in 1830, and 3,366,000 bales in 1860. The United States raised six million bales in 1880, and at the beginning of the twentieth century raised eleven million bales annually."

Besides performing agricultural labor the Africans (slaves and freed men) in the United States were employed as miners, ironworkers, sawmill hands, house and ship carpenters, wheelwrights, coppers, tanners, shoemakers, millers and bakers, and mechanics. After the abolition of slavery, Africans continued to work at these trades as well as in the developing service industries and professions among their own people.

It is ironic that despite the economic contribution that Africans made to the economic development of the New World, they are accused of "laziness" and their contribution either belittled or denied. Of course, the charge of laziness, whether levelled against the rebellious Africans in Haiti or the enslaved brothers in the other countries, was very much a rationalization for slavery, and a device to assuage white guilt. But more insidious is the conclusion of some white economic historians that the labor (performed by the early African slaves) was more costly than the labor of free men, and that the early slave traders and planters had all made a dreadful mistake. Of course, the implication is that the slaves and planters were more guilty of stupidity than of cruelty. U. B. Phillips, the most famous apologist for American southern slavery concluded: "Plantation had in strictly business aspects as many drawbacks as it had attractions. But in the large it was less a business than a life: it made fewer fortunes than it made men." The desire here is to ignore all the factors involved in the development of the New World, i.e., the shortage of labor for developmental work.

Africans not only contributed labor to the development of the New World economies, but they repeatedly showed that they had the genius to discover the properties of its Flora and Fauna and the skill to contribute to its technology. Africans had folk remedies for treatment of Yellow Fever, Yaws and human parasites, which, incidentally, they also introduced to the New World, but it is to a Koromante that cedit goes for being the first African to have a New World plant named after him. In 1730 "the Negro Gramman (i.e. Grand Man) Quacy" discovered the properties of "Bitter Ash" and it was named *Quassia amara* in his honor. About 200 years later on the North American continent, a boy born in slavery in 1864, and considered too frail to be useful, also became an agricultural chemist: George Washington Carver held patents for the manufacture of over one hundred products from sweet potato, nearly as many for the pecan, and one hundred and fifty for the peanut. Yet he did not become a wealthy man. In the United States Patent Office there is a record of over fifteen hundred inventions made by Negroes. But owing to the absence of similar institutions in other New World countries the contributions of Africans go unrecorded. According to Negro oral tradition, it was a man of African descent, and not Eli Whitney, who should hve received credit for inventing the cotton gin. The first Afro-American believed to have been granted a U.S. patent was Henry Blair of Maryland for inventing a corn harvester. Durham concluded that the Negro was forced into menial labor. He "had come to be associated with this kind of work, and his effort to secure the opportunity to do better is regarded with indifference or with a sense of helplessness. Thus, the Negro as a group is denied the work which it is capable of doing and detesting the work it is forced to do."

In most New World societies social and economic status is still linked to color. Nowadays, with the prevalence of the concept of *negritude,* the stigma is decreasing. The psychological aspect of the asymetrical relations of Africans and Europeans in the New World has not received the kind of treatment it deserves. True, we cannot do paleontology of the early African slaves to determine what their psychic state was, but we know from historical texts that they disliked their status. Some committed suicide, some dissembled, and some like the dreaded "Koromante" revolted. But we also found loyalty among the slaves and especially honor. If we go back into comparatively recent history, we shall learn more about the White man and the Negro in the New World by seeing them as teachers and pupils. According to Geneva Gay, "an area of American life in which the Black presence is most pervasive, and one that is generally ignored by formal education programs is popular culture. Recordings of contemporary Black pop and soul songs are a multi-million dollar business. The music many young Americans prefer for recreation and relaxation is unmistakenly Black American-centric. If it is not the music itself of Black performers, then it is the music of other performers whose styles and techniques have been influenced by Blacks. Contemporary fashions in clothes are influenced by the preferences and styles of Black "youngbloods." There is some credence to the belief that the way Black teenagers and young adults respond to a "new look" can turn it into a fashion craze or a failure. The Black imprint upon the contemporary language and communication of living — called by some "slang," by others "the vernacular of the youth culture" — is obvious, too. It can be seen in the vocabulary, the kinesthetic qualities, the rhythm and aesthetic-artistic manner in which language and behavior are interwoven, and act as essential complementary components of the communication act. Consider, if you will, the language usage — its structure, vocabulary, and style — in newspaper, magazine, and television advertising, and reflect for a moment upon its similarities to communication behaviors typically associated with Black Americans. This is just one concrete example of the penetrating presence of Black culture in contemporary American life. It also is illustrative of the inescapable fact that cultural modifications and adaptations of any cultural system are bound to occur as different ethnic an cultural groups interact, borrow, and exchange perceptions, ideas, habits, and artifacts. It should be remembered that as Blacks are influencing and helping shape American life and culture, so too are they being influence and shaped by experiences and contacts with the many other ethnic and cultural groups in the United States."

Few writers have dealt with the psychological impact of the African myth on the White man in the New World. Cayton, talking specifically of the White Americans, states: "White people, too, are anxious in their dealing with colored people. They, too, are fear ridden ... The white man suffers ... from an oppressor's phobia — the fear that there will be retribution from those he has humiliated and tortured. The mechanism involved with frightened White people is a guilt-hate-fear complex." Cash, a historian, spoke of the "tyranny" of the Negro over the customs and habits of White Southerners. He believed that the Negro "entered into the White man as profoundly as the White man entered into the Negro — subtly influencing every gesture, every word, every emotion and idea, every attitude." Jung, the famous psychologist, was amazed at what he considered to have been the Negro's psychological impact upon all Americans. "The first thing which attracted my attention," he was quoted as saying, "was the influence of the Negro, an obviously psychological influence regardless of any mixture of blood." Jung went on to say that "the influence of the Negro was apparent in the walking, laughing, dancing, singing, and even praying of White Americans."

The African's physical prowess has enabled him to dominate most sports in which he has had the opportunity to participate. His problem was that Europeans have often feared that permitting the African to compete with him might possibly prove the superiority of the African. The emergence of men of African descent as boxers challenged the dominance of the New World Europeans especially the Anglo-Saxons. When Tom Molineaux, a slave born in Baltimore, Maryland, fought Tom Crib for the heavy-weight championship of the world in England in 1810, the Whites felt threatened. Indeed the White American who was bare-knuckle champion in 1882 refused to fight all Black challengers. The White champion Corbett fought and defeated Peter Jackson, an African from the Virgin Islands, in 1891, much to the relief of the Whites, but the *New York Sun* commenting later on the fight wrote: "We are in the midst of a growing menace. The Black man is rapidly forging to the front in athletics, especially in the field of fisticuffs. We are in the midst of a black rise against white supremacy. Just at present we are safe from the humiliation of having a Black man world's champion, but we had a pretty narrow escape. ..."

Black athletes in other sports have had to fight racism to prove their prowess. Racism is still a barrier to blacks becoming champions in golf, and swimming. Hopefully those persons who will have an impact on those sports in the New World are already born. The only thing they need is the opportunity.

The great difference in the types of food eaten in the Northern states of the

United States of America and in the South can only be attributed to the presence of the African. Brazilians have been attempting without too much success to "de-Africanize" their cooking. They have started to emphasize meals prepared by important European cooks. A comparable process took place in other New World countries some years ago. In the United States middle-class Blacks became ashamed of eating "Negro" foods. However, with the rise of Black pride, Afro-Americans are not only attempting to retain "soul" food, but have been able to introduce it into "white" cafeterias and restaurants as well.

African languages have enriched all the linguistic systems in the New World. And people of African descent continue to be among the creative colloquialists found there. There is increasing evidence that the impact of African languages on European ones took place even before Africans were exported to the New World in large numbers. Afro-Spanish and Afro-Portuguese developed on the West Coast of Africa in the early sixteenth century and were certainly brought to the New World by slaves at that period. Later when Dutch and French were replaced by the English traders, their pidgins or "patois" developed also. When, in the seventeenth and eighteenth centuries, British traders became dominant, Afro-English became firmly established in West Africa from Gambia to the Cameroons, and also made the passage to the New World. These pidgin languages certainly formed the basis for the first communication between the colonists and their African laborers, and have co-existed with the African and European languages. The Africans in Brazil continued to use their native languages down through the centuries, and have made important lexical contributions to the Portuguese. The Afro-Portuguese creole language still survives, especially in the rural areas of the country. Some modern Brazilian linguists, probably out of racial chauvinism, "do not admit to grammatical influences from African languages on the Portuguese spoken in Brazil." They insist that African language could not influence the grammatical structure of Portuguese because "the Negroes arrived already speaking a 'Negroized' form of Portuguese." Nevertheless, even these scholars admit the influence of the African languages on the phonemes of the Brazilian language. They declare that "Portuguese became softened in Brazil, losing the hardness of the Portuguese spoken in Portugal, so difficult for Brazilians to understand in prammaphone records and films, and of which they make such fun because of the harshness of its pronunciation."

The persistence of Afro-English *(taki-taki* or *krioro* or *sranang-tongo)* in Surinam, and *papiomento* (Afro-Spanish) in Curacao reflects the history of these two areas, as well as the remarkable "retension and transmission of West African speech habits." The main contribution of African languages to Spanish in most of Latin America has been in lexicon and intonation. The Spanish dialects of Puerto Rico and Cuba are rich with African words, and intonations. Yoruba was spoken in Cuba as late as the 1940's and has contributed hundreds of words for religious subjects to the local Spanish. On the other hand, full-fledged Afro-Spanish creoles apparently did not develop in either Cuba or Puerto Rico, or the other Spanish-speaking areas of the New World.

In contrast to Spanish America, Afro-French Creole languages are present in Haiti, Guiana, Guadeloupe, Martinique, Trinidad, Louisiana, St. Lucia, and Dominica. Each of these regional Creoles has its own characteristics and influence in the various societies. For example, Afro-French is really the national, if not the official language of Haiti. Everyone in Haiti speaks and understands Creole. Nursemaids teach it to their elite charges, so that children know it from infancy; elite lovers lapse into its expressive phrases in order to say something particularly intimate which might sound sentimental in French; priests must use it in their parish work if they are to be understood at all. Even the elite presidents have found it wise to speak often to the countrypeople in their own tongue.

The Africanness of the Afro-French of Haiti has been questioned by some scholars just as they question the effect of any West African trait on the New World. Leyburn believed that the African influence on Creole was almost negligible, while Suzanne Sylvain, a Haitian, believed that the language has many African characteristics. Nevertheless, even Leyburn admits that there are African elements in the vocabulary of Vodun, and that the language has the "onomatopoeic" and especially the "duplication" qualities of many African languages.

African languages have had differential impact on the English dialects of the New World. There is wide variation in the African elements in these dialects, even within the same territory. This is due to history and social class. Thus in eighteenth century Jamaica there were: speakers of Creole "Negro-English," the ancestor of Jamaican Creole by local born slaves; speakers of various African languages by newly-imported slaves; speakers of creole English by freed colored people and poor Whites; speakers of regional dialects of English by newly arrived indentured servants, etc.; speakers of English "with a Jamaican accent" and of course, expatriates. Today, Jamaican Creole, a real pidgin, is spoken by most members of the working class, and is at one end of the linguistic spectrum with "English with a Jamaican accent" or standard Jamaican at the other. Nevertheless, "virtually every Jamaican is at least bilingual" in the sense that he understands the "patois" as well as the standard dialect of the island. "Jamaican Creole" has the usual African phonemic elements, tones, and given the importance of the "Koromantee" element in the society it is not surprising that, of the African loan-words in common use, "the greatest number are from Twi or one of its related Ghana (Gold Coast) languages." In addition to Twi, there are words from Mende, Mandinka, Ewe, Igbo, Efik, Yoruba, Kongo and Kimbundu, and possibly Swahili.

Attempts to ascertain the linguistic impact of Africa on the United States of America have always led to controversy, and the contemporary quarrel about "Black English" highlights the political as well as the linguistic aspects of the problem. No one tried to preserve the languages of the African during slavery. Indeed there was fear that the ability of the slaves to communicate in their own languages would lead to rebellion. The aim was to teach the African the local English dialect and people did not consider the possible effect of the African linguistic system on this process. Linguists are now also subjecting the speech of Southern Whites (quite different from that of Northern Whites) to close scrutiny to determine the nature of Africanisms in it. They have called attention to the "musical" quality of the speech of both Southern Blacks and Whites — similar to the musical characteristics found in French and Portuguese influenced by African languages. Linguists have also identified the characteristic "you-all" or "y'all" of the Deep South as an Africanism. The suspicion that "O.K. (oh kay)," that most American of all slang terms, may have been derived from the Wolof words *waw kay* ("all right," "certainly") has recently stirred up a great debate in both the *New York Times* and the *London Times*. It has certainly demonstrated, once again, that the issue of the African's contribution to New World cultures is as much a political as a cultural matter. But while scholars could debate the derivation of "O.K." they cannot question the African's pre-eminence in creating slang both in America and New World societies. American Blacks create slang and the Whites adopt. Even the President of the United States now feels the need to "tell it like it is." This verbal artistry is found elsewhere among the New World Africans whether it be in the "Speech Band" of Tobago whose members vie with opponents in speech contests, or the "Tea Meetings" in Antigua and Nevis. The "Sweet talk" and the satires of the Calypsonians of Trinidad are cultural elements which have been adopted by the Whites of that Island, and the other populations as well.

The impact of Africa, especially West Africa, on the folklore traditions in New World societies has now been recognized. Not too long ago, the tendency was to suggest that New World Africans only re-interpreted the Grimm's Fairy Tales and diffused them. But the African elements in New World folk-lore were so easily demonstrable that even the most reactionary detractors have had to admit their influence. The strong African element in the folklore of Surinam, Guiana, and the West Indies is readily apparent, especially the *Anansi* or *"Nansi"* stories of the Akan peoples. These stories have adapted to their milieu and thus have undergone some interesting transformations: In Jamaica this descendent of the West African semi-diety seems to take on special significance in a society which has its roots in a system of slavery — a system which pitted the weak against the strong in daily confrontation. ... It is as though every slave strove to be Annancy and he who achieved the Spider-form became a kind of hero ... This picaresque character misses no chance for chicanery ... as though he lives in a world that offers him no other chance for survival ... to cope with an unstraight and crooked world one needs unstraight and crooked paths.

The Anansi folk-lore complex has become part of the folk-lore tradition of the United States of America. But characteristically, it gained its reputation as a series of stories used by "Uncle Remus" to entertain the "Young Master." To the slave in his condition the theme of weakness overcoming strength through cunning proved endlessly fascinating.

African musical traditions have influenced all the musical styles found in the New World, and form an integral part of an original music the people of that hemisphere ever produced. What is more remarkable is that there are important African elements in the music of such Latin American countries as Peru, Bolivia, Uruguay, Chile and Argentina where the African population has almost disappeared. These elements appear even in the so-called "Indian" music of these countries. Despite their ability to create popular music Afro-Americans have not been able to profit from it. Whites still run most of the recording houses publishing phonograph records, and they are still the "critics" of the Negro music. W. C. Handy lived long enough to hear Leonard Bernstein and the *New York Philharmonic* play the "Saint Louis Blues" in his honor. What Jones wrote about the plight of the Afro-American musicians in the 1940's is still painfully true: "Even at the expense of the most beautiful elements of Afro-American musical tradition, to be a successful (rich) swing musician, one had to be White. Benny Goodman was the 'King of Swing,' not Fletcher Henderson, or Duke Ellington, or Count Basie." The *Beatles* who admitted that they imitated the music of Afro-Americans probably made more money in their short lives than almost all the "successful" Black musicians that ever lived. The drive of the contemporary Afro-American is not only to influence the evolution of music in the United States, but to gain a just reward for doing so.

Africans have had as much an impact on the dances of the New World as they have had on its music. Herskovits states that "it is a commonplace that many American Negro forms of dancing are essentially African ..." The dances of the Caribbean exhibit many more African characteristics than those in the United States. The *rhumba* of Cuba, the *mambo* of Puerto Rico, and the *merengue* of Santo Domingo have all become national dances of their islands. African dances are the basic elements in almost all Brazilian dances. Luciano Gallet, a musicologist and folklorist, once identified some seventeen types or series of "Negro dances transplanted to Brazil."

While Africa's music has had a great impact on the New World, its religious systems have had unequal effect. Except for the neo-Yoruba religion found in temples in Harlem, organized African religious systems never became established in the United States. In the Caribbean area, where a more indulgent Catholicism predominated, African religious elements survive and play an important part in the lives of the people. For example, two systems of divination are found in "Afro-Cuban religious cults ..." These divinatory systems form part of an Afro-Cuban religion known as *santeria*. The priest (santeres) and priestesses (santeras), also known as *babalorisha* and *ivalorisha* after the Yoruba *babala,* preside over cult houses and venerate Yoruba entities such as Orula, (also identified with St. Francis of Assisi). Cubans of all ethnic origins and of all colors are members of this religion and consult its dinors.

The *vodun* cult in Haiti is primarily a folk religion even though Presidents of Republic have been numbered among its devotees. There has been a great deal of syncretism between its African (Dahomean and local) dieties and the Catholic saints. There are vodun priests and priestesses and services of the cult are well-structured. However, the divination found in Cuba (and of course in Dahomey) has disappeared except that people sometimes consult the cowries of Legba. What has given *vodun* a questionable reputation in Haiti (but what has also accounted for its influence among a large number of people), is the magical practices allegedly associated with it. These magical elements of vodun are also reported for Martinique and Guadaloupe.

The African religious elements in Trinidad have had difficulty surviving owing to the opposition of the colonial government and of the upper social classes. Nevertheless, *Shango,* the Yoruba God of Thunder is worshipped on the island and gives his name to the African religion. In addition to *Shango* there is the family of African Gods. These Gods have their days of worship, special foods, colors and paraphernalia, and some are associated with Catholic Saints.

African religious elements have had such an impact on Brazil that they have mutated over time and are even found in "high-rise" apartments in Rio de Janeiro. The ordinary Brazilians believe that in time and with education the cults will die out.

Let us look back and see how far we have come in this discussion. We began by suggesting that one of the most important relationships between groups was educational and that much history could be viewed in terms of the movement of ideas from one group to another.

In looking for examples of this, the first we found was the rise of Japan through learning and assimilating foreign ideas; and we saw that Japan had made this important step three times — once in the Dark Ages of the seventh century, once in the nineteenth century, and now again under American tutelage in the twentieth.

Another example was Turkey. A third was ancient Rome, which made itself a pupil of Greece; and we saw how Rome had passed its knowledge on to the barbarians. Finally we traced the psychological impact of the African myth on the White man in the New World.

No doubt many other examples of the movement of ideas between national and racial groups could be found in the realm of society and politics; but these will suffice at present to demonstrate that although the history of contacts between civilizations deals principally with contacts involving violence or disruption — so much so that it occasionally views interacting civilizations as assailant and victim — it does bring out the importance of peaceful and educative relationships between different cultures and sketches certain laws of cultural radiation which explain these relationships in terms of the migration of ideas. "It is stimulating to approach history teaching and learning in the schools from this point of view. To consider the movement of thought throughout the world is, in a way, like making a new map, in which we can see distant countries connected by invisible tides, intellectual currents moving by strange paths around the whole globe and uniting the manifold minds of men int something like a single, mighty, super-human Reason. It is as though the earth were thinking."

REFERENCES

BURNS. C. DE LISLE *The Contact Between Minds,* Macmillan 1923; and *Industry and Civilization;* Allen (London) 1925.

LELLO. A.J.E. AND WOOD, J.E. The Teaching of History and Geography. In *Techniques of Teaching, Volume 2, Secondary Education.* Edited by A.D.C. Peterson; Pergamon Press, (Oxford, London, New York) 1965.

GOLDSCHMIDT. WALTER *Cultural Anthropology,* American Library Association, 1967.

HIGHET. GILBERT The Migration of Ideas. *Three Lectures delivered on the North Foundation at Franklin and Marshall College;* Oxford University Press (New York) 1954.

SKINNER. ELLIOTT P. *The Impact of Africans on the New World.* Paper presented to the Multicultural Conference, Universidad Autonoma de Santo Domingo, Dominican Republic. 1972.

DUBOIS. W.E.B. *The Gift of Black Folks,* Boston, 1924.

HERSKOVITS. M.J. *The Myth of the Negro Past,* (Boston), 1950.

DOWD. J. *The Negro Races,* New York, 1907-1914; and Daniel J. *In Freedom's Birthplace: A Study of the Boston Negroes.* (Boston and New York).

WEATHERBY. U.G. The West Indies as a Sociological Laboratory, *American Journal of Sociology,* 1923.

WILLIAMS. ERIC *The Negro in the Caribbean,* Washington, 1942.

EPPSE. M.R. *The Negro, too, in American History,* Nashville, 1943; and Woodson, C.G. *The Negro in our History,* Washington, 1928 (Fifth Edition)

HELPS. A. *The Spanish Conquest in America,* London and New York, 1900-1904, Vol. 2 and Vol. 3.

WRIGHT. R.R. *Negro Companions of the Spanish Explorers,* Amer. Anthro. Vol. IV, No. 2, 1902.

PRESCOTT. W.H. *The Conquest of Mexico,* (Philadelphia) 1892.

RAMOS. A. *The Negro in Brazil,* (trans. R. Pattee), (Washington, 1939).

DUBOIS. W.E.B. *The Suppression of the African Slave Trade,* (New York) 1969. (First published in 1896); First Schocken edition, 1969.

WILLIAMS. ERIC *Capitalism and Slavery,* (First published in 1944, New York), 1966.

MCCLOY. S.T. *The Negro in the French West Indies,* (Kentucky) 1966.

GREAVES. I.C. *The Negro in Canada (National Problems of Canada),* McGill University Economic Studies, 1930.

RENS. L.L.E. *The Historical and Social Background of Surinam's Negro-English,* (Amsterdam), 1953.

CURTIN. P. *The Atlantic Slave Trade: A Census,* (Madison, Milwaukee and London), 1969.

BOAHEN. A. *Topics in West African History,* London, 1966.

PAGE. J.D. *Slavery and the Slave Trade in the Context of West African History,* Journal of African History, 1969.

PHILLIPS. U.B. "Plantation and Frontier Documents: 1649-1863", *A Documentary History of American Industrial Society,* Vol. 2, (Cleveland), 1909.

BROWNING. E.B. "Negro Companions of the Spanish Explorers in the New World", *Howard University Studies in History,* No. 11, 1930.

WAGENHEIM. K. *Puerto Rico: A Profile,* (New York), 1970.

WRIGHT. I.A. *The Early History of Cuba,* (New York), 1919; and Humbold, A., *The Island of Cuba,* (New York), 1969.

SCHOMBURGK. R. *Travels in British Guiana, 1840-1844,* (trans. Walter E. Roth), (Georgetown, Vol. 1, 1922).

TANNENBAUM. F. *Slave and Citizen: The Negro in the Americas,* (New York), 1946; and Harris Marvin, *Patterns of Race in the Americas,* (New York), 1954.

ROMERO. FERNANDO "The Slave Trade and the Negro in South America", *The Hispanic American Historical Review,* Vol. 24, No. 3, 1944.

FRAZIER. E.F. *The Negro in the United States,* (New York), 1949.

DUBOIS. W.E.B., 1924: Dubois states: Negro labor has played a peculiar and important part in the history of the modern world. The Black man was the pioneer in the hard physical work which began the reduction of the American wilderness and which not only hastened the economic development of America directly but indirectly released for other employment thousands of white men and thus enabled America to grow economically and spiritually at a rate previously unparalled anywhere in history."

JOHNSTON. SIR HARRY *The Negro in the New World*, (1910), (New York and London), 1969.

STAMPP. KENNETH M. *The Peculiar Institution: Slavery in the Anti-Bellum South*, 1956.

DUBOIS. W.E.B. *The Philadelphia Negro*, (New York), 1899.

PHILLIPS. U.B. *American Negro Slavery*, (1918), (Baton Rouge), 1969.

JAMES. C.L.R. *The Black Jacobins*, (New York), 1963.

APTHEKER. HERBERT *American Negro Slave Revolts*, (New York), 1969.

CAYTON. HORACE R. "The Psychology of the Negro under Discrimination," in *Mental Health and Mental Disorder: A Sociological Approach*, (Ed. Arnold M. Rose), (New York), 1955.

BENNETT. JR.. LERONE *The Negro Mood*, (Chicago), 1964.

JUNG. C.G. *Civilization in Transition*, (Princeton), 1970.

DAVIS. JOHN P. "The Negro in American Sports", in *The American Negro. Reference Book* (ed.). John P. Davis, Englewood Cliffs. 1967.

SPORTS ILLUSTRATED. January 18, 1971. "Black i Best".

RODRIGUES. JOSE HONORIO "The Influence of Africa on Brazil and of Brazil on Africa", *Journal of African History, Vol. III, No. I*, 1962.

VANSERTIMA. IVAN "African Linguistic and Mythological Structures in the New World," in *Black Life and Culture in the United States*, (ed.) R. I. Goldstein. (New York) 1971.

RENS. L.L.E. *The Historical and Social Background of Surinam's Negro-English*, (Amsterdam), 1953.

LEYBURN. JAMES G. *The Haitian People*, (New Haven and London), 1966.

SYLVAIN. SUZANNE *Le Creole/Hatien*, Watteren, 1936; and Price-Mars, *Ainsi parla l'oncle*, Essais de'ethnografic, Port-au-Prince, 1928.

HUGHES. LANGSTON AND BONTEMPS. ARMA (ed.) *Book of Negro Folk-lore*, (New York) 1958.

SKINNER. ELLIOTT P. *Ethnic Interaction in a British Guiana Rural Community: A Study in Secondary Acculturation and Group Dynamics*, Ph.D. Dissertation, Columbia University, 1955.

HERSKOVITS. M.J. *Man and His Works*, (New York), 1950.

ALLEN. W.F., WARE. C.P., AND GARRISON. LUCY *Slave Songs of the South*, (New York), 1968.

GEORGE. ZELMA "Negro Music In American Life", in *The American Negro Reference Book*, ed. John P. Davis, Englewood Cliffs. 1967.

JONES. LE ROI *Blues People*, (New York), 1963.

PUCKETT. NEWBELL N. "Religious Folk-Beliefs of Whites and Negroes" in *The Journal of Negro History, Vol. XVI, No. I*, January, 1931.

COURLANDER. HAROLD "Gods of the Haitian Mountains" in *The Journal of Negro History*, Vol. XXIX, No. 3, July, 1944.

BASTIDE. ROGER *Les Ameriques Noires*, (Pares), 1967.

HOROWITZ. MICHAEL M. *Morne-Paysin: Peasant Village in Martinique*, New York, 1967.

HERSKOVITS. M.J. AND HERSKOVITS. FRANCES S. *Trinidad Village*, New York, 1947.

RELATIVE POWER
AND STRATEGIC ETHNICITY
IN MIAMI

By Anthony P. Maingot
Florida International University

INTRODUCTION

In the 1950's immigrants accounted for 11% or 1 in every 9 additional Americans. In the 1970's immigrants have been contributing 21% — or more than 1 in every 5 new Americans. 1980 was the year of highest immigration in U.S. history.

Citing numbers of immigrants is but one way to indicate that immigration and its accompanying processes (acculturations, assimilation and ethnic relations) have traditionally been critical issues in American history.

Immigration has been a consistent fact; what has changed have been the ethnic characteristics and attitudes of these new arrivals and the reception extended by the host groups. Not only are the proportions changing, so are the type of immigrant: between 1965 and 1974 fully 35% of the total immigrants came from two groups, Asians and Cubans. Both groups are characterized by their determination to retain their ethnic identity while at the same time succeed in the American system.

Cubans contribute to the fastest growing minority in the U.S.: Hispanics. In 1976, Hispanics accounted for 5.29% of the U.S. population (11,195,000 out of 211 million); by 1979 they had grown to 12,079,000 or 5.59% of the then population of 215,935,000.

More important than this overall growth, however, is the concentration of these groups in specific areas. Hispanics now account for over 16% of the population of California and more than 21% of that of Texas. In Dade County, Florida, for example, the growth of the Hispanic sector is made all the more dramatic because it is both absolute as well as relative to the proportion of other groups in the county. Table No. 1 shows the dimensions of this change.

TABLE NO. 1
DADE COUNTY: POPULATION AND ETHNICITY, 1950-1985

Year	Blacks	%	Latins	%	Non-Latin Whites	%	Total
1950	64.9	13.1	20.0	4.0	410.2	82.9	495.1
1960	137.3	14.7	50.0	5.4	747.7	79.9	935.0
1970	189.7	15.0	229.2	23.6	778.9	61.4	1,267.8
1975	208.0	14.4	467.0	32.3	770.0	53.3	1,445.0
1980 (est.)	233.0	14.5	617.0	38.3	760.0	47.2	1,610.0
1985 (est.)	260.4	15.0	746.5	43.0	729.1	42.0	1,736.0

Sources: Dade County, Planning Department

The fact is that since 1975 virtually the totality of Dade's population growth was due not only to net migration but specifically to net migration of Hispanics. This movement of Hispanics and specifically of Cubans into Dade County will probably continue for two reasons (other than natural growth): (1) resettlement: in 1980 30% of the Cubans in Dade County had moved from other parts of the U.S.; (2) Cuba has now become a "Caribbean" country in the sense that Cuban migrations today — at least a significant proportion of it — are similar to that of other Caribbean islands in that people are seeking a better life rather than fleeing *direct* political persecution. Like the other islands in the Caribbean, Cuba's economic development has not been adequate to the kind of population growth and expectations which it is experiencing. Cuba's population size is second only to that of Mexico in the area so it can be expected that the pressures for migration to the U.S. will continue strong for the immediate future. What will be the significance of this large scale immigration influx into South Florida and that of the Cubans specifically? What is — and, more importantly, what will be — the significance of this growth and concentration of Cubans in Dade County?

It is crucial to understand that any discussion of Cubans and other immigrants to the United States has to deal not merely with the issue of the place of Haitians or Cubans or Central Americans in this society, but more fundamentally with the whole question of what kind of society it will be for its people. But there is also the intellectual side of the issue. While the contributions of Cubans to the *shaping and molding* of this society take place primarily on the crucible of action, theoretical discussion and analysis helps shape the broad ideologies and theories of acculturation which do have a long range impact on practice and theory.

BASIC CONCEPTS

Any analysis of immigration assimilation and acculturation should take the following factors into account:

1. The type of culture and society from which the immigrants came: the existing social and cultural conditions; and the sense of identity existant;
2. The degree of organization and sophistication of the immigrant group, its type of occupational structure at settlement, its collective set of identifications with a particular style of life;
3. The particular intellectual milieu regarding immigration (acculturation and integration) which exists in the host society.

Characteristics under number one can be called the group's *capability for acculturation,* those under number two, the *capability for integration.* The first deals with culture and the ability to communicate, interact and negotiate successfully in it. The second deals with social structure: the capacity to "penetrate" the system, occupying important social, economic and political statuses. It is clear that *some degree* of acculturation is necessary for integration but that no degree of acculturation can guarantee integration.

This clarification of concepts leads to the statement of two propositions:

General Proposition: In periods of ethnic revitalization integration can proceed without the need for total acculturation (a condition known as assimilation).

Specific Proposition: The Cuban migration from 1959 to 1979 was characterized by a high capacity for integration and a high capability for that degree of acculturation necessary for that integration. This latter process we call "strategic acculturation", one element of a broader process of strategic ethnicity. This requires some elaboration.

Despite the reservations often raised about the significance of ethnicity, it appears quite important that the particular *ethnic* dimensions of the immigrant group be analyzed both in terms of the way in which *they* define themselves and the way in which the majority group of the host society defines them. This is fundamental because it is an established fact of ethnic groups (at least since Max Weber defined them)[1] that their identity is based on sets of assumptions: of common traits, of common origin, of common values — whether these be *real* or *imaginary.* It is a good idea to divide these ethnic traits into *voluntary* and *involuntary* ones: over a given period of time an individual can voluntarily change his language and speech patterns, his dress and eating habits and break the other practices or rules of the ethnic group. These are all voluntary traits. What he cannot do is change the color of his skin, the texture of his hair and other physical features. These are involuntary ethnic traits. The country of origin lies somewhere in between since it is an historical and now-a-days, recorded, fact but one which the individual might be able to conceal in certain cases.

It is clear from this working definition that the larger the number of options regarding its use of ethnicity the greater the potentiality for acculturation and integration. What is being suggested here is that ethnicity (including acculturation) can be utilized *strategically* by both minority and majority groups. Obviously, the greater the number of voluntary traits which make up a group's ethnic identity, the greater its strategic capabilities in ethnic bargaining.

The ability and the disposition to emphasize or deemphasize some or many ethnic traits — *not out of self-hatred* but for advantageous bargaining — I call strategic ethnicity.[2] The concept takes into account the fact that the participants behave not only on the basis of *values,* largely derived from their ethnic identity, but also on the basis of *interests,* derived from their class position and membership. In other words, an awareness of their class interests within given power contexts, allows them to use their ethnicity selectively, i.e. politically. Strategic acculturation is an integral part of strategic ethnicity in that the group is then allowed to adopt those traits of the dominant group necessary for successful integration while also retaining those original ethnic traits necessary for group cohesion as well as bargaining. At this time, and in this particular environment, ethnicity enhances power capabilities. The group purposefully retains not only major parts of its ethnic identity but perhaps more significant politically, its ethnic identifications.

Clearly this set of hypotheses and the assumptions derived therefrom bring into question the universality of many traditional approaches to the study of race and ethnic contact and relations in the U.S.A. Specifically, it challenges the "race relations cycle" theory.[3] This theory postulates a progression of stages in ethnic group contact with the following sequences:

> (1) contact — (2) competition — (3) accommodation — (4) assimilation (i.e. the complete acculturation and assimilation of the new immigrant group).

The discussion here challenges this interpretation since it hypothesizes that the most fundamental dimension in the study of acculturation and ethnic relations is the relative power of the parties in contact. In an age of ethnic revitalization it is wrong to assume a priori that the "majority-minority" dichotemy between the groups in contact is always and across-the-board an asymmetric one. The strategic use of ethnicity, we hypothesize, can "reverse" the situation of power in specific instances.

The question of the ethnic factor in the study of power thus cannot be treated lightly; it requires a working definition of power which takes into account the ethnic factor. This paper suggests a working definition which takes into account the relative and the situational aspects. In other words, power relationships are hardly ever absolute since more often than not the relative distribution of power will vary according to the situation, especially the object or goal of the competition. As such, power can be measured in terms of the range of decision-making options which a particular group has in a given situation. The research question is then: does the ethnic factor expand or curtail the number of these options?

The answer to this question calls for a restatement and elaboration of Point No. 3 above since one of the very critical aspects in the analysis of *"strategic ethnicity"* is the particular intellectual milieu regarding immigration, acculturation and ethnicity which reigns at the time of entry of the ethnic group.

Logically, it is the already established majority group (or at least its intellectual spokesmen) which has the largest say in this matter. And yet, it is an ironic aspect of an ideology of ethnic revitalization that negative attitudes towards minorities can be converted into advantages by those groups; a kind of "reverse dependency" can take place. For instance, it is important to recognize that very often before contact both groups might well have deep-rooted stereotypes about each other. Naturally, these stereotypes will play an important role in the formulation of theories or ideologies of immigration and acculturation which precede, accompany or follow large scale immigration settlements. But it is precisely these stereotypes which play two functions: on the one hand they allow the group to be identified as a "minority" by the majority (and thus a candidate for special treatment) while at the same time they act to reinforce a sense of group identity (and thus purpose) in the minority. In a period of ethnic revitalization, negative stereotypes can have a crucial latent consequence thus.

There is today a new awareness of the role of competition and conflict in all social relationships. This includes, and perhaps especially so, ethnic relationships. Certainly, the social sciences have already provided us with sufficient evidence of this reality.[4] The seminal works of Daniel P. Moynihan and Nathan Glazer[5] and Herbert Gans[6] point precisely to the role of competition and conflict in the original creation and maintenance of ethnic group identity and cohesion. These groups came into being because they discovered in their common origin and cultural background the strength to confront major challenges. Ethnic groups maintain their integrity because in this society and at this time their members have found them to be the best means of advancing their individual and group claims to power and privilege. To be sure, ethnic groups represent more than that to their members, but one ignores this interest group function of the ethnic group at the peril of ignoring the true dynamics of U.S. society in the 1970's and 1980's.*

An analysis of the status and role of the Cuban immigrant in South Florida will show that the hypotheses stated are at least plausible.

CUBANS IN DADE COUNTY

Between 1970 and 1980 the total population of the United States grew by 9.6%. During the same period the Hispanic population of Dade County grew by 121% and 85% of these were Cubans. These figures do not include the 125,000 Cubans who came with the boat-lift from Mariel in mid-1980.**

One of the very important aspects of Cuban-U.S. relations before the 1959 Revolution was the fact that few Cubans actually immigrated to the U.S.

---

*The business world is seldom slow in understanding the cultural aspects of their potential market. A recent marketing handbook advises its customers that: "The recent surges of immigrants from Latin America coincide with the upsurge in individual human rights. Each person is encouraged to take pride in and recognize his/her own roots and heritage. Thus, rather than being encouraged to become strictly "American," immigrants/ethnic groups are encouraged to maintain their heritage and culture." (Antonio Guernica /ed./, *U.S. Hispanics: A Market Profile.* NASB/Strategy Research Corp., 1980. P. 18.

**Even more phenomenal has been the Hispanic population's growth in neighboring Broward County: from 15,500 in 1970 to 92,700 in 1980 or an increase of 498 percent.

The figures in Table No. 2 show that prior to 1950 there were many more West Indian immigrants to the United States than Cuban. Since 1959 the picture has changed to show both Cuba and the West Indies as major sending countries. Rather than being a country of migration, Cuba was a country of immigration. So many Spaniards, other Europeans, Americans, Haitians and West Indians migrated to Cuba in the early 20th Century that by 1919 fully 20% of the population were of foreign birth. In fact a major factor in the Revolution of 1933 was anti-foreign feelings and the 1934 "50% law" (along with the Great Depression) effectively reduced this immigration to a trickle. By 1953 only 4% of the population was foreign born.[7] Even after this nationalistic social movement of the early 1930's, however, there was no escaping the presence and contact with foreign cultures, predominantly North American. Two aspects of this contact has been noted by Nita R. Manitzas. The first was economic; rather than the landed gentry of other Latin American countries, the Cuban upper class was composed of urban businessmen, bankers, merchants and professionals. Their interests were tied directly to U.S. interests, from sugar to tourism. The other dimension was cultural: both the upper and the middle classes were comfortable with North American life-styles and cultural traits. Trade unions tended to follow the lead of North American unions and even the Cuban Communists took their cues from the U.S. Communist Party.[9] "The achievements and aspirations of Cuba's upper and middle classes," note two Cuban sociologists, "were more closely tied to the U.S. economic, political, and social institutions than to those of other nations in the hemisphere."[10] The Cuban capability for acculturation was clearly present.

TABLE NO. 2
U.S. TOTAL IMMIGRATION
BY AREA OF LAST RESIDENCE
1820-1977

	1820-1901	1901-1950	1951-1960	1961-1970	1971-1977	Total
Latin America & Caribbean						
Mexico	27.959	810,841	299,800	453,900	438,500	2,031,000
West Indies	—	356,000[1]	29,800	133,900	169,300	689,000
Cuba	—	1,400[2]	78,900	208,500	208,200	497,000
Other	139,896	242,704	210,400	506,800	386,200	1,486,000
Total Latin America & Caribbean	167,855	1,410,945	618,900	1,303,100	1,202,200	4,703,000

[1]Includes 1820-1950
[2]Prior to 1951, included with West Indies

Source: U.S. Immigration & Naturalization Service
          Strategy Research Corporation

The point is an important one: the urban middle and upper class Cuban already had had significant contact with North American culture and economy before they emigrated. When one adds to this the fact that 81% of economically active refugees during 1959-62 were professional, managerial, clerical or skilled people[11] one understands that the original "settlers" were eminently equipped to establish a solid "social network" in the United States. Table No. 3 shows the high rate of transferability of skills from Cuba to the U.S. Fully 63.63% of those in the $25,000+ category in 1974 had the same jobs in Cuba. Of those in that income bracket, Solis and Wogart discovered that 63.63% had completed either high school or college in Cuba. Education, like actual skills, was highly transferrable into the new society.

TABLE NO. 3

Income Category	Occupation in Cuba	N=76
	Same Occupation	Other Occupation
$ up to 9,999.	50.0%	50.0%
$ 10,000-14,999.	42.42	57.58
$ 15,000-24,999.	43.75	56.25
$ 25,000 +	63.63	36.37

Source: Solis, Humberto J. and Wogart, Jan Peter.
"Study on Cuban Entrepreneurs and Administrators in the Private Sector".
University of Miami, Coral Gables, 1974.

The fact that 96.5% of these Cubans were white also was critical in easing their entry into a Southern state such as Florida.[12] It also helps explain another crucial aspect of successful penetration: outgroup marriages. In their study of Hispanic intermarriage in New York City, Joseph P. Fitzpatrick and Douglas T. Gurak found that while only 29.5% of Puerto Ricans married non-Puerto Ricans, 63.4% of Cubans married outside their group.

The authors are careful to point out that while inter-marriage is a powerful indicator of assimilation, that by assimilation "we do not mean a one-way process by which one group loses its ethnic identity and assumes that of another."[13] They correctly note that high rates of intermarriage can only occur when structural conditions — i.e., social class factors — do not inhibit everyday social interaction at various levels between different groups. This interpretation, which is supported by other sociological studies,[14] points clearly to the Cuban's *capability for integration* into the American Society.

One indication that Cubans retain important dimensions of their ethnicity even as they marry out is the fact that they have the highest rate of marriages with Roman Catholic ceremonies of any of the other Hispanic groups studied.[15]

If outmarriage is an indicator of the *capability for integration,* so is the process of naturalization. A crucial indicator of Hispanic civic-culture is the trend toward acquisition of citizenship. Since what is involved is a purposeful act to acquire that status, the figures on the trends contain broader implications for the collective behavior of this community. While the rate of naturalization (in 1979) among Mexicans who had been in the U.S. since 1967 was 4.8%,[16] by 1970 25% of Dade County's Hispanics were citizens.[17] By 1980, 43.3% of a representative sample of foreign born Hispanics in Dade County had become citizens, and 77.2%e with Permanent Resident status indicated their intention of becoming citizens. The trend towards citizenship clearly provides another indicator of permanence in the U.S. and in Dade County and of the capacity to integrate. Perhaps the most significant features of this process is, however, that it symbolizes the crowning of a successful political journey rather than the beginning of it. Not surprisingly, the rate of naturalization is correlated with residence: the higher the social status area, the higher the rate of naturalization.[18] Power, thus, was achieved prior to citizenship not because of it.[19] It appears then, that the step towards citizenship has caused little erosion in the depth of ethnic attachments and loyalties which after all were and are the true foundations of political action. Citizenship is a matter of strategic choice, not primordial attachment. The following case is illustrative: When asked about her attempt to become a U.S. citizen, Juanita Castro (sister of Fidel Castro and resident in the United States for 17 years) responded: "I do not wish to speak of unimportant things ... I will keep on being Cuban until I die." Castro's sentiments seem to be widely shared.[20]

It is vital to understand that this process will continue with little loss of ethnic identities. In fact the identities will be intensified by the increased participation in ethnic bargaining through direct political participation as well as interest group activities.

Direct participation in the political process, thus, explains only part of the story. While it is true that fully 86.9% of Hispanics in Dade County who are citizens are registered for the vote and of these an amazing 85.4% had actually exercised that vote in the most recent national and local elections, other political actions have to be considered. This is so because in sheer numbers, Hispanics remain a minority of registered voters in Dade. As of 1979 the figures were: Blacks 113,881 (15.9%); Hispanics 111,032 (15.5%); Non-Hispanic Whites 489,257 (68.3%).[21] Also significant is the fact that the highly concentrated residential pattern of the Cuban-Americans gives them a majority in less than 5% of the electoral precincts in Dade County. This has meant that the Cuban has had to use benefits secured by other groups. These benefits have been an important source of Cuban political strength and point to the significance of ethnic politics in an era of ethnic revitalization.

Dade's Cubans benefitted quite early from nationwide minority group pressures which had generated a social and political climate propitious to ethnic bargaining. Many groups, including many non-minority liberal ones, made this new environment possible. But in the Hispanic population it was the Mexican-American sector more than any other which had stretched the boundaries of political participation, further reducing the weight of citizenship as a resource. Commenting on the 1977 Silva case involving Mexican illegal aliens, a Houston observer painted an accurate picture of the new socio-political milieu in which "the ability of illegal aliens to challenge the Government and win" was accompanied by what was described as "the proliferation of 'store front' legal agencies that have taken their cause in hand."[22] The new climate is not purely emotional, thus, but rather informed by precise political and legal advice as well as sympathetic legal talent.

Cubans, relative latecomers to the movement of ethnic minorities, have been able to gain from the advances of others. The Voting Rights Act of 1965 was a direct result of Black Civil Rights agitation but the "Hispanic amendment" of 1975 to that Act was due mostly to Mexican-American lobbying. The latter provided for bilingual voting materials and instructions as well as bilingual poll-workers in any precinct with more than 10 Latin voters.[23] It is significant that the defeat in 1980 of the Bilingual statute of Dade County in no way affects these Federal regulations which indicates the value of ethnic bargaining which targets Federal, rather than local, legislation.

Language is by far the most important factor in the retention of ethnicity, but in Dade County it certainly is only one of many. Crucial is the development of the private school system, Catholic and very "Latin," organized sports and the continued celebration of their own heroes, patriotic figures, and other elements of the ethnic group's collective mythology.

The most important indication of *capability for integration*, however, is economic success and the measures of this for the Cuban Community are clear. A few are listed in summary fashion:

> Aggregate annual income of the Cuban Community in Dade County in 1978 was $2.2 billion.
>
> The median family income in 1978 was $13,644 (higher than Dade County "Anglos" and much higher than Blacks.)
>
> 61.4% own their own home.
>
> 67% have credit cards.
>
> 34% of household heads have some college education. The median number of years of schooling completed (in 1978) was 11.3.
>
> In 1975 the Dade County Cuban family outspent its Anglo counterpart for groceries: $64.10 vs. $42.39 per week.

One of the areas of most spectacular success was the expansion of Cubans in manufacturing. Between 1969 and 1972 the number of Cuban-owned manufacturing industries increased from 166 to 267 (a 60.8% increase) but their gross receipts per firm increased from $59,632 to $500,520, or 739 percent. In explaining this spectacular success of immigrant group entrepreneurship, the Commission on Spanish Speaking Populace of Florida cited the following three points:[24]

> 1. A higher rate of return on investment than in the retail sector.
>
> 2. The impersonal relation existing between the manufacturers and the ultimate consumer. This enables the Hispanic manufacturers to serve both an Anglo and Hispanic market regardless of language barriers.
>
> 3. Availability of managerial knowhow and past experience in industrial enterprises among Hispanic entrepreneurs.

Point No. 1 underscores the immigrant group's capacity to make sophisticated judgements and decisions regarding investments; point No. 2 the absence of barrier — cultural or otherwise — to the utilization of existing skills, and No. 3, the actual existence — prior to immigration — of these skills.

Previous ethnic group contact in Cuba and adoption of urban industrial society life-styles combined with high social class and occupational status as well as racial (white) homogeneity tended to guarantee the Cubans' capabilities of acculturation and integration. Their high rates of outmarriage and naturalization are expressions of the capability for integration. The retention of their ethnic identities in turn indicates that this integration has taken place while they not only kept their ethnic identity, but indeed selectively used it to enhance their power. As a major marketing agency noted, "In spite of signs of increasing assimilation into the American economy, the Latin life-style resists conversion in many areas." The agency noted such facts as the ongoing use of Spanish in 80% of Cuban households, the preference for "Latin" goods and merchandising milieus (especially the ability to speak Spanish), and generally a preference for things with "a Latin taste."

It is interesting to speculate what this same set of characteristics did for a group which shared a "double" minority status: Cuban women. Not only do Cuban women in the United States have a higher rate of participation in the labor force (in 1970, 55.1% compared to 54.3% for Black, 46.8% for white, 39.1% for Mexican and 34.2% for Puerto Rican women), it compares dramatically to the 11.6% rate existing in Cuba before the Revolution.[25] The following comparisons made by Fagen, Brody and O'Leary attest to the upward mobility of those women after immigration to the United States.

OCCUPATIONAL COMPARISON
OF CUBAN WORK FORCE
AND CUBANS IN THE UNITED STATES.*

OCCUPATION	PERCENTAGE OF CUBAN 1953 CENSUS	PERCENTAGE AMONG CUBANS STUDIED
Lawyers and Judges	5%	3%
Professional and Semi-Professional	4%	22%
Managerial and Executive	5%	12%
Clerical and Sales	14%	31%
Domestic Service, military and police	8%	9%
Skilled, semi-skilled and unskilled	27%	20%
Agricultural, fishing	41.5%	3%
	N = 1,938,228	N = 55,354

Source: Richard Fagen, R. Brody, & T. O'Leary, *Cubans in Exile: Disaffection and the Revolution,* Stanford University Press, Stanford, 1968.

*The sample of migrants considered in this study consists of registrants at the Miami Cuban Refugee Center only until 1963.

Reinforcing these various dimensions of the Cuban capability for integration without complete loss of cultural identity is their concentration in Miami, the "unofficial capital of the Cuban community" as a Cuban academic called it.[26]

In 1972, 27.4% of the Hispanics in Dade had lived elsewhere before moving to that county; by 1977 the figure had increased to 34.6%. Interestingly, the reasons for moving were those which traditionally tend to guarantee a continued trend regardless of other factors: climate, 45.6%, family-related motives, 21.7%.[27] Not surprisingly, in 1977 fully 93.2% intended to remain despite that year's economic recession and despite the fact that Dade registered a higher unemployment rate among Hispanics (10.1%) than the rate for Hispanics nationwide (9.0%). The decision to move to Dade revolves around issues other than jobs or economics; the decisions are grounded in primordial attachments and an intense sense of group identity. Once in Dade, the remarkable permanency of marriage among Hispanics[28] eliminates divorce as a cause of outmigration. These trends among Hispanics take on additional weight as they are accompanied by the exact opposite attitudes on the part of non-Hispanic whites and thus on their decisions to move out. The outmigration of this sector combined with the phenomenal growth of the Latin sector virtually guarantees the trend toward Hispanization of Dade County.

CONCLUSION

What the performance of Cuban immigrants would have been under previous historical periods and less liberal ideologies of acculturation, I leave to the reader's imagination. I would venture the educated guess that the ideology of ethnic revitalization suits the Cuban immigrant well. There is some evidence that the same ideology has been counterproductive to the Black ethnic group, as Martin Kilson has warned. He is of the opinion that Blacks' perceptions of the relationship of ethnicity to power is distorted. Kilson has argued that, "Today ethnicity, in the hands of a new set of Negro leaders — bent like their Irish, Polish, Jewish, Italian historical counterparts on the ethnic redress of differentials between subordinate and superordinate groups — might well lead to profound political crisis at many levels of the American political system."[29]

The politics and ideology of ethnic revitalization is a dangerous double-edged sword for a minority with major involuntary aspects of ethnicity, such as Blacks. Skin color and general phenotype are involuntary and these reduce the options for the use of strategic ethnicity for the individual and more so for the group.

This is not the case with the American Jew or the Cuban. The practice of anglicizing Jewish names was a frequent occurrence because it had a positive result. The fact that Blacks were forcefully given anglicized names in no way has affected their status; the practice of adopting Islamic names might be physically comforting but perhaps little else. Interestingly, there is no evidence of the changing of Cuban names.

In short, as long as the majority continues to control major degrees of power, the process of ethnic revitalization will benefit only those whose ethnicity contains enough elements of choice, of voluntarism, that they can turn it on or off according to the situation vis-a-vis that majority: those groups with the capacity to engage in strategic ethnicity. This is a vital point because as the history of major ideologies on acculturation in the United States shows, a previling ideology can be changed rather rapidly. The strategies which succeed in one period might well be quite counterproductive in another.

FOOTNOTES

[1]Max Weber, "Ethnic Groups", in Talcott Parsons, et. al. (eds.), *Theories of Society*, Volume 1 (New York: The Free Press, 1961), pp. 305-309.

[2]I first developed the concept of "strategic ethnicity" in a paper presented to the International Congress of Applied Anthropology, Amsterdam, March 28, 1975, ("Privilege and Anxiety: The White Creole in Trinidad"). Since that time I have benefited (despite major disagreements) from Orlando Patterson's essay, "Context and Choice in Ethnic Allegiance: A Theoretical Framework and Caribbean Case Study," in Daniel P. Moynihan and Nathan Glazer (eds.), *Ethnicity, Theory and Experience* (Cambridge, 1976), pp. 305-349.

[3]Cf. Robert E. Park, *Race and Culture* (paperback ed., New York, 1964), p. 150. A good discussion of the various theories of "race relations cycles" is contained in Brewton Berry, *Race and Ethnic Relations* (Boston, 1958), pp. 129-149.

[4]Those not all social scientists are of one mind about the significance of ethnicity as an independent variable. Piere van der Berghe claims, for instance, that race and ethnic relations have "no claim to a special place in a general theory of society." They do not, in his opinion, warrant special theoretical treatment. *(Race and Ethnicity* [New York, 1979], p. 9). R. A. Schermerhorn is not quite as categorical yet he maintains that "basic research in macrosociology should have priority in the understanding of ethnic and racial pluralities." *(Comparative Ethnic Relations* [New York, 1970], p. xii.)

[5]*Ethnicity: Theory and Experience* (Cambridge, Mass., 1976)

[6]*The Urban Village* (1962)

[7]Sergio Diaz-Briquets and Lisandro Perez note that the majority of the migrants during this period were former migrants returning to their country of origin — not the United States. *(Cuba: The Demography of Revolution.* Population Bulletin, Vol. 36, No. 1 (April, 1981), p. 4. One can assume that those who succeeded remained. They and/or their children would be an important element among those who would later migrate to the U.S.A. In a way 1959 was the migration of the successful migrant.

[8]"Social Class and the Definition of the Cuban Nation," in D. P. Barkin and N. R. Manitzas (eds.), *Cuba: The Logic of the Revolution* (Mass: Warner, 1974), pp. 1-17.

[9]Cf. Anthony P. Maingot, "The Struggle for Socialism and Democracy in the Caribbean," in Howard Wiarda (ed.), *The Continuing Struggle for Democracy in Latin America* (Westford, Conn. Greenwood Press, 1979).

[10]Diaz-Briquets and Perez, p. 29.

[11]Juan M. Clark, "The Exodus from Revolutionary Cuba (1959-1974)," Ph.D. Dissertation, University of Florida, 1975.

[12]It must be understood, however, that Miami was not then, and is certainly not now a "Southern" city. The State was also governed by such progressive southerners as LeRoy Collins and Reuben Askew.

[13]*Hispanic Intermarriage in New York City: 1975* (New York: H.R.C., Fordham University, Monograph No. 2, 1979), p. 1.

[14]Milton Gordon found that degrees of interaction were higher among people of the same social class, regardless of ethnicity, than among people of different social status of the same ethnic group. *(Assimilation in American Life.* New York: Oxford University Press, 1964).

[15]Fitzpatrick and Gurak, pp. 60-64.

[16]*Staff Report.* Select Commission on Immigration and Refugee Affairs. Washington, D.C., 1980, p. 264.

[17]Strategy Research Corporation, *Dade Latin Market,* (Miami, 1970), p. 26.

[18]Cf. Anthony P. Maingot, "Ethnic Bargaining and the Non-Citizen: Cubans and Haitians in Miami," Report to the U.S. Coordinator of Refugee Affairs. 1979, p. 23.

[19]A study of a multi-ethnic neighborhood in Miami shows that Puerto Ricans appear to derive no bargaining edge from their U.S. citizenship. Noting that the other Latin groups cannot vote because of their present citizenship status, they were nevertheless "the ones most watchful of American politics — on all levels — and legislation which could affect them." Puerto Rican Opportunity Center, *Wynwood: Perspectives on a Multicultural Community,* (Miami, Florida: August, 1977) p. 58.

[20]*The Miami Herald* December 10, 1981, p. 26. The highly ethnic emotions present even at citizenship swearing-in ceremonies is evident in the following description of a Cuban eyewitness and participant: "Only when a representative of the Dade County Bar Association closed his speech with Cuban patriot Jose Marti's words, 'Honrar, Honra' ... did the audience respond with fervent applause ... Technically, it took me 10 years / to become a citizen /. Emotionally, it may take me forever." (Fabiola Santiago, "Journey to Citizenship," *(The Miami Herald,* June 5, 1980, p. 1C).

[21]Dade County Elections Department, 1980; *The Miami Herald,* August 19, p. 1.

[22]John M. Crewdson, "The New Migrant Militancy," *The New York Times,* April 16, 1978.

[23]Priority number one on the 1981 agenda of the Mexican-American Legal Defense and Education Fund (MALDEF) continues to be renewal of the 1965 Voting Act; immigration issues come a close second (Cf. *Miami Herald,* January 19, 1981, p. 4).

[24]C.S.S.P., *First Annual Report,* 1977, p. 93.

[25]George L. Wilbur, Daniel E. Jaco, Robert J. Hagen and Alfonso C. del Fierro, Jr., *Minorities in the Labor Market,* Vol. I (Kentucky: University of Kentucky Press, 1976), p. 19.

[26]Pastora San Juan Cafferty, "The Cuban Experience," in Foundation News, *Hispanics and Grantmakers* (Washington, D.C. 1981), p. 17. San Juan's description fits the analysis of this paper: "Cuban communities keep the Spanish language and Cuban traditions while actively participating in the new English language society in which they have become integral members."

THE IMMIGRANT AND THE PEDAGOG

By Asa Grant Hilliard III
Professor of Urban Education
Georgia State University

... the book is a study of one of those unattractive "isms" which taught our forbearers how to make up their minds, and also how to act, most often without awareness of the confused meanings of their thinking or of the ambiguous consequences of their deeds. The lesson we may learn, I suggest, is that we have learned the lesson too well. The apologetics entailed is still too much with us. We are still confronted by "savages"; we are still the bearers of "civilization"; we still seek ever to develop a theory of the relations of the one to the other, a theory whereby the violence that has inevitably ensued will be at once rationalized, understood, and excused — above all, made bearable. I have said that we are not in a position to instruct the past. But I continue to think, in a history such as this one, we may well be instructed by it.
(Pearce, 1965, p. x)

Thinking in multicultural education has tended toward richness in anecdotes, information, ideas, and prescriptions. Yet it has at the same time been theoretically and philosophically poverty stricken. Consequently our analyses of problems which fall under such headings as multicultural education, "Title I education," "disadvantaged education," and "education for the linguistically different" are frequently without power and clarity. Moreover, the diversity of names or labels for the problem area ("multicultural," "bilingual," "culturally deprived," etc.) reflect a diversity of implicit and explicit assumptions and conceptions about the nature of pedagogical problems. These must be made explicit if options are to be exercised without wholesale confusion.

The atheoretical and, I might add, ahistorical orientation and approach in multicultural education leaves us with the knowledge that pedagogical problems appear to be manifest in several areas:

1. Culture;

2. Oppression;

3. Social Economic Class;

4. Pedagogical Strategy.

Yet descriptions, expression, and ideas do not provide coherent explanations as to *how* such problems emerge. Without a theory of problem *dynamics*, pedagogical intervention strategies cannot be theory guided. For example, *how* does culture enter the teaching-learning process to impede or facilitate learning? What evidence is there for this? Does the juxtaposition of cultural groups generate conflict? What are the conditions under which it does or does not?

Clearly, educators need:

1. A theory of cultural *functioning* and its relationship to pedagogy;

2. A theory of the *dynamics* of oppression and its relationship to pedagogy;

3. A theory of socioeconomic class *functions* and their relationship to pedagogy;

4. A theory of pedagogical *dynamics*.

These theories must be grounded empirically. *Then criteria can be established for the selection of pedagogical approaches. At this point multicultural theory is at a crisis stage simply because multicultural educators have not given theory building a high priority. For that reason, much of our work has been both impractical and of suspect validity.*

It is unfortunate that most multicultural education practice is ad hoc and speculative. There are hundreds of examples of success in teaching all types of cultural groups in all types of conditions. These natural experiments should serve as the sources for the development of theory. This is seldom the case. As a consequence we witness certain predictable absurdities. While academics are at work on such crash projects to discover the cure for the "disease" of illiteracy which seems to strike certain cultural groups, other educators quietly go about their regular work of teaching, with the highly successful results which one would expect from good teaching. While our United States academic community strives to give tortured explanations for the failure of so many citizens to achieve high academic goals, other nations demonstrate that they can produce high academic achievement among nearly all their population. If there is one place where there are blinders being worn in education, it is in this area. The origin of theory must come from the observation and explanation of successful practice, not from armchairs.

If valid theory existed, I feel certain that we would be forced to say goodbye to many of our hidden operating assumptions. These hidden assumptions derive from our national history, which includes slavery and our close identification with the thinking of former colonial powers about formerly colonized people. Such thinking includes such elements as the following:

1. There are "civilized" and "uncivilized" peoples;

2. There are Christians, Jews, Islamics, and other major religions, and there are "pagans";

3. High "technology" is equivalent to Western technology. Traditional societies are not *technical;*

4. Some societies are cognitively deficient or underdeveloped;

5. There are many "primitive" people in the world.

If valid theory existed, we would begin to ask entirely different types of questions. For example, if we had a theory of culture in education, we would be forced to extend our view from a restriction of attention to students to a look at both teachers' and students' cultural dynamics.

America is unique in its makeup among nations in the world. Perhaps its central characteristic is its diversity under a unified national unbrella. Fully 10% of the population of America are the descendants of slaves from Africa. A lesser percentage of the population are the descendants of the original occupants of the continent — American Indians. The remaining part of the American population is made up of immigrants and the descendants of immigrants from all parts of the world, with the exception of a very small group of descendants of slaves and indentured servants from Europe.

The interaction of such diverse cultural and national groups over a relatively long period of time has produced an emerging common culture with its own unique distinguishing characteristics — *a common culture* which is unlike that of any culture presently associated with previous homes of the diverse populations. And yet the sensitive observer will have no difficulty whatsoever identifying numerous pockets of cultural diversity throughout the land. These pockets of cultural diversity are *within* the common general culture. There are also significant examples of cultural uniqueness among groups. In some cases the uniqueness is barely perceptible. In other cases it is quite visible.

The national experience of diversity, even in the face of hostility toward some of the cultural groups who now occupy a place under the national umbrella, has produced certain mechanisms for incorporating members of groups who are new to the American scene. It is important to note that the reception of diverse national groups on the American scene varies greatly dependent upon the national origin of the group (Daniels, 1971; Collier, 1973; Forbes, 1977; Chase, 1977; Jacobs, Landau & Pell, 1971; Prucha, 1978; Montagu, ; Stuart,). Both legally and socially, the signals and practices are quite clear. The accommodation of newcomers occurs most easily when they arrive from Northwestern Europe or from colonized lands which are populated with the descendants of Northwestern Europe who are in political control of those lands. The accommodation is most harsh, on the other hand, for those who come from the nations of the so-called "Third World." The quotes below are descriptive of the American Indian experience.

> A powerful education can be obtained with no school at all. In a lifetime experience with Indians in the Southwest, I have been impressed by the acuteness and intellectual effectiveness of unschooled Pueblo and Navajo Indians who often respond to complex modern legalistic challenges with more grasp than school-trained Indians. Does this suggest that Indian children can lose intelligence by going to schools? Or is it simply very difficult to use Indian intelligence in white programs? Throughout this study, total education rater than the interlude of school is the large concern. We want to know *how schooling affects education,* additively or subtractively. In the same reference we are concerned with how schools affect learning and the development of intelligence.

> California school teachers frequently view their Indian students as unintelligent or retarded. This impression may have a basis of accuracy, for certainly Indian students perform at a low level. The question the anthropologist must raise is: Do they enter school retarded, or do they become retarded through schooling? One of the casualties of acculturation, moving from one system of values to another, is that effective intelligence can be left behind.
> (Collier, 1973, p. 3)

> All three of these main lines of Indian policy reform converged in one ultimate goal: the total Americanization of the Indian. All were aimed at destroying Indian-ness, in whatever form it persisted. The aim was to do away with tribalism, with communal ownership of land, with the concentration of the Indian on reservations,

> with the segregation of the Indians from association with good white citizens, with
> Indian cultural patterns, with native language, with Indian religious rites and
> practices — in short, with anything that deviated from the norms of civilization
> practices and proclaimed by the white reformers themselves. Failing to perceive a
> single element of good in the Indian way of life as it existed, they insisted on a
> thorough transformation. The civilization which they represented must be forced
> on the Indians if they were unwilling to accept it voluntarily.
> (Prucha, 1978, pp. 7-8)

In short, there have been and there continue to be implicit and explicit messages
and practices which indicate that the preference for indigenous cultural groups
and newcomers coincide with the place of national origin, skin color, linguistic
similarity to English, level of education, etc. An examination of United States
immigration laws including quotas for various nations around the world will
provide the data to support these contentions. All of these things and more
contribute to the character of the context within which any new immigrant is to
be educated. Clearly, then, there can be no standardized formula for answering
questions pertaining to the education of all immigrant populations.

FACTORS AFFECTING THE RECEPTION
AND EDUCATION OF THE IMMIGRANT

Given the background above, we may anticipate that there will be a number of
factors which will determine the nature of the educational experience for any
immigrant population in the degree to which educational efforts will be
successful. Among these factors will be the following:

1. *Images* of the immigrant nation. It can be shown that the names of
such nations as Northern Ireland, England, Haiti, Cuba, the Philippines, Israel,
Jamaica, South Africa, China, Australia, Japan, by their very mention, are
likely to stimulate clear-cut feelings, attitudes, and images in the minds of
present American citizens. Those images, attitudes, and feelings will be
determined in part by the national and cultural background of the perceiver.
Some nations tend to be viewed overwhelmingly as positive sources for
immigration, while others tend to be perceived quite negatively (Chase, 1977;
U.S. Civil Rights Commission, 1976). Much "civilized" belief is still infected
with egocentric and self-serving notions that there are "primitive" people. There
are not now, nor have there ever been a "primitive" people in the sense that our
scientists and general population have tended to believe.

> First let us look at the empirical picture. There are small societies that are highly
> urbanized in Europe. There are predominantly rural societies of enormous scale
> such as China. The kinship system of the Americas of the highly complex industrial
> society of the United States is extremely simple, but the kinship system of the
> Australian aborigine whose main tools for production are the digging stick and the
> boomerang must be rated in general among the most complex in the world. There
> are societies with highly organized political structures such as that of Uganda and
> Dahomey which share the lack of a written language with others with no trace of

centralized government whatsoever, such as those of various branches of Eskimoes or Kaska Indians. Barter as a main form of trading is found among the Toda with their polyandry, and among diverse other people, including the Chuckchee of Siberia, Congo Pygmies, Bantus, Melanesians, and many Indians of the New World. As for the importance of the sense of personal security and cohesiveness of communal life, compare such people as Dobans and Alorese, on the one hand, and Zuni and Fox Indians, on the other. Religion and religious rituals are far more homogeneous and important among Catholics in the world as a whole, than among the widely divided and various Protestants as a whole. This contrast holds true whether we compare them intrasocietally or intersocietally. Who among us have observed that Catholics are therefore more primitive than Protestants? Even the criteria of abstract thinking versus concrete thinking are not foolproof for differentiating the primitive from the civilized. Is the Arunta or Murnging type of social organization less abstract than the Arab or Chinese traders' profit calculations? (Hsu, 1968, p. 49)

Even though the concept of "primitive," like so many other pejorative labels for less favored cultural groups, is without meaningful content, yet the image remains.

2. The *socioeconomic status* of immigrants from the national group presently in the United States. If an immigrant population has succeeded in developing a strong economic and political base within the nation, the image of that group in the eyes of other Americans and the leverage which that group can exert on behalf of additional immigrants from its home base will be factors in the reception of new immigrants from the same country.

3. The *number* of immigrants and the *rate* of their immigration. A trickle of immigrants from a favored nation is very likely to go unnoticed. However, a large number of immigrants, even from a favored nation, or a large number of immigrants from an unfavored nation entering the nation within a very short period of time will cause serious reaction.

4. The *dispersion* of immigrants. If an immigrant population arrives and remains in a small geographic area, the reception will be quite different than would be the case if immigrants were dispersed evenly throughout the nation. Both the reaction to the immigrant and the immigrant reaction as an immigrant are affected by numbers, rate, and dispersion.

5. The *socioeconomic status of the new immigrant.* Immigrants who come from wealthy professional classes in their native land are more likely to be accommodated than would be the case with the more impoverished immigrant.

6. *Single* immigrants or immigrant *families.* If immigrants come alone, such as large numbers of male immigrants without families, the reception is likely to be quite different than if whole families come together.

7. *Ethnic communities.* If a national ethnic community exists in the place where immigrants settle, the reception of the immigrant from that group will be facilitated.

8. *Linguistic match.* Immigrant accommodation will be facilitated if the linguistic match between the immigrants' language and English is high. On the other hand, immigrants who speak a language different from that spoken in the United States are more likely to have a difficult time in direct proportion to the degree of difference.

9. *Political economy of the immigrant's own nation.* The political importance of a particular nation to the national interests of the United States is a definite factor in the way in which immigrants will be accommodated within the United States.

10. *Racism.* Within the past two centuries, racism has developed as a malignancy and has filtered through human relations throughout the world (Hodge, Struckman, & Trost, 1975; Blanner, 1972). It became an overriding factor which will still affect the reception of indigenous, African and immigrant populations (Chase, 1977; King, 1971; Spivey, 1978).

Examples of the points above are seen easily as we note the experience of diverse immigrant groups within the nation at the present time. The Hmong, an Asian population who in their country were quite poor, and who did not for the most part have opportunities for formal education, had a reception here which was quite different from that accorded to the first Vietnamese immigrants, who tended to be from South Viet Nam and who tended to be perceived as a part of the allied struggle in that area, at least until large numbers of Vietnamese began to appear, primarily on the West Coast. Similarly, most of the first Cuban refugees, being in many ways more closely identified with European culture than was the case with some of the more recent Cuban immigrants in the "freedom flotilla," encountered a distinctly different reception upon their arrival. Even more extreme has been the experience of our Haitian population, who come from a nation which does not figure prominently in the foreign policy picture for our nation, which is also linguistically different, and which has a low status because of its race, in addition to being economically disadvantaged. A number of factors combine together to make for more extreme difficulty of accommodation of Haitians than has been the case of affluent, white British citizens who immigrated in small groups, almost invisibly, within the limits of a very favorable national quota for immigration.

PRIMARY ISSUES AND PROBLEMS

The factors above are but a few of the things which must be considered by educators as we attempt to assess the situation for immigrants and educational opportunities. Together they create for the immigrant a number of important problems, problems which educators tend to overlook. Among them are the following:

1. Problems of *identity;*
2. Problems of *assimilation* and the issue of whether to assimilate or not;
3. Problems of *cultural understanding;*
4. Problems of *mobilization for self-determination.*

Problems of identity. Culture is to a group what personality is to the individual. The importance of the personality to an individual is well recognized in our nation, a nation which more than any other glorifies the individual (Lasch, 1978).In psychotherapy, for example, it would be unthinkable to proceed to help an individual without reference to that individual's personal history and special style. Psychometry is full of devices to assess different aspects of individual behavior; such things as intelligence, self-concept, and personality are all of interest. Variations in individual behavior are expected. On the other hand, we live in a nation which has a peculiar culture-blindness. (Hall, 1977; Levi-Strauss, 1966; Turner, 1949; Vass, 1979). In general, cultural behavior tends not to be recognized or acknowledged, nor do instruments exist to assess cultural "quotients," cultural "concepts," or the "personality" of a given culture. If culture is attended to at all, it is culture in what, to us, is its exotic form, primarily in foreign lands. The plain fact is that every person is a part of both a cultural and an historical stream (Cole & Scribner, 1974; Hall, 1977). It is not a matter of "should they be?" The fact simply is that they are. It is the history and culture of a group, combined almost as raw material in a matrix, from which persons are continually being created (Flores, Attinasi, & Pedraza, 1981). The attempt to understand or to explain either individual or group behavior without reference to information on history and culture is an empirical fallacy and will generate certain error.

The political importance of strong cultural identity is well understood by all dominating cultures. It is seen most clearly in its negative and virulent racist form in the educational planning of South Africa. The Broederbond is a secret group of white South Africans which has institutionalized a modern system of slavery and has sought to maintain it through calculated use of cultural chauvinism.

> Four years later, the Chairman of the Broederbond reaffirmed the Bond's commitment to the principles and education for which it has fought so ardently during the years. "The heart of the successful program of action to achieve Afrikaner unity on the basis of our own distinctive Afrikanerdom," he said, "is naturally how we educate and train our children and youth. As Christian Afrikaners, we undertake, when our children are christened, to educate and have them educated in Christian faith and to the honor of our Creator. This education begins in the family life and must be continued in our schools and institutions of higher education.
>
> "At the same time we teach our children Afrikaans as their mother tongue in our homes and adjust them in this way to their own Afrikaner cultural assets, a process which is also continued in and through our educational institutions. To achieve one's own mother tongue and thus one's own culture is at the same time to achieve awareness of one's own distinct Afrikanerdom. Education whereby one's own Christian Afrikanerdom is achieved and enriched is the key to Afrikaner unity. If Afrikaner parents, teachers, and lecturers fail in this task or carry it out defectively, Afrikaner unity will suffer irreparable damage."
> (Wilkins & Strydom, 1979, p. 264)

Strong cultural identity need not and indeed should not be negative and racist. One thing is certain: a confused cultural identity is a prelude to vulnerability.

The immigrant to America runs into the awkward position of being a product of history and an exemplar of a culture in a nation where perceptions have evolved away from the capacity to perceive cultural diversity. Where cultural variety can be seen, it can sometimes be appreciated temporarily as an exoticism; or, since usually it is neither expected nor understood, the presence of cultural variety can be the source of great discomfort for some Americans. In either case, the general expectation in our nation is that the appearance of distinct cultural forms and content will be but temporary.

The immigrant to America will encounter many formal and informal beliefs and practices which operate to negate cultural identity. For example, the immigrant may experience a strange array of naming practices: having been a *Filipino,* a *Haitian* or a *Spaniard* on the day before immigration, the person may arrive in the United States to become at once a "minority," "disadvantaged," or may find a confusing new label for their cultural identity. For example, a *Filipino,* a *Cuban,* a *Spaniard,* and a *Mexican* may become simply "Hispanic." A *Hawaiian,* a *Japanese,* a *Chinese* (Cantonese or Mandarin) may become simply "Asian." The name of the cultural group more often than not will be in the eye of American beholders who seek economy in communication more than accuracy. It is a matter of *external attribution* of identity. All people have real cultural and personal boundaries, even when they are unaware of them. Though both small and large adjustments in those boundaries may be made consciously or unconsciously at any given time, they are both real and important.

A real question arises for every immigrant. How and to what extent will one's cultural identity be modified?

Assimilation. The presence of different cultural groups in the United States is a consequence of diverse causes. American Indians were already here and were dominated by Western European colonizers. African-Americans were forcibly removed from their homeland and brought to labor as slaves. European-Americans elected to come, for the most part. Some Chinese-Americans and Mexican-Americans have sought permanent homes, while others have seen their movement as a temporary necessity for the purpose of taking advantage of available economic opportunities. Regardless of the reasons for the existence of cultural populations in America, a choice of cultural identity ultimately must be made by each group or by group members. Does one assimilate and reject the old culture, or does one maintain the old culture to some degree and assimilate to some degree, or does one attempt to maintain the old culture at all costs? Some groups have plunged into the American mainstream willingly, becoming assimilated to an emerging national culture. Others have been much more reluctant to do so. Still others have not had the option of doing so.

For some Americans, "American culture" is regarded as equivalent to some version of Western European cultural tradition. For them, to become "American" is to adapt to cultural traditions of Western Europe as modified in America. For them, "American culture" and "Western civilization" are synonymous. Much could be said about the accuracy of the points of view or about the desirability of any of the choices. However, the important point for discussion is this: Can the nation maintain a *democracy of culture,* or is a national culture a prerequisite to citizenship? Is being an "American" more a statement about culture or citizenship? Some of the tensions which exist in the accommodations of immigrant populations and in the education of immigrants are centered upon the absence of a clear resolution for this problem.

Cultural understanding. Wherever two cultures come into contact with each other, there is a temporary dissonance. The *meanings* which are attached to such dissonance will vary. For the culturally sophisticated, such disonance is nothing more than what should be an expected temporary set of inconveniences or mismatches in experiential content or rule systems which precede the opportunity for cultural accommodation and harmony, sometimes even fusion. Cultural diversity in and of itself is not a cause of conflict. When conflict occurs concurrent with the meeting of cultures, it is almost always the case that political agendas lie underneath the conflict, and cultural features will serve merely as *signs* to determine who the "we" and the "they" are. It is important for the educator to understand the distinction between culture as the source of conflict and culture as a marker for determining treatment. For many educators have assumed falsely that conflict among cultural groups is a natural and inevitable consequence of cultural contact. Such is not the case.

The temporary social and communication dissonances which occur do so because every culture creates its own cognitive and perceptual *structures,* which are nothing more than habitual ways of handling certain human transactions. For example, we may expect diversity among cultural groups in terms of patterns of intimacy, patterns of openness, patterns of mutuality, and patterns of religion, etc. In the absence of raw political agendas, cultures are usually able to accommodate to each other quite easily and quickly.

Self-determination. The economic and political status of immigrant populations will determine the degree to which self-determination is possible. It is my firm belief that no group of people will be happy to exist under the domination and control of another group of people, either by force or because of economic or political dependence. I assume that self-determination is a universal goal. The capacity for self-determination is determined not only by economic and political status, but by the character and strength of a cultural system as well. Where cultures have a strong sense of identity and tradition, the basis for ethnic group collaboration and mobilization for self-determination is likely to be quite strong. Where cultural cohesiveness has been destroyed or has simply eroded, the basis for self-determination is correspondingly weakened (Cabral,   ;Prucha, 1978; Pearce, 1965).

TEACHING STRATEGIES

One of the lessons of the past decade in the United States is that where cultural groups exist who occupy disadvantaged economic or political positions in the society, educators have invented theories of education which appear to be tied *uniquely* to particular groups on the basis of their condition. We hear, for example, of special pedagogy for the "disadvantaged", or special pedagogy for "Title I children." Sometimes we hear of special pedagogy for "Head Start children." In my opinion, such reasoning is faulty at its core and is without empirical evidence to support the theories. I believe that sound pedagogical principles are *generic* for all learners. What varies is the content through which the pedagogical principles are applied. The reason for the variation in the content has to do with the history and culture of the particular group which is involved. Every person or group is the product of his, her, or its own special experience. These experiences are the raw materials which provide building blocks for future experience. For that reason, a fundamental principle of pedagogy is that all persons must be approached in such a way that they are allowed to utilize their own center as the basis for learning (Asante,   ). Given that *cultural and historical core as a pedagogical necessity,* we would expect the pedagogical differences in treatment among groups in education to be largely differences of content, and not differences of strategy or process. Julius Nyerere has summarized an approach which is powerful in producing results.

An Alternative Philosophy of Education
congruent with the ideas of Paulo Freire

(This is a re-ordered summary of a philosophical statement by His Excellency Julius K. Nyerere, President of the United Republic of Tanzania, in June, 1976. Nyerere gave the keynote speech at the International Conference on Adult Education and Development, sponsored by the International Council for Adult Education. The text of his address was adopted by the 400 participants from over 80 countries as the Conference's own basic statement on objectives and strategies for adult education and development. This is a restatement of part of his speech; in its entirety, it is known as the Declaration of Dar es Salaam. It is reprinted in *Convergence,* Vol. IX, No. 4, 1976.)

An adult learner
1) can only educate him/herself. Education cannot be accomplished for, or by, someone else;
2) knows something about the subject s/he is interested in, even if s/he is not aware that s/he knows it. S/he may indeed know something which the teacher does not know;
3) learns through a process that includes all three components of thinking, deciding, and acting (Freire calls this process praxis.);
4) must relate to and cooperate with others in order to act. For this reason, achievement is never individual.

Adult education
1) enlarges people's understandings, activates them, helps them to make their own decisions and to implement those decisions for themselves;
2) is not self-contained within informational subject areas, but reinforces connections between different areas to make a coherent whole;
3) is a highly political activity because it affects how people look at the society in which they live and how they seek to use it or change it. Because education always includes some action on the part of the learner, it is never "neutral," or free of values and consequences;
4) should include a desire for change and an understanding that change is possible, and should help people to work out what kind of change they want, and how to create it.

An educator of adults:
1) must involve learners in their own education and in the practice of it from the very beginning. What is important is that the adult learner should be learning by doing;
2) is a leader and guide along a path which teacher and learner travel together. They share a task which is of mutual benefit; the teacher is always also a learner.

This egalitarian basis is a necessary prerequisite of full use of existing human resources in the learning situation.

3) draws out the things the learner already knows and shows their importance to the new thing which is to be learned. This establishes the learner as confident and capable of contributing, demonstrates the relevance of experience combined with thought and analysis, and shows that people extend understanding and control over their lives by sharing knowledge. (Moriarty & Wellerstein, 1979)

It is because we are unfamiliar with or are confused about these matters that we tend to identify problems of temporary cultural dissonance as if they were fundamental pedagogical issues. For example, differences in language may be overcome relatively easily. Cultural unfamiliarity is usually a temporary problem. But neither differences in language nor differences in the degree of familiarity with a culture are in any way suggestive of pedagogical diversity as a necessity. Options do exist in pedagogy; however, they are *not* tied to cultural identity. For example, *we may choose a pedagogy of liberation or a pedagogy of slavery* which is independent of the culture of the learner. However, the choice of pedagogy is a political not a cultural necessity. Freire speaks to us of the pedagogy of dialogue and liberation.

Literacy makes sense only in these terms, as a consequence of men's beginning to reflect about their own capacity for reflection, about the world, about their position in the world, about their work, about their power to transform the world, about the encounter of consciousness — about literacy itself, which thereby ceases to be something external and becomes a part of them, comes as a creation from within them. I can see validity only in a literacy program in which men understand words in their true significance: as a force to transform the world. As illiterate men discover the relativity of ignorance and of wisdom, they destroy one of the myths by which false elites have manipulated them. Learning to read and write has meaning in that, by requiring men to reflect about themselves and about the world they are in and with, it makes them discover that the world is also theirs, that their world is not the price they pay for being men but rather a way of loving — and helping the world to be a better place. (Freire, 1973, p. 81)

I regard the pedagogy of liberation as that pedagogy which recognizes, values, and utilizes the *critical powers of learners as a central part of its operation.* For example, Paulo Freire in *Education for Critical Consciousness,* John Dewey in *Democracy and Education,* and Jean Piaget in his discussion of the development of cognitive structures, all share a common faith and interest in the creative learner. On the other hand, I see as pedagogies of domination and control such things as *behavior modification* (when used as a general approach rather than as a temporary remedial approach), *indoctrination,* and *propaganda.*

Having said these things, it is now possible to point out that for many educators the education of immigrant populations constitutes no pedagogical puzzle whatsoever. They neither expect nor find that it is unduly difficult, different, or strange to reach diverse cultural groups (Hilliard,   ). Remarkable success is possible when fundamentally sound generic pedagogical principles are applied. If educators are impeded in the application of fundamental liberating pedagogical principles, then students will fail to learn. At that point, the point of failure, the educator must analyze pedagogy, not the learner or the culture. Was the pedagogy applied in a high quality manner? Was it a democratic pedagogy or a pedagogy of critical consciousness?

> Freire insists that methodological failings can always be traced to ideological error. Behind the practice of agricultural extension, he sees an (implicit) ideology of paternalism, social control, and non-reciprocity between experts and "helpees." If on the other hand one is to adopt a *method* which fosters dialogue and reciprocity, one must first be ideologically committed to equality, the abolition of privilege, and to non-elitist forms of leadership wherein special qualifications may be exercised but are not perpetuated. (Goulet, 1973, xi-xii)

Educators who misunderstand the dynamic importance of history and culture are quite likely to misapply or fail to apply fundamental generic pedagogical principles, such as the principle that all earners should be taught in such a way that they use their center. What this means in terms of strategy is the following:

1. The *content* of education for immigrant populations must be a content which, where the immigrant population is concerned, is *truthful* and *respectful* of the learner. A brief trip to almost any library would be sufficient to convince the careful reader of how little truthful and respectful content exists as information on many nations and cultures from which immigration has occurred. The pre-colonial history of many nations is totally ignored; the dynamics and impact of colonialism is biased or ignored; indigenous populations are exoticized; the accounts in our libraries are almost never from the perspective of indigenous people; and so forth (Forbes, 1977). Above all, the real problems and conditions of learners are often ignored.

2. The *goals* for immigrant education must be comprehensive; that is to say, they should not be limited to the development of low-level vocational skills. The full gamut of educational opportunities should be made available as soon as possible to every immigrant group. Moreover, the focus must be on action, *praxis,* or critical consciousness. A general approach to a pedagogy of liberation is described by Moriarty and Wallerstein.

> Sometimes, as in the case of ESL classes where the teacher does not share a common language with students, identifying central issues necessitates a special kind of listening. This differs from most educational needs assessments in that it employs an approach much like anthropological fieldwork. The teacher becomes a participant-observer, using tools like body language and systematic note-taking to focus on themes that are most timely or problematic for students. Students participate as co-investigators, anthropological informants and members of a team whose task is to choose the starting points for discussion. The teacher can use curriculum development to test the reaction of the larger group to these themes; s/he enters an ongoing process of listening, feedback, and refinement.

> Whether it is used to facilitate dialogue among teachers or within their separate classrooms, this method of problem-posing moves through three necessary states: listening (choosing the issues to discuss; creating and revising codifications to focus on these questions) dialogue (the questioning process outlined above, moving from individual experience to awareness of the larger issues involved), and action (doing something to try and resolve the problems discussed; gaining new information and insight as the result of that concrete interaction). Freire calls this listening/dialogue/action process CONSCIENTIZATION, and emphasizes that

action — following through to consequences — is essential to any real learning: "... Knowledge is not a fact but a process. And what is more, it is a process which determines the praxis of men and women in their reality. Because of this, knowing implies transforming. We know when we transform." (Moriarty & Wallerstein, 1980. p)

This general approach is as suitable for young children as for adults.

3.   The educational materials for literacy, cultural familiarization, etc. can easily be tailored so as to take advantage of the nearness of immigrants to real human problems such as problems of immigration, public welfare, citizenship rights and responsibilities, and employment. Indeed, it is just such content which has been utilized effectively by such people as Lotte and Allen Marcus in their highly successful literacy program for migrant farm workers in California. The program was called *English on Wheels*. Not only is such content contemporary and meaningful; it provides an opportunity to engage learners in a critically conscious way.

> Although cultural issues transfer inevitably into adult classrooms, teachers often try to avoid raising serious questions with their students. Understandably, many feel unprepared to handle the complexity of conflicting values, emotions, and ways of communicating. What Kan's teacher to do when a standard ESL question — "How many children do you have?" — brought tears and a halting story of two babies still in resettlement camps in Thailand? We would argue that cultural differences and emotional experiences are not only inevitable in adult teacher-student and teacher-teacher groups but that they create a kind of energy that can be handled with sensitivity and respect and channeled toward motivated and effective learning. Freire-style codifications and questioning strategies serve as useful tools in this process. (Moriarty & Wallerstein, 1980. p.)

CONCLUSION

It is important that the educators rightly divide the word of truth; that is to say, where the problems of educating immigrant populations are concerned, it is very important that problems which are primarily problems of pedagogy be sifted out from a whole array of other problems which are not primarily pedagogical. The immigrant who is unemployed and who is hungry, under stress, and depressed as a consequence, does not require a new pedagogy for learning. He or she merely requires that basic human needs be met and that he or she be active in solving problems to meet them. The immigrant who is the victim of racism as evidenced by the denial of an opportunity or any say in the development of educational policy which affects his or her life, or as reflected in the professional literature which may suggest a genetic basis for inferior performance in school (Hirsch,   ; Jensen, 1980; Chase, 1977), or which is reflected in low expectations and irrelevant goals for his or her education, is not in need of a unique pedagogy; rather, he or she is simply in need of protection from those who are unable to apply *normal high quality pedagogical* procedures to immigrant populations.

We do a disservice to immigrants and indeed to the education profession itself when we suggest that there is some *mystery* pedagogy *uniquely* suitable or waiting to be discovered for each new cultural group, or for all immigrant populations as a whole. Usually we find that the idea of a mystery pedagogy or pedagogical "puzzle" is associated with less favored cultural groups. The assumption is implied that "normal" cultural groups should receive "normal" pedagogy. We need to determine first the extent to which sound generic pedagogical principles *are or are not* applied to immigrant populations. Perhaps in times of high unemployment in the nation, the incentive for the production of even more well-educated graduates at all educational levels, including immigrants who would be among those graduates, is very low. If that is the case, once again, it is not a matter of pedagogy but a matter of politics. At the same time, educators must be prepared to work on the appropriate problem, but through the appropriate mechanisms. The immigrant is a person — no more and no less than are or were all those immigrants who preceded him or her. With the exception of American Indians and African slaves, America is itself a nation of immigrants. If any nation is specialized to ease the problems of transition for immigrant groups, it ought to be this one. The "culture" of the nation should certainly be no barrier to that end; for it is a culture which is just as African, Mexican, Asian, Cuban, and Haitian as it is English, German, French, and Scandinavian. The pool of common American culture which we experience consciously or unconsciously could not by any stretch of the imagination have been created out of the narrow and lonely experience of any *one* national group. Perhaps conscious attention to that fact will ensure greater levels of tolerance, understanding, and skill among educators as we approach the problem of ensuring the greatness of the nation for its new sons and daughters. The proper pedagogical strategy for immigrant populations is to ensure that they receive the same culturally sensitive normal liberation pedagogy which should be offered to all members of a free society. In 1933, Carter G. Woodson highlighted the deep meaning of education for freedom. At the time he focused on the plight of African-Americans.

> It may be of no importance to the race to be able to boast today of many times as many "educated" members as it had in 1865. If they are of the wrong kind, the increase in numbers will be a disadvantage rather than an advantage. The only question which concerns us here is whether these "educated" persons are actually equipped to face the ordeal before them or unconsciously contribute to their own undoing by perpetuating the regime of the oppressor.

> Herein, however, lies no argument for the oft-heard contention that education for the white man should mean one thing and for the Negro a different thing. The element of race does not enter here. It is merely a matter of exercising common sense in approaching people through their environment in order to deal with conditions as they are rather than as you would like to see them or imagine that they are. There may be a difference in method of attack but the principle remains the same. (Woodson, 1933, p. xxxi)

REFERENCES

The All-African People's Union, *Education to Govern: A Philosophy and Program for Learning Now,* Detroit: Advocators Press, 1974.

APTHEKER. HERBERT. ED. *The Education of Black People: Ten Critiques, 1906-1960,* by W.E.B. DuBois. New York: Monthly Review Press, 1973.

ASANTE. MOLEFI KETE *Afrocentricity: The Theory of Social Change,* Buffalo, New York: Amulefi Publishing Co., 1980.

BATTLE. VINCENT M., LYONS. CHARLES H. EDS. *Essays in the History of African Education.* New York: Teachers College Press, Columbia University, 1970.

BIBBY. CYRIL. *Race, Prejudice, and Education.* New York: Praeger, 1960.

BLAUNER. ROBERT. *Racial Oppression in America.* New York: Harper and Row, 1972.

CABRAL. AMILCAR. *Return to the Source.* New York: Monthly Review Press, 1973.

CARDENAL. FERNANDO S.J., Nicaragua, Valerie Miller 1980: The Battle of the ABC's. *Harvard Educational Review, 51* (1), 1981, 1-26.

CARLSON. LOUIS H., COLBURN. GEORGE A., EDS. *In Their Place: White America Defines Her Minorities.* New York: John Wiley & Sons, 1972.

CHASE. ALLAN. The Legacy of Malthus: *The Social Cost of the New Scientific Racism.* New York: Alfred Knopf, 1977.

COLLIER. JOHN JR. Alaskan Eskimo Education: *A Film Analysis of Cultural Confrontation in the School.* New York: Holt, Rinehart, and Winston, 1973.

CRUSE. HAROLD. *The Crisis of the Negro Intellectual.* New York: William Morrow, 1967.

DANIELS. ROGER. *Concentration Camps, USA: Japanese-Americans and World War II.* New York: Holt, Rinehart and Winston, 1971.

FLORES. JUAN. ATTINASI. JOHN. AND PEDRAZA. PEDRO. JR. LaCarretta Made a U-Turn: Puerto Rican Language and Culture in the United States. *Daedalus,* Spring 1981, *110* (2), 193-213.

FORBES. JACK. *Aztecas Del Norte: The Chicanos of Atzlan.* Greenwich, Connecticut: Fawcet Publications, 1973.

FORBES. JACK D. *Racism, Scholarship, and Cultural Pluralism in Higher Education.* Davis, California: Native American Studies Tecumseh Center, University of California/Davis, 1977.

FREIRE. PAULO. *Education for Critical Consciousness.* New York: Seabury Press, 1973.

FREIRE. PAULO. The People Speak Their Word: Learning to Read and Write in Sao Tome and Principe. *Harvard Educational Review, 51* (1), 1981, 27-30.

HERNANDEZ. DELUVENA. *Mexican American Challenge to a Sacred Cow.* Los Angeles: Aztlan Publications, Chicano Studies Center Monograph I, University of California, 1970.

GRANGER. ROBERT C., YOUNG. JAMES C. *De-Mythologizing the Inner-City Child.* Washington, D.C.: National Association for the Education of Young Children, 1976.

HALL. E.T. *Beyond Culture.* New York: Anchor, 1977.

HILLIARD. ASA G. The Pedagogy of Success. In Sunderland, Sylvia (Ed). Washington, D.C.: Association for Childhood Education International, 1979, pp. 45-52.

HILLIARD. ASA G. Equal Educational Opportunity and Quality Education. *Anthropology and Education Quarterly, 9* (2), 1978, 110-126.

HILLIARD. ASA G. Straight Talk about School Desegregation Problems. *Theory Into Practice, 17* (2), 1978, 100-106.

HODGE. JOHN L., STRUCKMAN. LYNN D. TROST. *Cultural Bases of Racism and Group Oppression: An Examination of Traditional "Western" Concepts, Values, and Institutional Structures Which Support Racism, Sexism, and Elitism.* Berkeley, California: Two Riders Press, 1975.

HIRSCH. *Unfrocking the Charlatans.*

HSU. FRANCES L.K. Rethinking the Concept of "Primitive" In Ashley Montagu (Ed.), *The Concept of the Primitive* New York: Free Press, 1968.

Institute of the Black World (Ed.) Education and Black Struggle: Notes from the Colonized World. *Harvard Educational Review,* Monograph #2, 1974.

JACOBS. PAUL. LANDAU. SOL. PELL. EVE. *To Serve the Devil. Vol. 1: Natives and Slaves, Vol. 2: Colonials and Sojourners.* New York: Vintage Books, 1971.

JENSEN, A. *Bias in Mental Testing.* New York: Free Press, 1980.

KING, KENNETH. *Pan-Africanism in Education: A Study of Race, Philanthropy and Education in the Southern States of America and East Africa.* Oxford: Clarendon Press, 1971.

KITANO, HARRY H.L. *Japanese Americans: The Evolution of a Subculture.* Englewood Cliffs, N.J.: Prentice-Hall, 1969.

LACY, DAN. *The White Use of Blacks in America: 350 Years of Law and Violence: Attitudes and Etiquette, Politics and Change.* New York: McGraw Hill, 1972.

LASCH, C. *The Culture of Narcissism: American Life in an Age of Diminishing Expectations.* New York: W. W. Norton, 1978.

LEVI-STRAUSS, C. *The Savage Mind.* Chicago: University of Chicago Press, 1966.

LOPEZ, ANDRE. *Pagans in Our Midst.* Rooseveltown, N.Y.: Akwesasne Notes Mohawk Nation, 1980.

MEMMI, ABERT. *The Colonizer and the Colonized.* Boston: Beacon Press, 1967.

MILLER, STEWART KRATEN. *The Unwelcome Immigrant: The American Image of the Chinese, 1785-1882.* Berkely, California: University of California Press, 1969.

MORIARTY, PIA, WALLERSTEIN, NINA. By Teaching We Can Learn: Process for Teachers, *California Journal of Teacher Education,* Winter 1980, Vol. 7, 1, pp. 39-46.

PEARCE, ROY, HARVEY. *Savagism and Civilization: A Study of the Indian and American Mind.* Baltimore: John Hopkins Press, 1965.

PIVIN, FRANCES, FOX, CLOWARD, RICHARD, A. *Regulating the Poor: The Functions of Public Welfare* New York: Vintage Books, 1971.

PRIETO, LOUIS, B. *Simon Bolivar: Educator* New York: Doubleday, 1970.

PRUCHA, FRANCES, PAUL. *Americanizing the Indians: Writings by the "Friends of the Indians," 1880-1900.* Lincoln, Nebraska: University of Nebraska Press, 1978.

RAMIREZ, MANUEL III, CASTANEDA, ALFREDO. *Cultural Democracy by Cognitive Development and Education.* New York: Academic Press, 1974.

SANDMEYER, ELMER CLARENCE. *The Anti-Chinese Movement in California.* Chicago: University of Illinois Press, 1973.

SERFONTEIN, J.H.P. *Brotherhood of Power: An Expose of the Secret Afrikaner Broederbond.* Bloomington, Indiana: Indiana University Press, 1978.

SEXTON, PATRICIA CAYO. *Education and Income.* New York: Viking, 1964.

TACHIKI, AMY, WONG, EDDY, ODO, FRANKLIN, WONG, BUCK (EDS.) *Roots: An Asian-American Reader.* Los Angeles: University of California/Los Angeles Asian-American Studies Center, 1971.

WILKINS, IVOR, STRYDOM, HANS. *The Broederbond:* New York: Paddington Press, 1979.

SPIVEY, DONALD. *Schooling for the New Slavery: Black Industrial Education,* 1868-1915. Westport, Connecticut: Greenwood Press, 1978.

U.S. Commission on Civil Rights. *Puerto Ricans in the Continental United States: An Uncertain Future.* Washington, D.C.: Report of the United States Commission on Civil Rights, 1976.

VASS, W.K. *The Bantu Speaking Heritage of the United States.* Los Angeles: University of California, Center for Afro-American Studies, 1979.

WEINBERG, MEYER. *Minority Students: A Research Appraisal.* Washington, D.C.: U.S. Department of Health, Education and Welfare, National Institute of Education, March, 1977.

WOODSON, CARTER G. *The Miseducation of the Negro.* Washington, D.C.: The Associated Publishers, 1969.

WOODWARD, C. VANN. *The Strange Career of Jim Crow.* London: Oxford University Press, 1966.

ACCULTURATION:
A COMPARATIVE ANALYSIS
OF ALTERNATIVE FORMS

By J. W. Berry
Psychology Department
Queen's University at Kingston

The goal of this paper is to explore some variations in the process of acculturation of immigrant peoples, in the hope that such an exploration of alternatives will assist the current search for solutions to problems now facing this region. There is no claim on my part of knowledge about your particular situation, and no intent to advise; rather, my position is that a comparative overview and analysis might possibly inform your present work.

THE CONCEPT OF ACCULTURATION

When viewing a complex phenomenon such as acculturation, it is often useful to return to the early, original conceptualizations; these may serve both as anchors and as beacons in the ensuing search. Use of the concept of acculturation appears as early as 1880; there are, however, four classic formulations: Redfield, Linton, and Herskovits (1936), Herskovits (1938), Linton (1940), and the Social Science Research Council (SSRC) Summer Seminar (1954). Redfield et al. (1936) define acculturation in the following way:

> Acculturation comprehends those phenomena which result when groups of individuals having different cultures come into continuous first-hand contact, with subsequent changes in the original culture patterns of either or both groups ... under this definition acculturation is to be distinguished from culture change, of which it is but one aspect, and assimilation, which is at times a phase of acculturation. It is also to be differentiated from diffusion, which while occurring in all instances of acculturation, is not only a phenomena which frequently takes place without the occurrence of the types of contact between peoples specified in the definition above, but also constitutes only one aspect of the process of acculturation.

> In the 1954 formulation by the SSRC, acculturation was defined as: ... culture change that is initiated by the conjunction of two or more autonomous cultural systems. Acculturative change may be the consequence of direct cultural transmission; it may be derived from noncultural causes, such as ecological or demographic modification induced by an impinging culture; it may be delayed, as with internal adjustments following upon the acceptance of alien traits or patterns; or it may be a reactive adaptation of traditional modes of life. Its dynamics can be

seen as the selective adaptation of value systems, the processes of integration and differentiation, the generation of developmental sequences, and the operation of role determinants and personality factors. (p. 974).

From these classic statements, we may derive a number of features and dimensions of the phenomenon for our contemporary use. One is the basic nature of the phenomenon, a second is the characteristic course of acculturation, another is the levels at which it takes place, and a fourth is the issue of measurement. In the discussion which follows, there will be no attempt to encompass the worldwide features of acculturation; *rather the focus will be upon the impact of dominant contemporary societies in North America upon groups varying in cultural characteristics.*

Nature.   Acculturation requires the contact of at least two autonomous cultural groups; there must also be change in one or other of the two groups which results from the contact. Although, in principle, change can occur in either of the two parties (Bailey, 1937), in practice one group comes to dominate the other and contributes more to the flow of cultural elements than does the weaker of the groups.

The apparent domination of one group over the other suggests that what happens between contact and change may be difficult, reactive, and conflictual rather than a smooth transition. For some reason that is not clear, studies of intergroup relations and conflict research in the fields of sociology, psychology, and political science which could provide insights have usually been omitted in the study of acculturation. Nevertheless, the assertion may be ventured that between the initial contact and the resultant change in the contact arena, relationships are likely to be those of conflict.

The eventual form of the accommodation between the groups in contact and in conflict is not necessarily one of assimilation, as the initial formulation pointed out. A variety of relationships may develop which may best be comprehended in relation to the concept of adaptation (Berry, 1976a). This concept will be discussed in some detail later, but for the time being it may be viewed as the reduction of conflict within an interacting system.

Course.   This brief discussion suggests that there may be a characteristic three-phase course to acculturation: *contact, conflict* and *adaptation.* The first phase is necessary, the second is probable, and some form of the third is inevitable.

At the core of the notion of acculturation is the contact (physical or symbolic) between two groups; this can occur through trade, invasion, enslavement, educational or missionary activity, or through telecommunications. Without contact, there is no acculturation; so this condition is centrally important. Such variables as the nature, purpose, duration, and permanence of contact contribute to acculturation phenomena. The least acculturation may take place where there is no purpose (contact is accidental), where trade is mutually desired, or where contact is short-lived; *the greatest acculturation will take place where the purpose is a deliberate takeover of a society (e.g., by invasion) or of its skills or beliefs (e.g., by education and evangelization) over a long period of time (e.g., by settlement).*

Conflict will take place only in the case of some degree of resistance, but common experience shows that groups do not lightly give up valued features of their culture. Thus conflict, at some point during contact, has been the general rule.

Finally, as we have noted, *adaptation refers to a variety of ways in which to reduce or stabilize conflict.* This will be considered in detail in a later section of this paper.

Level. Although the *concept of acculturation originated within the discipline of anthropology* and *has most often been treated as a cultural group phenomenon,* the original formulations included the *term "individuals"* in their discussion and *referred to such psychological elements as "personality factors".* Thus, *acculturation may be treated as a two-level phenomenon* — that of the group and that of the individual (cf. Graves's, 1967, use of the term "psychological acculturation"). When *considering the three phases during the course of acculturation, it is apparent that contact, conflict, and adaptation are all phenomena which are of equal relevance to group* and *to individual levels of analysis.*

Measurement. A good deal of confusion surrounds the measurement of acculturation. One way to deal with the confusion is to carry out independent measurement of all three phases and at both levels of acculturation. Thus, any comprehensive study should consider at the group level the history, persistence, and purpose of the cultural contact, the nature of the group conflict, and the adaptations achieved by the two groups. Then the study should turn to the individual's exposure to the other culture, the interpersonal and intrapersonal conflicts and crises experienced, and the personal adaptations made to the situation.

Often, psychologists and others wish to comprehend an individual's adaptive behavior in a particular acculturation arena. We can begin to understand the individual's behavior only after (a) the group's experience of contact and conflict have been assessed, (b) the group's general mode of adaptation has been examined, and (c) the individual's exposure and conflict experience have been gauged. This suggests a multivariate measurement procedure that may be generally applicable to all individuals undergoing acculturation in North America. (Olmeda, 1979)

VARIETIES OF ACCULTURATION

Adaptation is a useful concept in the study of acculturation (Berry, 1976a, 1976b). If adaptation is viewed as the reduction of conflict, then the group and individual options taken to lessen acculturative conflict may be used to examine possible variations in this third phase of acculturation. Three varieties or modes of adaptation maybe outlined: adjustment, reaction, and withdrawal. In adjustment, changes are made which reduce the conflict by making cultural or behavioral features more similar; homogenization (as in the "melting pot") or assimilation of one group into another are examples of such adjustment. In reaction, changes are made which attempt to reduce the conflict by campaigning or retaliating against the source of the conflict; ethnic group political organization or aggression are examples of such reaction. In withdrawal, changes are made which essentially remove one element from the contact arena; moving back to the Reserve or setting up "nativistic" communities are examples of this mode. These three varieties of adaptation are similar to the distinctions in the psychological literature made between moving with or *toward*, moving *against*, and moving *away from* a stimulus.

One way to explore these three varieties is by giving dichotomous "yes" or "no" answers to two questions of crucial importance to all groups and individuals undergoing acculturation: "Is my cultural identity of value to be retained?, and "Are positive relations with the larger (dominant) society to be sought?" In this manner, four distinct varieties of acculturation may be identified: *Assimilation, Integration, Rejection,* and *Deculturation* (see Figure 1).

ADAPTIVE OPTIONS AVAILABLE TO NON-DOMINANT
GROUPS DURING ACCULTURATION

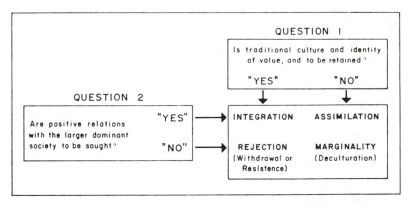

By answering "yes" to the question, "Are positive relations with the dominant society to be sought?", we have two positive varieties of acculturation (moving toward) which are distinguished by the contrasting value placed on the retention of cultural identity: Assimilation and Integration. In the case of *Assimilation*, relinquishing cultural identity and moving into the larger society is the option taken. This can take place by way of the *absorption* of a non-dominant group into an established "main-stream", or it can be by way of the *merging* of many groups to form a new society (the "melting pot"). In a detailed analysis of this form of acculturation, Gordon (1964) has distinguished a number of sub-varieties or processes: most important among these are "cultural or behavioural assimilation" in which collective and individual behaviours become more similar, and "structural assimilation" in which the non-dominant groups penetrate the social economic systems of the larger society. Other forms outlined by Gordon include marital, identificational and civic assimilation, by way of intermarriage, ethnic identification and the reduction of power conflict.

Integration, in contrast, implies the maintenance of cultural integrity as well as the movement to become an integral part of a larger societal framework. Therefore, in the case of integration, the option taken is to retain cultural identity and move to join the dominant society. In this case there is a large number of ethnic groups, all cooperating within a larger social system (the "mosaic"). Such an arrangement may occur where there is some degree of "structural assimilation," but little "cultural and behavioral assimilation".

Let us consider the types of acculturation that are identified by answering "no" to the question of establishing or maintaining positive relations with the larger society. *Rejection* refers to self-imposed withdrawal from the larger society. However, when imposed by the larger society, it becomes one of the classical forms of segregation. Thus, the maintenance of ones traditional way of life may outside full participation in the larger society be due to a desire on the part of the group to lead an independent existence (as in the case of "separatist" movements), or it may be due to power exercised by the larger society to keep people in "their place" (as in slavery or "apartheid" situations).

Finally, there is an option which is difficult to define precisely, possibly because it is accompanied by a good deal of collective and individual confusion and anxiety. It is characterized by striking out against the larger society and by feelings of alienation, loss of identity, and what has been termed acculturative stress. This option is *Deculturation,* in which groups are out of cultural and psychological contact with either their traditional culture or the larger society. When imposed by the larger society, it is tantamount to ethnocide. When stabilized in a non-dominant group, it constitutes the classical situation of "marginality" (Stonequiest, 1935).

CONTEXT OF ACCULTURATION

These four varieties of acculturation have been presented up to this point as if the acculturating groups were free to opt for one or another. However, these choices do not take place in a vacuum: the nature of the host society is clearly a major factor to be considered; so too is the nature of the particular acculturating group. With respect to the acculturating groups themselves, important variations are present in such factors as freedom of contact and mobility, while host societies vary greatly om a dimension of tolerance for diversity. Let us examine these two contextual factors.

Acculturating Group Variation. In the literature on acculturation (e.g., Price, 1969) reference is often made to the freedom inherent in culture contact: in some cases individuals and groups voluntarily seek out contact by migration, while in others contact is imposed as in the case of native peoples. Another dimension involves mobility: in some cases culture contact occurs because the acculturating group moves to the host society, while in others the group remains in place and contact is brought to them. These two dimensions are illustrated in Figure 2, by crossing two levels of each and providing a single illustration of each of the four resulting types.

FOUR TYPES OF ACCULTURATING GROUPS DUE TO
VARIATIONS IN FREEDOM OF CONTACT AND MOBILITY

Freedom		Mobility	
		Mobile	Sedentary
of	Voluntary	IMMIGRANTS	ETHNIC GROUPS
Contact	Forced	REFUGEES	NATIVE PEOPLES

The purpose here is to suggest that the nature of acculturation is likely to vary according to the type of group we are considering. The case of free or voluntary contact (indicated by the desire to migrate, or to have positive relations with the larger society), suggests that immigrants and ethnic groups may be more likely to Assimilate or Integrate than refugees or Native Peoples. In the case of sedentary groups, there is the possibility of establishing protective institutions and barriers which enhance the likelihood of maintaining ones identity, language and culture, and thus of following the Integration or Rejection modes of acculturation. To my knowledge, no empirical studies have been carried out systematically which indicate which modes of acculturation are more likely to be present in which type of acculturating group. The purpose of this analysis is merely to suggest that, with all four types present, one might reasonably expect not to find similar varieties of acculturation among all groups. (And it should be obvious that individual differences are likely to be present as well, but this issue is beyond the scope of the present discussion).

Larger Society Variation. A second contextual factor is that of the tolerance for cultural diversity in the host society. In some host societies, there has been the expectation, and a policy, which have tended to reduce extant cultural diversity; in others the position has been taken that diversity is valuable, is a resource rather than a problem, and has been tolerated, even encouraged. This dimension is one of *Multiculturalism,* and host societies may be placed along it between the two poles "multicultural" and "unicultural" (Berry, 1979a). This concept is not identical to that of "cultural pluralism", for even in plural societies attitudes and policies can still vary from homogenizing efforts to support for heterogeny. For a society to be multicultural, it requires the presence of both pluralism *and* of a multicultural ideology (Berry, Kalin and Taylor, 1977) in public attitudes and policy.

Societies which are culturally plural, *but* have been pursuing a unicultural goal, such as Australia *and the U.S.A.* have usually found that some reorientation in policy is required. For example, Australia has recently espoused multiculturalism as a public policy, and in the U.S. the fundamental work of Glazer and Moynihan (1963; 1975) has shown how the pursuit of the "melting pot" has not worked. In contrast, societies which are culturally plural *and* have been pursuing a policy of multiculturalism (such as Canada) have achieved a closer match between their sociocultural and policy situations.

At the 1956 UNESCO Havana Conference on "The Cultural Integration of Immigrants" (Borrie, 1959), the official Canadian paper argued that Canada's policy reflects "a society built upon the ideas of individual worth and cultural difference ... The pressure of one dominant group to assimilate, that is to absorb others, is therefore impracticable as a general theory". In 1971, a policy of multiculturalism was adopted in Canada by the Federal Government (and similar ones later by most Provinces). This policy asserted that "although there are two official languages, there is no official culture, nor does any ethnic group take precedence over any other". It sought to encourage the retention and development, by those groups wishing to do so, of cultural features of each group, and the sharing of these with all other groups. Programmes in support of this policy, such as grants to the ethnic press, the support of ethnic organizations and centers, and of research grants in ethnic studies, all gave concrete recognition to the value placed on diversity. A national survey of individual attitudes (Berry, Kalin and Taylor, 1977) established general support for the official position.

The purpose of this discussion has been to argue that the degree of tolerance for cultural diversity which is present in a host society will obviously be a major factor in the mode of acculturation which is likely to take place. In societies which attempt to reduce diversity, Assimilation or Deculturation are likely to take place, while in those more tolerant of diversity, Integration or Rejection are more likely. However if intergroup attitudes are hostile in the host society, Rejection (particularly the classical segregation form) and Deculturation are more likely than Assimilation and Integration.

From the point of view of the analysis of context, then, modes of acculturation are likely to vary according to both the variation in the type of acculturating group, and in the tolerance for cultural diversity in the host society.

BEHAVIORAL RESPONSES

In this section, an examination will be made of some of the literature which has attempted to assess psychological (individual level) responses to acculturation of the group. It should be clear, from the discussion of varieties of acculturation that psychological effects are unlikely to be only linear. Such a linear gradient would exist when there is a direct and linear relationship between experience of acculturative influences and degree of behavioral change; this pattern would typify only the Assimilation mode of acculturation. In contrast, some other psychological adaptations are more likely to take place to resolve the crisis in the Integration or Rejection modes, such as a judicious synthesis or a reaffirmation of traditional ways. Thus, with many varieties of acculturation possible at the group level of analysis, the psychological responses are likely to be at least as varied.

SCHEMATIC DIAGRAM OF PSYCHOLOGICAL RESPONSES
OVER THE COURSE OF ACCULTURATION

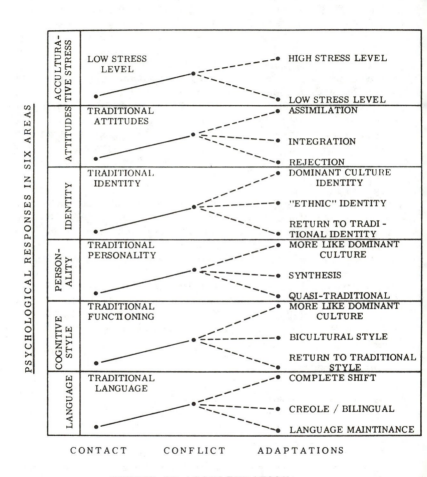

To help in conceptualizing these psychological responses, Figure 3 indicates six different areas of psychological functioning: language, cognitive style, personality, identity, attitudes, and acculturative stress. These are schematically diagrammed as a function of the course of acculturation. This figure is based upon a broad review of the literature (Berry, 1979b) and is presented here with only a few illustrative examples rather than with full documentation.

To begin, it should be clear that no single diagram can do justice to the wealth of available materials or to their complexity. Indeed, the attempt in Figure 3 violates the very purpose of Figure 1 which was designed to point up the variety of acculturation modes. Nevertheless, Figure 3 proposes that there is a common course across all six psychological areas: a traditional (precontact) situation at the left, and a gradual change in psychological characteristics until some hypothetical conflict or crisis point is reached that is followed by a variety of adaptations.

Language.   Perhaps the least complicated example is that of language use. It is a common experience that following contact, a language shift typically occurs which is more likely to take place in the nondominant group. In the Assimilation mode there is likely to be a complete shift away from the groups' own language to that of the larger society. Alternatively, individuals or the whole group may maintain or reinstate their traditional language by taking deliberate steps to protect, purify and institutionalize it. Intermediate options of bilingualism or linguistic merging into a creole are also commonplace. Classic examples of all three are readily available in the literature of acculturation in French Canada, colonial Africa, and among various ethnic groups in the Western Hemisphere.

Cognitive Style.   Included here are all perceptual and cognitive behaviors in addition to the work on the field dependent-independent cognitive style (see Witkin & Berry, 1975, for a review of cross-cultural studies). A general finding has been that most perceptual (e.g., illusion susceptibility), cognitive (e.g., intellectual abilities) and cognitive style test performance shows shifts toward the norms found in the dominant group. The most effective agent for these shifts appears to be the experience of formal, technical education (Berry, 1976b). There is, however, some work among Mexican Americans (Buriel, 1975) which suggests that there may be some acculturation to the *barrio* (cf. Rejection); this is indicated by the return to a traditional style mode. And finally, there is some impressionistic evidence that there may be a "switching" between styles, or a "bicultural" style, depending upon whether one is operating for the moment in the traditional or in the dominant group.

Personality.   An early study exemplifying the linear gradient pattern in personality was that of Hallowell (1955). In that study, three groups of Ojibway Amerindians, with three different degrees of contact with Eurocanadian society, exhibited a gradual shift in modal personality characteristics. However, such a gradient is not always found (e.g., Peck, Manaster, Borich, Angelini, Diaz-Guerrero, & Kubo, 1976) which may be due to the existence of a crisis point. The work of Spindler and Spindler (1957) has brought to the fore the anthropological basis for the crisis experience. Spindler (1968), working with the concept of reactive movement, and Linton (1943) and Wallace (1956), in a discussion of reaffirmation and revitalization movements, showed how some individuals and groups continue on the course toward the dominant culture (the Assimilation mode), while some move toward a native-oriented pole (cf. the Rejection mode). Still others achieve a synthesis in their personality (cf. the Integration mode), merging elements which are characteristic of both groups (Wintrob & Sindell, 1972). The psychological basis for dealing with the crisis experience is rooted in the work of Stonequist (1935), who noted that one possible course for the marginal person is to "swing about" and engage either wholly or partially with their traditional culture.

Identity. A review of the literature available on ethnic identity during the course of acculturation by Brand, Ruiz and Padilla (1974) indicates that there is often a fairly clear preference for an identity associated with the dominant group; however, numerous problems exist in this literature (e.g., experimenter's ethnicity/race) which make such an overwhelming shift toward the Assimilation mode somewhat suspect. Follow-up work by Levine-Brand and Ruiz (1978) considered some of these problems experimentally and found identification with the dominant group to be lower.

Work promoting a view of Canadian society as multicultural has demonstrated wide-spread identity with actual ethnic descent (Berry, Kalin & Taylor, 1977). For example, among those of French ancestry, about half identify as French-Canadian and another third as Quebecois. Overall, there is a substantial proportion of persons in the society maintaining a regional or ethnic identity, distinct from a national one. Thus, the reaffirmation of cultural heritage, either by claiming a traditional identity or a hyphenated "ethnic" identity, is clearly in evidence.

Attitudes. Research conducted over the past few years has attempted to assess a group's attitudes toward the various acculturation modes (Berry, 1970, 1976b; Sommerlad & Berry, 1970). Three scales have been developed, one each for attitudes toward the Assimilation, Integration, and Rejection modes. In the first study (Sommerlad & Berry, 1970), it was found that the critical difference between favoring the Assimilation mode and the Integration mode was identity as an "Australian" or as an "Aborigine". Subsequent work (Berry, 1970, 1976b) in Australia and northern Canada has attempted to show that these are fairly independent attitudes, that they can vary from group to group, and that the variation is to some extent dependent upon cultural and psychological characteristics of the two groups in contact. For example, favoring Assimilation now is positively related to initial cultural and psychological similarity between the two groups in contact, while favoring Rejection is negatively related. Favoring assimilation also is positively related to the degree of contact already experienced, but so, too, is favoring Rejection: among the younger, better-educated, and more exposed people, there is often evidence for a crisis followed by reaffirmation, leading to the Rejection mode. A similar pattern is found among Francophone Canadians who identify as Quebecois. Thus, a traditional identity choice, which probably contains an element of the Rejection mode, is favored by those who are young and, better educated.

These attitudes, then, can be assessed in acculturating groups, and their variations can be explained to some extent. Note that these attitudes are conceptually unrelated to the constructs of modernization or modernity (which assume some universal Assimilation mode); rather, they are attempts to cope (conceptually and empirically) with variations in acculturation modes.

Acculturative Stress. The five psychological responses considered up to this point have all been classed as "shifts"; that is, they are behaviors which are largely extensions of, or variations on, precontact behaviors. Another class of behaviors has been termed "acculturative stress," and includes those behaviors and experiences which are generated during acculturation and which are mildly pathological and disruptive to the individual and his group (e.g., deviant behavior psychosomatic symptoms, and feelings of marginality). Two main areas of research (adaptations of migrants and of native peoples) provide evidence that such stress is common, but not inevitable (Berry, 1979b).

With respect to immigrant adaptation, one argument (Murphy, 1965, 1975) is that migrants experience less stress in multicultural societies than in unicultural societies, and indeed may have better mental health than local-born residents. In multicultural societies, it is possible for groups to maintain a supportive cultural tradition, while in unicultural societies (those pursuing the Assimilation mode), there is a single dominant culture with a clear set of national attitudes and values which all immigrants must either adjust to or oppose, leading to greater conflict and higher rates of stress and perhaps eventually to psychological breakdown.

There is a clear difference in the adaptation of native peoples: they were inundated, rather than seeking out a new society. (An often-told comment of an Amerindian wit is that the only mistake they ever made was to have a lousy immigration policy!) Once again, the literature suggests that increasing stress is not inevitable as contact and conflict increase; stress levels are associated with both the cultural and psychological characteristics of the groups and individuals in contact, and may decline after a crisis point. For example, Chance (1965), working with Alaskan Inuit, found that high stress was associated with low contact but high identification with western life, while those with greater congruence between these two variables exhibited less stress.

In northern Canada (Berry, 1976b), work with nine different Amerindian communities has provided the following pattern of evidence: communities with high acculturative stress are those with least initial cultural similarity to the dominant society, are intermediate in contact (perhaps at the crisis point), and are most in favor of the Rejection mode. Conversely, those communities with the least stress are those with more initial cultural similarity, are highest in contact (perhaps past the crisis point), and most in favor of the Integration mode.

Putting the immigrant and native adaptation studies together, the following generalization may be proposed: acculturative stress will be highest when the cultural distance is greatest and when the insistence that the journey be taken is strongest. Obviously what we need now is a series of comparative studies of these stress phenomena, in which a range of traditional cultural groups adapt during acculturation to a range (unicultural through multicultural) of dominant societies. Only then will we be in a position to understand the relative contributions of these numerous variables to this very real problem of acculturative stress.

CONCLUSION

This paper has attempted to show that acculturation is not only Assimilation. The fact that much acculturation research has found Assimilation to be the predominant mode may be due to the culture-bound nature of the research; even in unicultural societies, Assimilation may be predominant, but is not the only mode.

Beyond the unicultural setting, though, the other varieties of acculturation, along with a large range of psychological responses, will almost certainly be more in evidence. It is the task of all of us to ensure that research reflecting the cultural panorama of human life is actually accomplished.

Needless to say, this paper solves no problems for you; indeed, because it has spread things out, it may have created some. Nevertheless, work elsewhere, and the conceptual underpinnings of that work, may stimulate your own understanding of your problems, and may give you new insights into their nature and their solution.

REFERENCES

BAILEY, A.G. *The Conflict of European and Eastern Algonkian Cultures 1504-1700: A Study in Canadian Civilization*. St. John: New Brunswick Museum Monograph Series, No. 2, 1937.

BERRY, J.W. Marginality, stress and ethnic identification in an acculturated Aboriginal community. *Journal of Cross-Cultural Psychology*, 1970, *1*, 239-252.

BERRY, J.W. Individual adaptation to change in relation to cultural complexity and psychological differentiation. Paper presented to American Anthropological Association, Washington, D.C., 1976a.

BERRY, J.W. *Human Ecology and Cognitive Style: Comparative Studies in Cultural and Psychological Adaptation*. New York: Sage/Halsted, 1976b.

BERRY, J.W. Research in multicultural societies: Implications of Cross-cultural methods. *Journal of Cross-Cultural Psychology*, 1979a, *10*, 415-434.

BERRY, J.W. Social and cultural change. In H. C. Triandis and R. Brislin (Eds.) *Handbook of Cross-Cultural Psychology, Vol. 5*. Boston: Allyn and Bacon, 1979b.

BERRY, J.W., KALIN, R. AND TAYLOR, D.M. *Multiculturalism and Ethnic Attitudes in Canada*. Ottawa: Government of Canada, 1977.

BORRIE, W.D. (ED.), *The Cultural Integration of Immigrants*. Paris: UNESCO, 1959.

BRAND, E.S., RUIZ, R.A., AND PADILLA, A.M. Ethnic identification and preference: a review. *Psychological Bulletin*, 1974, *81*, 860-890.

BURIEL, R. Cognitive styles among three generations of Mexican American children. *Journal of Cross-Cultural Psychology*, 1975, *6*, 417-429.

CHANCE, N.A. Acculturation, self-identification, and personality adjustment. *American Anthropologist*, 1965, *67*, 372-393.

GLAZER, N. AND MOYNIHAN, D.P., *Beyond The Melting Pot*. Cambridge, Mass.: Harvard University Press, 1963.

GLAZER, N. AND MOYNIHAN, D.P. (EDS.) *Ethnicity: Theory and Experience*. Cambridge, Mass.: Harvard University Press, 1975.

GORDON, M.M. *Assimilation in American Life*. New York: Oxford University Press, 1964.

GRAVES, T.D. Psychological acculturation in a tri-ethnic community. *Southwestern Journal of Anthropology*, 1967, *23*, 337-350.

HALLOWELL, A.I. *Culture and Experience*. Philadelphia: University of Pennsylvania Press, 1955.

HERSKOVITS, M.J. *Acculturation: The Study of Culture Contact*. New York: Augustin, 1938.

LeVINE-BRAND, E.S., AND RUIZ, R. An exploration of multicorrelates of ethnic group choice. *Journal of Cross-Cultural Psychology*, 1978, *9*, 179-190.

LINTON, R. (ED.) *Acculturation in Seven American Indian Tribes*. New York: Appleton-Century, 1940.

LINTON, R. Nativistic movements. *American Anthropologist*, 1943, *45*, 230-240.

MURPHY, H.B.M. Migration and the major mental disorders: a reappraisal. In M. B. Kantor (Ed.) *Mobility and Mental Health*. Springfield: Thomas, 1965.

MURPHY, H.B.M. The low rate of mental hospitalization shown by immigrants to Canada. In Zwingmann and Pfister-Ammende (Eds.), *Uprooting and After*. New York: Springer-Verlag, 1975.

OLMEDA, E. Acculturation: A psychometric perspective. *American Psychologist*, 1979, *34*, 1061-1070.

PECK, R.F., MANASTER, G., BORICH, G., ANGELINI, A., DIAZ-GUERRERO, R., AND KUBO, S. A test of the universality of an acculturation gradient in three culture triads. In K. Riegel and J. Meacham (Eds.), *The Developing Individual in a Changing World*. Mouton: Den Haag, 1976.

PRICE, C. The study of assimilation. In J. A. Jackson (Ed.) *Migration*. Cambridge: Cambridge University Press, 1969.

REDFIELD, R., LINTON, R. AND HERSKOVITS, M.J. Memorandum on the study of acculturation. *American Anthropologist*, 1936, *38*, 149-152.

SPINDLER, G. Psychocultural adaptation. In E. Norbeck, D. Price-Williams, and W. McCord (Eds.), *The Study of Personality: An Interdisciplinary Appraisal*. New York: Holt, Rinehart and Winston, 1968.

SPINDLER, G. AND SPINDLER, L. American Indian personality types and their socio-cultural roots. *Annals of American Academy of Political and Social Science*, 1957, *311*, 147-157.

Social Science Research Council Summer Seminar. Acculturation: An exploratory formulation. *American Anthropologist*, 1954, *56*, 973-1002.

78   Berry

STONEQUIST, E.V. The problem of the marginal man. *American Journal of Sociology*, 1935, *41*, 1-12.
WALLACE, A.F.C. Revitalization movements. *American Anthropologist*, 1956, *58*, 264-281.
WINTROB, R. AND SINDELL, P. Culture change and psychopathology: the case of Cree adolescent students in Quebeck. In J. W. Berry and G.J.S. Wilde (Eds.), *Social Psychology: The Canadian Context*, Toronto: McClelland and Stewart, 1972.
WITKIN, H.A. AND BERRY, J.W. Psychological differentiation in cross-cultural perspective. *Journal of Cross-Cultural Psychology*, 1975, *6*, 4-87.

SHARED PROBLEMS OF CULTURALLY DISTINCT PEOPLES SEEKING A PLACE IN THE EDUCATIONAL PROCESS

By Frank B. Wilderson, Jr.
Professor of Educational Psychology
and Vice President for
Student Affairs
University of Minnesota

I would like to begin today by telling you a story. It is based on a children's story called "The Snow Kings". The characters and plot have been changed somewhat to fit our needs as advisers to minority students. In the original story the snow kings were white, black and yellow. Today, however, the story's kings are Hispanic, Native American and Black.

Each lived in his own kingdom and his people avoided those of other kingdoms, holding strong to their racial and cultural distinctiveness. There was, however, an uninhabited area bordering the three kingdoms and occasionally the kings, each from within the borders of his own kingdom, would survey that area, thinking that it should be explored.

On one particularly snowy, blowy day, the three kings each independently made a decision that they would, indeed, explore the area. Each thought that on that day there would be no possibility of a chance of meeting with either of the other two kings. Not that they were truly enemies, it was just that not knowing each other except to know that they were racially and culturally different, they instinctively decided that it would be in their best interest and the interests of their kingdoms that they not associate. Therefore, a great deal of mutual distrust and animosity had grown between them.

Well, each king bundled up, stepped across the borders of their lands into the uninhabited area and began his exploration. Each saw things that would be beneficial to their people there. However, each assured by the weather conditions that he would not be confronted by one of the other kings, did not take proper precautions and walked carelessly not heeding the dangers that might exist for a lone person in an unknown area. And one by one they fell into a large open pit in the center of the area too far from their borders to call for help. First the Black, and shortly thereafter the Hispanic, and then the Native American King found himself at the bottom of the same pit. The sides of the pit were glazed with ice and snow. Instinctively, each found an area of the pit to which they laid claim and excluded the others from their thoughts and efforts to scale the slippery walls. Finally, despairing of ever being free, each sat down distressed and hopeless over his fate and the fate of the people whom he had hoped he would be able to lead out of the limited area of his separate kingdom to partake of some of the resources he had found in the bordering area. Daylight began to wane. It grew colder. Fear of freezing drew the men closer together, until they were huddled in one tight mass to ward off the cold. Finally, the Native American King spoke, "We are warmed because we have shared the heat of our bodies. Perhaps together we can think of a way to get out of this pit, save ourselves and return with our knowledge of this area to our kingdoms." They thought. The Black King spoke, "We've not been successful in our attempts alone, but if I stood and you, indicating the Hispanic King, stood on my shoulders and you, indicating the Native American, stood on his, one of us would be able to reach safety." Finally, the Hispanic King spoke, "No, all of us would be able to reach safety because I could then be pulled up by the first king and we could form a chain of our bodies by which to bring you to safety."

And so the three kings working together were able to pull themselves out of the pit and they recognized that when people share the same problems and work at a solution together, none need lose his identity and all may benefit.

Represented here today are the racial, cultural minorities of that story and each of us wants not only to retain our racial cultural heritage, but to be assured that that heritage becomes a part of the mosaic of a pluralistic society, a part that is represented and respected in our educational institutions as well as in the daily lives of our people. In order to assure that this occurs we must be prepared to explore the area of education and develop the resources that will enable us to retain our distinctiveness and yet acquire the skills that will allow us to survive in a technocentric society.

The problems that each of us share in this society are not problems we have created either for ourselves or for each other, but those imposed upon us by the larger majority. It is then beneficial for us to look at those problems from the standpoint of our similarities rather than from the standpoint of our racial/cultural differences. No matter how rich or distinctive our individual cultural or racial heritage we form together another minority within the American Society. Not only that, but jobs, housing, and education are less accessible to us.

Economic factors have a great deal to do with the incidence of the numbers of us who are ill housed and there is a direct relationship with the high incidence of our miseducation and undereducation as well as the inaccessibility of higher education to us as an economically disadvantaged group.

In 1973 Mercer conducted an intensive study in one school district of the incidence of minority placement in special classes. He found that the incidence of placement of black children was three times greater than would be the case on the basis of their numbers in the population at large and that for Hispanic Americans the placement rate was four times greater than would be expected. The League of Women Voters of Minnesota found that recently there were seven elementary schools in Minneapolis with an enrollment of over 10% Native Americans. In these schools, 39% of the children were in the below average reading comprehension group in 6th grade. At the 8th grade level of the two junior high schools with the highest Native American enrollment, 43% of their students classified as below average although the City-wide percentage for both elementary and junior high students remained at 23%.

The minorities, represented here today, throughout the history of their participation in the public educational system have been consistently miseducated, uneducated, and undereducated. The miseducation has become more and more apparent to us as we have each begun to reassess our lives and our aspirations in terms of our roots. Realizing as we did so that our children were being destroyed in an educational process that either did not recognize their existence or taught them that their cultural and racial heritage was unacceptable if not altogether despicable. More often than not what happened in this process was an ambivalence that caused many of our students to turn off completely and leave the educational process without ever acquiring what the dominant society accepts as a suitable level of education to allow participation on the economic level except in the very lowest paying most menial occupations. Others of our students have stayed on in the process with the majority of these being undereducated.

It is this undereducated population of minority students toward whom the following portion of my remarks will be directed.

Let's begin then by examining similarities in the characteristics of minority students entering higher education. As a group they are more apt to be deficient in computational and reading skills. While the aspiration level of minority students may be high, many have an accompanying fear of the educational process, a fear of failure and an ambivalence toward higher education, coupled with financial difficulties that make it difficult for them to function up to their potential. Most will come from environments which will have given them little if any model identification with those who have gone on and succeeded in higher education.

A basic assumption is that nationally minority students are presented with a relatively low representational figure of model identification. A figure which will continue throughout their career in higher education. In all probability, they will encounter fewer numbers of their own racial or cultural group as they proceed in their education, not only as role identification models but as peer associates. In addition, they will continue to find themselves among the most financially disabled in the campus population which is predominantly representative of the White middle class socially, culturally, economically. Thus, minority students face not only a period in which they must be helped to overcome deficiencies in their preparation for college, but a period of time when already battered self-esteem will be put to the ultimate test in terms of both the academic and social climate of the small world of the college campus.

In order to gain access to most colleges and universities students are subjected to standardized achievement or intelligence tests. Most minority students succeed less well on them than do majority students. These tests are constructed using the norms for acceptable responses to specific items as determined by the largest segment of the sample which is white middle class. The basic assumption of such tests then is that there is a commonality of experiences shared by all those who take the test. The assumption ignores the reality of distinctly different arrays of cultural and social experiences that each ethnic group in this country enjoys or is subjected to by virtue of that ethnicity. Further, it ignores the fact thaty not all have equal facility with the English language and that not all have been exposed to the same quality and level of written or verbal communication in the English language. Implicit in these assumptions is the expectation that all who take the test will comprehend the word usage and the context of the questions in exactly the same way and that all students share the same value system. There is no recognition then, that differences in cultural background, the economic conditions of one's life, and the value of one's family and culture will influence responses to such questions.

While the specific difficulties which are presented to each of us as distinct racial cultural groups may show variance, we share commonly the problem that questions on standardized tests rarely reflect the experiences of Hispanics, Native Americans or Blacks.

In a recent survey of students in the Martin Luther King Program, a support program for minorities and disadvantaged students at the University of Minnesota, it was found that those minority and disadvantaged students who profiles were most like those of the majority population were most likely to finish their college educations within the normal four year limit with academic performances very similar to that of the majority population. It further found that those students who by virtue of test scores were considered to be high-risk students also showed no significant academic variance from the norm or majority group. However, high risk students were more apt to carry fewer course hours and take longer to complete graduation requirements than four years. While my conclusion may not be very scientific, I would say that the most essential characteristics of the successful minority student is determination and the determining factor in his success is the ability to perservere in the face of adversity.

The role of guidance counselors then in preparing minority students for the college experience I see as twofold:

1) Early identification of those students who not only show ability which would make them potential college aspirants, but of those students who academic profiles may not be as impressive but who exhibit either through extra curricular participation or some other indication a strong determination and drive to "make it".

How many of us have heard teachers say, "Johnny isn't too bright, but he sure works hard." Well, Johnny may be brighter than he's given credit for because the standards used to test his brightness may be those which have little validity for him. Or he may have other problems that preclude his efforts. Seek his out and give some meaning to his hard work. Turn these people on to all the resources, public and private, that may be available to them to help them make it financially and academically.

Secondly, you are that minority student's role identification model. In you, he sees the possibility of success in the educational setting. It is imperative that you not only give guidance to his academic needs, but work to bolster his self-esteem and feelings of self-worth.

You work with the minority student in preparing that student for the college experience differs from that in preparing the majority student in a significant way; that is, in the student's ability to identify with someone who is to him a role identification model as well as someone who expresses a personal interest in his/her social/academic well being. John K. Coster did a study in 1958 on "attitudes toward school of high school pupils from 3 income levels." His purpose was to study the relationship of specific attitudes toward school and income level. The study was of 3,000 students in 9 Indiana high schools. His conclusions were: There was no difference between students of different income levels on items pertaining to attitudes toward school, the school program, and the value of education. Differences were found on items pertaining to interpersonal relationships: or social life, being liked by other pupils, feelings of parental interest in school and *personal interest* of the *teacher*. In another study done in 1964 under the auspices of the Institute for Social Research at the University of Michigan, the authors sum up their findings by saying "The results indicate that pupil perceptions of *the teacher* far outweigh all other influences on the level of utilization of intelligence for both boys and girls.

Minority students in their preparation for college need not only be able to get supportive services in reading comprehension and computational skills in which they may well be difficient, but their achievement in those academic areas is directly tied to their feelings of being liked, and accepted in the school environment. You can give them this!

Finally, I would like to mention briefly, and more specifically than in passing references I have made heretofore in this address, the financial plight that will exacerbate the problems faced similarly by us as we advise students about college preparation.

While there has recently been a significant increase in the numbers of minority students enrolling in colleges and universities nationally completion or retention has been another matter. Here we seem to have lost ground. While other factors might prove relevant to the decrease in percentages of minorities students completing college, we can be sure that finances is one of the most critical factors. If today our students are facing an economic crises and economic advances of minority groups are disproportionately affected by adverse national economic trends, the economic condition of students in the next few years will be not better and may certainly be worse. Therefore, more minority students will come to institutions of higher education needing to have made available to them financial support in terms of loans, grants and part-time jobs. More of them will in all probability be forced to "stop-out" to earn the money necessary to finance their educations. Because the relative economic level of minorities is not keeping pace with inflation and the gap between minority median income and majority income is widening, more minority students will be forced to be independent of parental financial support.

Implications are that the lowering of the age of majority may also cause minority students greater concerns in the market place for funds to see them through their college educations. In today's college campuses students from white middle class income families are exerting their independence from parental influence to and including financial independence. More of them are seeking part-time employment on campuses or "stopping out" to take the non-skilled jobs which financially disadvantaged traditionally sought. More students from White middle income families are seeking financial aid from educational funding sources previously reserved for the economically disadvantaged, and their independence from parental resources makes them eligible for those funds.

Whether in response to greater numbers of white middle income students seeking financial aid or to a real concern relative to providing opportunity to more academically gifted students, more colleges are reinstating the merit or no-need scholarship. A recent survey of 859 colleges and universities around the country found that a little of 20% of the scholarships given freshmen in 1975 went to academic achievers, regardless of their family finances. Growing numbers of students needing the limited funds now available, the entry of middle income students in the funding market place, and the resurgence of no-need scholarship programs present a prospect far from promising for the financial future of minority college students in the near future.

It begins to sound, as I categorize the areas of minority student similarities, that the future for these students is all but impossible. This is not my purpose, nor is it true. However, in all of these areas the future for minority students is difficult and as counselors to these students you must appraise them of the difficulties as well as help them to seek solutions to them. Indeed, there are debits, particularly for the student who must borrow against his future earnings in the terms of educational loans in a period of economic recession. There is no assurance that a college degree will assure the student reaching employment goals. Students must be prepared to accept the fact that while college education may give some leverage toward acquiring economic stability, it holds no guarantees.

They should also be made aware that most colleges and universities today are beginning to show some responsiveness to the social and cultural needs of Hispanic, Native American, Asian and Black students.

Many minority students are intimidated by the initial college experience and fail to take advantage of those services available to them.

Note: Particularly in instances where services are offered on a cooperative basis. It is imperative that students be encouraged to seek out not only those support programs set up for his particular cultural group, but to interact with other minorities so that cooperatively they can begin to formulate ways in which solutions can be found to shared problems.

It is the responsibility of minority counselors, not only to help students decide on which schools best meet their needs, but to be comfortable enough in that experience to take advantage of every available support service the school offers, particularly those in which their experiences might lead them to the realization discovered by the Snow Kings. We must also be committed to reinforcing that student's feeling of self-esteem at every opportunity to prepare him for the college experience. In closing I would like to reiterate that as advisers to potential minority college students that it is the responsibility of the counselor

1) to know what services are offered

2) to apprise the student of them, and

3) to reinforce his/her feeling of self-esteem to the extent that the student feels comfortable about seeking and using these services. Beyond this, minority counselors must

1)   Actively seek not only the minority student who conforms to the norms as perceived through standardized testing, but actively seek out those students whose will and determination may make them successful college candidates; 3) use every resource available to prepare these students for the college experience, both academically and socially; 4) be a role model with which the student can identify; and 5) perhaps most importantly, use every resource available to you to reinforce that student's feelings of self-worth. For while education may not necessarily solve the problems we share within the American Society, it will certainly equip us with some of the knowledge which has been used to subject us and the skills necessary to begin our quest for self-determination with a society that must become responsive to the pluralistic nature of its composite parts.

PART TWO
PERSPECTIVES ON
THE ETHNIC BACKGROUND AND
PATTERNS OF IMMIGRATION

HAITIAN IMMIGRANTS IN SOUTH FLORIDA: ECONOMIC, SOCIAL AND CULTURAL ISSUES AND PROBLEMS

By Sandra L. Woods, Ed.D.
Florida International University
Miami, Florida, U.S.A.
and
Adolph A. Thompson
Former Jamaica Ambassador to the
Republic of Haiti and the Dominican Republic

PREAMBLE

One assumes that by now it is common knowledge in the villages and teeming towns of Haiti that there is scant welcome in South Florida for "boat people"; that at the other end of that terrible 500-mile sea journey there lies arrest and detention in a crowded camp. But they still come. Even at risk of being stopped and turned back, they come. Such is the strength of an idea whose time has come.

The influx of Haitian immigrants to South Florida has made for many social, educational, economic and political problems. The effects are felt in the pressure upon governmental agencies, social security systems, driver license and food stamp offices; but most especially upon the schools, hospitals, work training programs, and employment facilities throughout the inner-city areas of Dade County and South Florida in general. The aim of this paper is to outline a perspective which can form a background for a greater understanding of this issue.

In examining, in a just, fair, humane, and race-free manner, the complex economic, social and cultural issues and problems that have been spawned by the intrusion of at least 60,000 Haitian men, women, and children who are estimated to have landed on Florida shores illegally by sea since 1971, and between 1,000 and 1,500 arriving each month, we must ask what the motives were which induced so stubbornly conservative a people to accept an unfamiliar idea. The psychologists and the sociologists have already worked out some of these. A very obvious one is fear. It was fear that their country would be invaded that caused some of the Japanese scholars to interest themselves in the organization and skills of the outside world. It was fear which led America to develop the applications of atomic fission. War, said Thucydides, is a violent teacher; but fear is a quick and efficient teacher. Human intelligence was developed largely through fear.

A second motive is pride, the desire for prestige. It seems that to have ideas originating outside one's own circle often demonstrates one's possession of a larger and more sensitive mind than one's fellows possess — like having foreign furniture or imported clothes. This motive may be healthy, for some, if not all, societies are too limited; but it may also be mean and selfish even when its results are good.

A third motive is appetite, the desire for pleasure and comfort. Witness the way in which tobacco and chewing gum have spread all over the world. There are other motives which the psychologists consider less important, and yet they also are effective. One of them is the interest in play; both active games and purposeless ingenuity, the play of the mind. Still more important, and more permanent than fear or pride or appetite, is the desire to learn, simply for its own sake: not in order to grow rich or to insure one's safety or to get more enjoyment from physical life, but simply to learn. Aristotle begins his *Metaphysics* with: All men desire knowledge. And in spite of all our depression over Haitians caught in the decline of their culture and the abrasive effects of false educational theories, we may always console ourselves with that truth.

INTRODUCTION AND BACKGROUND

Ideas of race, color and national independence have played a central role in the history of Haiti. Independence was declared and maintained by men who saw Haiti as a symbol of redemption for the whole African race. Haiti became independent in 1804, after several years of struggle. National independence was regarded by Haitians themselves, as well as by foreign observers, as a symbol of black independence and 'regeneration'.

Some of the important laws of the newly independent country (particularly with respect to land ownership and citizenship) were explicitly 'racial'. If ideas of race have provided a bond, linking Haitians together and strengthening their determination to achieve effective independence and economic development, color divisions dating back to colonial times, and the ideologies which developed out of them, have been one of the principal threats to national independence. Color divisions between black and mulatto have been reinforced by other factors such as class, religion, education and region, and first one group and then the other has been willing to invite foreign intervention in Haiti, rather than permit its opponents to gain political power. Thus, while ideologies of race have provided one of the principal bases of national independence, color factors have frequently been important causes of foreign intervention. The regime of Dr. Francois Duvalier can be understood only in the light of this history.

The island of Hispaniola in the Caribbean sea was once ruled by the two most maligned "caesars" of the western hemisphere, Generalissimo Rafael Leonidas Trujillo in the Dominican Republic, for 31 years, and President Francois Duvalier in Haiti, for 14 years. Now both are dead. Most of their old terror is gone. But neither country is a happy place, for neither can escape its past. In fact, Francois Duvalier's son, 29-year-old Jean-Claude Duvalier, is now the President-for-Life of Haiti. Hispaniola's problem is that it is trapped by its past and the fretting closeness of the United States.

The name *Ayti* is used to refer to the whole island in pre-Columbian times. *Hispaniola (Espanola)* is the name given to the whole island by the Spanish. *Saint Domingue* refers to the French colony existing on the western third of the island from 1697 to 1803. *Santo Domingo* is also the name of the capital of the eastern part of the island, but it should be clear from the context which entity is referred to; the city was called *Ciudad Trujillo* from 1936 to 1961. *Haiti* is the independent republic consisting substantially of the former French colony of *Saint Domingue*, but also including the eastern part of the island from 1822 to 1844. The *Dominican Republic* is the independent state consisting substantially of the former Spanish colony, existing from 1844 to 1861 and from 1865 to the present.

For a visitor who has seen both countries in the days of their best known "caesars," a return is depressing. In the early 1960s, in the heady and naive optimism of those times, it was possible for a visitor to feel that, without their "caesars," both Haiti and the Dominican Republic might succeed and prosper. Now both "caesars" are gone, and both countries have accomplished little.

THE HAITIANS AND THEIR COUNTRY

In the ten thousand square miles of Haiti's mountains and valleys more than six million people are crowded together. Some are black, some light-skinned, but less than five thousand are white, and these are almost all recent immigrants to the country. According to James G. Leyburn, modern Haiti has its racial roots primarily in Africa, but its social roots lie as much in Europe as in Africa; if it is "American" at all, geography and a few fairly superficial characteristics are the only American qualities it displays.

Carrying our own cultural interpretations with us when we visit our Caribbean neighbor, we are likely to misunderstand what we see in Haiti, for it is very easy to think of all colored people in terms of our own. To do so is to remain completely ignorant of Haiti. Whereas in the United States we use "Negro" and "colored" indiscriminately as synonyms, making a real distinction only between "black" and "mulatto," all four terms are taboo in polite society in Haiti. A new descriptive vocabulary, an entirely new frame of reference, must be acquired by the friendly foreign visitor to this West Indian republic.

Probably the most striking phenomenon in the country is its division into two social groups. So rigidly are the class lines set that *caste* is the only word to describe the effective separation of aristocrats from the masses. The caste system is a vivid fact, for it regulates a person's profession, speech, religion, marriage, famly life, politics, clothes, social mobility — in short, his whole life from cradle to grave.

In winning its freedom from the France of Napoleon, Haiti became the second independent state in the Western Hemisphere. It had been during the eighteenth century France's most prosperous colony, its wealth depending upon slavery and the plantation system. With the whites driven out, social distinctions which actually had their roots in colonial times began immediately to develop among the people, all of whom had some proportion of African blood in their veins.

During the course of the next century the criteria for aristocracy slowly assumed recognizable form, so that now even the most casual observer is aware that Haiti cannot by any stretch of the imagination be called a democratic country, with an open class system. The two castes are the elite and the masses. They are as different as day from night, as nobleman from peasant; and they are as separate as oil and water. The elite are generally reckoned to compose at the outside not more than three per cent of the population.

The elite do not work with their hands. This is the cardinal rule of Haitian society. Upon it rests the whole economic structure of the country, and to this the course of national history has led. All the professions, most governmental and military offices, and the large business enterprises are effectively closed to young men of the masses. Indeed, so completely accepted are caste rules, so practically difficult would it be for peasant youths to acquire the money and education necessary for such careers, that at birth a boy's future place in economic life is, within narrow limits, already predetermined. For the elite, law is the most popular of the professions, partly because it is the quickest avenue of approach to high political office; government, in turn, is the only career which can make a man rich within a few years. Next in popularity to law comes medicine. Teaching is not lucrative enough to attract many promising youths, and the priests of the Roman Catholic Church are almost all white Frenchmen. An effort was once made by the Catholic church to train native Haitian priests, but the peasants would have none of them after they were ordained. They drove them out, saying, "Go away! How do you expect God to listen to you? You are not white, you don't know anything." And the Haitian priests had to be transferred as missionaries to Africa.

The distinction between castes on the basis of occupation is nowhere more clearly seen than in the feminine sphere. The peasant woman, from childhood onward is an indefatigable laborer, absolutely indispensable to the economic life of the country. She not only performs the usual domestic functions but works in the fields as well. She carries marketable goods, sometimes for miles, to the town for sale. The aristocratic woman, on the other hand, is rarely active in business. Indeed, until recent years no career was open to her outside the home, nor would custom have allowed her to follow one; even now, teaching and a few clerical positions in government service are her only business opportunities. She directs the household economy but has servants if she can possibly afford them. Her place is definitely in the home.

The second infallible test of membership in the elite caste is education and an ability to speak French. When Haiti was a slave colony belonging to France, the hundreds of thousands of blacks imported from Africa had no common tongue, coming as they did from wide stretches of the continent; the French spoken by their overseers, a development of the Norman dialect, became their own language known as Creole. Every Haitian, high and low, knows and uses this language, for nursemaids speak it to the upper-class children in their charge and all servants speak it. The elite consequently learn it at a tender age, and must use it in all their dealings with the lower orders. Among themselves, however, they speak French. The official language of the country is French. To speak correct

French is an immediate announcement that one has had the advantage of schooling and has been in contact with the aristocracy. Theoretically, Haitian education is free and democratic; actually, no peasant could be spared from labor long enough for schooling or find money for proper clothes to go to school in.

In the last few decades, however, a new Black class began to develop, a kind of middle class. Despite their impoverished background, this small group of Blacks had managed an education and were aspiring to some of the positions held by the elite. Francois Duvalier, a medical doctor, was a member of this class. He also belonged to a group of anti-mulatto writers who tried to turn Haitians toward their African roots.

In 1946 the Black middle class made a breakthrough when Dumarsais Estime began opening the elite-dominated bureaucracy to the Blacks. Duvalier was his minister of Labor.

Duvalier, who came to power as president in 1957, with all the rhetoric about a Black social revolution, finished the job that Estime had begun. The Haitian civil service is now heavily Black, and other signs exist to show that Blacks have benefited from Duvalier's regime. The top secondary school in Port-au-Prince, which had an enrollment of only 10 per cent Blacks when Duvalier came to power, is more than half Black now. Many prominent Blacks insist that they have an entree into elite social life which would have been unthinkable in the 1950s.

But the Black entry into power under Duvalier was selective. In a sense, a new Black elite developed. Duvalier ruled like a potentate, favoring those who pleased him at the moment, turning against them at the next moment. His *ton ton macoutes* (which in Creole literally means the bogeyman) killed many more Blacks than mulattoes. Some mulattoes, in fact, had power under his rule because he trusted them. The mulatto-elite control of the economy was never broken. Duvalier didn't even try.

Added to this, the Black masses of Haiti — the peasants who make up more than 80 per cent of the population — did not benefit from Duvalier's so-called revolution. Haiti now competes with such countries as Bangladesh, Chad and Upper Volta for the desperate distinction of being the poorest place in all the world and ranks tenth among the most hungry countries. The average Haitian eats 400 to 500 fewer calories a day than the minimum of 2,000 calories considered necessary for good health. Haiti has the highest death rate in Latin America.

Under Duvalier, Haiti did not develop. He did not take over a rich country and make it poor. He took over a poor country and left it poor, at least as poor as he found it. For the impoverished masses, this was hardly a social revolution. Inevitably the standard of living is a reflection of caste membership. The elite wear shoes. When a man of the masses dons the castoff shoes of some aristocrat, the logical assumption by everyone is that this man is preparing to try to move, one step up the social ladder. Shoes are a symbol: wearing these, one must also wear a suit instead of a faded shirt and patched trousers; the suit demands personal cleanliness and a better home; all of these lead the country man to town life with its additional expenses. So arduous a climb does not allure many of the

Haitian common folk.

Because the standard of living, with its tangibles and intangibles, clearly separates the castes, the elite observe all the rules with rigor. Their etiquette is formal. Culture (in the popular, not the anthropological meaning) is respected with almost religious devotion.

Since the maintenance of a high standard of living is costly, it is obvious that another source of caste distinction lies in the inequalities of wealth and property. Wealth is a relative term, however, and the Haitian peasant is so poor that by contrast a few hundred dollars' income a year will seem like riches. The elite live economically by American standards, yet even parsimonious spending of money may, when governed by a consciousness of social distinctions, make the peak of aristocracy unassailable.

The elite live in towns. Many of them own country estates, but regard these as secondary to their residences in Port-au-Price (population, 900,000), Petionville (population, 35,000), Cap-Haitien (population, 48,000), Gonaives (population, 29,000), Jeremie (population, 29,000), and the other few towns. To live a rural life is to be isolated, out of the stream of fashion, news, social activity. What profession can one follow in a rustic valley? One who is class-conscious must see and be seen by others of his class, otherwise he would be forgotten by "those who count." In the towns are the schools; there French is spoken; there and there only, financial and social opportunities exist. True, plebeians form the majority of the population even in the towns, so that urbanization alone is not a mark of caste; it must be taken in conjunction with the others.

Formal marriage is another requisite for membership in the elite. Sex relations in Haiti are quite casual, as judged by American standards. The majority of Haitian families are established by parents who have gone through neither a civil nor a religious ceremony. This is not to imply that spouses are unfaithful to each other, or that there is not mutual respect within the family circle; it merely means that most poeple regard formal marriage as a luxury which hey cannot afford, or in any case as a ceremony which custom has made superfluous. Once again, however, the aristrocratic holds to the form. If a family can point to legal marriages among several generations of ancestors, there can be little question of its high scoial position.

Religion affords still another distinction between high and low. Haiti has a folk religion which American tourists call Voodoo (a name which makes them think immediately of superstitious emotionalsim or some kind of occult balderdash but which is more properly called Vodun). It is a true religion in that it answers for the native the questions arising in the world he knows, while giving him confidence to face the crises of life. Vodun is African in origin, Creole in its language, and homely in its creed and practice; none of these makes it any less a religion. The official religion of the country, on the other hand, is Roman Catholicism. Few members of the elite, however their hearts may yearn for the consoling securities of Vodun, dare openly either to acknowledge their "atavism" or to participate in the cult. They must be Catholic or agnostics. It is often remarked that below the surface many a professing Catholic aristocrat cherishes Vodun beliefs; the important fact is that he keeps his folk worship secret. Because the outside world ridicules Vodun as superstition, and because the approved Catholic church fights it, government restrictions effectively keep its ritual out of the public gaze. All of the discriminatory laws, however, have not weakened its hold upon the masses. It is because Vodun is a *folk* religion that the elite cannot permit themselves to adhere to it openly.

The final and most complicated distinction between the two castes is skin color. Any generalization on this matter is open to numerous exceptions; moreover, the whole question of color in Haiti touches the most sensitive nerves of the upper classes. One must begin by such casual observations as these: the vast majority of the lower orders are definitely dark or even black; the lighter the skin, the more likely a person is to belong to the elite. It is true that there are black aristocrats, and it is equally true that numbers of peasants have light complexions. At almost any function in high society, however, the proportion of dark-skinned persons is decidely small. Among the youth, the tendency is always to select a spouse whose skin color is light; marriages are often made between aristocrats and white foreigners resident in Haiti, so that the children may lighten the family complexion. While it is therefore inaccurate to assert that no full-blooded Negroes belong to the elite, it is also clear that lighter persons tend to have social advantages.

Modern usage, having borrowed the word "caste" from India, employs it loosely to mean a rigid class system of which the people are conscious. In India caste was always endogamous and connected with occupation. Kroeber defines it as "an endogamous and hereditary division of an ethnic unit occupying a position of superior or inferior rank or social esteem in comparison with other such subdivisions." Castes, as distinguished from social classes, "have emerged into social consciousness to the point where custom and law attempt their rigid and permanent separation from one another." by each of these criteria, Haiti has castes.

The elite are endogamous in that they would not consider marriage into the masses. The one exception to the endogamic practice is marriage with a white foreigner. Whereas in India all members of a caste had the same general occupation, in Haiti several occupations are open to caste members; but the distinction between honorable and demeaning work is understood by all, so that no person has free choice as regards the two larger categories. Haitian law does not name the social divisions, nor does it legislate the masses into a subordinate position — for the simple reason that there is no conceivable need to enact what already exists. The laws of Haiti are administered by elite officials; these men make the definitions and interpretations. The judge always knows the custom, so that (as in most countries) the same offense brings different penalties for upper- and lower-class offenders. Custom holds sway, and custom is more tyrannical than any body of the law.

Inside the castes may be found social distinctions familiar in democracies and in every other kind of society. Interest in politics, business, literature, or sport draws people of like minds together and makes cliques. There are well-to-do families who outshine their neighbors, just as there are peasant landholders who dominate their rural communities. A high civil official has more prestige than a doctor with a small practice, just as among the masses a house servant for an elite family outranks a beggar.

For the majority of Haitians, life is too elemental to be concerned with artificial wants. The peasant talks, unfettered by rules of grammar or any schoolmaster's correction; he behaves like his fellows; he learns by trial and error, by imitation, by the praise and ridicule of his elders, what to do and what not to do. What really matters in life is having food to eat, avoiding bad luck in health and crops, having a wife and family, keeping on the right side of the spirits, and being able at night to dance, sing, and tell tales with his friends. He wears no tight-fitting clothes, never bothers about fashions, certainly never puzzles his brain to reconcile his theological and philosophical views with each other. This is by no means a poetic or idyllic existence for him, however. The peasant is so poor that misfortune may be catastrophic; the soil he has to farm is worn out by decades of erosion and crude tillage; disease is so widespread that most people know misery. A man cannot, even if he would, save up for a rainy day; he lacks the necessary implements to plough deep while sluggards sleep. One is safe so long as he does what everyone else does, and if this rule breaks down, at least misery will have company. Keep out of harm's way, if possible, but bear it stoically when it comes. Avoid what is strange — particularly all legal documents, courts, politics, city ways, and people who shout orders. The peasant is conservative because radical changes, such as come from revolutions, for example, dislocate his life, leaving him worse off than before. Progress and improvement are to him only vague abstractions, much less real than the struggle for mere existence.

For the elite, on the other hand, life is rather a struggle to maintain and improve the standard of living. It is always easier to predict what a person will not do than what he will. It would be hard to define, therefore, a typical aristocrat. In one basic matter, however, the high-class Haitian is poles removed from the peasant. Instead of accepting things as they are ("*Bon Dieu bon*," runs the peasant saying: God is good — and the inflection of the voice implies that the second "bon" may also mean "inscrutable"), the elite person is restlessly dissatisfied with the conditions of life: economic, social, political. His unexpressed ideal is to be accepted as an equal in the cultured circles of Western society, to have the same entree to courts, clubs, and parties abroad as cultivated white Europeans and Americans.

Since the country has never had an accurate census, it is not possible to say precisely how many persons belong to each caste. By the most generous estimates, not one out of twenty-five Haitians is elite — and such a figure stretches the category to a point which no literate citizen would admit. The few cities and towns of Haiti do not contain more than 1,000,000 people in a total population which the atlasses generally put around 6.1 million. Since to live in the city is one necessary mark of aristocracy, and since obviously not every town- or city-dweller is an aristocrat, it is probably nearer the mark to infer that not more than two or three per cent of the people are of the elite.

A slightly larger group would fit neither category. This intermediate section would consist chiefly of those who have taken a few steps toward the upper stratum; they may wear shoes and keep a small shop and speak a few words of French, but not yet be accepted in "respectable" society; aristocrats will look down on them while the masses will regard them with curious interest. Yet these are not what Europeans would call a middle class. In their own generation, they are rootless and insecure. Their children will have as many advantages as the parents can afford, so that the next generation may increase the distance between itself and the common folk. Included in this intermediate group are also a few who, having once been up, are now on the way down.

If the terms "masses" and "peasants" are used interchangeably in these pages, it is because the vast majority of the people get their living from the soil. Haiti is, as it has always been, an agricultural country. Only one town, the capital, Port-au-Prince, has more than 100,000 people.

At least nine out of ten Haitians, therefore, lead rural lives and easily fit the designation of peasant. They live in little communities, generally of less than a hundred persons, rather than in scattered houses. A detailed map would be dotted with place names of these tiny communities, some of them designating "villages" of only four or five houses. For numbers of peasants hidden away in the valleys or on mountain farms, the only contact with the larger world comes through visits to the nearest market town which itself may count only a thousand souls. The peasant is thus effectively isolated. the smallness of the average annual income of the Haitian limits his material contacts with the outside world. Rural schools are few; consequently, all but a small percentage of the rising generation is growing up illiterate. Although education is compulsory, the Haitian illiteracy rate is apt to remain at eighty-five per cent. Education statistics are: 2,083 primary and secondary schools, with a combined enrollment of 368,414 (1971). Enrollment in higher education is 1,526 (1972). Education expenditure accounts for 0.7 per cent of the Gross National Product. There are 26 radio stations with 81,000 receivers (1972), and one television station (11,000 television sets) (1972). There are 4,500 telephones (1972), and six daily newspapers (1972) provide five copies per one thousand inhabitants.

Lack of mental stimulus completes the isolation. Bound to the soil by the need of wresting a livelihood from rocky, gullied, and increasingly unproductive land, harassed by ill health (the Haitian health statistics are: 1,344 inhabitants per hospital bed; 8,505 per physician (1973). The birthrate is 35.8 per 1,000 of the population (1975); deathrate, 16.3; life expectancy, 50 years; infant mortality, 200 per 1,000 births (1973), and governed by a group whose own security would be threatened by improving his lot, it is little wonder that the peasant is unprogressive or that he struggles along at a bare subsistence level.

Haiti is rural and agricultural, then, with a population density of about 500 per square mile. The 6.1 million people must get their living from 10,741 square miles, not of lush tropical soil but of rocky, mountainous country which after more than a century and a half of poor farming has been stripped of most of its forests and much of its topsoil.

A glance at a relief map of the West Indies would show clearly that the islands are the tops of a mountain range whose lowlands were long since submerged by the Caribbean Sea. Looked at from above, Haiti seems a jumbled mass of mountains running in all directions. Down their slopes flow many small streams which after rains become torrents, washing away crops and top soil. Brooks which run most of the year the Haitians dignify by the name of "reviere"; not even the largest, however — the Artibonite, which drains over a fifth of the country — is navigable for anything above a rowboat. The second largest "river," Les Trois Rivieres, is only 96 kilometers long. Many of the smaller streams disappear into sinkholes or caves in limestone, veritable lost rivers. Even some of the lakes are ephemeral.

Most of the best land of the country lies in its few plains flanking the mountains near the coasts or extending like wedges into the mountainous regions. In the northeast in the country back of Cap-Haitien is the Plaine du Nord; here in colonial times were the most flourishing of the French plantations; the palatial residences, and the slaves who in 1791 began the insurrection which ultimately led to Haiti's independence. In the middle region are the Artibonite Plain near the coast, and the Central Plain back fo the Black Mountains. Eastward from Port-au-Prince, the capital, is the Cul-de-Sac; and in the southwestern peninsula is the small plain of Les Cayes. All over the country in French days sugar cane grew in abundance, making white men wealthy. The irrigation systems have long since disappeared; fertilizer is far too costly for use; trees have been cut down to make room for hundreds of tiny farms to support the increasing population.

Not even all the plains are naturally productive. Many of them, on the contrary, are arid, sterile and forbidding, covered with cacti and other spiny plants. Indeed, the most arid areas of Haiti, including its salt marshes, are lowlands.

Although the country is wholly in the tropics, the usual preconceived notion of the tropics does not apply. There are no impenetrable rain forests or jungles, no wild beasts, and very few snakes. Because of the mountains, there are wide differences in rainfall, soil, and vegetation within a short distance. Occasional hurricanes do great damage to shipping and the water fronts. Infrequent droughts sometimes last for two or three months. Hailstorms that damage growing crops are fairly common. Taken as a whole, the country has an ample but not heavy rainfall; coming generally from the east and northeast, the trade winds strike the high ridges in the north and there deposit the greater part of their moisture in the Plaine du Nord. By the time they have passed down the western slope and across the Central Plain they are dried and rarified, so that this region becomes increasingly arid as its altitude decreases. Next to the Plaine du Nord, the best-watered part of Haiti is the southwestern peninsula, which projects far beyond the shelter of the mountains in the rest of the island.

When one subtracts from the 10,741 square miles all the sterile wastes of cactus, the salt marshes and brackish lakes, and the rock barren, one realizes the inevitability of a low standard of living for the mass of the people. Other nations buy little from Haiti, local industries never reach even the proportions familiar to small-town Americans. Not even the elite are well-to-do by American small-town standards; it is only by comparison with the masses that they can be said to constitute a favoured economic class. They rule the country, however, and what benefits accrue to Haiti rarely get beyond their pockets.

The resident of Haiti can never lose sight of the social distinctions between the two castes, for they permeate every phase of Haitian life. It has been so since the first hours of the republic. Indeed, the origins of the caste system lie in the French colonial days of the eighteenth century.

ECONOMIC TRENDS: THE HAITIAN SCENE OF THE EIGHTIES

All indications are that Fiscal Year 1981 (October 1, 1980-September 30, 1981) is proving to be difficult for Haiti. Earnings from coffee and bauxite exports, the major sources of foreign exchange, are significantly below FY 80 levels. Imports, spurred by increasing demand and prices for foodstuffs, petroleum products and consumer goods, will result in a projected commercial trade deficit of U. S. $151 million. The projected trade deficit, coupled with unbudgeted capital expenditures last year, has set the stage for severe foreign exchange difficulties. In response, the Government of Haiti (GOH) has enacted decrees on February 26, 1981, prohibiting or restricting the importation of certain products. In addition, wholesale prices of gasoline, flour, and tobacco were increased on March 17, 1981, in a further attempt to increase government revenues and dampen demand for imported goods. While demand for U. S. products continues strong, especially for construction equipment and materials, foodstuffs and health care products, the current financial situation makes increased U. S. exports unlikely this year.

In spite of these economic difficulties, the attractiveness of Haiti as a site for U. S. investment in labor-intensive assembly and transformation industries remains excellent. Haiti's greatest resource is its abundant supply of skilled and cheap labor; the current minimum wage rate is $2.64 per day, about one-third that of the English-speaking Caribbean. Haiti's proximity to the U. S. market, in a time of increasing fuel costs, should make Haiti relatively more attractive for U. S. firms currently engaged in offshore assembly operations. Recognition of the improving investment climate has resulted in plans for an investment mission to Haiti in December, 1981, sponsored by the Overseas Private Investment Corporation (OPIC) and the U. S. Embassy.

BACKGROUND

Haiti is the porest country in the hemisphere and one of the poorest on earth. It has extremely limited natural resources and severe deficiencies in infrastructure. Agriculture is the most important sector of the economy, producing about 40 per cent of gross domestic product (GDP) and employing aobut 70 per cent of the poplation. Manufacturing contributes 12 per cent of GDP, government 11 per cent, and commerce 10 per cent. Approximately 6 million people live within Haiti's mountainous 10,741 square miles (about the size of Maryland). Seventy-five to eighty per cent live in the countryside, many farming marginal land. While only about 30 per cent of the land is suitable for cropping, more than 40 per cent is actually under cultivation. The World Bank estimates that 85 per cent of the rural population exists below the absolute poverty level. Approximately 23 per cent of the population is literate. Coffee, sugar, rice, corn, sorghum, millet, beans, cocoa, sweet potatoes, manioc, nuts, vetiver, sisal, cotton, bananas, plantains, mangoes, oranges, limes and grapefruits are the major agricultural products. Agriculture is primitive and there is inadequate internal distributionof goods resulting in local shortages and wide price fluctuations. Coffee, vetiver and mangoes are the only agricultural exports. Of these, coffee and mangoes are exported by commercial buyers, not producers.

Haiti faces major development problems. Bilateral and multilateral aid, which will total over $142 million in FY 81, is being directed primarily to improve agriculture, education, health and transportation. Sanitation and health are major problems, particularly in the rurual areas. Infant mortality at the rate of 130 per 1,000 is second highest in the hemisphere. Hospitals are rudimentary. Unemployment and underemployment are broadly estimated by the GOH as 14 per cent and 65 per cent respectively. Unemployment in the urban areas of Port-au-Prince is generally acknowledged to be at more than 50 per cent of those who want jobs. Urban migration to Port-au-Prince is the other side of the rural migrant problem, the most publicized aspect being the flight of Haitians to the Bahamas, the Dominican Republic and the United States. This migration will continue as long as the countryside lacks employment opportunities and even the most rudimentary services in health, educationand public services. Job creation, therefore, must continue to be one of the economy's prime aims as Port-au-Prince is expected to swell form its current level of just under a million to more than 5 million by the year 2000. Just five short years ago Port-au-Prince was a city of fewer than 300,000.

There are about 3,000 kilometers of roads in Haiti of which about 600 would be classified as first class. Not all regions of the country are accessible by car, though most can be reached in a four-wheel drive vehicle. Total electric generating capacity is about 102 MW. Most of the major provincial cities as well as Port-au-Prince have electricity. However, occasional blackouts and current fluctuations cause most industries to install standby generators. The telecommunications network is limited and erratic internally but generally adequate for international calls.

The industrial and commercial sector is small and heavily concentrated in the Port-au-Prince area. Investment capital is limited. There are a few medium-sized basic industrial plants, including a cement factory, flour mill, small electric steel mill, match factory, canning facilities and three sugar refineries. Locally manufactured goods include cement, steel-reinforcing bar, shoes, plastic pipes, sisal twine, ceramic tiles, rum, denim, paint, foam rubber, matches, cotton fabric, soap, flour, cigarettes, machetes, enameled cookware, car batteries, mufflers, handicraft items and processed foods such as fruit juices, pasta, jellies, jams, peanut butter and canned fruit. There are over 200 firms engaged in assembly or light industrial transformation operations. The majority of these companies are Haitian-owned and produce a gamut of goods from baseballs to textiles to missile components for the U. S. market.

ANALYSIS OF MAJOR SECTORS

Haiti's major trading partner is the United States, which is the source of over half of both imports and exports. Other important partners are Canada, France, Belgium and Japan. In FY 80 Haiti exported about $184 million worth of coffee, assembled components, handicraft items, bauxite, cocoa, essential oils and other goods. During the same period about $284 million worth of food, vehicles, manufactured goods and other products were imported. In FY 81 exports should be worth $181 million and imports $320 million. Due to low world coffee prices and a decline in coffee production aggravated by Hurricane Allen, as well as rapid increases in public and private consumption, for the first time in six years Haiti's chronic balance of trade deficit will not be offset by the continued favorable capital account position and strong transfer payments account.

AGRICULTURE

Haiti is not self-sufficient in food production. Farming techniques are primitive and productivity per acre is quite low. In general, the average size of the plots is submarginal (.48 hectare) and a particular farmer will own a few, widely separated plots (average land holding is .77 hectare) planted with a number of different crops to minimize the risk of failure. Only an estimated six per cent of cultivated land is irrigated. Deforestation continues as farmers seek more land for food production. Production of charcoal, the major cooking fuel, also contributes to erosion and increased soil salinity, which in turn decreases the amount of arable land. There are a few larger sized agricultural holdings.

Coffee — Coffee is the most important export crop in Haiti, generating 40 per cent of export revenues. It is the major source of money income for about two million people or one-third of the population. In addition, coffee export taxes are the government's largest single revenue source. Because of an excellent growing season in FY 80, Haiti was able to export 411,000 60-kilo bags of coffee at an average price of $1.65 per pound. The value of the FY 80 coffee exports exceeded U. S. $89 million, resulting in GOH tax revenues of approximately U. S. $22 million. Because of the cyclical nature of Haiti's coffee production, caused by poor agricultural methods, and the effects of Hurricane Allen (August, 1980), FY 81 exports are expected to fall to the 200,000 bag range. Coupled with the precipitous decline in coffee prices (currently averaging around $1.20 per pound), FY 81 coffee export revenues and government tax receipts are expected to decline to U. S. $25 million and U. S. $5 million respectively. FY 82 looks promising thus far for Haitian coffee production. However, declining consumption patterns and bumper coffee harvest worldwide make short-term prospects for significant price recovery remote.

Sugar — Plagued by declining extraction rates brought about by sugar cane diseases (smut and rust), lack of irrigation and the limited use of fertilizers, the FY 80 sugar crop declined to an estimated 55,000 MT of raw sugar (down from 61,000 MT in FY 79). Less than 30 per cent of the cane grown is processed in the centrifugal mills. The vast majority is processed in the estimated 1,700 artisanal mills used to make clarin, a country variety of rum, or eaten straight from the fields. In 1980 local sugar consumption continued to increase, necessitating net sugar imports of 8.700 MT at a time when world sugar prices are approaching all-time highs. The government has announced plans to put an additional 6,000 hectares into sugar cultivation, primarily to supply a fourth sugar mill with a 3,000 MT (of cane per day) capacity, scheduled to open in December, 1981.

Essential Oils — Haiti produces a variety of essential oils, among them vetiver, lime, amayris and citronella. A government policy which set the price of Haitian vetiver well above the world price, and significantly decreased sales, has been adjusted somewhat. Exports of essential oils declined from $10 million in FY 78 to $6.5 million in FY 79. They were at about the same level in 1980 and will remains o in FY 81. A return to the FY 78 level will require further adjustments in policy, pricing and marketing.

Sisal — Sisal production is being actively encouraged by the GOH. Average production is about 1,200 tons per year and expected to increase in FY 81. Although much land is currently planted in sisal, in recent years harvesting has not seemed profitable to the producer. The price paid to the producer has been increased; machine decorticators have beenpurchased and are being used. As the price of petroleum drives up the cost of substitute materials, sisal becomes increasingly attractive.

Meat — Beef production is estimated at 6,600 MT for FY 81. Exports to the United States should increase significantly from 2.6 million pounds in FY 80 to 3.4 million pounds this year. African swine fever entered Haiti from the Dominican Republic in late 1978, and has substantially decreased the pig population. A swine fever eradication program is expected to be undertaken, beginning in November, 1981.

Grain — Demand for grain has been rapidly increasing and grain prices have been high. Rice production is projected to reach 105,000 MT, a slight (1%) increase over FY 80. The GOH is attempting to increase production of corn and other locally produced grains. The demand for flour, which has increased 52 per cent over the past two years, should be about the same in FY 81 as it was in FY 80. Wheat is totally imported and should exceed 135,000 MT in FY 81.

Mineral Resources — Reynolds now plans to close its bauxite mining operation in 1983. It has been producing about 640,000 tons per year with an export value of about $18 million. Calendar year 1981 exports willdecline to the 400,000 ton level and remain there during the final years of operation. There are deposits of copper, silver, gold, marble, lignite and natural asphalt which are not profitable to mine at current market rates.

INDUSTRY

In recent years the transformation and assembly industries have been the most dynamic sector of the economy. Taking advantage of U. S. Customs Code Sections 806 and 807 and low Haitian wage rates (current minimum wage is $2.64 per day), many companies have been sending U. S.-made components to Haiti for assembly and return to the United States. This has created 60,000 jobs over the past 10 years requiring only a minimum of capital expenditure. The recent recessionary slowdown in the United States has had a mixed effect on this activity. While firms engaged in assembly of electronic components used in vehicles or construction have experienced a drop in orders, the textile, toy, handicraft, and leather operations are booming. A number of firms are going ahead with expansion plans, but it is likely that there will be a decline in the number of new factories established in 1981 as compared with the past years. This could well exacerbate the already difficult local employment problem.

The government has been working on a new investment code which will consolidate many of the provisions already in place, including tax holidays, duty-free entry for goods which are to be re-exported, guaranteed repatriation of a percentage of profits, import protection for industries satisfying 75 per cent of the local demand and meeting certain quality and pricing requirements, and discrimination-free status for foreign firms. The National Office for Investment Promotion (ONAPI) is trying actively to promote investment in Haiti. Recent changes in the banking laws should provide some relief in the area of investment capital.

INFRASTRUCTURE

The completion in early 1980 of the southern highway linking Les Cayes with Port-au-Prince opened up a rich agricultural area. In addition, a number of secondary roads in the northeast and central parts of Haiti have been completed. Improvements in the airports at Port-au-Prince and Cap Haitien as well as the port of Cap Haitien are underway. Cabotage ports are under construction in Jeremie, Port-au-Prince and Port-de-Paix, the first part of a World Bank project to improve the coastal shipping network. There are proposals to repair and extend irrigation systems, build more roads, construct low-cost housing in Port-au-Prince, and continue the electrification of the countryside.

Port facilities in Port-au-Prince include a container port as well as roll-on, roll-off facilities. These should remain adequate for some time. Air passenger and cargo service meet the present demand.

FISCAL AND MONETARY SITUATION

The GOH FY 81 budget of U. S. $375.7 million (1,878.5 million gourdes) is 10.5 pr cent larger than last year's. The foreign assistance component, which at $142 million represents 38 per cent of the total budget, declined four per cent. Net Haitian budgeted expenditures for investment (formerly called development) increased by 37 per cent from FY 80 to about $87.5 million. Operations expenditures are budgeted at only 5.9 per cent above the previous year and receipts are projected to decline by 11.5 per cent because of projected declines in coffee and bauxite production as well as declines in income tax revenues and excise tax receipts. Agriculture, energy, transportation, community development, housing, education and health are the most important sectors and together will receive 77 per cent of the total investment budget.

Haiti has no exchange controls or restrictions and U. S. dollars circulate alongside gourdes, at an exchange rate of 5 gourdes equal $1. In spite of severe foreign exchange shortages, no significant currency black market has yet appeared. This may be attributed inpart to foreign exchange reserves held outside the domestic banking system, in the form of dollar holdings in cash or deposited in United States banks. It is also a reflection of general business confidence in the system. Extensive changes in the banking laws, which split the national bank into a central and commercial bank in 1979, now allow banks to accept titles to properties offered as loan collateral. During 1980 interest rates and reserve requirements were changed to help slow the outflow of interest-sensitive capital and to provide better control over monetary policy.

Haiti signed an agreement with the IMF in 1978 which makes balances of payments funds available under the Extended Fund Facility (EFF) as long as it fulfills certain conditions. The GOH is currently undertaking additional measures including the switch to ad valorem duty rates at the suggestion of the IMF to counteract the expected shortfalls in government revenue.

TRENDS

There will be about one per cent real growth in the gross national product (GNP) of Haiti during FY 81, led by continuing growth in the handicraft, light manufactured goods and construction sectors. Direct private investment in FY 81 should increase only marginally over FY 80.

INVESTMENT POSSIBILITIES

Despite the bleak current account picture, investment and assembly type opportunities in Haiti are excellent because of Haiti's low labor cost ($2.64 per day minimum), favorable tax incentives and proximity to U. S. markets. The relatively stable political climate and the low level of crime seem to enhance Haiti's good investment climate. The best investment prospects are in the labor-intensive assembly industries producing lower cost non-luxury goods. An existing U. S.-Haiti bilateral textile agreement limits exports in a few categories but places no restrictions on the majority of items. Haiti is a beneficiary of GSP (Generalized System of Preferences) which provides duty-free entry into the United States for over 2,000 items if more than 35 per cent of their value added is Haitian. Insurance for U. S.-owned investment is available from the Overseas Private Investment Corporation (OPIC). Individuals or corporate representatives wishing to explore investment opportunities may wish to participate in the OPIC investment mission to Haiti planned for December 1-December 5, 1981.

Investment opportunities in agriculture are limited by restrictive provisions of the land law, acute population pressure on land resources and lack of infrastructure. There is a need, however, for more investment in agro-industry and the government is willing to consider offering special benefits to serious proposals.

While the Haitian Government may be described as extremely receptive to foreign investment, it examines larger investment proposals carefully in light of national interests. It is currently reviewing proposals for a milk canning facility, cement factory, petroleum refining complex and fertilizer plant. In general, it prefers some Haitian involvement in large-scale operations. Private investment in the assembly industries has generally been approved without delay. Commercial disputes are usually referred to courts or formal arbitration. The GOH has become more sensitive to the consumer and reserves the right to control prices and quality on essential items.

FOREIGN ASSISTANCE

Haiti's longer term economic prospects are brightened by virtue of projected increases in foreign economic aid from multilateral and bilateral sources. External assistance will amount to about $142 million in FY 81. Multilateral aid donors to Haiti include the World Bank, the United Nations Development Program, the Inter-American Development Bank, and the Organization of American States. Bilateral donors include the United States, France, West Germany, Taiwan, Canada and Israel. Development programs carried out with the assistance of both multilateral and bilateral donors span a wide variety of fields, including agriculture, education, public health and transportation.

The program of the U. S. Agency for International Development is concentrating on agricultural development and rural infrastructure and on raising the level of public health and nutrition among Haiti's rural poor.

TRADE

U. S. Exporters usually supply more than 50 per cent of Haiti's imports. Haiti's proximity to the United States, Haitian familiarity with U. S. products, and established distribution channels are the main factors. While demand for U. S. products continues strong, the current financial situation makes increased U. S. exports unlikely this year.

A presidential decree published on March 14, 1981, banned further importation of locally produced goods for a period of two years. Groceries and foodstuffs banned are: coffee, candies, milk, macaroni, noodles, spaghetti, soaps and detergents, crude and semi-refined vegetable oils, vinegar, canned fruit juices, bread, biscuits and cookies. Consumer goods banned are: canvas shoes, mattresses, aluminum, enamel, and plastic housewares, small gas portable stoves, polyester fabrics, rum, alcohol and beer. Other prohibited items include: used newspapers, matches, jute bags and PVC pipe.

In addition, quotas (unspecified) were established for a host of other foodstuffs, consumer goods, and light industrial products. Such products can no longer be imported without first obtaining a license from the GOH Ministry of Commerce and Industry. Products for which quotas were established are: ham, bacon, hot dogs, salamis, sausages, fish, fresh and frozen seafood, beef, mutton, goat, pork, chicken, honey, yogurt, butter, fresh milk, corn, rice, wheat flour, manioc flour, corn flour, roasted nuts, soya oil and lard, sugar, cigarettes, toothpaste, disinfectant, deodornat, scourer, shampoos, cigars and shoe polish, shoes and leather articles, ceramic products, varnish, enamel paint, paint for swimming pools, industrial and special paints, anti-corrosive paints with lead oxide and minium, hydrofugal liquid, thinner, protection products for woods, insecticide and fungicide, stain for woods, glue, sanitary napkins, paper table napkins, paper and tissue handkerchiefs, metal zippers, iron shavings, paper and synthetic fiber bags, frozen fruits and vegetables, wooden furniture and fiberglass furniture, wrappings in paper, plastic or cardboard, hygienic paper, toothbrushes, flat irons, lead batteries, fruit preserves, jelly, metal containers, nails, sheet iron and bottle caps for soft drinks, flat irons utilizing charcoal, grey Portland cement, mosiacs, cotton thread not conditioned for retail sale, blue cotton denim, siam fabrics, carbella fabrics, regular socks and sport socks, underwear, clothing, marble.

The purpose of the presidential decrees prohibiting or restricting the importation of certain goods is two-fold. First, it is an attempt to reduce the enormous demand for imported goods, and thus the deficit in the balance of trade. Secondly, it is an attempt to protect and encourage local production. Goods prohibited are those for which it is deemed that local production is sufficient for the domestic market. Goods for which quotas have been established are those which are also produced locally, but in quantities insufficient for local needs.

The limited budget resources of the Haitian Government restrict possibilities for direct sales of U. S. goods to the government. There is no central purchasing agency and most purchases are made by the government ministry concerned. Purchases are generally made directly from suppliers or their agents, but competitive bidding is usually required for larger procurement actions. Equipment required for the larger, international projects financed by external donors is almost always obtained after seeking competitive proposals.

The best prospects for U. S. to Haiti exports in 1981 will be foodstuffs, building materials and construction equipment, consumer durables and medical supplies.

Demand for U. S. foodstuffs will remain strong, spurred by changing tastes, the concessional export financing of basic foodstuffs under PL-480, increasing population, and static or declining agricultural production.

Building materials and construction equipment demand should benefit by plans in the Fiscal Year 1981 GOH investment budget for two moderate-income housing projects (budgeted at U. S. $16.75 million) and some 2,000 low-cost housing units. In addition, private sector housing construction remains strong. The growth in housing, combined with a rising standard of living in the small, but expanding, middle class should also result in increased demand for consumer durables.

Major efforts by various bilateral and multilateral donor organizations (including the U. S. Agency for International Development) and the Haitian Government in the areas of nutrition improvement, malaria eradication and urban and rural health delivery systems should offer good opportunities for exporters of medical equipment and supplies.

HAITIAN KEY ECONOMIC INDICATORS

Income and Prices

	FY 1978	1979[1]	1980[2]	1981[2]
Population (millions)	5.8	5.9	6.0	6.1
Cost of Living Index (1975 M 100)	111.0	125.4	151.7	182.0
GNP Current Market Prices				
(millions U.S. $)	1,269.0	1,500.0	1.785.0	1,995.0
GNP 1955 Prices				
(millions U.S. $)	448.8	450.0	463.0	469.0
GNP Percaput (1955 dollars)	77.4	76.0	77.0	76.8
GNP Percaput (current dollars)	223.4	254.2	297.0	327.0
GDP (millions current dollars)	1,162.9	1,275.0	1,560.0	1.744.0

Balance of Payments and Trade

	FY 1978	1979	1980[1]	1981[1]
Exports (f.o.b)	154.8	138.0	207.1	166.7
Impports (f.o.b.)	208.9	227.2	268.4	318.5
Trade Balance	-54.2	-89.2	-61.3	-151.8
Services, Transfers, Investment Income	33.0	35.9	47.8	48.1[4]
Capital Account	41.6	68.0	40.0	57.1
Changes in Reserves	M14.2	M16.2	-6.0	-23.0

Money Supply and Central Government Resources
(millions of U.S. dollars)

M1	97.9	122.6	135.1	145.0
M2	236.4	276.6	303.1	320.0
Central Government Budget[3]	131.0	159.0	192.0	233.0

[1]Provisional
[2]Estimated
[3]Haitian Resources in Operations and Development Budgets
[4]Based on information available up to April 30, 1981, private transfers could reach $80 million in 1981.

THE HAITIAN COMMUNITY ABROAD

The qustion is frequently asked as to why so many Haitians endure so many hardships in order to leave their homeland. There are three basic reasons which are true regardless of the socioeconomic status of the emigre: political oppression; administrative incompetence which results in impoverishment of the country; and the uncontrolled growth of the population.

The first wave of emigres left primarily because of direct brutal political oppression during the first decade of the rule of "Papa Doc" Duvalier, from 1957-1967. This was during the period when "Papa Doc" was openly proclaiming a revolution inside Haiti, which meant systematic elimination of all opponents, real or suspected.

In the second decade of "Papa Doc's" rule, political oppression was still overt, but this was accompanied by manifest administration incompetency leading to a waste of natural resources. Many Haitian companies went bankrupt. This affected the lives of the skilled workers, including those living in rural areas. The second wave of migration consisted of skilled craftsmen — carpenters, tailors, mechanics, stonemasons, farmers, and the like. These emigres, from the middle and lower middle classes, including some of lower socioeconomic background, went elsewhere looking for better conditions of life. Some went to the islands around Haiti, such as the Bahamas and the French islands of Martinique and Guadeloupe. Those who were able to obtain visas to the united States continued to go to the northern cities such as New York, Chicago and Boston.

After 1970, during a period of recession in the United States, many American factories moved to Haiti in search of cheap manpower and low production costs. At the same time, the Haitian political and economic models, which were based to a large extent on corruption, led to dispossession of many peasants whose land was offered to large outside companies for exploitation. Although a few jobs were created, the companies' presence disrupted the balance of life for the poor people by raising prices of food and rent for many more than could be employed in the factories.

After the death of "Papa Doc" in April, 1971, and his replacement by his son, Jean-Claude, political oppression continued but in more subtle form. Mediocrity and waste of national resources persisted. The recent marriage of Jean-Claude Duvalier to Michelle Bennett cost five million dollars, allegedly diverted from international aid funds to Haiti.

The third wave of emigration consisted of poor peasants dispossessed of their land or unable to make a living on the deteriorated soil. Also, unemployed laborers were attracted by the myth of full employment and high wages in the United States. These were the "boat people" who saw the United States as their final destination, even though many stopped in the Bahamas en route. This temporary stop occurred either because of navigation problems or by design. In the Bahamas, many could make contact with smugglers who would bring them to the United States incognito.

Usually a poor peasant wishing to emigrate will sell his land to be able to pay passage. Laborers will sell all their possessions. Others receive passage money from family members who have gone before, and in the traditional way of immigrants, worked long hours to raise the cash for their relatives. As a rule, most newcomers arrive penniless because they have sold everything to get to the United States.

There are two categories of Haitian immigrants in Miami. A minority of legal residents, or Haitian-American citizens, are dispersed throughout Dade County, with significant clusters in Southwest Dade and in Carol City. Legal residents are estimated as numering up to 10,000.

The majority of the refugees are forced to live in limbo because their claim for political asylum has been denied. In fact, they are individuals without status in the United States, which makes them ineligible for any type of direct assistance from public funds. The only way they can receive help is through specially designed programs to assist refugees.

The refugees themselves include two subgroups: First, there are those who have had encounters with Immigration and Naturalization Service (INS) whose cases await a court decision. These are called Haitians with pending status. The second group are those with no encounters with INS, who have been brought here incognito by smugglers. These are called undocumented Haitians.

It is estimated that there are about 50,000 Haitians in Dade County. About 35,000 are concentrated in the Edison-Little River, Wynwood and Overtown areas. The others are in Model Cities, Opa Locka, Hialeah, El Portal, Miami Shores, and North Dade.

There is a vast range of problems faced by any group undergoing acculturation to a new society. Haitian problems include the following:

1. *Education* — The Haitian educational system is very authoritarian. Parents delegate their authority to the school and expect the school professionals to take full responsibility for educating their children. Since parents typically abdicate their responsibility to the schools, there are two sources of conflict with the American system. First, Haitian parents are not used to participating in P.T.A. or even in meetings with teachers to discuss their child's progress. Second, Haitian parents do not usually expect or know how to help their children with homework, which leaves the children without home stimulation or support.

Up to now in the school systems few attempts have been made to understand the problems of acculturation and identity faced by the newcomers. A large number of Haitian students are confronted with materials they cannot understand in a system from which they feel alienated. Many experience feelings of profound discouragement and as a consequence drop out of school prematurely to enter the job market.

Under an international UNESCO agreement, to which the United States is a signatory, all minor children are entitled to an education as a basic right regardless of status. However, this changes when a youngster attains his majority at age 18. Up until now nothing has been done for Haitian youngsters who are over 18, when they finish school. They are now considered adults, but because they have no legal status it is impossible for them to be admitted to a college or university. For this a legal document from INS is required. This leaves many bright young Haitian youngsters without hope or prospects for the future.

Many parents feel confused about how to raise their children. Their old authoritarian patterns are disapproved of in the new world. They perceive American society as too permissive. Many feel the atmosphere of the public school system is perverting their children who have now become exposed to early sexual initiation, drugs, and aggressive behavior. In Haitian culture, parents whip their children to discipline them. In the United States, some of these beatings may be perceived as child abuse. The Haitian childrearing system did not focus on dialogue between parents and children, but on linear authority and automatic obedience. Stripped of their old methods of correcting misbehavior, Haitian parents feel even mor epowerless in understanding how to raise their children and fear disruption of the family.

2. *Changing Sex Roles* — The opportunities offered here for women to become income providers, together with observation of different male-female interactional styles, has led many Haitian women to reject their old sub-servient role. Women now demand more participation in decision-making in the administration of their homes and in budget-planning in their homes. Conflicts

arise in this area in particular, since Haitian men expect to have control of the money and consider this part of the macho role. Many Haitian women now ask for separate bank accounts so they can have more control over their own earnings. Much marital conflict arises over this thrust for financial autonomy.

In other cases, women confined to the home who had accepted the equilibrium of poverty in Haiti now demand more of the consumer goods that they see all around them. Easy credit has created many conflicts. Usually the complaints of "Femme exigente" is frequently heard in marital counseling of Haitian couples, with the man insisting that he is being impoverished by his wife's greed. The wife, on the other hand, may claim that the husband is diverting the family budget toward external pleasures.

3. *Employment* — People without authorizatio to work from INS were forced to work illegally in order to susbist. Haitians took menial low-paying jobs that most Americans, even when unemployed, refused to accept. Recent court decisions, however, have enabled Haitian refugees to work openly. Among the refugees, Haitian women for the most part are working as maids or aides in hotels or hospitals. Some are operating machines in the garment industry, working in laundries, or in packing plants. Men are laborers, factory helpers, busboys in hotels and restaurant workers. A large number of Haitian refugees, boh male and female, have gone to the Belle Glade and Indian River areas to work as migrant canecutters and farm laborers. A few skilled workers can work in their professions, but usually as helpers rather than master craftsmen.

4. *Food* — The majority of Haitians retain their habits regarding food and recreation. A basic Haitian meal might consist of rice and beans, boiled plaintains, salad made of lettuce and tomato and stew meat. The ingredients are similar to those used by Cubans, but cooking styles are different. A real Haitian delicacy is a dish composed of fried plantains, called "bananes pesees" and fried pork called "Griot."

Haitians like to eat at home, and their prefer to cook their own food. They take pride in introducing their children to Haitian food and tend to disparage fast food places.

5. *Recreation* — Leisure habits in Miami are the same as in Haiti. People like to gather to play dominoes and cards, or just to chat. In Creole, chatting is called "bay odians" and this means a group of people telling stories, recounting daily events, and the like. On the weekend, when there is a Haitian band performing, people like to go to dance.

Haitian youngsters, more acculturated than their parents, are more familiar with disco, bars and clubs. Many Haitians feel comfortable in places where they can enjoy Latin-American or Caribbean music.

Youngsters attend the movies, but older Haitian refugees because of linguistic and cultural barriers are not cinema goers. Television viewing is a leisure activity primarily for children, who understand the language, and for women confined to the homes.

Generally Haitian people are soccer fans. Weekend games between local teams are the occasion for animated gatherings in the neighborhoods. Haitians enjoy home parties where friends and relatives get together to eat, drink and listen to modern Haitian "mini-jazz" music. Christenings, weddings, and first communions are joyfully celebrated. They provide an opportunity for reunion of friends and relatives, and are accompanied by heavy eating. These are also the very rare occasions when Haitians may drink heavily.

6. *Vodou* — Vodou practices are still prevalent among Haitians here in the United States. Formerly practiced in secrecy, the ceremonies are becoming more visible. The *Vodou Sevis*, as they are called in Creole, fulfill a double function. They satisfy religious needs and are also an occasion for socializing.

Despite many difficulties in establishing a Haitian community, Haitians in Dade County have been challenged to develop a speedy economic base. Haitian investors have opened small businesses in all the area between 79th Street on the North, 54th Street on the South, N.W. 2nd Avenue and N.E. 2nd Avenue. This is one of the reasons that this geographical rectangle and its immediate environs has come to be called "Little Haiti."

SOCIAL MOVEMENT DIMENSIONS

Ethnic minorities, like racial groups, are produced primarily through the process of migration — either through the movement of a colonial elite which subordinates an indigenous population of the same race as itself, or the voluntary migration of ethnic groups into a society to improve their economic situation. In both cases, however, economic factors are paramounts. Haitians have migrated to the United States for both reasons. Of crucial significance in their position are three major factors: (1) the historical circumstances under which they entered the society; (2) their degree of perceived cultural similarity to the dominant elite such as skin color; and (3) their economic role in the host society (low or high economic-occupational status and degree of economic resources.)

Haitians have entered the United States under negative historical circumstances and therefore are perceived as culturally different from the society's mainstream and have been assigned low economic status with few resources, experience the most discrimination, remain highly segregated, and experience low levels of political, economic, and social assimilation into the new society.

Fear of deportation limits Haitians in any type of revolution. Young people in the schools are constantly harassed, and looked down upon. Systems exploit the Haitian. It is said that within the next three years, Haitians will have a greater understanding of the American system and begin to develop their own political, social and economic base.

CONCLUSION

It is reasonable to assume that the most pressing social problem in contemporary society is not simply inflation and unemployment, but of a value system which will end exploitation, degradation, and destruction of human beings. For, even if economic difficulties were to decline, the problem of creating a humane society would remain. Failure to deal with it results in devastating human damage and intergroup conflict. The continued degradation and exploitation of the Haitian people testifies to the relatively low development of human society. Much needs to be done if the wide gap between technological and human society is to be closed. An appreciation of the problem's significance and magnitude is but a small step in this direction. Its costs have been profound and dramatic, as the Haitian "boat people" have, unfortunately, had to learn.

REFERENCES

LEYBURN, J.G. *The Haitian People*, New Haven and London, Yale University Press, 1966.
AMERICAN EMBASSY, HAITI *Economic Trends Update for Haiti (April, 1981)*

THE ETHNIC
POLARIZATION OF MIAMI*

By John F. Stack, Jr.
and
John G. Corbett

Miami has always been a city of great contrasts — of enormous wealth and desperate poverty; the carefree "Magic City" of sun, surf, and sand, and a nightmare of organized crime, prostitution, and narcotics; a model of non-partisan urban and suburban reform-oriented government and a corrupt semi-tropical Dodge-city; a crossroad of cultural diversity and a staid Anglo-Saxon southern town. The central paradox of Miami is that its leadership and citizenry seldom anticipated the potential for conflict which these disparities suggest. It is ironic that one of the most culturally diverse communities in the United States discovered its ethnicity a full decade after ethnic polarizations defined political, economic, and cultural relations throughout the United States and much of the world.

This chapter is an attempt to unravel a number of dimensions affecting the crystallization of ethnicity and ethnic conflict in Miami during 1980 and 1981. Our thesis is based on three assumptions. First, that the creation of ethnicity is the product of the convergence of the distinctive cultural values of the ethnic group which interacts with the political, socio-economic, and cultural organizations and institutions of the broader society. We do not suppose ethnicity to be an immutable primordial bond that is possessed by all groups but rather as a fluid grouping based on a sense of peoplehood or shared values that may intensify or abate depending upon specific conditions. Ethnicity, therefore, combines both affective ties — a sense of peoplehood — with instrumental goals — individual and collective interests.[2] In a pluralistic society ethnicity may intensify or diminish depending upon the mesh of the ethnic group with the values, organizations, and institutions of the broader socity. It is, indeed, conceivable for class or socio-economic affiliations to take precedence over ethnicity and vice versa. Our model of interethnic relations is essentially fluid and dynamic.[3]

The second assumption is that ethnicity is significantly affected by the penetration of the international system into the local setting.[4] It is our contention that the impact of international events, activities, and choices increasingly shape the context in which local priorities are ordered and examined. In this context

*We would like to acknowledge the assistance of Anthony Maingot and Christopher Warren who provided useful comments on an earlier draft of this paper and to Antonio Jorge who assisted us in our search for data on Miami's Latin community.

we are witnessing the "internationalization" of an American city with few parallels in twentieth century American history. The polarization of interethnic relations must be investigated from the perspective of international politics in which investment strategies, political instability, and natural disasters in the Caribbean and Latin America directly affect political, economic, and cultural factors in Miami. The dependence of Miami on the broader Caribbean-Latin American regional environment helps to define the cultural and socio-economic divisions of labor in Miami that are expressed in the city's economic growth rate, the cost of real estate, and the existance of sizeable exile communities with distinctive political agendas — Cubans, Haitians, Nicaraguans, and Salvadorians. The progressive internationalization of Miami means that local political and economic decision-making is becoming sensitive to the manner in which policy content and outcomes affect international linkages and perceptions of Miami abroad.

Third, ethnic polarizations are fueled by two processes. the *first* is economic competition based on perceptions of different distributions of opportunities and costs which reinforce existing ethnic cleavages. For example, it is difficult to bridge the isolation of the Latin and Black economies because of the divergent tastes, goods, and services which reflect different constituencies and cultural outlooks. A keen sense of competition, therefore, lingers especially as perceptions of Latin upward mobility intensify. *Secondly*, economic competition and ethnic differences heighten a "seige mentality" in which all ethnic groups perceive their stake (current or anticipated) as vulnerable to and threatened by the actions and interests of other groups. The principal danger is a rapidly escalating upward spiral of conflict which is defined in zero-sum terms. The social and political fabric of the community would indeed be threatened as events and issues are increasingly defined in zero-sum terms. While we can offer no sound predictions for the future, it is our contention that the polarization of Latins, Anglos, and Blacks must be seen as an important, if not a crucial, vairable in any discussion of contemporary Miami.[5]

This chapter provides an overview of the interplay of heightening ethnic conflicts amid domestic political and economic upheavals brought about in party by the increasing penetration of the international system into the local setting. It is organized in four main sections: The Setting of the City, The Internationalization of the Economy, The Polarization of Interethnic Relations, and The Anatomy of Conflict.

THE SETTING OF THE CITY

In the aftermath of the Liberty City riots of May 1980, the arrival of over 125,000 Cuban refugees during the Mariel boatlift, daily arrivals of scores of Haitian immigrants, and the fastest rising violent crime rate for any city in the United States, the salience of ethnicity has dramatically increased for many residents of Miami. While ethnic cleavages historically have characterized the demographic landscape of South Florida, particularly after the arrival of nearly 500,000 Cuban exiles in the 1960's, it is clear that ethnicity has never so completely dominated the area's political, economic, and cultural institutions. The difficult quest for economic security, especially of the Cuban population during the initial years of resettlement in Miami, tended to reduce the visibility of ethnicity outside of business activities and areas of residential settlement. The civil rights movement, the politicization of Hispanic identities, most notably Puerto Rican and Mexican-American, and the revitalization of white ethnic affiliations in the northern and midwest sections of the United States — Italian, Irish, Polish, and Jewish — tended to raise the consciousness of Cubans and coincided with their rising socio-economic affluence during the 1970's.[6] As the 1970's drew to a close, all the necessary ingredients for a vibrant ethnic community were established: a flourishing cultural life which displayed an extraordinary ability to adapt to living conditions in the United States while maintaining and, in some cases, intensifying traditional ethnic symbols; the continuing arrival of new immigrants; the establishment of cultural organizations including the mass media — newspapers, books, magazines, radio and television stations — social clubs and fraternal organizations, and an impressive educational system; the rapid growth of the business and financial sector (which will be analyzed in much greater detail below); and involvement in politics.[7] In less than twenty years, a viable Cuban community was established that exhibited a high degree of institutional completeness and, thus, underscored in subtle and explicit ways the importance of ethnic distinctiveness in the group's life.

The salience of Black ethnic identities crystallized in the turbulence and upheaval of the 1960's and ealy 1970's. While political and socio-economic achievements resulting from the civil rights movement and government programs affected segments of Black neighborhoods, many of the direct political and socio-economic benefits of the 1960's clealy apparent in the larger cities of the United States, did not materialize in Miami. Socio-economically, Black businesses were overshadowed by the spectacular achievements of Cuban and Latin entreprenuers. Politically, the Black community historically has been underdeveloped. It is a young community by the standards of the United States, the major cities dating only to the 1920's when Blacks came to South Florida in order to work in service sector jobs that were created by an expanding tourist industry. As the most socio-economically marginal ethnic group in Dade County, political achievements have been limited. The 1970's witnessed some progress, however. The growing eminence of Dr. Johnny Jones, the Superintendent of the Dade County Public School System, throughout South Florida suggested the possibility of new dynamic departures from the past. Jones' vast popularity within the Black community and his credibility and acceptance in the Miami establishment augered well for future political and socio-economic achievements. With his conviction for theft and his implication in a contractor-kickback scheme less than a month before the May 1980 riots broke out, the Black community lost its most powerful and charismatic leader. The 1970's, therefore, were an unsettling decade for Miami's Blacks. They were marked by perceptions of downward mobility vis-a-vis the Latin and Cuban community as well as by a series of more immediate events in 1979 and 1980 that illustrated the existence of pervasive institutional racism in the police, courts, the political system as a whole.₈ It became apparent to Miami Blacks that the gains derived from the civil rights movement for many Blacks were retarded by a worsening political, socio-economic, and cultural climate in Miami where Blacks were directly penalized for Latin economic mobility and continuing Anglo dominance.₉

In this context, the rapid population growth and increasing ethnic heterogeneity of Miami since 1950 provides insight into the ethnic polarization of Latins, Blacks, and Anglos. In 1950 the Anglo population made up almost 83 percent of the total, with the Latin share barely 4 percent. Even though the Black and Latin populations more than doubled during the 1950's, massive migration from elsewhere in the country meant Anglos accounted for 79 percent of total growth during the 1950's, and their share of the population declined only marginally. As the figures in Table I show, however, the ethnic profile changed radically during the 1960's as waves of Cuban refugees entered the United States, while internal migration failed to sustain the former ethnic distribution. Recent estimates suggest an even more radical change, with the Anglo population perhaps 60,000 less than it was a decade ago, and below the 1960 enumeration.₁₀ With approximately 43 percent of the population, Anglos barely outnumber Latins, and it seems likely that within two years Latins will be the largest single ethnic group in Dade County.

TABLE I
Population

	Total	Black	Latin	Other
1950	495,084	64,947 (13.1)	20,000 (4.0)	410,137 (82.8)
1960	935,047	137,299 (14.7)	50,000 (5.3)	747,748 (79.9)
1970	1,267,792	189,666 (15.0)	299,217 (23.6)	778,909 (61.4)
1980	1,665,000	263,000 (15.8)	687,000 (41.2)	715,000 (43.0)

Data for 1950-1970 from U.S. census. 1980 figures based on preliminary census data. Percentages in parentheses may not add to 100 percent due to rounding. "Other" includes Anglos and Asians.

At the municipal level the ethnic shift is even more noticeable. The burgeoning Latin population has spread far beyond early concentrations in Hialeah and Miami's Little Havana; both cities are now more than 50 percent Latin. The Latin population also spread into the unincorporated areas of the county; the middle class Westchester area in west-central Dade County changed from 30 to 70 percent Latin between 1970 and 1980, with many of the predominantly Jewish former residents moving to more distant suburbs or out of the county entirely. Although there are some signs of "white flight" at a county-wide level, the Anglo population tends to cluster in the more recently developed unincorporated portion of south Dade County and in the older upper-middle class suburbs near Broward County, e.g., North Miami. Census estimates show a limited tendency for Blacks to move out of Black neighborhoods and ghettos — Opa-Locka is now at least 70 percent Black — but soaring housing costs sustain *de facto* segregation. Blacks and Anglos share the view that numerical and spatial expansion of the Latin population is a major factor in the rapid rise of local housing prices.

Although most discussions of ethnicity in Miami, our own included, make use of a three-fold distinction among Blacks, Latins, and Anglos (or Whites), ethnic and cultural heterogeneity divides this tripartite classification even further. While the terms "Latin" and "Cuban" are frequently treated as synonymous, at least by non-Latins, almost 20 percent of the Latin population is non-Cuban. Colombians, Nicaraguans, and other Central and South Americans total more than 100,000. Increasingly, one hears street references to "old" Cubans and "new" Cubans, the distinction being between those who arrived in the 1960's or early 1970's, and the recent arrivals via the Mariel boatlift. Many of the "old" Cubans, although initially instrumental in facilitating the boatlift, now perceive the "new" Cubans as different and contributing to a backlash against Cubans in general.[11] The presence of 25-30,000 Haitians, many of whom are in the country illegally or on a tenuous immigration status, and smaller groups of Caribbean Blacks, adds complexity to the Black population. Even the Anglo population displays a significant difference between retirees, often Jewish former residents of the New York or Chicago metropolitan areas, and a somewhat diffuse Anglo population which includes migrants from the Deep South and upstate Florida, retired Canadians, and even an occasional Miami native. Class differences contribute to differentiation; "old" Cubans commonly have middle class backgrounds, while "new" Cubans are predominantly unskilled and lower class. Wealthy Anglo retirees in the condominium enclave of Bal Harbour have little in common with impoverished Anglo retirees in Miami Beach or Anglo working class families in Homestead. To the extent class cleavages reduce the size of one's reference group vis-a-vis the general population, it enhances a sense of isolation and threat.

THE INTERNATIONALIZATION OF THE ECONOMY

The 1970's and the last five years in particular fundamentally transformed Miami's economy while that transformation has affected every significant aspect of life in the South Florida region. Before the mid-1960's, the economy revolved around domestic tourism, service to retirees, and the construction needs of an increasing population. It was of marginal significance to the national economy which frequently led to cycles of rapid growth and contraction. The 1960's and the 1970's constituted an extraordinary period of growth in which local sectors of the economy were transformed by the financial, trade, investment, and service needs of a regional and international economy. Miami's geopolitical and cultural climate served as a favorable setting for North American, European, Middle Eastern, and Latin American business interests to interact. These activities encouraged the establishment of a wide array of intermediary and brokerage firms. Miami has become the Latin American and Caribbean headquarters of over 100 multinational enterprises and scores of U.S. corporations. The total value of the goods and services of these and other enterprises geared to the international market should top five billion dollars in 1981. The progressive internationalization of Miami's economy in 1979, 1980, and part of 1981 stimulated an economic boom resulting in more than two billion dollars in private funding slated for downtown redevelopment and luxury condominiums selling out before construction was finished while many of the United States experienced recession.

Miami has become such a major center for foreign investment in the United States that Florida now ranks third in the country in the dollar value of foreign ownership of real estate.[12] These investment patterns reflect the diverse and varied needs of a number of international investors: for example, the long-term development needs of Canadian involvement in condominium construction or conversion; the search for speculative profits through the buying and selling of raw land in Dade County by Netherlands Antilles and Cayman Island firms; or shelters for flight capital from Latin America and Europe. Moreover, there are allegations that Miami's real estate market is used to launder significant sums of monies from the flourishing drug trade. Over 40 per cent of all real estate transactions in excess of $400,000 during 1980 were on behalf of foreign investors. The total value of these purchases was $1,064,000,000. There is little opposition to the inflow of direct foreign investments because foreign investors appear to strengthen the local tax base without adding to the service demand although economist Mira Wilkins has challenged this view noting the inflationary potential of such investment.[13]

The changing distributions of visitors to Dade County is another indication of the rapidly rising importance of international economic linkages. While reports of civil disorders and violence may have slowed the growth of domestic tourism to Miami in late 1980 and early 1981, foreign tourism remains strong. Latin American tourists alone are expected to spend over $2.8 billion in 1981 in shopping areas almost completely targeted to Latin tastes and needs. Downtown Miami epitomizes this strategy and has assumed the character of a Latin American city with Spanish the dominant language and where events and decisions in Buenos Aires, Rio, Caracas, and Bogota are far more important than those in Tallahassee, Atlanta, and, in many cases, even Washington.[14] City and County officials vigoriously pursue foreign linkages — particularly those to the Caribbean and Latin American markets — promoting port expansion, convenient air travel, and the largest free trade zone in the United States. If current trends hold, it is estimated that by 1985 one-third of all employment in metropolitan Miami will be related, directly or indirectly, to international economic transactions.

Undoubtedly, the pace, breadth, and vigor of local economic growth draws heavily upon the demographic and economic expansion of Miami's Latin population. The convergence of new economic opportunities in the Caribbean and Latin America with the entrepreneurial talents, professional skills, and the resources of the arriving Cuban exiles during the 1960's generated much of the impressive growth of the 1970's. The availability of cheap labor, federal assistance to Cuban refugees, a growing quasi-captive Latin market through ongoing immigration, and the institutional completeness of the Cuban enclave laid an important foundation for Miami's spectacular economic growth during the 1970's. The Cuban population in 1981 includes 16 bank presidents, approximately 250 vice-presidents, 3,500 doctors, and thousands of small and medium size business owners.[15] It is, of course, easy to romanticize the Cuban exile experience by overestimating the rate of upward mobility. A growing and important body of literature is helping to adjust the notion that Horatio Alger is living in Miami and speaks Spanish through investigations of downward mobility and under-employment for significant segments of the Cuban professional classes as a result of their relocation in Miami.[16] The growth of the Latin, and, in particular, the Cuban business community undoubtedly has strengthened the economy of Miami as a whole. The hispanicization of Miami in language and culture has provided Cuban and Latin entreprenuers with the inside track — in many respects, a crucial competitive edge — on many new business relations with Latin America and the Caribbean, thus, enabling them to identify and exploit opportunities not as readily available in other areas of the sunbelt, for example, New Orleans, Atlanta, or Houston.

These achievements are not uniformly applauded, however. Latins argue their abilities and dynamism account for much of the growth in the Miami economy, but many Blacks and Anglos believe Latin penetration comes at their expense. Blacks have been arguing since the mid-1960's that Latins compete with them for employment, displace them from housing, and display considerable insensitivity to the systemic constraints on Black progress in Miami. Competition for blue-collar jobs both blocks much-needed low skill employment and depresses wages, while Latin competition for public sector employment angers Blacks who regard such positions as fruits of the civil rights movement and Black-led efforts to secure affirmative action programs. "Let a Cuban through the door, there'll soon be many more; let a Latin through the door, you won't be here no more" captures the sentiments of many Blacks. Others just see the Black economy, never strong in Miami, as pressed even further to the margin as a consequence of Latin aggressiveness and superior resources.

TABLE II

	Black			Latin		
	1969	1972	1977	1969	1972	1977
Number of Firms	1.166	1,530	2,148	3,447	4,847	8,248
Gross Receipts	28.7	75.0	95.0	121.0	363.0	688.0
(Millions)						
Receipts per Firm	49	49.1	44.1	35.0	75.0	83.4
(In Thousands)						
Manufact. Firms	17	20	26	166	267	295
Manufact. Receipts	.91	5.97	6.93	9.89	133.64	188.75

Source: Survey of Minority-Owned Business Enterprises, 1972 and 1977, U.S. Bureau of the Census.

These figures are merely suggestive of the rather slow growth of the local Black economy and the dynamism of the Latin. Latin firms are expanding in both size and receipts; impressionistic data suggests that Latin manufacturers may employ between fifty and one hundred times the workers employed by black manufacturers (Latin-owned garment manufacturing alone reportedly employs 25,000 workers).[17] While there are no formal barriers to cross-ethnic employment, locational and cultural considerations do impose significant constraints. To the extent that the ethnic identity of owners provides a clue as to the ethnic identity of the work force, the tentative data above suggest far more opportunity at the blue-collar level for Latins than for Blacks.

Concern over employment competition has become much more pronounced within the Anglo population (the very shift in terminology from "White" in a straight racial sense to Anglo, which incorporates a language dimension, indicates the social implications of spreading Latinization), as the demand for bilingualism, particularly in rapidly expanding service areas such as finance or trade management, leaves the largely-monolingual Anglo population at a serious disadvantage. "Bilingual" is generally regarded as synonymous with Latin, as few Anglos and even fewer Blacks have the Spanish language capability to perform successfully in the workplace on a daily basis. The use of Spanish as a working language has spread far beyond tourism and trade, and increasing numbers of employers consider an inability to speak Spanish a major liability, even where the job does not normally entail foreign contact. Calvin Trillin recently commented, "A Black secretarial school graduate who might have throught her handicaps in the job market would be limited to her color and an occasional problem with verb endings now has another handicap, she can't speak Spanish".[18] There is a certain irony in the success of bilingual education (which has meant teaching English to Spanish-speakers) in Miami, where between 1975 and 1980 the number of Latin households reporting equal use of Spanish and English rose from 13.8 to 21 percent. Far from aiding a subordinate and disadvantaged group to assimilate into the dominant culture, it has given the Latins a critical competitive edge on the local job market.

THE POLARIZATION OF INTERETHNIC RELATIONS

The absence of stable well integrated ethnic communities intensifies the social-psychological parameters of multi-cultural conflict in Miami. Ethnic bonds may also become a convenient vehicle for the mobilization of ethnic grievances real or imagined, legitimate or specious. The principal danger is that once ethnic antagonisms crystallize they are not easily abated. Thus, once collective and individual ethnic sentiments are mobilized they tend to be carried over into the principal institutions and values of a society.

principal institutions and values of a society. Cultural conflicts can be most effectively managed through the coordinated efforts of several institutions, ethnic and civic. as the history of machine politics demonstrates.

In Miami, the structure of the Black and Latin communities provide little in the way of effective elite leadership or cohesive institutions. The diversity of the Cuban community, as merely one segment of an immensely complex Latin community, is staggering. Socio-economic and cultural differences further fragment Miami's Cubans especially in light of the recent Mariel boatlift. Similarly, there are many Black communities in Miami ranging from the desperate poverty of Liberty City, Overtown, Carol City, and the Goulds to the relative affluence of South Dade's Richmond Heights area.

Anglos dominate Miami's principal economic, political, and socio-cultural institutions. The Greater Miami Chamber of Commerce is the preeminent elite institution which draws representatives from every significant economic, political, and ethnic sector. It represents the Anglo dominated Miami establishment better than any other county-wide organization. However, the fictional nature of a coherent, unified Anglo community is apparent as soon as one moves outside of less than a handful of elite institutions (the Bankers Club, the Miami United Way, the Tiger Bay Club). On a more general county-wide level the non-Latin and non-Black community reveals a bewildering array of groups and individuals, some possessing distinctive identifications based on race, region, class, culture, or religion.

What we may be witnessing is the creation of a new ethnic group — the Anglos — a residual category binding non-Latins, non-Blacks, and non-Haitians together on the basis of language and a familarity with traditional American culture broadly defined. Perhaps the most interesting aspect of evolving Angloness is that its character is defined on the basis of the supposed negative un-American attributes of Latins, Blacks, Haitians, and other non-European immigrants to Miami, and ongoing international immigration have heightened a sense of common cause among Miami's disparate Anglos. The strength of an Anglo sense of identity, therefore, is directly attributable to threat perceptions — a state of seige mentality — based on the progressive internationalization of life in Miami. Undoubtedly, an Anglo identification draws some of its vitality from extant traditions of nativism, zenophopia, and racism. Historians John Higham and Richard Hoftstadter have illustrated how the convergence of international uncertainies and domestic political, social, and economic upheavals triggered anti-foreign sentiments in 19th and 20th century America ultimately culminating in the immigrant restriction legislation of the 1920's.[19] A similar dynamic is at work as southeast Florida confronts problems that are by definition beyond its control. Given the absence of credible community-wide institutions capable of reassuring all segments of the Miami community, Anglos, Blacks, Haitians, Cubans, and Latins, that their most vital interests will be safeguarded, the fundamental danger is that Miami's underdeveloped civic institutions and fragmented ethnic groups will reduce the possibility of effective conflict management which may itself encourage the intensification of ethnic conflicts.

The one institution that tries to promote county-wide interests without regard to ethnicity, class, or political affiliation is the *Miami Herald*. The *Herald* self-consciously attempts to synthesize the strengths of Miami's culturally diverse groups while it simultaneusly works to stabilize Miami's political, socio-economic and cultural institutions. All too frequently, and not unexpectedly, the *Miami Herald* epitomizes the limitations of both assimilationist precepts and cultural pluralist pretentions. What results, therefore, are superficial attempts to delineate the contributions of Blacks, Cubans, and Haitians to greater Miami as well as preoccupation with problems that have clear ethnic overtones: crime, institutional racism, and the integration of refugees.

The *Herald's* difficult, perhaps even untenable, position was illustrated in its coverage of the Dr. Johnny Jones larceny trial and the implications of the McDuffie murder case. The *Herald's* investigative reporters reconstructed the central aspects of the Jones case indicating the possibility of ten thousand dollars worth of graft (in plumbing fixtures) for Dr. Jones' vacation home. As the highest ranking Black man in South Florida politics, Jones' trial constituted a devastating blow to morale in the Black community. The *Herald's* reporting was highest ranking Black man in South Florida politics, Jones' trial constituted a devastating blow to morale in the Black community. The *Herald's* reporting was pecise, accurate, and non-sensational. It led directly to Dr. Jones' arrest and, as many Blacks maintain, to his incredibly swift conviction.[20]

The *Herald's* careful scrutiny of the murder of Arthur McDuffie by four Metro-Dade policemen and their subsequent acquital was precise and non-sensational as well. What the *Herald* uncovered was the logical progression of a history of police brutality and racism which culminated in Arthur McDuffie's brutal death. In its reportorial functions and in its constructive editorial opinions, the *Herald* helped to legitimate the outrage of Black Miamians. Similarly, the *Herald* cast serious doubt on the legitimacy of Miami's central political, legal, and judicial institutions.[21]

In the absence of other county-wide institutions and the fragmentation of Miami's Black neighborhoods, the *Herald* frequently found itself under fire. Black accused it of conspiring with the white dominated power structure in its coverage of the Jones' scandal. Anglos perceived it as undermining Miami's political system and, in some respects, contributing to the Black riots of May, 1980, in its coverage of the McDuffie case and in its analysis of the riots.[22]

The tendency to use symbols laden with explosive ethnic overtones, therefore, has become common place in Miami. Johnny Jones and Arthur McDuffie became symbols for Blacks and non-Blacks. The intensity of the Black response when viewed within the framework of the May riots and when placed in a context of heightening economic insecurities vis-a-vis Mariel refugees offers some important insights into the nature of multicultural conflict in greater Miami.

While the acquittal of the four police officers who beat Arthur McDuffie to death was the immediate cause for the riots of May, 1980, the seething frustrations of the Black community would not have been likely except for the structure of race relations which consistently placed Blacks at the bottom of the pile. When compared to the socio-economic success of Miami's Cubans and the general Latinization of Dade County, civil rights in Miami meant Latin rights gained at the expense of the Blacks. Indeed, just as the impact of the civil rights movement diminished in the late 1960s, Miami was pushed into the 1970s by frantic Latin economic activity. On May 6, 1980, eleven days before the McDuffie verdict was announced and the riots began on Saturday, May 17, 1980, the Dade County Community Relations Board accurately assessed the level of frustration within the Black community.

> From every angle, every perspective, the community relations board perceived that Dade County is in a state of crisis . . . In our law enforcement agencies, there is police brutality, including murder; there are allegations of police corruption involving alliances with drug dealers and the theft of confiscated money . . . In our school system, there are charges of official corruption at the highest level . . . In our neighborhoods there are drug-related, gangland-style killings, joblessness, inflation and juvenile delinquency . . . Fear and anger are prominent among our citizens . . . Many of them feel they can no longer trust their police, their neighbors, their government officials nor even the news media . . . The potential for open conflict in Dade County is a clear and present danger.[23]

Deep-seated frustrations of a rather different sort exist in both Latin and Anglo communities and have increasingly spilled over into the political area through the use of ethnic symbols. Although the Anglo population feels vulnerable and threatened, it continues to dominate metropolitics. At present the Anglo population is but 43% of the county total while 65% of the registered voters would be considered Anglo. The Latin population is substantially under represented because many Latins have not become citizens. In addition to the ethnic distribution of voters, the structure or political organization of the county also favors the Anglo population. County commissioners are elected through county-wide elections but they are elected to represent specific districts. In addition, boundaries between districts divide Black and Latin populations in a way which assures minority status within districts as well as the county as a whole. County elections are nonpartisan and the strong county manager system gives a sense of technocratic government. Increasing demands to revise the county charter so as to elect county commissioners on a district basis are rejected as too parochial or politically backward but an underlying concern is that such a change would reduce the power of the political majority. To date no Latin has been elected to the county commission and the only Black commissioners who have served have been appointed by the Governor to fill unexpired terms of office after which time they have competed for office successfully, running as the incumbent commissioner. Political strength may be one of the most valuable resources of the Anglo community, it is unlikely to be surrendered readily.

The continued power of the Anglo political majority may be seen in the November 1980 anti-bilingualism referendum. A referendum so named because its purpose was to deny the county authority to extend county funds to utilize any language other than English or to promote any culture other than that of the United States. The thrust of this referendum was to eliminate insofar as possible county expenditures to provide publications and services in Spanish. In practice the vote was far more symbolic than substantive as it makes little real difference in the operations in county government, it does not prevent county employees from speaking Spanish on the job nor does it help monolingual English speaking residents to get jobs in the public or private sector. The vote against bilingualism approximately 60% favoring the ordinance, 40% opposing it must be seen as largely symbolic in nature as an expression of the frustration of the Anglo population with regard to what it sees as continuing expansion and penetration of community life by Spanish speaking residents. One clear outcome of the vote on the bilingualism ordinance was to heighten the seige mentality, the sense of being a beleaugered minority among the Spanish speaking population. An expression of frustration on the part of English speaking and largely Anglo voters found a counter expression in increased resentment on the part of Spanish speaking voters and in the Latin population at large.[24] The anti-bilingualism referendum helped to solidify anti-Latin and anti-Cuban stereotypes convincing many that no matter how hard they try, they will not win respect and acceptance from non-Hispanics. Anti-Cuban prejudices have undoubtedly increased in the wake of wide-spread perceptions of the criminal activities of Mariel refugees.[25] The immediate consequences of the Mariel boatlift has been to strain Miami's already overloaded municipal governmental system that has been pushed to the limits in its attempt to provide specialized services to Cuban refugees as well as to increasing numbers of Haitian immigrants.[26] The ultimate victor of the Mariel boatlift was Fidel Castro who humiliated Cuban Americans when he revealed that mental defectives, homosexuals, and hard core criminals were indiscriminately mixed with the vast majority of refugees. The inability of the federal government to find viable solutions to the problem posed by the Mariel refugees and the disparities in the treatment of Haitian immigrants inevitably tends to polarize even further Miami's strained interethnic relations.

Multi-ethnic conflict emerges at other levels in the public arena. The Miami City Commission, divided among a Puerto Rican, Black, Anglo, and two Latins, required 42 ballots and seven months of political maneuvering before naming a Black to be city manager. Latins constitute a slight majority of the population in the City of Miami, although they account for only 35 percent of the electorate, and some Latins urged a concerted attempt to defeat the Black commissioner in the November, 1981, city election. Such a defeat would deprive Blacks of one of their most prominent spokesmen and further reduce their political influence. Ethnic considerations have become prominent in every local personnel decision, and personnel managers in most public agencies are as sensitive to ethnic representation as any ticket-balancing politician. The City of Miami Police Department is under such pressure to increase minority representation on the force that it is offering a five hundred dollar bounty to anyone recommending a minority applicant who makes the force. Public policies, personnel selection, and social programs have become subject to a pervasive ethnic bargaining which becomes increasingly complex as more groups enter the political arena, more claims are advanced, and more resources deployed.

THE ANATOMY OF CONFLICT

The internationalization of Miami as reflected in rising levels of ethnic heterogeneity, the transnational dynamics of its economy, the immediate and long-term consequences of international migration, and the city's progressive Latinization helps to establish a framework for significant levels of ethnic polarization and the potential for an escalating upward spiral of multi-ethnic conflict. For the communal battle lines that emerged during the Black riots and their aftermath delineate not only the cumulative effects of collective group fears of Blacks but rising frustrations and group resentments for Latins and Anglos. What makes Miami's ethnic conflicts so potentially explosive is the clarity of readily identifiable communal symbols used to polarize Miami's divergent and, by no means, monolithic ethnic communities.

The continuous intrusion of significant international and transnational processes and actors as well as U.S. federal governmental policies, over which Miami's underdeveloped and communally fragmented multiethnic political system offers little effective control, complicates an uneasy ethnic setting. It may well prove true that Miami increasingly exhibits symptoms of a disease that will institutionalize communal conflicts that make the orderly exercise of its political system untenable. In this scenario, Miami may constitute the Western Hemisphere's Beirut — international, cosmopolitan, and physially threatened system untenable. In this scenario, Miami may constitute the Western Hemisphere's Beirut — international, cosmopolitan, and physically threatened by interethnic hostilities. It would not be difficult to predict greater levels of communal conflicts as Miami's political, social, economic, and ethnic stability are steadily affected by heightening levels of international penetration.

Alternatively, and more optimistically, Miami's successful survival amid the onslaught of domestic and international problems may foreshadow a new era of domestic and international challenges confronting strategically located sunbelt cities amid rising levels of hemispheric and global interdependence in economics, politics, and demograph shifts. If Miami can work to stabilize its political system and to integrate successfully its culturally diverse groups, Miami may well offer a convincing variant of consociational democracy. It appears that these alternatives or perhaps some middle ground yet to be defined are possible. However, we must urge some caution in accepting the easy assumptions of assimilationists or cultural pluralists — the future of Miami remains very much in a state of evolution. Indeed, the very intensity of transnational influences may result in significant challenges to traditional notions of state sovereignty and ultimately the governance of urban political systems. The somewhat troubling analogy of an American Beirut seems strangely plausible within our interpretive context — an analogy ironically proposed by Miami Mayor Maurice Ferre:

> The situation here is even better than it was in Beirut. Because in Miami you have the American flag, the American Constitution, American laws, American products, the American economic structure . . . and all in Spanish. You can come here and buy a computer, an airplane, a house or an apartment; you can invest in the stock market or buy United States bonds . . . and all in Spanish. What you have in Miami is a total infrastructure that's unique in the American experience.[26]

FOOTNOTES

[1]"Miami" has three referents: (1) City of Miami, (2) Metropolitan Miami, or Dade County, and (3) urbanized South Florida from Palm Beach to the Florida Keys. Our usage conforms to the second referent, and when we speak of referents (1) or (3) we will be specific, e.g., City of Miami.

[2]Daniel Bell, "Ethnicity and Social Change" in Nathan Glazer and Daniel P. Moynihan, eds., *Ethnicity, Theory and Experience*, (Cambridge: Harvard University Press, 1974), pp. 140-174.

[3]Our conceptualization of ethnicity is substantively indepted to the work Andrew M. Greeley, especially, *The American Catholic, A Social Portrait*, (New York: Basic Books, 1977), pp. 22-30.

[4]See, for example, John F. Stack, Jr. *International Conflict in an American City, Boston Irish, Italians, and Jews, 1935-1944* (Westport, Ct: Greenwood Press, 1979) and John F. Stack, Jr., ed., *Ethnic Identities in a Transnational World* (Westport, Ct: Greenwood Press, 1981).

[5]H. Jerome Miron and Robert Wasserman, *Prevention and Control of Urban Disorder: Issues for the 1980's*, (Washington, D.C.: University Research Corporation, 1980), p. 4.

[6]For an excellent analysis of Cuban ethnic identity within the South Florida socio-economic and political context, see, Antonio Jorge and Raul Moncarz, "Cubans in South Florida: A Social Science Approach," *METAS* (Fall, 1980), Vol 1, No. 3, pp. 37-87.

[7]*Ibid*, pp. 63-87; Antonio Jorge and Raul Moncarz, "International Factor Movement and Complementarity: Growth and Entrepreneurship Under Conditions of Cultural Variation," *Research Group For European Migration Problems*, (September, 1981), (The Hague: The Netherlands) pp. 2-10, 21-49. Alejandro Portes makes an important conceptual contribution to the study of Cuban ethnicity in Miami through the notion of the immigrant enclave, "Modes of Structural Incorpoartion and Present Theories of Labor Migration" in Sylvano Tomasi, *et al International Migration* (New York: Center for Migration Studies, 1980).

[8]Miron and Wasserman, *Prevention and Control of Urban Disorders*, pp. 8-13.

[9]Herbert Burkholz, "The Latinization of Miami," *New York Times Magazine*, September 21, 1980, p. 46.

[10]"Prospectus of Dade County Growth," Strategy Research Corporation, Miami, 1980, p. 10.

[11]Judith Valente, "Clashing Waves of Cuban Refugees," *Washington Post*, September 10, 1981, pp. C1, C4. Reliable data on the overall socio-economic characteristics of Mariel refugees has not yet been gathered or analyzed. The absence of such data only supports the wide-spread stereotyping of Marielitos as criminals, homosexuals, mental defectives, and social deviants. For a non-random preliminary an analysis of Mariel refugees and recent Haitian immigrants, see, *Metropolitan Dade County* "Social and Economic Problems Among Cuban and Haitian Entrant Groups in Dade County, Florida: Trends and Indications; Phase 1 Entrant Interviews; Phase 2 Key Persons/Agency Interviews;" 1981; Sylvia M. Unzueta, Special Projects Administration for Refugees Affairs for Dade County, has analyzed the implications of Mariel refugees in "The Mariel Exodus. A Year in Retrospect," (April 1981), Mimeo.

[12]Mira Wilkins, "Foreign Direct Investment in Florida, Costs and Benefits." See also, Mira Wilkins, *New Foreign Enterprise in Florida* (Miami: Greater Miami Chamber of Commerce, 1980); Emmanuel N. Roussakis, *Miami's International Banking Community: Foreign Banks, Edge Act Corporations and Local Banks* (Miami: Peat, Marwick, Mitchell and Co., 1981).

[13]Wilkins, "Foreign Direct Investment in Florida," pp 37-38.

[14]Burkholz, "The Latinization of Miami," p. 46.

[15]Carlos J. Arboleya, "The Cuban Community 1980," Barnett Bank, 1980, p.2.

[16]See, Jorge and Moncarz, "Cubans in South Florida," pp 56, 60, 61-65.

[17]U.S. Department of Commerce, Bureau of the Census, *Survey of Minority-Owned Business— Black*, 1972 and 1977; U.S. Department of Commerce, Bureau of the Census, *Survey of Minority-Owned Business — Spanish Origin*, 1972 and 1977.

[18]Calvin Trillin, "Judging Johnny Jones," *New Yorker*, (April 21, 1980), pp. 81.

[19]John Higham, *Strangers in the Land, Patterns of American Nativism, 1860-1925* (New York: Atheneum, 1974); Richard Hofstadter, *The Age of Reform From Bryan to F.D.R.*, (New York: Vintage Books, 1955).

[20]Miron and Wasserman, *Prevention and Control of Urban Disorders*, p. 11.

[21]*Ibid*, pp. 8, 30.

[22]Kenneth I. Harms, Chief of Police of the City of Miami, best represented this point of view when he charged that the *Miami Herald* seriously undercut the effectiveness of the police. "You continue to shout about our failures while you whisper of our successes. Until you fully accept your total responsibility to the community, you will continue to be a divisive force within South Florida." *Miami Herald*, February 1, 1981, p. 6M.

[23]Miron and Wasserman, *Prevention and Control of Urban Disorders*, p. 8.

[24]Roberto Fabricio, "Dade Cuban-Americans Becoming New Minority," *Miami Herald*, November 15, 1980, p. 61.

[25]Liz Balmaseda, "Tossing Power with Pride," *Miami Herald*, January 31, 1981, pp. 1C, 2C; Anthony P. Maingot, "Ethnic Bargaining and Non-Citizenship: Cubans and Haitians in Miami, p. 56 in John F. Stack, Jr., ed., *The Primordial Challenge: Ethnicity and the State in the Modern World* (manuscript in preparation).

[26]*Florida Senate*, Select Committee on the Impact of Recent Refugees on the State Budget, Jack D. Gordon, Chairman, Report on Public Hearing held October 22, 1980, Dade County, Florida, Mimeo; pp. 5-6, 10-37, Unzueta, "The Mariel Exodus," pp. 13-19; *Metropolitan Dade County*, Social and Economic Problems Among Cuban and Haitian Entrant Groups, Phase 2, pp. 2-23.

DADE CUBAN IMMIGRANTS: INTEGRATION PATTERNS AND SPECIAL EDUCATIONAL NEEDS
By Guarione M. Diaz

CHARACTERISTICS OF CUBAN IMMIGRANTS

Although Cuban immigration to the U.S. dates back to the 19th century, the present Cuban community in Dade County and in other states of the union is formed and shaped by recent immigrant waves that began arriving to South Florida in the early sixties, and have continued settling in the area up to the present decade.

By the late 1800's there were about one hundred thousand Cubans mainly concentrated in Tampa, Key West and New York City, but also noticeably in other Florida cities. Fleeing the Cuban wars of independence (1868-1895), this first massive exodus established the tobacco industry in South Florida, and remained here as the first large enclave of Cuban-Americans. Not only did those early immigrants establish permanent roots in the U.S., but they also held public offices in local government, became a significant aspect of the area labor market and, yes, established a lively bilingual and bicultural community where "Spanglish" was not uncommonly used by the first generations.

After the Spanish American War (1898), scores of political exiles sought asylum in this country, several other thousands immigrated in small family groups in search of economic opportunity, and large numbers of Cubans visited simply as tourists. Those who lived in or visited the States brought back to Cuba their knowledge and experience of American institutions and culture. In fact, developments here have steadily reached Cuba's urban population by means of consumer products, machinery, the arts, and the media. Given this historical perspective and the geographic proximity of the two countries, it is not surprising that a new Cuban exodus to the U.S. ensued upon the establishment of Castro's socialist regime.

The exodus of the 1960's began under particular social and political conditions, both in Cuba and in the United States.* For the first time in Cuban history, waves of professionals, entrepreneurs, and skilled technicians left their country, hoping to return but nevertheless unwilling to live in socialist Cuba.

*In this paper, Cuban immigration is separated in three stages or immigration waves, the first from 1959-1965, the second covering the airlift period 1965-1972, and the third the Mariel exodus of 1980. Clearly, this is an artificial construct which is helpful only to highlight demographic and socio-economic characteristics of each wave, as well as to suggest events and relationships affecting the Cuban community at different time periods.

Many left with their entire families. Others sent their children unaccompanied. The vast majority were from Havana and other provincial capitals. Up to the late sixties, Cuban immigrants showed rather homogeneous characteristics. About a third had been managers and professionals in Cuba. With a middle class orientation and previous exposure to life in a modern urban setting, these early immigrants were not unfamiliar with life in Miami or other American cities. One third to one half of first wave immigrants were resettled in states other than Florida through a massive refugee settlement program. Those who stayed in Florida mostly in Miami's Little Havana and in Hialeah, found a city with a tourist and small scale service economy, available rental units at moderate prices, relatively low unemployment rates, and a native population generally sympathetic to their situation (perhaps a temporary one) as exiles from a socialist country.

Indeed, some traits of the Cuban population in the United States began to change prior to the Mariel exodus of 1980. From 1965 to 1972 over a quarter million Cubans were airlifted into the U.S. The airlift wave was considerably larger in size than the group arriving to the U.S. between 1959 and 1965.

While a third of the first wave Cuban refugees (in the labor force) were professionals and managers, the rate was reduced by half in the early seventies, and has not shown significant changes to date. Also, by the mid seventies the proportion of Cuban refugees from Havana decreased by half as compared to the previous decade. Over the same ten year interval, the number of refugees from all other provinces in Cuba doubled. The airlift had brought to the U.S. tens of thousands of Cubans from small towns and medium sized cities throughout the island. About the same period, there were large groups of rural residents who escaped the island in small boats, rafts, automobile tires, or anything that would float.

Second wave arrivals overrepresented students, children and housewives, as well as older persons, and showed a relative increase of persons from lower socio-economic strata.

During the summer of 1980 about 125,000 Cubans migrated to the United States aboard some two thousand boats of all sizes, both private and chartered. About half of them had relatives in the U.S.

Most of these "Marielistas" came willingly to the U.S. A noticeable minority consisted of common criminals pressured by the Cuban government to abandon the island. The freedom flotilla included hand-picked homosexuals, and a few lepers and mentally ill.

As a whole, the boatlift immigrants of 1980 increased diversity to the already changing Cuban community of the sixties and seventies. Unlike previous Cuban immigrants (52% female), about two thirds of the Mariel "entrants" (status defined by the U.S. government) are male. At a median age in the low 30's, the Mariel exodus is six years younger on the average than the rest of the Cuban-American community. Also, the group has a larger proportion of Blacks (10%) than previous Cuban immigrants, and lower educational and skills levels than previous immigration waves.

The vast majority of them did not speak English. Having lived in a closed socialist country for twenty years, they are the least familiar (of all Cuban immigrants) with the American way of life.

As the last decade came to an end, a new generation of Cuban Americans born in the United States accounted for almost 20 percent of the Cuban community. If one adds to it other thousands of youngsters and adults who were raised in this country, about one in every five Cubans attended U.S. schools and were exposed to and influenced by non-Cuban peers as well as American institutions during their formative years. Conversely, these Cuban Americans had little or no personal experience of life in Cuba before or after the revolution.

THE PROCESS OF SOCIAL INTEGRATION

As described above, waves of Cuban immigrants have settled in the U.S. since the early 1960's. Although twenty years is a comparatively short period of time, the integration patterns of Cuban immigration into the U.S., particularly in Dade County (Greater Miami Area), involve a succession of several complex factors, some related to the group characteristics, some exogenous to the Cuban community, and still others resulting from social and material structures shaped by Cubans in South Florida.

Social integration is considered in this paper as a process of coordination of social elements (class, ethnicity, etc.) into a unified whole. Integration of a large group of immigrants is rarely achieved in a few years. It does not require total relinquishment of customs, language, and beliefs from the mother country. At different points in time we regard an immigrant as having integrated more or less satisfactory into a host society. Thus, rather than trying to determine whether Cubans have "in toto" integrated themselves or not into American society, I will discuss below relative patterns of social integration as suggested by commonly used social indicators.

Let us begin with language. As a group with relatively high educational levels and from middle class extraction, first wave immigrants in Miami would have been expected to learn and use English, the host country's language.

Moreover, the use of English was particularly necessary to them as one could not speak of a Cuban community in Miami prior to the 1960's. Although there is no available data relating use of English to date of arrival, survey data collected during the past five years, and particularly in 1980, shows that usage of English and language preference by Miami's Cubans varies according to age and activity. Overwhelmingly, Cubans prefer to speak Spanish at home. English is used more at work, and is the predominant language in school. Differences in language preference also exist in the use of printed or electronic media. On the whole, these data suggest that the first two waves of Cubans use language alternatively depending on factors that are both quite practial as well as culturally-related. Available data also indicates that usage of English is related to a higher level of education (in the U.S.); but even among Cuban college graduates, Spanish is spoken more in Miami than in other cities with large Cuban populations (e.g. Union City).

While the Miami Cuban community has nourished the use of Spanish through the media (Spanish) and at home, there is no indication that the private teaching of Spanish is becoming predominant in Dade. This is shown by the fact that over 80% of Cuban children attend the Dade public school system.

While it is an observable fact that "Cuban neighborhoods" in Dade are filled with thousands of small stores owned or operated by Cubans, the majority consist of family businesses with few other employees. Although the Cuban community is making a substantial contribution to Dade County's economic development, the majority of Cubans in the labor force are employed by businesses not owned by other Cubans. By and large Cubans workers are integrated with the area's work force. It is also interesting to consider that whatever entrepreneurship Miami Cubans have shown, it is in keeping with prescribed goals and values of the host society's and thus a positive sign of social integration. Yet, the development of a ghetto economy which precludes the usage of English to obtain goods, services, and/or employment, acts as a deterrent to integration with the society at large.

Patterns of residential integration in the Cuban community have changed as new immigrant waves established residence in Dade County. From initial heavy concentrations in Miami's Little Havana and in Dade's City of Hialeah, Cubans are establishing residence in most county areas. Residential patterns are an interesting example of how interrelated factors within and outside the Cuban community can affect the development of this immigrant group.

The arrival of a massive second wave of Cubans (1965-1972), together with a massive number of returnees, created a relative housing shortage in Miami's neighborhoods with large Cuban concentrations.* This factor combined with a healthy economy, estimulated local builders to develop large numbers of new housing units throughout the county.

Additionally during this period, Cubans with several years of residence in the U.S. began to look for housing facilities suitable for larger families and of a more permanent nature.

During the 1970's, as Cubans with an increased buying power moved to areas further south and west, tens of thousands of non-Hispanic whites moved out of the county.

As a result of these population shifts, the cities of Miami, Sweetwater, and Hialeah now have a majority of Latin residents, most of whom are Cuban. Nonetheless, Dade's half million Cubans can be found in most county neighborhoods. Residential integration between Cubans and non-Cubans is likely to increase unless the exodus of non-Latin whites reaches new unexpected proportions. Given the sagging economy of the early 1980's and the expected income and language limitations of the new Mariel entrants, one can also anticipate that members of this recent immigration wave will remain concentrated in traditional or new neighborhoods densely populated by Cubans such as Little Havana or South Miami Beach.

Naturalization indices are another sign of social integration. During the decade of the 1960's the number of Cubans who became American citizens increased fivefold from 1,824 in 1960 to 9,182 in 1969. In 1970, 22,000 Cubans became American citizens. Yearly, naturalization figures remained at the same

*More than one of every four Cuban Dade residents have lived in the U.S.

or higher levels during the rest of the decade.

In the cities of Miami, Hialeah, and Sweetwater, Cubans make the largest number of registered voters from a single ethnic group. However, the last Miami municipal election, Cubans did not vote as a compact ethnic block thus, providing another example of the selective nature of the Cuban vote.

One could speak of social integration in terms of the degree to which an immigrant group clings to national celebrations and institutions of the mother country or adapts the ones from the host country. Again, Cubans show a mixed bag in this respect. Anyone barely familiar with the Dade Cuban community realizes Cubans maintain their traditional Christmas Eve dinner while also celebrating with a Christmas Day meal. Presents are exchanged on Christmas Day, but the Three Magi-gift bearing Spanish tradition is celebrated community-wide with a big parade where thousands of children participate. Cuban children celebrate Halloween as enthusiastically as other children in the U.S.

Cuban culture in the U.S., and particularly in Miami, shows typical elements of Cuban traditional culture which may be disappearing in Cuba itself. These are commonly found in eating patterns and recipes which are transmitted from older Cubans to young restaurant and food industry workers. The same is true for religious events involving small town patron saints as well as Afrocuban rituals only held secretly in today's Cuba. A visitor of any large Latin festival on Little Havana's Calle Ocho (Southwest eighth street in Miami) will hear typical latin music being played not far from a discotheque crowded with Cuban youth dancing to disco beats. He will see pedestrians dressed in typical guayabera garments, and still others in youthful T-shirts, jeans or walking shorts and sandals. The canvas includes long hair, moustaches, chaperones, and signs advocating the freedom of Cuban political prisoners or asking voters to favor a political candidate. The setting, increasingly typical of Miami, is bicultural: boxing from Latin America, Miami Dolphins football and local Little League baseball; its words, frequently bilingual, sometimes at the expense of the canons of both languages.

As would be expected multi-organizational contacts with non-Cuban groups are more prevalent among Cuban groups and individuals from the professional and business community. In this respect, one can speculate that Cubans from a lower socio-economic background are less socially integrated, at least on terms of contacts with non-Cubans through formal organizations.

SPECIAL EDUCATIONAL NEEDS OF CUBAN IMMIGRANTS

Recent Cuban immigration continued unfolding as recently as one year ago. Second generation Dade Cubans are still a young population, under twenty years old. Consequently, it is to be expected that the Cuban community is very much in the process of finding its own patterns of integration into American society.

Surveys conducted in the Cuban community indicate that learning English ranks among the most important needs felt by the group. Greater availability of language training programs became specially important when over 90,000 of the Mariel Cuban immigrants established residence in Dade County. Presently, there are several programs offering language training to Mariel entrants in Dade. Although adequately funded to service thousands of entrants, these programs offer potential participants the alternative of badly needed employment income or unsubsidized class enrollment for a period of several weeks. Moreover, federal funding available to these programs will terminate within a year, thus leaving Florida's state and local government with the burden of financing these needed services.

Pre-Mariel data shows that scores of professionals trained in Cuba have been unsuccessful in practicing their professions in the United States due to language barriers and licensure problems. This group has been enlarged by ex-political prisoners freeed from Cuban jails in 1979, and by other professionals arriving to the U.S. through the Mariel boatlift.

In addition to the problems of re-training and certification of professionals and technicians, there are other educational issues of concern to the Cuban community, particularly since the latter part of the 1970's.

During the 1978-1979 school year, Hispanic high school students (80% of whom are Cuban) enrolled in the Dade County public school system had an 18.76 percent dropout rate. This rate represented a 27.9 percent increase from the previous year, while the comparative rate for Blacks dropped by 2.2 percent, and the rate for non-Hispanic whites increased by 3.5%.

Gradual but steady increases (preceding the Mariel arrivals) in school dropouts, juvenile delinquency, and number of Cuban families seeking or receiving mental health services in Miami suggest that cultural adaptation and intergenerational problems within Cuban families could benefit from an increased availability of bilingual, culturally sensitive, educational and mental health services. The growth and orientation of service delivery systems in the Miami area has not kept pace with the recent growth of the Cuban and Latin communities in Dade County.

Whether it is due to the unavailability of Cuban professionals, entry qualifications in this field, or perhaps due to a simple matter of unequal employment opportunity, Dade Cubans are significantly underrepresented in the ranks of teachers and administrators, both in the County's public school system and in major institutions of higher learning. For instance, between 1977 and 1980, Hispanic students composed about one third of the student body of Dade's School System (grades K-12). Yet only 11% of the faculty, and less than 10% of the administrators were Hispanic.

Educational issues affecting the Cuban community are not solely related to instruction or staffing. The universal need for parental involvement in school affairs is especially important for Cuban families, and essential for the last wave of Mariel immigrants.

This is probably more simply said than done. Families recently arrived from Cuba came from a society where parental involvement in school affairs is neither practical nor encouraged. Secondly, there is the problem of a language barrier, and parental unfamiliarity with the American social system's role expectations.

Thus, even if parents and relatives were committed to play an active role in educational activities and scholastic progress, how would they keep pace with the children's progress?

In most likelihood the academic community has not had enough time to even ponder the problem, let alone its possible solutions.*

Nevertheless, coping with this and similar problems affecting the education of Cuban children will require much greater involvement of the Cuban community as a whole and hopefully greater use of the resources within it.

A good example of this could be a new and imaginative use of Spanish media as a vehicle of communication between educators and community members.

FINAL COMMENTS ON SOCIAL INTEGRATION

Throughout this paper, I have discussed social integration as a multi-dimensional process. Further, it is a dynamic process influenced by forces within and outside an immigrant group itself.

Clearly, I have found it more useful to review multiple patterns of social integration than to try to determine in absolute terms whether Cuban immigrant have integrated or not to American society. If one envisioned an ideal state of social integration by the Cuban immigrant group, it would probably not be achieved during most of the lifetime of the first generation. Hence, after a relatively short period of twenty years during which three successive first generation waves have reached American shores, such an attempt would seem premature.

Secondly, the speed of social integration may depend on factors exogenous to the Cuban community such as the permanence of non-Cubans in predominantly Cuban neighborhoods.

What the process of social integration of Cubans seems to tell us so far is that Cubans have established roots in the United States, particularly since the 1970's. In doing so, the Cuban community has been a significant factor in shaping the social, economic, and cultural life of entire communities, such as Dade County.

Integration patterns are not alike for all Cuban immigrants. Moreover, when several integration variables are analyzed, it appears that within each immigrant wave there are elements both accelerating and retarding the incorporation of Cubans into the mainstream of American life in Dade County. Likewise, each immigrant wave received different degrees of support from residents of the host community (both Cuban and non-Cuban), received differential levels of government assistance, and found different states of well being in the local and national economy as well as in the Cuban community itself.

The social integration of Cubans in Dade County is likely to continue showing pluralistic features unique to this area of the United States. Cubans have exercised a strong influence in the expansion of Florida's trade with Spanish speaking countries, in the increase of Latin American tourism, and in the growth

---

*In fact, the Dade public school system faced enormous short term problems in just absorbing over 10,000 Spanish speaking students during the period 1980-81.

of services: banking, real estate insurance, and in small manufacturing. The economic advantages brought to the area by these developments are closely related to the existence of a social and economic infrastructure of a bilingual and bicultural character.

On the other hand, there is no indication that the use of Spanish or the existence of the above mentioned infrastructure in Dade necessarily acts as a deterrent to the social integration of Cubans into American society.

Perhaps it is worth remembering that ours is an open, dynamic and pluralistic society. In this respect, the United States is a unique nation. It has a seemingly inexhaustible capacity to change its customs and values, preserve its traditions, mix its population, and yet maintain its national American character. As we have seen for the last twenty years, Hispanic customs themselves are neither fixed, nor isolated. They change with the times and with the land and are influenced by the pervasive richness and appeal of American life.

Turning these historical and cultural tenets into a reality of meaningful social integration will require the depolitization of issues such as bilingualism which we must begin to treat as a practical mechanism to help us face social, political, and economic changes in Dade County.

This is the social and educational challenge that we, as citizens of this community, will face in the years to come.

BIBLIOGRAPHY

Strategy Research Corporation, *The Dade Latin Market,* Miami, Florida, 1978.

RICHARD R. FAGEN, RICHARD A. BRODY, AND THOMAS J. O'LEARY. *Cubans in Exile: Disaffection and the Revolution,* Stanford University Press, Stanford, California, 1968.

GUARIONE M. DIAZ, (ED.). *Identification and Evaluation of Health Education and Welfare Needs in the Cuban Community,* Cuban National Planning Council, Inc., Miami, Florida, 1980.

JUAN M. CLARK. *The Exodus from Revolutionary Cuba* (1959-1974): *A Sociological Analysis* (Ph.D. Dissertation), University of Florida, 1975.

For references on the professional adaptation of Cuba-trained professionals in the U.S. see Raul Moncarz, "Professional Adaptation of Cuban Teachers in the United States, 1959-1969", *International Migration,* 1970(a), 8, 110-116. (DC), and "Cuban Lawyers: Ten Years Later", *International Migration,* 1972(b), 10, 3, 109-114 (D.C.). The same author has conducted similar research on Cuba-trained physicians, veterinarians, pharmacists, and other professionals.

THE MARIEL EXODUS
AN UNFOLDING EXPERIENCE

By Silvia M. Unzueta, B.A.
Coordinator - Refugee Affairs
Metropolitan Dade County Government
Miami, Florida, U.S.A.

This paper is an attempt to start unravelling the interrelation between the Cuban "entrant", here called *Marielitos,* or Marieleros or persons from Mariel, and the community life of Dade County, Florida, where large numbers of the Marielitos reside.

Before their arrival, the population of Dade County was 35 percent Hispanic, 16 percent Black American, and 49 percent White. The Black Americans are about equally divided between those from the Islands and those from the deep South. After the initial arrival of the Cubans through the Mariel boat lift in April, 1980, the Hispanic population increased by a half of one percent. More than most other metropolitan areas, Dade County, Florida, was a community of descendants of immigrants or immigrants themselves.

The exodus of over 125,000 Cuban men, women and children started when more than 10,800 Cubans moved into the grounds of the Peruvian Embassy in Havana on April 4, 1980. After the Cuban government guards were removed from the Peruvian Embassy, the word quickly spread throughout the island. The removal of the guards was Castro's response to a dispute between the Cuban and Peruvian governments, when the previous week a small group of dissident Cubans broke into the Embassy seeking asylum.

At that time, no one predicted that the removal of the Cuban militia guard from the Embassy was to be interpreted as anything but "teaching a lesson" to Peruvian authorities. Instead, in less than 24 hours, over 10,800 Cubans jammed into the small Embassy grounds seeking political asylum. Dramatic photographs of crowded men, women and children in trees, and on the Embassy roof without water, food and basic necessities hit the world press, creating embarrassment and pressure for their release.

After extensive third country negotiations and humanitarian requests from all over the world, the Cuban Government agreed to allow the departure of the Cubans holding the Embassy. Peru, Spain, and Costa Rica, along with the United States, agreed to give refuge to the 10,800 Cubans seeking political asylum. During these negotiations, spontaneous demonstrations of support by Cuban-Americans in the Miami area and other cities of the United States as well as other countries, and extensive coverage of the world press, helped to highlight the incident and eventually helped to achieve the release of approximately 1,500 of the 10,800 originally held in the Peruvian Embassy in Havana. Upon the arrival of the initial groups in San Jose, Costa Rica, and Madrid, Spain, the Cubans shared with the world media the horrors lived while at the Embassy. This exposure generated a negative opinion for the aging Cuban Revolution. A few days later, in a skillful and talented show of strategy, Fidel Castro announced the opening of the Port of Mariel and invited Cuban Americans to come to Mariel, Cuba, and pick up their relatives who wanted to leave the Island.

The announcement was well received by the Cuban-American community in the United States. Immediately there began what appeared to be an endless flotilla through the Florida Straits to bring relatives and friends from Cuba.

After a few weeks it was evident that the Cuban Government had no intention of fulfilling their promise. Instead, some individuals released from jails and mental institutions became part of the human flow that constituted the Mariel exodus. During the month of May, 88,817 Cubans arrived. This figure constitutes a larger number of Cubans than had arrived in any single previous year.

During May, 1980, a number of other factors converged to create a very special situation. President Carter stated that: "We will continue to provide an open heart and open arms to refugees seeking freedom from Communist domination." That statement was qualified less than a week later. Decisions surrounding the handling of the Mariel exodus became entangled in the United States political scene.

In Dade County, Florida, the initial processing and housing of refugees was skillfully handled by a handful of local, state and federal officials under the coordination of Metropolitan Dade County Government and the City of Miami. At Tamiami Park, a 24-hour processing center was set up where more than 1,500 Cubans were scrutinized by Immigration and Naturalization Service, fingerprinted, X-rayed, and released to family, friends and other supporters. Food, clothing and shelter were generously donated by individuals, local businesses, and civic groups. The processing and housing operation involved more than 1,500 volunteers daily who worked day and night in a unique and heart-warming show of care and good will. The Tamiami Park opened its doors on Monday, April 21, and operated until the evening of Friday, May 9, when the Center was moved to an old hanger near the Opa Locka Airport.

That same month, a state of emergency was declared by the President and the Federal Emergency Management Agency (FEMA) was mobilized into action. FEMA is the arm of the federal government responsible for coping with natural disasters and emergencies. FEMA's efforts were plagued by a lack of staff with knowledge of the language and culture of the people arriving, changes in personnel, policy inconsistencies, lack of clear direction, and clashes among various federal agencies. A Cuban-Haitian Task Force was appointed by the President to guide federal efforts during the emergency.

Although many errors were committed and severe criticism of the management by various levels of the federal bureaucracy has been voiced, many individuals were served because of the work and dedication of workers and volunteers who, side by side, worked in what was an unprecedented chapter in the history of U.S. immigration.

FEMA's presence attempted to bring the needed federal dollars and the recognition of the exodus as a national emergency. Meanwhile, the Cuban Government had turned what had been a negative internal situation for Cuba into a serious emergency for the United States Government. The masses of humanity continued arriving in Key West and other parts of Florida. In Cuba, one of the results achieved by the Mariel boat lift was to alleviate serious internal administrative and political problems for the Cuban Government by exporting a high-risk population to its political rival, the United States. The exodus freed jobs, houses, and prison space for the Cuban establishment, and these were critically needed in the Island. The departure of dissidents and other marginal persons undoubtedly relieved Cuba from explosive internal pressures.

At this time, still in the month of May, 1980, another phenomenon took place: FEMA opened four refugee camps in Florida, Arkansas, Pennsylvania and Wisconsin:

1. Elgin Air Force Base in Northwest Florida, housing 10,025. This was the first camp, a "City of Tents."
2. Indiantown Gap, in Pennsylvania, with a population of 19,094 Cuban refugees.
3. Fort McCoy, in Wisconsin, housing 14,243.
4. Fort Chaffee in Fort Smith, Arkansas, with 19,060 refugees.

The continued human migration and the inability of authorities to cope with the large numbers at their immediate point of arrival offered little alternative but to use these four military installations as a temporary housing of the hundreds who continued to arrive.

Life in camp began another chapter in the lives of these new immigrants. Physical and psychological abuse, beatings and rapes were happening along with riots as the weeks went by and many Cubans remained tangled up in the red tape of federal bureaucratic management. At one point during the month of June, 1980, in excess of 62,000 Cubans were housed in the four camps.

The processing and resettlement of these individuals was delayed while diverse Voluntary Resettlement Agencies (VOLAGS), contracted with the Department of State, tried to seek sponsors to place the Cubans throughout the United States. In expediting their placement, credentials and careful matching with potential sponsors were not always followed. As a result, the rate of broken sponsorships was estimated to be as high as 30 to 40 percent of those resettled. Most of those without relatives and who had broken away from their sponsors or "padrinos" gravitated to areas of high Hispanic populations. Florida, New York, New Jersey, and California became primary targets where homeless Cubans sought refuge.

In the Miami, Dade County area, where the largest number is still being concentrated, their presence created another emergency for public officials. Emergency temporary housing measures included opening up the Orange Bowl stadium and making cots available to those with no place to stay. The Orange Bowl was opened by the City of Miami in the second week of June, 1980. On June 20, Metropolitan Dade County obtained a special appropriation from

Washington to feed refugees breakfast and one hot meal a day.

Those staying at the Orange Bowl were certified for food stamp assistance by the State of Florida Health and Rehabilitative Services, Food Stamp Division. But as the stadium is the home of the Miami Dolphins, the City of Miami decided to establish another temporary facility, erected by July 21 — a "Tent City" under a downtown expressway. Up to 800 Cubans were housed in Tent City at one time, and more than 4,000 lived there during the two months it was open. Tent City remained open until September 30, 1980. Simultaneously with the operation of Tent City, the increasing number of broken sponsorships and the hardships encountered by Cuban Mariel refugees as they faced life in the United States, the wave of weekly hijackings of commercial planes by Cubans seeking a return to the Island (up to three in one day) made national headlines.

Reflecting on the Mariel flotilla, it is clear that its final chapters are still unfolding. More than 700 still remain in Fort Chaffee, Arkansas, now a modern-day concentration camp, where primarily young men and a few women and their children await the opportunity to enjoy life in the United States. Efforts to relocate the last refugees and close the camp have failed. Major communities heavily impacted by the Mariel refugee population have demanded careful planning and screening on the part of the federal agencies handling their resettlement. The hard-core cases have posed special resettlement problems and the final outcome of their fate remains uncertain.

DEMOGRAPHIC CHARACTERISTICS OF THE MARIEL REFUGEES

One of the most severe problems surrounding the Mariel population has been the lack of factual information as to the characteristics of this group.

In a brief six-month period, 125,266 Cubans entered the United States. Now, close to 20 months later, accurate demographic information about the group remains unavailable. To date, one of the few official data released on the total group is the one obtained of the first 61,569 Cubans who arrived and were processed in Miami, Florida.

Initial Group — Processed in Miami, Florida

Males	55.2%	
Females	44.8%	
Age group 15-45	54.7%	
Age group 23-35	29.2%	
"Immediate Family" in the U.S.	28.5%	TOTAL 61,569

Key elements in the composition of the Mariel population are age, race, educational level and family ties. Although no conclusive figures are available, individuals familiar with the group place the number of non-Whites as high as 30 to 40 percent, and males making up approximately 60 to 70 percent of the overall population. The average educational level is estimated to be between the sixth and the ninth grade with few of the arrivals being able to communicate in any language but Spanish.

Perhaps the most serious problem this group faces is a lack of attachment to family and friends outside of Cuba. This apparent lack of a support system has often inhibited effective resettlement efforts.

Juan Clark, in *"The 1980 Mariel Exodus: An Assessment and Prospect,"* estimates that "about 50,000 men came without their families." He further estimates that about 20,000 men were forced by the Cuban Government to be separated from their spouses in coming to the United States, in violation of their human rights.

UNACCOMPANIED MINORS

Dr. Jose Szapocznik, Director of CAMP, Cuban Adolescent Management Program, University of Miami, Department of Psychiatry, Spanish Family Guidance Center, which provided services to Cuban unaccompanied minors, reports their total in the camps at 672. Of those, more specific information was obtained on 549 cases: of these

55 or 10% were females.

43% were non-Whites.

18% have been or were in a marital or paired relationship.

12% reported coming directly from jail.

50% reported having been in jail at some point of their lives.

59% reported having some relative in the United States, but only about half of these could give any portion of an address.

Parental occupation and education was reported to be:

70% labor/agricultural.

20% skilled labor.

10% professional.

Szapocznik reports that a large portion of the interviewees appeared to have poor adjustment to school. Sixty-five percent stated that they had stopped going to school. The rough literacy assessment turned up approximately eight percent illiteracy rate.

Six of the fifty-five female minors stated that they thought or knew that they were pregnant at the time of the interview. Fifty-six, or almost ten percent, reported sexual abuse, venereal disease, or multiple sexual problems in their recent or distant past.

Clinical judgments of a series of psychiatric symptoms and conditions reported the following characteristics:

47% had experienced behavioral problems in Cuba.

14% had experienced hallucinations.

8% had experienced delusions.

31% were or had been clinically depressed.

22% had experienced suicidal tendencies.

14% had made a suicide attempt.

Although much publicity has been given to the criminal record of this population, reliable information is not available. The Immigration and Naturalization Services had 1,761 or 1.4% in custody, charged with committing felonies and other serious crimes in Cuba. Most of these remain at the Atlanta Penitentiary for crimes committed outside of the United States. A total of 23,927 were considered by INS as non-felon criminal and political prisoners, representing 19.1% of the total arrivals. It is very unfortunate that both categories were lumped together into a single total figure.

Much has also been said about the percentage of homosexuals in those arriving from Mariel. However, no data is available as to the actual number of homosexuals in the Mariel population.

The Mariel Boat Lift ended in the same abrupt manner in which it had started, with Fidel Castro's instruction on September 26, 1980, that boats waiting to pick up relatives in Mariel Harbor in Cuba return to the United States empty. On September 26, 1980, the exodus that had brought to our shores 125,266 men, women, and children in 2,011 boats and one airplane was concluded. In final negotiations between the United States and the Cuban governmental officials, at the end of September, 1980, the Cuban Government advised the United States Interest Section in Havana, Cuba, that an additional 600 Cubans were stranded as a direct result of the abrupt closure of the Port of Mariel, officially requesting that they be cleared for admission into the United States. The United States accepted the Cuban Government's request and agreed to fly these Cubans to Miami after careful screening by United States authorities in Havana. These individuals were granted full "refugee status" rather than being legally classified as "entrants", as was the case with others who came as part of the Boat Lift.

LEGAL IMPLICATIONS

Throughout this paper, reference is made to "refugees." Legally, however, the individuals coming in the Mariel Flotilla have been granted the new administrative category of "entrant". This technicality rendered them ineligible for assistance available through the U.S. Refugee Act of 1980. Many experts believe that the denial of refugee status to these people greatly contributed to the many problems encountered in the handling of the group. It was through legislation known as the "Fascell-Stone" Amendment (named after two senators from the Florida delegation) that special funding allocations were authorized, in the form of cash assistance and health care, which reached the entrants during the latter part of February, 1981.

The Mariel experience highlighted and dramatized the need to look at the newly adopted Refugee Act. The Select Commission on Immigration, created by the President to review U.S. immigration matters, undoubtedly felt a wave of public pressure as a direct result of Mariel. The Commission's final report was issued in March, 1981, in Washington, D.C. The Commission made important recommendations in the area of U.S. immigration procedures.

DADE COUNTY, FLORIDA

Official estimates put the number of Mariel refugees in the Dade County area at over 90,000. Despite resettlement activities aimed at the relocation of refugees out of this area, it is estimated that many have not left Dade County and others, resettled out of the State of Florida, have returned.

By August, 1981, a total of 92,030 Cuban and Haitian entrants were officially added to the total Dade County population figures in an update of the 1980 Census.

It is difficult to overstate the impact that this wave of refugees has had on the social, economic, and institutional framework of the Dade County-Miami community. The emergency nature and the short span of time involved in the arrival of many thousands of people has been particularly taxing to the existing governmental entities, and to the residents of the community. Their arrival coincided with an increasing flow of Haitians, seeking freedom from Haiti and relocating from the Bahamas, and the increasing conservative trend felt throughout the nation.

GOVERNMENTAL SERVICES

Social security, driver license and food stamp offices, as well as social service agencies became overwhelmed by the great number of people requesting services. Lines at the Immigration and Naturalization Office began forming daily in the early hours of the morning. Medical care demands at the County hospital and in community mental health centers and other social service programs, have increased substantially.

UNEMPLOYMENT

Although the official unemployment figures for Dade County are reported at 6.7%, these exclude an estimated 50,800 unemployed Cuban and Haitian entrants who actually double the unemployment rate for the area. Many of the Cubans require a substantial upgrading of their employment skills before they are able to find and retain jobs.

As of mid-March 1981, the Little Havana Manpower Agency reported 3,046 individuals on a waiting list. The same agency reports having employed, from April to March 1981, a total of 2,165 persons, in a variety of jobs. Of these, only 285 or 13.1% were Mariel refugees. These figures confirm the severe unemployment problems experienced by the newly arrived group.

HOUSING

Dade County's rental housing market has a vacancy rate of less than one percent. Overcrowding indices in Hispanic communities were high even prior to the Mariel influx. It was to these same areas that many of the new refugees came, adding to the severe housing crunch. Rent has skyrocketed, further curtailing the ability of the new arrivals to secure adequate and safe housing.

EDUCATION

By the end of December 1980, the Dade County Public School System was hit with approximately 13,800 Cuban refugee children in grades K through 12 (ages 5 to 17). The children, fluent only in Spanish, came into an already overcrowded school system, the fourth largest system in the nation, which in spite of severe funding constraints, continues to make every effort to respond to community needs.

CRIMINAL JUSTICE SYSTEM

The increase of local criminal activity has been one more item often blamed on the Mariel refugees. As of December 26, 1980, of 163 Cubans charged and/or convicted of felonies in the Dade County Main Jail, 103 or 63.9% are Mariel refugees, 11 or 6.8% are Cuban expolitical prisoners, and 47 or 29.1% are Cuban-Americans. Mariel refugees represented 9.8% of the total number of individuals in the Main Jail. In the Women's Detention Center, where females either charged or convicted of felonies or misdemeanors are housed, eight or 4.6% Cuban-American women were housed along with eight or 4.6% Mariel Cuban women and seven Mariel Cuban homosexual males. Mariel refugee women represent 4.6% of the total females, while Mariel homosexual males represent 4.0% of the total number of individuals housed in the County's Women's Detention Center.

The increase in criminal activity has been a severe stress on the entire Dade County and State judicial system.

DEATH OF MARIEL CUBANS

While no specific data is available on the total number of deaths of Cubans who came through Mariel, a study of dead Mariel refugees who were taken to the Dade County Medical Examiner's Office throws some light on this question. It is estimated that the Medical Examiner's Office deals with approximately 33% or one-third of all County deaths, and *all* homicides and suicides that occur in the Dade County area. An analysis of the Medical Examiner's records for the period of April 21, 1980 to March 31, 1981, indicates that 101 Cuban Mariel casualties were processed.

Homicides represented fifty-seven or 56.4% of those cases, followed by natural deaths, which represented twenty-three or 22.7%; accidents, eleven or 10.8%; and ten or 9.9%, suicides. Of the dead, seventy-eight or 77.2% were white and twenty-three or 22.7% were black. Eighty-eight or 87.1% were males, while thirteen or 12.8% were females. The average age of the Cuban Mariel dead was 41.8 years.

In spite of well-intentioned efforts to discuss and to provide some statistical information on the Mariel population, attempts to clarify and sharply focus the dynamics involved in the Mariel-Key West Boat, are still unfolding in the streets of Dade County, Florida.

Since the late seventies, multi-ethnic Dade County has been home to close to half a million Hispanics, primarily Cuban-Americans who came to the United States in the early sixties and seventies. The Cuban-American's contribution to the wealth of Dade County life which has been substantial, is confronted head-on with the "new" Cubans, those who are primarily the product of life in the Island, under the Communist Government of Fidel Castro. This fact, compounded with the complex population mix achieved by the Cuban3 Government, when convicted criminals, severe mental cases and other maladjusted individuals from the island were added to the thousands that came in the Boat Lift, has helped to add confusion, apprehension, and suspicion to the ability of Cuban Americans to relate with the newly arrived Cubans.

The overall community climate has eroded further when other members of the community are venting their frustrations against the presence of illegal aliens, against old and new Cubans alike, and anything that is other than the traditional image of non-Hispanic Whites. The atmosphere of fear and rejection of foreigners, even American citizens of Cuban origin, is perceived by Cuban Americans as an over-reaction that places stress on ethnic relations. On the economic arena, Cuban-Americans continue to grow and share in the "American dream"; their advancement in other areas however, has deteriorated greatly as a direct result of the Mariel Boat Lift.

These events and what has been perceived as inadequate leadership on behalf of Cuban-Americans has helped to polarize residents of the area to the point that dialogue at present is more difficult to achieve.

While future ethnic relations in Dade County remain uncertain, major efforts are going to be needed to improve communication among both Cuban-Americans and Mariel Cubans, and other ethnic/cultural groups in the area.

REFERENCES

Metropolitan Dade County Planning Department, 1979. Statistical Analysis of Cuban Refugees -
   Cumulative Statistics through 14:53:40; September 12, 1980, John Lasseville, Statistical Analyst.

CAMP — *Cuban Adolescent Management Program* — Report prepared by Spanish Family
   Guidance Clinic, Jose Szapocznik, Director, University of Miami Program.

Impact of Cuban Entrants on Dade County, Florida. Paper presented at the National Conference on
   Feminist Psychology, Boston, Mass. Prepared by Dorita R. Marina, Ph.D., and Silvia M.
   Unzueta - March 1981.

The 1980 Mariel Exodus: An Assessment and Prospect prepared by Juan Clark, Ph.D. for the
   Council of Inter-American Security, Washington, D.C.

*Study of Hispanic Inmates at the Three Metro Dade County Corrections and Rehabilitation
   Department.* Memorandum prepared by Sylvia M. Unzueta on December 31, 1980.

Study of Mariel Deaths from April 21, 1980 to March 31, 1981 — Dade County Medical Examiner's
   Office, Memorandum prepared by Sylvia M. Unzueta dated April, 1981.

Survey of Cuban Refugees: Exodus, Employment, Housing prepared by Dr. Jose Ignacio Lasaga,
   Miami, Florida, presented at the Congress of Dissidents in New York, Summer 1981.

Violent Death Stalks the Boat Lift Refugees, by Helga Silva and Carl Hiaasen, article from The
   Miami Herald, May 31, 1981.

*Social and Economic Problems Among Cuban and Haitian Entrant Groups in Dade County,
   Florida: Trends and Indications* — Metropolitan Dade County Government, Office of the
   County Manager, September 11, 1981.

*Clashing Waves of Cuban Refugees — Cuban refugees head for the United States in May, 1980.
   The stiffest prejudice the newcomers face is from those who came first* by Judith Valente — The
   Washington Post, Sunday, September 20, 1981.

AN INVESTIGATION INTO THE ECONOMIC, SOCIAL AND CULTURAL PATTERNS OF WEST INDIANS, RUSSIAN JEWS AND INDO-CHINESE IMMIGRANTS IN SOUTH FLORIDA

By Shelly Goldman
and Stephen M. Fain

INTRODUCTION

To be sure, in the last three hundred years America has received its share of immigrants. Obviously each wave of newcomers faced significantly different challenges as they sought their place within the country of their choice. Oscar Handlin's *The Uprooted* tells the story of the great exodus from Europe in the nineteenth century.

The following excerpt from Handlin captures both the problems of the particular subjects of his book as well as speaking to what we think are universal problems facing virtually all immigrants.

> ... To the immigrants America seemed unstable; it lacked the orderly elements of existence. Without security of status or the recognition of rank, no man, no family, had a proper place in the social order. Only money talked, for Americans measured all things in terms of gold and invariably preferred the superficial and immediate to the permanent and substantial.
>
> These reactions reflected the urge to strengthen old values and to reaffirm old ideals. Precisely because migration had subjected those to attack, it was necessary aggressively to defend them, to tolerate no change because any change might have the most threatening consequences. In that sense all immigrants were conservative, dissenters and peasants alike. ... (Handlin, 1951, pp. 115-116)

Although Handlin is examining the period of immigration to the United States which is described as the great European migration, his description could be applied to South Florida today. No one is really surprised at the effective assimilation of those who came from Latin America with money and often English. These individuals and groups were able to create linkages between two cultures with relative ease. "Natives" were equally interested in "building bridges" which provided a kind of "cultural romance" afforded significant opportunities for financial gain.

However, all recent immigrants have not made the journey with the same ease. Today, South Florida also recognizes that a vast majority of the newcomers journeyed to our communities in search of freedom and opportunity. These people have a great deal in common with the Europeans Handlin wrote about. Generally without affluence and English they, as did their historical counterparts, are slower to assimilate as they are dependent on their old culture ("old country ways") for personal and social security.

Although there exists great similarities between the immigrants of "then" and "now" it would be foolish to assume that all things are the same. We all recognize that the raw frontier open to the ways of European immigrants is no longer present. Going west with the railroads or other forms of "pioneering" associated with the past have virtually disappeared with the shift from industrialization to high technology. Further, social policy issues provide a broad spectrum of considerations that were not operative some one hundred years ago. Among the differences which have significantly impacted upon the assimilation of immigrants are such things as child labor laws, minimum wage, affirmative action, multi-ethnic issues, and the wide spectrum of issues touched upon by the "Great Society."

We are forced to wonder about the question of the status of minorities and immigrants among and between themselves as well as within the greater society. On the one hand there seems to be powerful forces directed at accomplishing social integration while supporting the maintenance of cultural differences. On the other hand, there seems to be limited economic and social service resources available. Obviously, the new frontier is significantly different than the one Handlin's immigrants faced. In the "old days" one did not want to be a "greenhorn" and the "melting pot" concept seemed to be accepted. Today we seem to have embraced the "salad bowl" concept. Perhaps the new frontier lies in being able to walk in many ways while keeping one's identity. Perhaps that always was the frontier and will continue to be the frontier in the future.

This paper considers social and cultural patterns of other minority immigrant groups and their relationship to acculturation in the multi-ethnic culture of South Florida, specifically looking at West Indians, Indo-Chinese, and Russian Jews.

FOCUS ON MIAMI: DISCUSSIONS ABOUT THE INDO-CHINESE, RUSSIANS AND WEST INDIANS

We shall discuss each of the groups above by using several types of data bases. In the case of the West Indian populations, much of the information is drawn from reports of West Indian resettlement. Our information and discussion of the Russian immigrants and Indo-Chinese comes from a more ethnographic perspective. We have attempted to learn about the people's expeiences as immigrants through their perspectives. We accomplished this by interviewing and observing people in their communities.

THE ENGLISH-SPEAKING WEST INDIANS

It is estimated that there are a fair amount of English-speaking West Indians immigrating to Miami. The people who come to Miami from the various islands in the West Indies are from a vast array of cultural groups. It has been noted that about all these peoples actually have in common is that they carry British passports and speak some form of the English language. Generally these immigrants come to Miami from Jamaica, Trinidad and Tobago, and several other islands in the Caribbean, each of which has its own customs, traditions and culture.

Most of the West Indians that emigrate do so for economic reasons since there is little employment opportunity in their home island. The West Indians who immigrate usually have higher educational and skill levels than the general populations in their home country.

The West Indians are generally linguistically and culturally closer to American culture than the other groups that will be discussed. They speak English and generally practice some form of Christianity. Surprisingly, the West Indian immigrants found emigration and assimilation into the British society extremely difficult. Most reports of the British experience with West Indian immigration report the great difficulties that West Indians had in entering the employment, social and educational structures. (Ogbu, 1978; Bowker, 1978).

When educators and sociologists analyzed the problems that West Indians had in Britain, they identified language as a great barrier to success. Additionally, it was found that cultural differences inhibited success of immigrant children in school. Lastly, racial discrimination was identified as a significant blocking barrier for West Indians, both in terms of success in school and in access to employment. (Ogbu; 1978)

The West Indian in Miami faces many of the same obstacles as the British immigrant did during the past twenty years. Language, race (most are black or Chinese), and cultural styles will affect their opportunities in employment markets and schools. The question we must ask is, "How can we learn from the British experience with West Indian immigrants?" We need to examine the situation that exists in Miami in relation to the West Indian immigrant.

Language was identified as the greatest barrier to school success. Unfortunately, in Miami, no program exists for West Indian students for remediation of language. West Indian students are considered to be English speakers and are not eligible for ESOL or BCC programs in the schools. Many West Indians actually speak a different dialect than we speak. This is a problem that needs to be recognized by the schools. This is especially important in light of the other cultural and racial adaptations the West Indian is making upon arrival in this country.

We found that the West Indians have generally blended into the existing multi-ethnic scene in Miami. It appears that the West Indian's economic, geographic and social familiarity with South Florida's culture (they are distinctly westerners) and their possible identification with several ethnic groups in Miami (e.g., Blacks, Chinese and other West Indians) could contribute to their ease in assimilating. Lastly, the West Indian who leaves his homeland tends to be educated, Christian and solidly middle class.

THE INDO-CHINESE

As a whole, the Indo-Chinese comprise the second largest minority immigrant population in Dade County. The largest group of Indo-Chinese is from Vietnam, although there are also Laotians, Cambodians, Thais, Koreans and Chinese here. Together these immigrants from this part of the world speak several languages and come from some vastly different cultures. It would be naive of us to attempt to link them together and classify them as one group as these populations are from different religious, political, and economic backgrounds, and have emigrated to the United States for a variety of reasons. We will examine the social and cultural adjustments of one of the Indo-Chinese groups, the Vietnamese.

For the most part, the Vietnamese have made steady progress in their adjustment to American culture. They are predominantly a people comprised of refugees from a war-torn nation. Their family, community, economic and political lives were devastated by the war, and prior to their arrival here, many resided in refugee camps.

Economically, most of the Vietnamese have fared well since their resettlement in Miami. Many of the refugees came unskilled and have entered jobs through training programs such as CETA programs; others have procured entry leve jobs which do not require skilled labor. The Vietnamese are working and making their way in the labor force, albeit in jobs at the lower end of our occupational structure. The exact reasons for this successful entry are unclear, although several people we spoke with contended this adjustment was easy because the Vietnamese culture itself is organized around trade and commerce. The people were familiar with competitive jobs and trade markets, understood the idea of "working into the system," and expected to start at entry level positions when they came to Miami. One immigrant, for example, said that he was eager to get a job as soon as he got settled. He was willing "to do anything" to earn a living. To this man, just gettign the opportunity to have a job and a place for his family to live was important. In fact, just being settled in Miami knowing that they would be able to stay here met his expectations.

The Vietnamese have established communities for themselves around Miami. They live in neighborhoods nearby each other and have a strong sense of comradery with each other. They look forward to bringing other "new" Vietnamese into their midst and would gladly offer food, shelter, and wherever possible, employment opportunities to other Vietnamese.

The greatest problem that the Vietnamese seem to have in adjusting to American life is that they are inexperienced with many aspects of an industrialized and technical culture. Their own background is different. Most of them come from small villages where life is simple and untouched by technology. Many of the Vietnamese children have lived only in camps or as migrants, and thus knew nothing of houses or schools, televisions, computers or telephones. Everyday life in the United States provided the Vietnamese refugee with cultural shock and new learning experiences at every turn. Teachers report that they had to spend time teaching the children how to eat with a fork and a knife, and how to use a toilet and a telephone. One case worker told of a time when she had worked with a group of Vietnamese who she found apartments for. Several days after they were settled in one building, the landlord called her and said that she would have to come down to the building and show the men how to live there. The men, not knowing how to use the appliances in the kitchen, had been setting campfires for cooking food in the middle of their living room floor. The landlord had called the fire department because he hadn't realized what was going on. The landlord and fire department needed the case worker and a translator to come down, explain that they could not safely cook-out in their rooms, and demonstrate how to use the kitchen. The immigrants were truly sorry, and "amazed" at the stove once they learned what it was.

Anecdotes like the aforementioned are not unusual for describing life for the Vietnamese refugee in America. They certainly emphasize the need for basic and comprehensive educational programs. Much of what we take for granted in our lives is totally unknown to the immigrant. The agencies and groups that work with these groups must be prepared to work with people at vastly different levels of sophistication vis-a-vis American culture. Presently, this need is being met through language programs and English instruction, where much of the program revolves around learning the language for everyday American experience.

The Vietnamese must adjust to American culture through their daily experiences and English programs. They receive much support and encouragement from their ethnic communities. They are faring well in the job market and most seem pleased that they have the chance to work and settle in a growing community.

THE RUSSIAN JEWS

Since 1978 approximately 600 Russian families have immigrated to the Miami area. Almost all of the families settled on Miami Beach where today the majority of them still reside. Most of the Russians left the Soviet Union because they were discriminated against for being Jewish. Their passports stated that they were Jewish, rather than stating what state they came from (as the passports of other Russians do). In addition, recent government policy in Russia was prohibiting Jewish students from taking university entrance examinations. Parents feared that their children would be denied opportunities for a productive life in Russia.

Some of the Russian immigrants we spoke with characterize their adjustment to this culture as being very difficult and frustrating. Almost all of the adults and children now speak English because they were enrolled in English classes as a condition of their resettlement program. Most of the Russians felt that language was a barrier for them, but cite other differences in cultural values and patterns as impediments to their acculturation.

The Russians came to the United States from a very restrictive society. They were inexperienced in dealing with a multi-bureaucratic system where they needed to make individual decisions. The Russians were unfamiliar with a competitive job market. One woman explained that in Russia, you are given a job when you finish your schooling or training. You do not have to go out to job interviews or compete with other people for a position. Once you are given the job, it is yours for life. While in the Soviet Union, a Russian does not have to worry about moving up the occupational structure, he/she certainly doesn't have to worry about moving down. This has been a problem for many of the Russian immigrants because they were not used to "looking for a job." The problem did not ease once the Russian immigrant procured jobs. As they started to earn a living the Russians were overwhelmed at the amount of money management they had to do. Arranging for services in their home from different utility companies such as the telephone company and the electric company seemed like "so much work" for them. They were, in short, unaccustomed to dealing with each company separately, since in Russia, everything was arranged for them. One case worker who helped many families settle remembers several of the immigrants crying and "pulling their hair out" because they could not figure out all of the different places they had to go to arrange for even their most basic necessities. These people had never lived in a capitalistic economy, and were basically disappointed when they realized that they had to pay for services and material goods in this country.

Most of the Russian Jews that came to the United States were educated, middle class, blue collar workers. Many of the men had college educations and worked as engineers (middle class-technical workers) in the Soviet Union. Many were disappointed with their immigration because they felt as if they had tossed aside their middle class existence only to become downwardly mobile in this country. Even though many of the men were engineers in their homeland, they now have low status jobs in this country. People must start their training again here if they want to work at their professional jobs. Many of the immigrants find that an extremely frustrating process. Some are studying in their professions, although many of the immigrants trained for jobs in unrelated occupational areas of CETA sponsored programs.

Unlike the Vietnamese, the Russian Jews are quite used to living in an industrialized and technologically advanced society. In some respects then, their adjustment to many aspects of life in the United States is easy.

It appears that the Russian immigrants have a very high level of education. They are generally quite sophisticated by our standards in the arts and sciences regardless of whether or not they attended colleges in their homeland. Even the young children are advanced in the sciences and math areas. This fact has proved to be a problem for the schools and a problem for the Russian children. Quite simply, teachers and students are working on different academic levels. When the children entered the schools, it became apparent that they were bored with the curriculum. In the third or fourth year of school in Russia, the students are learning algebra and geometry while here they are learning much more simple levels of mathematics. The elementary schools were able to adjust to this problem by offering more advanced curriculum through the BCC program. This was a successful tactic at the elementary level that, unfortunately, was less successful in the secondary school where there is a high truancy and drop-out rate among Russian students.

Boredom was not the only problem that the Russian students faced in relation to the schools. Like their parents in the employment market, the Russian students faced adjustment problems given the less restrictive cultural millieu in the schools. When the students first came to the schools, they expected a rigid environment. For example, they thought that they had to "rise" from their seats every time an adult (a teacher or administrator) walked into the classroom or each time they were asked to speak. They also expected that they would have to carry their "copy books," which contained their work and evaluations, with them at all times in case an adult wanted to inspect them. Several teachers told us that the Russian children feared authority when they first came and were overwhelmed by the amount of freedom they had in American schools. They also contend that this is where the greatest problems developed. Almost everyone we spoke with, including some students, told us that the Russian children had hard times adjusting to the school. At first, they thought the school was a place where they could "do anything they wanted to do." Generally, that attitude has created a great deal of discipline problems, especially for the teenage population who feel bored with the curriculum. Many of those who are truant want to quit school and get jobs; others are finding ways of leaving high school and going to college.

In general, the Russian immigrants have made successful entry into the social and economic structures in Miami. They are mastering the English language, procuring jobs and planning for advances in the occupational structure. As they become more familiar with life in a free enterprise system, they (are becoming consumers as well as producers and are beginning to purchase cars and homes) feel less regretful and more optimistic about their resettlement.

OBSERVATIONS

The description of the three groups presented thus far indicate that there is stress within each immigrant community. And, as pointed out by Handlin earlier, old ways are often held on to for security. We see no evidence of significant political action within these groups. Rather, we see them quietly accessing the formal and technical systems of the society. (Hall, 1966)

Learning the language is a problem but it would appear that the Russian Jews and Indo-Chinese immigrants are mastering English. It appears that coping with a dialect is more difficult. The Russian Jews and Indo-Chinese seem to be drawn to occupations similar to occupations held in the "old country." It also appears that the West Indians who are either black or Asian are forced to confront the informal and very tough barrier set up by individuals and societies bent on sustaining various race and ethnic prejudices.

Schools are looked to as vehicles for acculturation by each group. However, schools seem to be "out of step" with the living styles and cultural expectations of the immigrants. "Dropping-out" is viewed as a viable move for securing employment; even at a young age it seems to be an accepted way of "making it."

Obviously, social status is unclear as individuals seek social and economic advancement ("the American Dream"). Without a clear sense of where one belongs it is difficult to feel comfortable in the greater society. However, it seems that each of these groups seeks to establish a place in the social order as individuals and not as a special group. We were constantly made aware of the fact that virtually none of the individuals in any of the three groups discussed felt our "label" applied to them (i.e., Russian Jews were Russian, Indo-Chinese said they were Vietnamese and West Indians said they were Jamaican.)

CONCLUSION

After considering our work it appears to the authors that there is much to learn from observing these groups in this moment in time and in this place. Immigration in Miami usually brings visions of Cubans and Haitians to mind. These groups are definitely the majority groups. These groups seem to be coming together as political entities. These groups are newsworthy and the media seems to make it clear that each of these groups is experiencing difficulty.

On the other hand, our efforts have convinced us that social progress is being made more effectively by Russian, Vietnamese and Jamaican immigrants. These groups seem to share something with the European immigrants of one hundred years ago. They are conservative and they are not "in tune" with a good deal of mainstream culture. They are building on their pasts to create a new future for themselves and the children. Their dream is the American dream and they want to dream it as Americans.

REFERENCES

BOWKER, GORDON. *The Education of Coloured Immigrants* (London: Longmans, 1967).

BURGEN, TREVOR AND EDSON, PATRICIA. *Spring Growth: The Education of Immigrant Children* (London: Oxford University Press, 1967).

GLAZER, NATHAN AND MOYNAHAN, DANIEL P. *Ethnicity: Theory and Experience* (Cambridge, Massachusetts: Harvard University Press, 1975).

HALL, EDWARD T. *The Silent Language* (Greenwich, Conn.: Fawcett Premier Book, 1966).

HANDLIN, OSCAR. *The Uprooted* (Grosset & Dunlap, New York, 1951).

McDERMOTT, R.P., GOSPODINOSS, KENNETH. "Social Context for Ethnic Borders and School Failure: In Wolfgang, A., Ed., *Non-Verbal Behavior* (New York: Academic Press, pp. 175-195).

OGBU, JOHN. *Minority Education and Caste: The American System in Cross-Cultural Perspective* (New York: Academic Press, 1978).

PERCEIVED SOCIOCULTURAL CHANGE AMONG INDOCHINESE REFUGEES: IMPLICATIONS FOR EDUCATION

By Liem Thanh Nguyen
University of Iowa
and Alan B. Henkin
University of Iowa

Social scientists suggest that minority immigrant groups will commonly experience cultural and behavioral changes in the course of adaptation and adjustment to new social settings. Such transitional phenomena may also apply to refugees under similar circumstances.

The purpose of this study is to inquire into concepts of culture and behavioral change among Indochinese refugees. Data related to the perception of changes in refugee lifeways and cultural patterns were collected. Study subjects include Vietnamese and Lao refugees in the United States. The sample consists of 332 male and female adults randomly selected from Vietnamese and Lao communities. Responses of the subjects to structured items of an instrument constitute the principal source of data for the study. Results of analyses suggest that Vietnamese and Lao respondents have perceived critical changes in behavioral patterns and cultural values within a period of time after resettlement in the United States. The attitudes of Vietnamese subjects toward these changes appear generally unfavorable. Although the attitudes of Lao subjects are more favorable, the social desirability factor remains in question. Intent to maintain major home culture characteristics has important implications for educational programs designed to serve these populations.

INTRODUCTION

What happens when minority group persons resettle in a new society and encounter the majority group of that society? Anthropologists suggest alternative responses depending on the context of the culture contact. In the case of colonialism, the culture of a majority group may be threatened by that of a minority (but dominant) group with control over military and political spheres. However, it is the culture of the minority immigrant group that appears subject to change in the case of migration, given inevitable involvement in the process of cultural assimilation (Spiro, 1955).

Sociologists further distinguish between voluntary immigrants and refugees. These two groups differ from each other in terms of motivation to migrate and circumstances under which migration occurs (Davie, 1947; Garkovitch, 1977). Immigrants are commonly motivated by the primarily economic attraction, or pull-force, of the host society, while refugees usually migrate because of the push-force related to social and political conditions in the home country. The former frequently have a destination in mind, a plan for migration, and some preparation for adjustment in the environment after migration. The latter enjoy few opportunities, if any, for planning, preparation or stipulation of ultimate destination (Davie, 1947; Kent, 1953). Refugees may experience lower levels of assimilation to the host society (Garkovitch, 1977), although no definitive confirmation of this assertion is currently available within the literature. Resettled refugees or immigrant groups, however, tend to experience changes in cultural patterns in the course of adaptation, regardless of the motivation to migrate (Gordon, 1964; Warner, 1945; Saenger, 1941; Davie, 1947; Kent, 1953). This tendency appears to apply to the target population of this study, Indochinese refugees (Kelly, 1977; Montero, 1979, Liu, 1979).

If, indeed, this is the case, what are some of the cultural patterns that have changed? Are the refugees aware of these changes? What are their attitudes toward these changes? What implications do these changes have for the education of refugees? This study is an attempt to respond, in part, to such questions. It is designed to explore perceptions of some sociocultural changes among adult Indochinese refugees, and to ascertain current attitudes toward perceived changes. We seek to examine these attitudes toward change, moreover, as important elements in socialization and integration processes within the host society.

METHODS

Numerous refugees from the three countries of Indochina — Vietnam, Laos and Cambodia — entered the United States and other receiving countries, after the fall of South Vietnam in April, 1975; a more controlled exodus from Indochina continues. Indochinese-origin persons constitute the first substantial refugee group to arrive from Southeast Asia and, in the aggregate, the largest group of incoming refugees to the United States over the last two decades. Six distinct ethnic groups and the countries of origin may be identified among Indochinese refugees; the Vietnamese (Vietnam), the Chinese-Vietnamese (Vietnam), the Lao (Laos), the Hmong (Laos), the Thaidam (Laos) and the Cambodians or Khmer (Cambodia). In this study, subjects are members of the two largest Indochinese ethnic populations in the United States; namely, the Vietnamese and the Lao. The sample consists of 400 Vietnamese and 400 Lao adults currently residing in the Pacific Southwest. Subjects were selected at random from available lists of members of Vietnamese and Lao organizations. The organizations assisted in the distribution of questionnaires to study subjects. The representativeness of this sample is not asserted, since all Vietnamese and

Lao refugees who live in this geographical area with high density populations of Indochinese refugees do not necessarily belong to one or more of these organizations.

The questionnaire was made available in either Vietnamese or Lao. Attention to item development principles, stylistic simplicity, and factors influencing reading ease, we posit, facilitated related ethnic group understanding of the questionnaire. Review and revision procedures were implemented prior to distribution.

The questionnaire itself is composed of 60 items. It is organized in three parts. Part 1 (10 items) inquires into demographic and related areas such as age, sex, education, family status, time in the United States, occupations in the home and host countries, and religion. In Part 2 (5 items), subjects are asked to rate life-circumstances in the host country in comparison with those in the home country, given several dimensions (material life, spiritual life, occupation, social status, and a composite rating of life-conditions in general). For each dimension, subjects relate perceptions on a five point continuum from "much worse" to "much better". Part 3 (25 items) consists of statements reflecting behavioral patterns and cultural values that are common to the Vietnamese and Lao in their home countries. Subjects are asked to react to these statements. Each item is presented in two contexts; that of the native country, and that of the host country. An example is in order: (Item) In Vietnam (or in Laos), the Vietnamese (or the Lao) always respect old people; (Item) In the United States, the Vietnamese (or the Lao) always respect old people. We note here that even though Laos and Vietnam are neighboring countries located on the same peninsula, they have received distinctly different external cultural influences. The Vietnamese culture was significantly impacted by the Chinese; the Lao received influence from India. The Hinayana Buddhist ethic has predominated in Laos, while the Confucian ethic constitutes the major sociocultural influence in Vietnam. Despite differences in terms of ethnic group, nationality, and certain aspects of culture, there are some salient similarities. Both Laos and Vietnam are developing countries. Their economies are based on agriculture with comparatively minor development in industrial sectors. Both countries were controlled by the French from the end of the nineteenth century to the end of World War II and, consequently, received some Western influences which are especially apparent in educational and public administrative systems. Extant similarities in cultural values and behavioral patterns will be detailed later. These similarities allowed us to construct the third part of the questionnaire appropriate for both the Lao and the Vietnamese.

Questionnaires were returned, after follow-up, by 45% of the Vietnamese subjects and 37.5% of the Lao subjects. Care should be exercised, of course, in generalizing findings beyond the study group to the general refugee population in the United States.

Data were processed by means of the computer. Besides descriptive statistics such as frequencies and crosstabulations, two nonparametric statistical techniques have been used to analyze the data. The first technique is the chi-square test for difference between the two subgroups on several aspects of culture presented in the questionnaire. The chi-square value of this test is rendered by using the following formula (Siegel, 1956, p. 107):

$$x^2 = \cfrac{N(AB-BC-2)^2}{(A+B)\,(C+D)\,(A+C)\,(B+D)}$$

Another technique is the McNemar test for the significance of changes (Siegel, 1956, pp. 63-67). The McNemar test is used separately for each subgroup on each aspect of culture from the home country to the host country contexts. The significance of the chi-square value of this test indicates subjects' perception of change from the home country to the host country.

RESULTS AND INTERPRETATIONS

1. *Profiles of the two respondent subgroups.*

    a. For both subgroups (Lao and Vietnamese), the percentage of male subjects is four or more times that of female subjects (80% - Vietnamese, and 83% - Lao). This distribution of subjects by sex is not attributable to a set of parallel circumstances in the general refugee population. It is, however, an indicator of male refugee involvement in the respective associations. An unequal distribution of refugees by sex is also found in previous studies where population distributions of Vietnamese refugees by sex, for example, are reported in ranges from 54% male and 45.3% female (Montero, 1979), to 77.4% male and 22.6% female (Kelly, 1977) and 78% male and 22% female (Nguyen and Henkin, in press). Multiple study distributions of Lao refugees by sex are not available; however, the sample in one research effort (Nguyen, Henkin, and Phommasouvanh, in press), provides a male to female ratio among Lao heads-of-household of about four to one.

    b. Many of the subjects are under 45 years old (76% - Vietnamese, and 85% - Lao). The sample is made up of relatively young people. This finding is consistent with previous studies on Lao and Vietnamese refugees. It is suggested that some 86.9% of Lao heads-of-household are under 45 years old (Nguyen, Henkin and Phommasouvanh, in press). There is a general consensus in the literature that the Vietnamese refugee population is also relatively young (Kelly, 1977; Liu, 1979; Montero, 1979; Nguyen and Henkin, in press).

    c. A classification of subjects' educational background by level reveals that 14% of the Vietnamese and 54% of the Lao subgroups are at the elementary level, 44% of the Vietnamese and 36% of the Lao are at the secondary level, and 44% of the Vietnamese and 10% of the Lao are at the higher education level. For this sample, then, there are more Vietnamese than Lao at the higher education level. The distribution of subjects in terms of educational background in this study does not differ substantially from that found in previous studies. There is general agreement that Vietnamese refugees as a group are atypical in terms of educational background when compared with the total South Vietnamese population of the early 1970's (Kelly, 1977; Montero, 1970; Nguyen and Henkin, in press). The same pattern of non-representativeness in the refugee group is also found among the Lao (Nguyen, Henkin and Phommasouvanh, in press).

    d.   Many Vietnamese subjects (56%) purportedly held white collar jobs in the home country. Only 28% of the Lao subgroup indicated former encumbency in white collar positions. The distribution among the subgroups for blue collar workers in the home country was 38% (Vietnamese) and 69% (Lao). Some subjects did not report their former occupations. The occupations of Vietnamese subjects in the United States are reported as 28% white collar, and 46% blue collar; those of the Lao are reported as 5% white collar, and 55% blue collar. The remainder are either unemployed, or are attending schools and/or transitional English language classes. In sum, more Vietnamese than Lao hold white collar positions when former and present occupations are considered. These circumstances appear consistent with the subgroups' educational backgrounds. Both subgroups experienced a diminution in occupation status from the home country to the host country.

    e.   Many of the Lao subjects (77%) in this study are Buddhist (Hinayana branch or lesser vehicle), a smaller number are either Catholic (9%), Protestant (6%), or are members of other sects (8%). Among the Vietnamese subjects, the number of Buddhists (Mahayana branch or greater vehicle*) is approximately equal to the number of Catholics (42%), while a small subset claim to be Confucianist (4%), Protestant (4%) or members of other groups (8%). The Lao are more homogeneous in terms of religion, both in their home country and in the United States. The large majority is Buddhist. In South Vietnam, Buddhist-Confucianists constitute approximately 80% of the population; there is no clear-cut differentiation between Buddhists and Confucianists among the Vietnamese. A high percentage of Catholics among Vietnamese refugees in the United States has been noted (Kelly, 1977; Nguyen and Henkin, in press).

    f.   Most Vietnamese subjects (78%) in this sample have been in the United States for more than five years. They came to the United States with the first wave of refugees after the collapse of the South Vietnam government in 1975. A smaller number (22%) may be counted among the second wave of Vietnamese refugees who arrived in the United States after 1976. This group is commonly referred to as "boat people". A significant migration of Lao refugees, on the other hand, was under way by 1976. Many Lao, however, were detained in camps in Thailand; hence, the absence of a mass immigration to the United States. For the Lao subgroup in this study, 70% have been in the U.S. for five years or less, while some 30% have been in residence for more than five years.

    Profiles of the two subgroups document some interesting similarities and differences. Both subgroups are relatively young, and include more males than females. They do differ, however, in terms of educational background, occupation, religion, and time in the host country. The Vietnamese subgroup includes more subjects at higher levels of education, more subjects with white

---

*For greater detail on Hinayana and Mahayana Branches of Buddhism, see Shoothill (1929), or Henkin and Nguyen (1980).

collar positions in their home country, a higher percentage of Catholics, and more subjects resident in the United States for a longer period of time. Profiles of these study groups appear to be similar to general profiles of Lao and Vietnamese refugees found in other studies. While there is no claim for representativeness of the study sample, it is apparent that the subgroups studied here are not unlike related refugee groups in the United States.

2. *Refugees' attitudes toward different aspects of life in the host country.*

When subjects were asked to compare aspects of their lives in the United States with those in their home country, they responded as follows:

a. For the material aspects, 52.8% of the Vietnamese and 72.4% of the Lao responded that their life in the United States is better, 25.0% of the Vietnamese and 7.9% of the Lao felt that it is essentially the same, and 19.5% of the Vietnamese and 14.5% of the Lao think that it is worse.* More Lao than Vietnamese perceive an improvement in the material aspects of their lives in the United States. This finding corresponds with previously reported educational backgrounds and former occupations of the subjects. Those subjects with higher levels of education and higher status in former occupations appear less satisfied with material aspects of their new lives.

b. On the subject of spiritual conditions, 16.6% of the Vietnamese and 33.5% of the Lao subgroups said that their lives here are better, 10.6% of the Vietnamese and 11.2% of the Lao felt that it is the same, and 70.0% of the Vietnamese and 50.7% of the Lao reported that their lives are worse in comparison with circumstances in the home country.

c. In terms of occupation, 27.8% Vietnamese and 30.2% Lao noted that their jobs here are better than those that they held in the home country, while 28.3% of the Vietnamese and 13.2% Lao felt that they are equivalent to former positions, and 40.0% of the Vietnamese and 48.0% of the Lao said that they are worse.

d. Comparative perceptions of social status in host and home countries yielded subgroup responses as follows: "improved" - 17.2% of the Vietnamese and 14.4% of the Lao; "similar or the same" - 27.2% of the Vietnamese and 29.6% of the Lao; and "worse" - 52.8% of the Vietnamese and 52.0% of the Lao.

e. Subjects were then asked for an aggregate appraisal of life-circumstances in the United States in comparison to those in the home country. In the Vietnamese subgroup, 39.5% perceived it as better, 21.7% felt it is the same, and 35.5% consider it worse, while in the Lao subgroup, 37.5% said it is better, 15.1% feel it is the same, and 43.4% think it is worse.

The material aspect of life in the host country appears to be the most satisfying to these refugees. Their spiritual lives and social status are perceived less positively. Subjects in the Lao subgroup seem to be more satisfied with their material and spiritual lives than those in the Vietnamese subgroup. There are more Vietnamese than Lao, however, who appear dissatisfied with their spiritual lives. The two subgroups do not differ much in terms of ratings on occupational

---

*Hereafter, the percentage of non-respondents will be deleted. If the total percentage is less than 100.0%, it may be assumed that the remaining subjects did not respond to the item(s).

and social status in the host country; there are, however, more Lao than Vietnamese on the negative side for this dimension. It seems that the Lao subgroup — with less highly educated people, with more experience with life under communist rule and in the refugee camps, with more people from lower social echelons, and with less time in the United States — is more satisfied with life in the host country than the Vietnamese subgroup. A related study (Nguyen and Henkin, in press) of two groups of Vietnamese refugees (those who came to the United States concurrent with the mass evacuation in 1975, the "first wave," and those who arrived later, the "boat people,") suggests that the first wave included many persons from the Vietnamese elite. They had strong educational backgrounds, high social status in their home country, as well as general success in the host country in terms of occupational achievement and economic status; nonetheless, they expressed dissatisfaction with their new lives. The second group, the boat people, included more persons with less education, lower social status, and less success in terms of occupational achievement and economic status; however, they appear to be more satisfied with their new lives.

3. *Perceptions of cultural changes.*

Subjects provided perceptions of changes in cultural and behavioral patterns.

a.   From ancient times, societies in Laos and Vietnam are best described as consisting of a set of hierarchies of social status. Under the monarchy, the Vietnamese owed respect, in rank order, to the king, the teacher, and the father. The order was modified in modern times to include the chief of state, the teacher and the father. By profession, the order is the scholar, the farmer, the artisan and the merchant. A woman, as an unmarried girl, must obey her parents; as a married woman, she owes obedience to her husband, and as a widow she must live with her children and worship her dead husband. In the extended family, the oldest generation retains the highest status. Older people are always respected by the young. In this social network, each individual acts according to his position, and conforms to the social hierarchy (Henkin and Nguyen, 1981). In Laos, there was "a lay hierarchy consisting of village and district level personnel, a royal hierarchy of monks leading to the king, and a religious hierarchy of monks leading to the supreme patriarch of the kingdom" (Chamberlain, 1979, p. 132). In such a hierarchical structure, each person behaves according to his well-defined position and corresponding role in order to keep the social order alive.

Such cultural similarities between the Lao and the Vietnamese facilitate structuring of a content base for certain items in this study. Of the Vietnamese subgroup, 78.9% perceived that people tend to behave in the home country according to his/her position. The percentage of subjects who agree on this study dimension in the Lao subgroup was 90.8%. A smaller number disagreed (18.3% - Vietnamese and 7.3% - Lao). The difference between the two subgroups is highly significant ($x^2 = 8.08/p.$ .01). Once in the host country, however, conformity to the social hierarchy is no longer confirmed by a large majority of the subjects. For the Vietnamese subgroup, the percentage of subjects who agree drops to 56.8%, and the percentage of subjects who disagree increases to 39.4%. For the Lao subgroup, the percentage of subjects in the "agree" category decreases to 64.5%, while the percentage of subjects in the "disagree" category rises to 26.2%. When the McNemar test for the significance of changes is applied, the chi-square value is 21.27 for the Vietnamese and 79.04 for the Lao subgroups; both are highly significant (p.   .01).

   b.   Another cultural similarity between the Vietnamese and the Lao is respect for older people. Derived from the filial piety tradition, on one hand, and from the belief that older people possess knowledge and wisdom, on the other, respect for older persons has been a hallmark of Vietnamese society for centuries. In Vietnam, older people were highly respected regardless of wealth or social status (Te, 1962). The hierarchical structure of Lao society (Chamberlain, 1979) and the concept of *"Kengchai,"* which relates to showing respect for others while maintaining a low profile for oneself (Outsama, 1977; Phommasouvanh, 1979), are bases for respect and consideration of older people. "Toward the Lao father one is obedient and always respectful, and by extension to all other men of his generation. The same deference is expected toward the mother and other women of her generation ... Respect is given also to an older brother, for the society regards the elder as having more authority than the younger" (LeBar, 1960, p. 67). Among the study subgroups, 95.5% of the Vietnamese and 98.0% of the Lao agree that older people are respected in both home countries. Only 1.7% of the Vietnamese and 1.3% of the Lao disagree with this perception. The difference between the two subgroups is not significant ($x^2 = 0.03$). The same behavioral pattern is confirmed when it is applied to refugees in the host country, in contrast, by 68.9% of the Vietnamese and 53.3% of the Lao subjects. It is not confirmed by 27.8% of the Vietnamese and 45.4% of the Lao subgroups. The difference between the two subgroups is significant at the .01 level ($x^2 = 9.60$). More important, however, is the result of the McNemar test of significance of changes. Here the value of x^2 is 93.06 and 69.47 for the Vietnamese and the Lao subgroups, respectively; both are significant beyond the .01 level.

   c.   The politeness of children and young people is related to study foci on conformity to hierarchical structure and respect for older people. At home and in school, Vietnamese and Lao children were socialized to act in a polite manner; especially when they found themselves in the presence of persons of higher social status or of older people. A Vietnamese proverb reminds us that education should emphasize politeness first, and literature (substantive materials) later *(Tien hoc le, hau hoc van).* "Regardless of their social origins, all children are expected to be polite to their parents and older persons and solicitous of their welfare ..." (Smith, 1967, p. 118). A similar pattern is apparent among the Lao (Outsama, 1977). "Children learn how to behave in the family, and at the same time learn how to interact in the social hierarchy. At an early age they learn to say *kuu* and *ming* to their younger siblings and *dooj khaaz mooj* to their parents, grandparents, aunts and uncles"* (Chamberlain, 1979, p. 38). Politeness is expressed in language and behavior. There are different styles of speaking for different classes of people, and special lexical items designate or refer to social relations between persons of different status. Personal pronouns vary with rank

---

Kuu means "I" and *ming* means "you" (singular), when speaking to a subordinate, a close friend, or a child; *dooj khaaz noojz* means "yes" derived from little slave (Lao transliteration).

and relative status. In Laos, as in Vietnam, the personal pronouns have many forms depending on the social status of the person who speaks and that of the person to whom the speech is addressed. The pronoun I, for example, can be expressed in a form demonstrating extreme humility, or at a higher level on the status continuum. In the Vietnamese language, there are special terms which may be used before questions or answers in order to denote politeness. Among these terms are *da, thua, bam*[2], *kinh, thua, kinh thua,* and *da thua* (Henkin and Nguyen, 1980). Children may not address older, respected people on an equal basis. In addition to use of polite language, there are certain behavioral patterns that children display as a matter of deference. In greeting older, respected people, children are expected to clasp their hands and bow slightly while smiling. When speaking, "restraint in gestures and quiet speech are considered desirable. Brusqueness or offhandedness in such matters is practically unheard of, particularly in the rural areas, and to copy Western casualness in polite expression is considered misguided" (LeBar, 1960, p. 98). These behavioral patterns in the home countries are confirmed by 91.7% of the Vietnamese and by 90.2% of the Lao subjects. Only 5.6% of the Vietnamese subjects and 8.5% of the Lao subjects disagree on this study dimension. The same patterns in the host country are not confirmed by a large majority of subjects (45.0% Vietnamese, and 60.6% Lao). The percentage of subjects who disagree has increased substantially (51.7% Vietnamese, and 38.2% Lao). The significance of change is beyond the .01 level ($x^2 = 86.49$ for the Vietnamese, and $x^2 = 36.97$ for the Lao subgroups).

d.   In Laos and Vietnam, as in the other South Asian countries, children are expected to obey their parents. A Vietnamese proverb confirms this expectation: The fish which is not preserved in salt will be rotten, the child who does not obey his parents will be corrupted in every way *(Ca khong an muoi ca uong; con cai cha me tram duong con hu).* "From childhood, the members of traditionally oriented families are taught the importance of discipline and of willing submission to parental authority, and their upbringing is extremely strict. Unquestioning obedience is demanded; offenses are promptly and rigorously punished" (Smith, 1967, p. 195). Parental authority among the Lao is well documented in the literature (LeBar, 1960; Outsama, 1977). This behavioral pattern in the home country is confirmed by 88.9% of the Vietnamese and 70.4% of the Lao subjects, while 8.4% of the Vietnamese and 27.6% of the Lao subgroups disagree. The same behavioral pattern is confirmed by only 36.7% of the Vietnamese and 66.4% of the Lao subgroups in the host country. The results of the McNemar test for the significance of changes show that for the Vietnamese subgroup the $x^2 = 81.32$, and is highly significant (p.   .01); for the Lao subgroup the value of x^2 is almost zero. The Vietnamese subjects perceive considerable change in terms of obedience to one's parents, while the Lao subjects do not.

e.   In Vietnam, obedience to one's parents is integral to the concept of filial piety that is extolled in the Confucian ethic system. However, filial piety also means solicitude and support to one's parents in their old age. It requires an individual to conduct his life so that his parents may be proud and satisfied with his behavior (Henkin and Nguyen, 1980). A person who does not conform to the ethic is said to "lack filial piety," and is commonly rejected and ostracized by the community. "The worst insult which a Vietnamese can receive, and by which he is mortally hurt, is to have the expression of lack of filial piety (do bat hieu) applied to him" (Te, 1962, p. 101). Even though there is no formal code for filial piety in Lao society, an individual's obligations toward his family do suggest expectations for behaviors similar to those of the Vietnamese. According to Phommasouvanh, "the tendency for Lao families to invest heavily in their children might be better explained through their complex reciprocal services" (p. 87). Services may include those rendered by a successful member to his family and to his older parents. It is extremely rare, for example, for an aged couple to occupy a separate household. Such an arrangement is unseemly in Lao society, and is viewed as a disgrace on the part of the children. Most of the Vietnamese (94.4%) and Lao (94.0%) subjects in this study do agree that in the home country people behaved in conformity with the filial piety ethic. The percentage drops to 67.8% for the Vietnamese subgroup, and 69.1% for the Lao subgroup when this behavioral ethic is perceived by refugee groups in the United States, while percentages of those who disagree increase from 2.8% to 28.9% for the Vietnamese subgroup and from 5.2% to 29.6% for the Lao subgroup. The significance of changes using the McNemar test is beyond the .01 level ($x^2 = 40.71$ - Vietnamese subgroup, and $x^2 = 60.24$ - Lao subgroup).

    f.   As the head of the family, the man plays a predominant role in both Lao and Vietnamese societies. Lao men make all critical decisions and oversee the general welfare of the family. They enjoy a great deal of privilege and power (Phommasouvanh, 1979; LeBar, 1960). In Vietnam, "great respect is given to men, especially to older men, and particularly to the head of the lineage who traditionally made all the important decisions for every member of the family. In the modern period family decisions, such as the choice of occupation or marital partner, are generally made by the head of the individual household with the concurrence of the wife and, perhaps, the grandparents; where decisions are made in this manner, unquestioned obedience on the part of the younger generation is demanded and received" (Smith, 1967, pp. 114-115). The dominant role of men in Vietnam and Laos is confirmed by a large majority of the subjects (80.6% - Vietnamese, and 90.8% - Lao). It is not confirmed by 16.1% of the Vietnamese subgroup and 7.3% of the Lao subgroup. This dominant role concept is not confirmed by the majority of study subjects in the United States. Only 37.8% of the Vietnamese subjects still agree on the subject of male role dominance, while 58.8% do disagree. For the Lao, 32.2% responded within the agree category, and 64.4% disagreed. The changes are highly significant (p. .01) for both subgroups ($x^2 = 70.53$ - Vietnamese, and $x^2 = 86.73$ - Lao).

    g.   Women in Indochina play a subordinate role to men. In Laos, their responsibilities are largely confined to the home. Women's domestic tasks may include "carrying water and wood, pounding rice, cooking, tending kitchen, gardens and livestock, spinning, weaving, and making clothes ..." (LeBar, 1960, p. 63). Vietnamese women, in accordance with the Confucian ethic, conform to the following three social obligations: (1) before marriage, she must live with her parents and obey her father, (2) after marriage, she follows her husband and obeys him, and (3) if widowed, she lives with her children. (Henkin and Nguyen,

1980). "Throughout her marriage a woman is expected to be dutiful and respectful toward both her husband and his parents. The wife is expected to become an integral part of her husband's family, to care for him and their children and to perform all household duties" (Smith, 1967, p. 115). Vietnamese women were not encouraged to participate in social activities. They were educated since childhood to be daughters, spouses, daughters-in-law, and mothers. The status of women in both Lao and Vietnamese societies is confirmed by 65.0% of the Vietnamese and 96.1% of the Lao subjects. Only 2.0% of the Lao subgroup disagreed, in contrast with 31.1% of the Vietnamese subgroup. Why does a general absence of consensus appear within the Vietnamese subgroup concerning the role of women in the home country? In fact, progressive ideas and educational reforms were introduced rapidly in Vietnam over the last two decades. Concurrently, accelerated development of the country occurred in terms of industrialization and urbanization. Conditions of warfare precipitated changes in the Vietnamese social structure. More women were enrolled in secondary schools and universities. Many of them became wage earners, and a small number of women became involved in social causes and political activities. The home may no longer be the focal point of activity for some Vietnamese women. Laos, in contrast, "remains basically agricultural and the traditional ways of life still prevail" (Phommasouvanh, 1979, p. 92), despite some changes in urban areas and influences from the West.

Do Vietnamese and Lao women maintain traditional roles in the host country? Among the Vietnamese subgroup, the number of people who agree with the concept is low (19.4%), while the number of those who disagree is considerable (77.2%); in the Lao subgroup 72.4% still agree with the traditional role concept, while 25.0% disagree. Changes in both subgroups are, however, highly significant (p.   .01).

h.   Individualism is not encouraged in either Vietnamese or Lao societies, despite exogenous influences. The individual had no place in Vietnamese society (Henkin and Nguyen, 1980). Most Vietnamese, especially those residing in the south, still feel that the family has first claim on their loyalties; the interests of each individual are subordinate to those of his common descent group (Smith, 1967, p. 105). "In accordance with his Confucian heritage, a Vietnamese identifies himself almost exclusively as a member of a particular family ... the strongest bond in the society has always been that of family loyalty, and the members of the kin group have been mutually responsible to and for one another. Family loyalty and filial piety have held the society intact for over 2,000 years, through periods of war, foreign domination and national disaster" (Smith, 1967, p. 192). The Lao family remains a strong, intact social unit despite Western influences. As an extended entity, the Lao family commonly includes the immediate family, the in-laws, blood relatives and relatives by marriage. The Lao maintain strong ties with their relatives. "The word relative or *phinong* in the Lao context is both broad and indefinite. It includes distant blood relatives of many generations and relatives by marriage ... tied in with the extensive but strong bond one has with relatives are obligations that he has to fulfill ... one is obliged to respond to the needs and problems of his *phinong*" (Phommasouvanh, 1979, pp. 87-89). The tendency to live for one's family in the home country is confirmed by 94.5% of the Vietnamese subjects and 84.2% of the Lao subjects. It is not confirmed by 2.8% of the Vietnamese subgroup and 14.5% of the Lao subgroup. Does this pattern remain the same in the host country? Some 72.2% of the Vietnamese and 61.9% of the Lao subjects agree that similar patterns continue among the refugees, while 25.0% of the Vietnamese and 36.2% of the Lao respondents do not agree on this point. The changes in both groups are highly significant (p.   .01).

i.   Both the Lao and the Vietnamese tend to actively seek to preserve and perpetuate their customs and traditions in the home country. This tendency is reflected, for example, in documents delineating fundamental foundations of curriculum development in the Vietnam educational system first published by the Ministry of Education, and later reiterated in the 1967 Constitution. "Education in Vietnam should be nationalistic education. Education must respect the traditional values related to all activities in the family, the professions, and on the national scene. Education should develop the national spirit by helping students to preserve traditional values and customs of the nation ..." (Nguyen and Henkin, 1981). Similar propensities were observed among the Lao prior to the communist takeover. The Lao have long-standing traditions and a rich heritage; Lao people wish to preserve the values that are so meaningful to them (Phommasouvanh, 1979). "The basic pattern of Lao values has been relatively unaffected by the years of French colonial administration and the more recent contact with other foreign nations," and "... a general satisfaction with their traditional way of life makes the Lao reluctant to change" (LeBar, 1960, p. 94).

This tendency in the home country is confirmed by 91.1% of the Vietnamese and by 96.7% of the Lao subjects in this study. A small percentage of subjects, however, disagree (6.1% - Vietnamese, and 2.0% - Lao). When the same study focus is viewed by subjects in the United States, 55.0% of the Vietnamese still agree, but only 16.4% of the Lao agree. Some 42.2% of the Vietnamese and 82.2% of Lao subjects disagree. Changes in both subgroups are highly significant (p.   .01).

j.   In general, considerable changes in the cultural and behavioral patterns appear to have occurred among the refugees since departure from the home country. Most of the Vietnamese and Lao subjects confirm these changes (82.3% and 93.4%, respectively), while 15.0% of the Vietnamese subjects and 5.3% of Lao subjects do not agree. The crosstabulation of subjects' responses on different aspects of cultural changes by age, sex, educational level, occupation and ethnic group shows no association of the perceptions of changes and these independent variables. Study respondents, we suggest, perceived changes in behavioral patterns and cultural values regardless of age, sex, educational level, occupation and ethnic group.

k.   What are subjects' attitudes toward these perceived changes? A large majority (71.1%) of the Vietnamese subjects expressed a negative attitude toward these changes, while only a small number (24.5%) favored the changes. In contrast, most of the Lao subjects (87.5%) were positive about these changes, and only 9.8% of the subgroup were negative. Caution should be exercised in interpretations of responses of the Lao subgroup. The general reputation of the

Lao is that they are polite to a fault. "Western observers have noted that such polite behavior has its negative side in that it is often difficult to get a Lao to give a frank opinion" (LeBar, 1960, p. 98). "A smile on one's face, a nod of the head, 'yes' or 'no', does not necessarily express the true feeling of a Laotian. He carries himself the way he is expected to, not the way he wants to" (Phommasouvanh, 1979, p. 91).

    4.   *Subjects' attitudes toward preservation of the home culture, and adoption of host lifeways.*

    What are subjects' expectations and hopes with reference to the adoption of lifeways of the host country and preservation of the home culture? Most of the Vietnamese (91.7%) and Lao (88.9%) subjects in this study agree that children should learn their home language and about the home culture. Only a small number (5.5% - Vietnamese, and 7.22% - Lao) were not in agreement on this study dimension. There is no significant difference ($x^2 = 0.18$) between the two subgroups.

    Most of the Vietnamese and the Lao (93.9% - Vietnamese, and 91.5% - Lao) agree on the need to preserve their respective home cultures in the host country. A small number (3.4% - Vietnamese, and 5.2% - Lao) do not agree. There is no significant difference between the two subgroups. Most subjects (83.9% - Vietnamese, and 92.3% - Lao) - wish to maintain their distinctiveness in the host country. These findings seem to corroborate findings in previous studies (Nguyen and Henkin, in press; Nguyen, Henkin, and Phommasouvanh, in press).

    There is a considerable difference between the two subgroups in terms of adoption of host lifeways. Among Vietnamese subjects, only 19.5% agree that the refugees should adopt American lifeways, while 77.7% do not agree. Among the Lao subjects, in contrast, a majority (59.2%) agree on the question of the need to adopt host lifeways, while only 36.2% do not agree. The difference between the two subgroups is highly significant ($x^2 = 57.2$; p.   .01). Again, the tendency toward tacit acquiescence may be operating here among Lao subjects, since the questions asked relate directly to the host population. Attribution of motivating factors remains to be determined. One may recall that "the Laotians used this technique effectively with French missionaries who tried to convert them to Christianity. The Lao were never overtly negative, when asked by missionaries to attend mass or preaching sessions. But they never showed up and always had excuses for not attending" (Phommasouvanh, 1979, p. 91). Perceptions associated with expectations and hopes to preserve their home language and culture are reiterated by Phommasouvanh: "One can only hope that the values that are so meaningful to the Laotians will be preserved" (p. 92).

    Table 1 provides compositive data of Vietnamese and Lao subject responses on several study dimensions. It also includes the value of the chi-square on the McNemar test of significance of changes for each aspect of culture from the home country context to the host country context. In sum, we suggest that both subgroups have perceived changes in most cultural patterns studied. Vietnamese subjects perceived considerable changes in politeness of children, the obedience of children, the subordinate role of women, the predominant role of men, the respect for older people, and the preservation of culture and customs categories.

The most obvious changes for the Lao subgroup relate to the preservation of culture and customs, the respect for older persons, the predominant role of men, conformity to the social order, the filial piety ethic, and the subordinate role of women. The Lao subgroup has perceived change with reference to the politeness of their children, but not in child response to authority (obedience). For the Vietnamese subjects, such changes in cultural patterns are perceived negatively, while the Lao are, in general, relatively positive.

THE EDUCATION OF INDOCHINESE REFUGEES: IMPLICATIONS OF STUDY FINDINGS

Adult and child deference to the authority and role of the teacher as the bearer and provider of the "gift of knowledge" are repeatedly cited in literature (Chamberlain, 1979; Nguyen and Henkin, 1981; Phommasouvanh, 1979). Study data on subjects' home country perceptions of patterns of authority and role behaviors further suggest considerable retention of traditional perception among refugee adults. While acculturation and adaptation of children to new social institutions and learning environments may be rapid (Nguyen and Henkin, 1980), adult progressions may be decelerated by problems associated with communications, social interaction, and organizational integration. Relationships between adults and children may be strained as a result of differences in the rates of transition to new life-circumstances in the host country. Educators should consider the possibilities for and consequences of a reactive surge of "reacculturation advocacy" when developing guidelines and policies. Programs that serve to facilitate social adaptation while allowing sufficient latitude to accommodate significant cultural differences are likely to have higher levels of success. The need for community involvement in the design, development and implementation of educational programs for adults and children is axiomatic.

Alternative positions of educators and sociologists support the provision of learning programs with either transitional or maintenance emphases. The argument for the latter type of program may be founded in the desire to preserve certain aspects of the native culture and language, as refugees acquire dominance in the language of instruction and learn the ways of the new social system. Regardless of the approach elected, however, service providers should assiduously avoid the two extremes where precipitous transition occurs without the benefit of complementary interrelationships with the social mainstream, or where incentives to return to the old ways emerge which may contribute to the formation of isolated communities.

TABLE 1
SS' RESPONSES AND SIGNIFICANCE OF CHANGES

Questions	Vietnamese			Lao		
	Agree %	Disagree %	x^2	Agree %	Disagree %	x^2
Conform to social order in home country	78.9	18.3	21.27**	90.3	7.3	79.04**
Conform to social order in host country	57.8	39.4		64.5	33.5	
Respect old people in home country	95.5	1.7	69.47**	98.0	1.3	93.06**
Respect old people in host country	68.9	27.8		53.3	45.4	
Politeness of children in home country	91.7	5.6	86.49**	90.2	8.5	36.97**
Politeness of children in host country	45.0	51.7		60.6	38.2	
Obedience of children in home country	88.9	8.7	81.32**	70.4	27.6	.01
Obedience of children in host country	36.7	60.6		66.4	31.5	
Filial piety in home country	94.4	2.8	40.71**	94.0	5.2	60.24**
Filial piety in host country	67.8	28.9		69.1	29.6	
Male predominant in home country	80.6	16.1	70.53**	90.8	7.3	86.73**
Male predominant in host country	37.8	58.8		32.2	64.4	
Female subordinate in home country	65.0	31.1	80.61**	96.1	2.0	58.53**
Female subordinate in host country	19.4	77.2		72.4	25.0	
Family/Individual in home country	94.5	2.8	33.15**	84.2	14.5	24.16**
Family/Individual in host country	72.2	25.0		61.9	36.2	
Preservation of value and customs in home country	91.1	6.1	65.45**	96.7	2.0	117.87**
Preservation of value and customs in host country	55.0	42.2		16.4	82.2	
Changes have occurred	82.3	15.0		93.4	5.3	
Changes are good	24.5	71.1		87.5	9.8	

**p.   .01

REFERENCES

CHAMBERLAIN, JAMES R. *A Contrastive Analysis of Lao and English Language and Culture* (Part II), unpublished manuscript prepared for the Mid-America Center for Bilingual Materials Development, Iowa City, Iowa: The University of Iowa, 1979.

DAVIE, MAURICE R. *Refugees in America,* New York, New York: Harper and Brothers Publishers, 1947.

GARKOVITCH, LORRAINE E. "The Indochinese Refugees: A Critique of Assimilation Theories," paper presented at the annual meeting of the Midwest Sociological Society on April 16, 1977, in Minneapolis, Minnesota.

GORDON, MILTON M. *Assimilation in American Life.* New York, New York: Oxford University Press, 1964.

HENKIN, ALAN B. AND NGUYEN, LIEM THANH. *Between Two Cultures: The Vietnamese in America,* Saratoga, California: Century Twenty One Publishing, 1981.

KELLY, GAIL PARADISE. *From Vietnam to America,* Boulder, Colorado: Westview Press, 1977.

KENT, DONALD PETERSON. *The Refugee Intellectual,* New York, New York: Columbia University Press, 1953.

LeBAR, FRANK M. AND SUDDARD, ADRIENNE, (EDS.). *Laos: Its People, Its Society, Its Culture,* New Haven, Connecticut: Human Relations Area Files Press, 1960.

LIU, WILLIAM T., LEMANNA, MARYANNE AND MURATA, ALICE. *Transition to Nowhere,* Nashville, Tennessee: Charter House Publishers, Inc., 1979.

MONTERO, DARREL. *Vietnamese Americans: Patterns of Resettlement and Socioeconomic Adaptation in the United States,* Boulder, Colorado: Westview Press, 1979.

NGUYEN, LIEM THANH AND HENKIN, ALAN B. "Determining Factors of Perceived Adaptation and Academic Standing of Indochinese Refugee Students: An Exploratory Study," *NABE Journal,* V. 1 (1980): 45-69.

NGUYEN, LIEM THANH AND HENKIN, ALAN B. *Vietnamese Refugee Students: Legacies of an Educational Past,* Iowa City, Iowa: National Center for Materials and Curriculum Development, The University of Iowa, 1981.

NGUYEN, LIEM THANH AND HENKIN, ALAN B. "Vietnamese Refugees in the United States: Adaptation and Transitional Status," *Journal of Ethnic Studies* (in press).

NGUYEN, LIEM THANH, HENKIN, ALAN

NGUYEN, LIEM THANH, HENKIN, ALAN B. AND PHOMMASOUVANH, BOUNLIENG. "Adaptation of Lao Refugees in America," (in press).

OUTSAMA, KAO. *Laotian Themes,* New York, New York: Center for Bilingual Education, Board of Education of the City of New York, 1977.

PHOMMASOUVANH, BOUNLIENG. "Aspects of Lao Family and Social Life," in *An Introduction to Indochinese History, Culture, Language and Life,* edited by John K. Whitmore, pp. 85-92, Ann Arbor, Michigan: Center for South and Southeast Asian Studies, University of Michigan, 1979.

SAENGER, GERHART. *Today's Refugees, Tomorrow's Citizens,* New York, New York: Harper and Brothers, Publishers, 1941.

SIEGEL, SIDNEY. *Nonparametric Statistics for the Behavioral Sciences,* New York, New York: McGraw-Hill Book Company, 1956.

SMITH, HARVEY H., ET. AL. *Area Handbook for South Vietnam,* Washington, D.C.: U.S. Government Printing Office, 1967.

SPIRO, M.E. "The Acculturation of American Ethnic Groups," *American Anthropologist* 57 (1955): 1240-52.

TE, HUYNH DINH. *Vietnamese Cultural Patterns and Values as Expressed in Proverbs,* unpublished doctoral dissertation, Columbia University, 1962.

WARNER, W. LLOYD AND SROLE, LEO. *The Social Systems of American Ethnic Groups,* New Haven, Connecticut: Yale University Press, 1945.

PART THREE
COUNSELLING, TESTING
AND PLACEMENT

CLASSIFYING AND PROGRAMMING ETHNIC MINORITY IMMIGRANTS IN THE PUBLIC SCHOOLS

By Ronald J. Samuda, Ph.D.
Faculty of Education
Queen's University
Kingston, Ontario, Canada

INTRODUCTION

In the course of preparing my notes and materials for this presentation today, I was repeatedly struck with the thought that in talking about the testing of minorities for almost ten years now, I find that I have been repeating the same themes: Tests are unfair to minorities. Tests lead to labelling and grouping procedures which operate negatively for minorities. Test results should not be interpreted to infer innate genetic or cultural deficits. Norm-referenced tests do more harm than good when used indiscriminately with minorities. Tests are ethnocentric and do not sufficiently embrace the social and cultural environment of minorities.

The list is long. I could go on repeating those statements which seem to me like to many truisims — almost trite. But, perhaps, what I have said so far is not quite so obvious to all of you here today. So I have tried to work on a new approach so as to illustrate, in a concrete manner, the issues, problems, and perspectives, by administering a short paper-and-pencil test and using the results to exemplify and illustrate the issues and problems inherent in the construction, validation, and selection criteria in assessing ethnic and linguistic minority students. I shall conclude my talk with some recent innovative approaches and methods in cross-cultural and multiethnic assessment.

ISSUES RELATING TO TEST CONSTRUCTION

For the average middle-class teacher, the Chitling Test must embody a set of concepts and information which are totally bewildering and alien. Yet, although you may be inclined to find the jargon and situations depicted in the test somewhat amusing, I would submit that this test accurately simulates some important facets of those regular norm-referenced instruments which claim to measure mental ability or intellectual aptitude.

The Chitling Test, like most group IQ tests, is objective, requiring you to provide a single response from a multiple-choice item format. It requires responses to questions essentially based more on your general knowledge of the sociocultural environment rather than on your familiarity with a particular course content. The items have been chosen specifically to reflect your degree of general knowledge and information, and to discriminate between those of you who are familiar with the Afro-American ghetto culture and those for whom the language and situations are quite alien. I submit also, that this test reflects more than ethnic group membership; it demonstrates the influence of social class difference, as well, since many of the words and situations are more indicative of the urban ghetto experience than that of the Black middle-class intellectual or professional. The point I want to emphasize here is that, while such a test as the Chitling requires the knowledge of such words as "preacher", "hoddi", "hully-gully", and "gas head", the common IQ test similarly comprises words and situations, and involves skills and processes, geared particularly, and selected from, the more typical middle-class American Anglo-Saxon home and social environment.

Social and cultural bias in the testing of ability was not incidental; it was deliberate. If we briefly recall the beginning of the testing movement at the turn of the century, we might well remind ourselves that Alfred Binet deliberately based his original items upon typical tasks, samples of information, and vocabulary derived from observing his own children and others like them whom he considered to be developmentally "normal". You will remember that in his attempt to discriminate between those children who could succeed in the regular classroom and those who required special instruction, Binet equated mental ages with the chronological ages of a population sample. In accordance with the performance of those children who were from an *essentially middle-class background,* Binet was well aware that his test *was culturally and socially loaded and that it could not measure innate capacity. He knew also that what the test measured was far more than mental ability but that the results were inevitably affected by "home-training, attention, motivation, habit of looking at pictures and scholastic exercise".*

Although pioneered in France, Binet's tests immediately caught on in the United States where even so competent and creative a person as Terman chose to ignore Binet's strictures. For when the test was translated, expanded and standardized by Lewis Terman and Maude Merrill at Stanford University, they not only chose the language and tasks typical of white middle-class school children at different age levels, but they also excluded from their norming population all ethnic and linguistic minority group children. Thus, that first test of mental ability which was so significant in spawning and proliferating the standardized objective-type of ability tests was, in some respects, as deliberately biased in content as the Chitling. Moreover, although no minority children participated in the original standardization sample, that instrument was used for more than half a century to rate the potential of Black, Hispanic, and other minority children to profit from instruction in the mainstream of the school. The most critical role of intelligence tests like the Stanford-Binet, and the Wechsler Intelligence Scale for Children, has been in the procedures for special education placement, and in the parallel system of homogenous ability grouping.

For over half-a-century, the majority-minority comparison of test results became a major preoccupation of American educators and social scientists to the extent that Shuey in 1958 and 1966 was able to draw selectively on more than 500 studies covering a period of 50 years concerned with issues in testing Black Americans. It would almost appear that psychologists in the United States were compelled by the obvious social injustice perpetrated by test results to find justifications based upon theories of innate genetic deficit, cultural/environmental deprivation or psycholinguistic function. As a result, the role of standardized tests — especially intelligence tests — became increasingly controversial because of three basic factors: 1) the disproportionate classification and placement of minority groups in classes for the mentally retarded; 2) the over-representation of Black, Hispanic and native-American students in the lower non-academic tracks in secondary schools; 3) the very limited number of ethnic minority students in programs for the gifted and learning disabled and in the institutions of higher education.

It is surprising to realize that as far back as 1923, the British psychologist, Gordon, compared the measured IQ's of English canal-boat children who hardly went to school at all, with that of the average English school children. Gordon found two things, namely, that the mean of the canal-boat children was 60, clearly below average, but even more interesting, Gordon found that the canal-boat people's IQ's declined with age. If IQ was a determinant of intelligence, the canal-boat people were becoming less intelligent, the older they became. As Segall (1979, p. 50) has pointed out, Gordon was right to conclude that the lessening IQ was due to cultural and environmental difference in life style between the canal-boat people and the average Englishman. But Segall also speculates that the test was probably not measuring the intellectual performance of the canal-boat children per se but an amalgam of motivation, degree of familiarity with the content of a culture other than their own, and such extraneous unknowns as the patience of the children to perform what they may have regarded as alien and silly games. The point to be underscored with this example is that tests of mental ability measure only the current capacity of individuals to participate effectively in the middle-class oriented school system of the majority culture. It is no wonder that the use of tests in the referral-placement process has been perceived as part of an overall pattern of ethnocentric assumptions underlying the educational process in the United States. In any consideration of testing, it should be remembered that standardized ability tests are constructed by educated, urban, majority-oriented social scientists and that those tests are directly linked to the kinds of learning, information, and processes which the middle-class, sociocultural environment and school enhances.

TEST VALIDATION

The three basic forms of validation are Construct, Content, and Predictive Validity. The first, Construct Validity is a measure of the degree to which certain explanatory concepts like intelligence can account for an individual's performance. It is, in effect, a check on the theory underlying the tests. However, as I have demonstrated in another place (Samuda, 1975), intelligence is still a vague and ill-defined term. Although many teachers still refer to the term intelligence quotient, they probably fail to realize that the term is really archaic since it was derived from the now outmoded relationship of chronological and mental age (the ratio IQ). But even many of those who are aware of the present deviation IQ concept may fail to realize that "the term is bound to myths that intelligence is fixed, unitary, and pre-determined". The fact is that IQ test results do not reflect innate potential and no test of mental abilities can be culture-free.

Let us remember that ethnic minorities in general and ethnic linguistic groups in particular have not had the opportunity to share fully in the goods of society. Minorities suffer the full impact of "the culture of poverty" to a higher extent than the general population. Cultural and linguistic barriers between the majority and minority groups are compounded by low income, unemployment, poor housing, prejudice and discrimination, and, more particularly, by a system of education which often ignores the reality of those linguistic and cultural differences or labels them as deficits.

Content Validity, as in the case of the Chitling Test, involves the skills and information required by an individual to perform on a particular test. As indicated above, the validation assumptions made with respect to mental ability tests are: 1) test takers have been exposed to and are familiar with the universe of information from which test items are drawn; 2) the language of the test is the language of the test taker. In the case of the Stanford-Binet, for instance, children are asked to identify "common objects" presented in the form of pictures or toy models to explain why certain objects are employed in daily living and to interpret pictorially presented situations. Yet, not unlike the illustration of the Chitling Test, the so-called common objects are not familiar to children who differ socially and culturally from the norm group.

In almost all tests of mental ability, strong emphasis is placed on the definition of abstract words, on sentence completion, on analogies which all presuppose a certain mastery in the comprehension and usage of standard English and ease with the subtleties of grammar. Not infrequently, linguistic and ethnic minority students (including those who speak an adulterated form of Spanish or the black vernacular), may give "nonsensical" answers simply because they did not understand what was required of them or because they are unfamiliar with the examiner's pronunciation and idiom.

In the case of Hispanic children, several language-related factors will necessarily affect assessment. The straight translation of English tests are inappropriate since many tests written in formal Spanish cannot be applied to students who speak substantially different Spanish dialects. Such translated versions would tend to ignore the linguistic differences among and within the various Hispanic sub-groups such as Puerto Ricans, Mexican-Americans, Cuban-Americans and those who originate from South America. Translation cannot yield equivalent forms because of the complex linguistic, cultural and psychological factors affecting the administration and content of the tests.

Even for those bilingual minority students, born in the United States, significant language-related factors will inevitably affect their performance on tests. Lexical, morphological, syntactical and phonological interferences may contaminate the results. Olmedo (p. 1078) has shown that "it is wrong to think that because someone can speak a second language they can also be tested in a second language" for, those who come from homes where parents speak Spanish may be merely functionally receptive bilinguals understanding the idiom but unable to express themselves in anything but English. To test the bilingual student, we must understand his kind and degree of bilingualism. The standard language tests fail to accomplish much for Black or Spanish-speaking children because they do not inform us about the students' language development. What they do reflect is the extent of linguistic acculturation and, as a consequence, they are less than worthless as valid indicators of basic ability. Also, let us remind ourselves that the performance of the minority individual is affected by far more than language. Other cultural factors, such as customs, interpersonal relationships, values, and especially cognitive style will be prime determinants of performance. As Mercer has so persuasively demonstrated, the inter-group differences in IQ, for example amongst Anglo, Black and Chicano children are related to sociocultural variables such as urban acculturation, socioeconomic status, family structure, and family size. Similarly, Berry's cross-cultural research has shown that there is no necessary cross-cultural equivalence of measurement. In terms of the emic-etic dichotomy, some phenomena can be explained in culture-specific categories but when we postulate universal (etic) constructs we are going beyond the valid use of standardized tests to assume generalizability across cultures.

The Predictive Validity of a test is based upon the extent to which the results can be correlated with a criterion. In such tests labelled intelligence, mental ability or scholastic aptitude, academic achievement is the criterion measure against which test scores are validated. It is undeniable that IQ tests and such screening devices like the SAT do correlate with academic achievement to a significant degree. However Fishman (1964) has identified three categories of factors that impair Predictive Validity with respect to minority test takers. First, such external variables as self-concept, anxiety, familiarity with test-taking, examiner-examinee rupport, motivation, and speed will all contaminate the minority child's performance. Second, school grades themselves depend heavily on such factors as personal appearance, classroom behavior, study habits and compatibility with the classroom milieu. Third, the fact of linguistic and sociocultural differences tends to invalidate the assumptions of innate abilities as predictive of achievement. As Anastasi has reminded us, the curriculum of the school and the teaching/learning climate and style operate as moderator variables to account for the correlation between the behavior sample (the test) and the criterion (school grades).

What is far more pernicious and demeaning, in terms of the ethnic and linguistic minorities, is the claim by certain genetically-oriented social scientists that the native mental endowment of minorities is properly measured by the tests of mental ability and that the substandard achievement in school is indicative of intellectual deficits. Fortunately, that ethnocentric view, tied to the institutional and structurally racist views, have lost their respectability, as evidenced in the latest issue of the APA Journal of November, 1981. Rather than using test results as the crutch to bolster the failure of the schools to educate minorities, we are now forced to find new directions and to face the challenge of an increasingly diverse school population.

SELECTION CRITERIA

We come now to that aspect of testing which I consider to be the most important. I am delighted that this paper required me to deal with this perspective of the topic because I have been quite frustrated for some time by my own unsystematic and insufficient treatment of what to do as opposed to what not to do.

By a special fluke of good fortune, the October, 1981 special issue of the *American Psychologist, 36*(10) has just been released and I have been able to draw heavily on the papers by Reschly (p. 1095-1101), Olmedo (p. 1078-1085), Sternberg (p. 1187-1188), Scarr (p. 1164), Garcia (p. 1180) and Gordon (p. 1170), each dealing with novel and significant elements of the issues concerning the testing of linguistic and ethnic minority individuals. It is an important work and I recommend it to you as an essential reference.

Rather than listing a series of do's and don't's, I would prefer to present a sort of overall design for assessment which summarizes my philosophy and from which will flow guidelines and more specific suggestions. But first, permit me to provide a gestalt of the whole notion of selection criteria by citing the words of so illustrious a psychologist and testing pioneer as Lewis Terman, commenting upon the test performance of a pair of Mexican-American and Indian children:

> Their dullness seems to be racial or at least inherent in the family stocks from which they come ... there will be discovered enormous significant racial differences which cannot be wiped out by any schema of mental culture.

> Children of this group should be segregated in special classes ... There is no possibility at present of convincing society that they should not be allowed to reproduce (quoted in Kanim, 1975, p. 318).

Such a statement epitomizes the view of some eminent leaders in the field and, as we found in a recent study (Samuda and Crawford, 1980), is not uncommon amongst teachers and administrators presently practicing in the school systems of the United States and Canada. But, in my view, it does little or no good to dwell on recriminations and merely to resort to negative labels such as racist and bigot. Such men were probably well-intentional but, despite their eminence, they were merely echoing the sentiments of men like Sir Francis Galton and what seems to us today to be the residual ethnocentric nineteenth-century beliefs and conclusions which were merely part of the fallacy of their time.

We need to bear in mind that the notions of cultural diversity and multiculturalism as a viable alternative to the American assimilationist model of the melting pot are very recent indeed. And so, from Terman's statement I want to draw some general principles: 1) that standardized tests of mental abilities have traditionally been embedded in a mold of racist and genetic explanations for inter-group differences; 2) that the differences in performance of ethnic minorities have been interpreted as innate deficits rather than as differences due to socio-cultural or environmental influences; 3) that dependence upon that model and perspective has led to the labelling and overrepresentation of minority students in those segregated classes for mild (educable) mental retardates and in homogenous groups in the mainstream of the schools; 4) that those classes, in general, merely provided holding centers and a means to shelve the real educational problem of educating the atypical student.

Those are precisely the views which have been challenged by a new wave of cognitive and cross-cultural psychologists who demonstrate 1) that culturally loaded tests are useless as determinants of intelligence proper; 2) that ethnic and linguistic minorities perform differently because of their difference in experience; 3) that ethnic minorities develop learning styles resulting from their adaptation to their cultural and ecological milieu; 4) that modes of cognition *are* modifiable and that teachers *can* be trained to help develop in students better ways of information-processing and problem-solving which can be generalized to learning in the broadest sense; 5) that the adjustment and motivational patterns of the minority student can be tested and progressively ameliorated; 6) that a culturally diverse school population will require new approaches and individualized programs of instruction based on information concerning the sociocultural, cognitive, and sensory-motor, and personality traits of the individual.

In other words, as Gordon (1981, p. 1170) has emphasized, the proper course of assessment is not merely to categorize but to describe the processes by which the individual functions in sufficient detail so that strengths can be identified and disabilities can be diagnosed to make it possible for developmental treatment to be prescribed. The work of Rubin Feuerstein (1979) is particularly significant in this regard whereby assessment becomes an aid to pedagogical and rehabilitative intervention.

This view of the selection criteria for assessment calls for a massive proliferation and expansion of different kinds of tests rather than a banning of their use. But it requires a new kind of professional orientation which will emphasize a real commitment on the part of teachers to change.

COMPREHENSIVE INDIVIDUAL ASSESSMENT

In the testing of minorities, the most offensive and demeaning aspect has been the labelling of some individuals as educable mentally retarded leading to special education placement and inappropriate programs of instruction. Such practices are not only unethical; they are pedagogically unsound, humiliating for the student, and frustrating for the teacher. To avoid simplistic non-solutions, let us recognize them immediately (Reschly, 1981).

1. To ban IQ tests without addressing the educational failure of students.
2. To use pluralistic norms with conventional tests, unrelated to programming and remediation.

3. To use IQ tests as screening or placement devices which lead to disproportionate classification of minorities in special education classes with resultant ineffective programming.

The most recent movements in the education of minorities call for reforms in the assessment procedures classification, as a concomitant and integral prerequisite to curricular programming for students. Traditional classifications based on the presumption of internal pathology or deficits should be abandoned. Unless for those very obvious and demonstrably evident cases of sub-normal physiologically-based pathology, such labels as mental retardation should never be applied and, instead, classes should be labelled in relation to the perceived needs of students in such terms as "English as a Second Language" or "special subject programs for low achieving students". But, such reforms should not be merely cosmetic; they should involve a serious effort in terms of in-service education for all teachers in urban, bilingual and minority education.

I agree with Reschly (1981) in his call for such assessment reforms as abandonment of the term IQ and the myths associated with it. The concept of comprehensive individual assessment would stress the need for a broad variety of information prior to making diagnostic decisions. The placement of minority students would require a team approach involving some measure of acculturation, adaptive behavior, primary language (or language dominance), social, economic and ethnocultural background. A comprehensive assessment program would be geared to provide an accurate appraisal of the student's present level and mode of functioning within the context of his cultural background and experience. It would identify the specific needs of the individual as well as focusing upon the particular assets and strengths he brings to the academic situation so as to form the basis on which new skills can be developed. Since it would go hand-in-glove with placement and programming, assessment would necessarily be an ongoing process helping to monitor and to reinforce academic progress and/or cognitive restructuring.

The process by which a diagnostic-prescriptive-intervention system might be operationalized has been outlined by Richard R. DeBlassie in *Testing Mexican-American Youth* (1980, p. 41) in the diagram on the following page.

Such a comprehensive assessment system would involve a team including the teacher, school administrator, counsellor or other professionals providing data through observation, consultation and formal testing procedures. Most important is that, in a humane and democratic society, it is the prior right of parents to become an integral part of the decision-making process. There are two other special characteristics to this scheme: 1) special education should be the very last option; 2) psychological assessment should come last after all other data have been collected and so that their results can be interpreted in the light of comprehensive and vital background information. Finally, notice that the data for the comprehensive assessment portfolio would be obtained from:

1. Observational data
2. Other data available
3. Language dominance
4. Educational assessment data
5. Sensory-motor and/or psycholinguistic data
6. Adaptive behavior data
7. Medical and/or developmental data
8. Personality assessment data, including self-report
9. Intellectual assessment data.

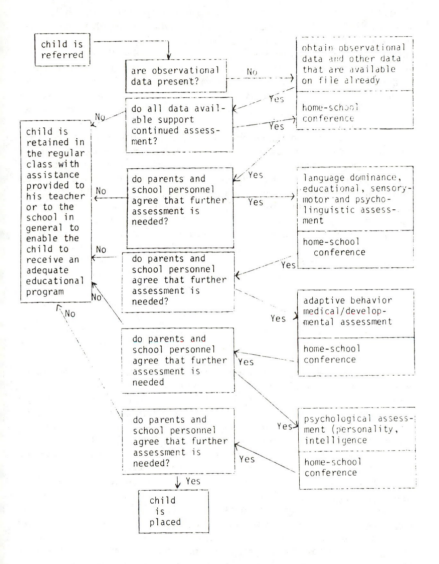

Specific descriptive data and validation criteria are provided for a whole range of tests and alternative information-gathering methods especially in such works as Sattler (1974), and Salvia and Ysseldyke (1978). It would be virtually impossible to state in the time allotted for this presentation the particular instruments appropriate for each category in the determination of learning disability. In any event, by consulting those sources, teachers can learn to make sound judgments as to the validity and practicality of tests for use with what one author has termed the "non-core-culture" Americans or more recent immigrants to these United States of America.

Further in-depth familiarity with the available instruments may require a special course in *"non-biased cross-cultural assessment"*. What I find most exciting is the new trend of effective endeavors in urban and minority education that we can now envision as we begin to develop and implement systems based upon criterion-referenced diagnostic-prescriptive, achievement-motivation; and curriculum-related systematic models of assessment. We have the elements of the system; we have already created much of the technology; what we need more than anything else is the sensitivity and the orientation in the use of these results. And, in addition, we are now on the fringe of a psychometric technology which can embrace information-processing testing procedures. Such data will open up new diagnostic possibilities. As Sternberg (1980, p. 1187) has indicated, factor or subtest scores from psychometric tests can identify the areas in which training should take place but they do not specify just what should be trained. We are at the point where component scores from information-processing linked to systematic computer technology, can pinpoint those particular skills towards which we would need to draw special attention if overall performance is to be effectively and swiftly enhanced.

In general terms, then, *psychometric tests — far from being the instruments of discrimination and social injustice in education and employment,* can become a boon for those who differ from the middle-class mainstream. *Testing can become a source of pride for those teachers who are struggling to cope with the atypical youngster in providing the means whereby effective pedagogy can take the place of teacher frustration and student despair.* But, above all, *we need more than an expansion of the testing technology.* We need a new orientation on the part of teachers, which *will include respect for those who are socioeconomically, culturally and/or ethnically different,* and a commitment to the notion which may be summed up as *"different strokes for different folks".*

Finally, I would like to underscore what Garcia (1981, p. 1180) has emphasized: *that single scores and dimensions should be deemed invalid as true representations of the minority individual's performance.* If the purpose of testing is to diagnose and augment the individual's achievement, then what teachers need are profiles bearing *some semblance to the individual's brain functions and having some relationship to concomitant curricular programs.* It goes without saying *that tests will have to be repeated to determine changes in the individual's profile.* And, as *we continue to identify and refine the factors and information-processing involved in each subject-area or cognitive structure, we can match the proper learning materials and procedures to the perceived needs of the individual student.*

BIBLIOGRAPHY

ASHWORTH. M. *Immigrant Children and Canadian Schools.* Toronto: McClelland and Stewart Ltd., 1975.

BANKS. J. *Multiethnic Education: Theory and Practice.* Boston: Allyn and Bacon, 1981.

BARATZ. S. AND BARATZ. J. "Early childhood intervention: the social science base of institutional racism." *Harvard Education Review, 40,* 1970, 29-50.

BEREITER. C. ET AL. "An academically oriented pre-school for culturally deprived children." F. M. Hechinger (Ed.), *Preschool Education Today.* New York: Doubleday, 1966, 105-135.

BERNSTEIN. B. "Language and social class." *British Journal of Sociology, 11,* 1960, 271-276.

CLARK. K. AND PLOTKIN. L. "A review of the issues and literature of cultural deprivation theory." K. B. Clark (Ed.), *The Educationally Deprived.* New York: Metropolitan Applied Research Center, 1972, 46-73.

COLEMAN. J. ET AL. *Equality of Educational Opportunity.* Washington, D.C.: Department of Health, Education and Welfare, 1966.

CROSSLAND. F. *Minority Access to College.* New York: Schocken Books, 1971.

DEUTSCH. M. "Minority groups and class status as related to social and personality factors in scholastic achievement." M. Deutsch et al., (Ed.) *The Disadvantaged Child.* New York: Basic Books, 1976, 89-131.

DREGER. R. AND MILLER. K. "Comparative psychological studies of negroes and whites in the United States: 1943-1958." *Psychological Bulletin,* 1960, 361-402.

DREGER. R. AND MILLER. K. "Comparative psychological studies of negroes and whites in the United States: 1959-1965." *Psychological Bulletin,* 1968. (Monograph Supplement 70, No. 3, Part 2.)

DUNN. L. "Special education for the mildly retarded. Is much of it justifiable?" *Exceptional Children, 35,* 1968, 5-22.

FEUERSTEIN. R. *Instrumental Enrichment: An Intervention Program for Cognitive Modifiability.* Baltimore. Md.: University Park Press, 1980.

FINDLEY. W. AND BRYAN. M. *Ability Grouping: 1970. Status, Impact, and Alternatives.* Athens, Ga.: Center for Educational Improvement, 1971.

GARCIA. J. "The logic and limits of mental aptitude testing." *American Psychologist, 36,* 1981, 1172-1180.

HAYNES. J. *Educational Assessment of Immigrant Pupils.* National Foundation for Educational Research in England and Wales, 1971.

HILLIARD. A. "Cultural diversity and special education." *Exceptional Children, 46,* 1980, 584-588.

HUGHES. D. AND KALLEN. E. *The Anatomy of Racism: Canadian Dimensions.* Montreal: Harvest House Ltd., 1974.

JENSEN. A. "How much can we boost IQ and scholastic achievement?" *Harvard Educational Review, 39,* 1969, 1-123.

JONES. R. (ED.) *Mainstreaming and the Minority Child.* Leadership Training Institute/Special Education Bureau of Adult and Occupational Education, United States Office of Education, Department of Health, Education and Welfare, 1976.

KAMIN. L.J. *The Science and Politics of IQ.* New York: Wiley, 1974.

LABOV. W. "Academic ignorance and black intelligence." *The Atlantic Monthly,* 1971, 59-67.

MANN. T. "Testing uses and misuses in education as related to minimal competency testing." *Proceedings of the National Conference on Testing: Major Issues.* Richard Bossone and Max Weiner (Eds.) New York: The Graduate School and University Center of the City University of New York, 1977, 138-146.

MERCER. J. "Institutionalized and anglocentrism: labelling mental retardates in the public schools." P. Orleans and W. Russell (Eds.) *Race, Change and Urban Society.* Los Angeles: Sage Publications, 1971.

MORRISH. I. *The Background of Immigrant Children.* London: George Allen and Unwin Ltd., 1971.

OLMEDO. E.L. "Testing linguistic minorities." *American Psychologist, 36,* 1981, 1078-1085.

RESCHLY. D.J. "Psychological testing in educational classification and placement." *American Psychologist, 36,* 1981, 1094-1102.

RIESSMAN. R. *The Culturally Deprived Child.* New York: Harper and Row, 1962.

SALVIA, J. AND YSSELDYKE, J. *Assessment in Special and Remedial Education.* Boston: Houghton Mifflin, 1978.

SAMUDA, R.J. *Psychological Testing of American Minorities: Issues and Consequences.* New York: Harper and Row, 1975.

SAMUDA, R.J., CRAWFORD, D., PHILLIPS, L. AND TINGLIN, W. *Testing, Assessment, Counselling and Placement of Ethnic Minority Students: Current Methods in Ontario.* Ministry of Education Contract #213. Toronto: OISE Press, 1980.

SAMUDA, R.J., BERRY, J. AND LAFERRIERE, M. *Educational Implications for Cultural Diversity.* Proceedings of the Invitational Symposium on Multiculturalism in Education, Queen's University, November 7-11, 1981. Allyn and Bacon (in press, 1982).

SATTLER, J. *Assessment of Children's Education. Revised Reprint.* Philadelphia: W. B. Saunders, 1974.

SCARR, S. "Testing minority children: why, how, and with what effects?" *Proceedings of the National Conference on Testing: Major Issues.* Richard Bossonc and Max Weiner (Eds.) New York: The Graduate School and University Center of the City University of New York, 1977, 71-101.

SCARR, S. "Testing for children: assessment and the many determinants of intellectual competence." *American Psychologist, 36,* 1981, 1159-1167.

SHUEY, A. "The testing of negro intelligence." Lynchburg, Va.: J. P. Bell, 1958. Second Edition, New York: Social Science Press, 1966.

STERNBERG, R.J. "Testing and cognitive psychology." *American Psychologist, 36,* 1981, 1181-1189.

TYLER, R. AND WOLF, R. (EDS.) *Crucial Issues in Testing.* Berkeley: McCutchan Publishing, 1974.

ASSESSING AND PLACING ETHNIC MINORITY IMMIGRANTS: CURRENT METHODS IN GREATER TORONTO

By Ronald J. Samuda, Ph.D.
Queen's University
Kingston, Ontario, Canada

PREAMBLE

This paper will deal with three aspects or perspectives concerning the ways in which ethnic minority immigrant students are being assessed and placed into the school jurisdictions of Metropolitan Toronto. First, I should like to present some of the background related to the study and to indicate why such a study was necessary. Second, I will briefly describe the design of the study and the instrument and methods used to derive the data. And third, I will provide a summary of the main findings from the field data and from the document analysis, and, in addition, I will state the recommendations flowing from the research.

INTRODUCTION AND BACKGROUND

Twenty years ago, it is highly unlikely that the government of the province of Ontario would have been sufficiently concerned with the issues and problems of assessment and placement to expend in excess of $600 00 to finance a research study. Up until the early sixties, people used to refer to the city as "Toronto the Good". The metropolitan area of Toronto spans some twenty or thirty miles of extensive housing developments, high rise apartment dwellings and commercial-industrial complexes. Like all great cities of North America, Toronto comprises a highly populated urban core which, until relatively recent times, was inhabited mainly by people of North European and British origin. The ghettoes of ethnic concentration, like the Chinatown area, were small and inconsequential for, like the immigration laws of the United States, Canadian policies had been expressly biased towards the encouragement of British and European settlers whilst selectively excluding persons from such areas as Asia, Africa and the Caribbean. Speaking in the House of Commons on May 1, 1947, Prime Minister Mackenzie King stated: "The people of Canada do not wish, as a result of mass immigration, to make a fundamental alteration in the character of our population". By that, he meant that Canada would continue to implement the kind of restrictive policies which ensured that people from the developing countries of Africa, South Asia, and the West Indies would be automatically excluded as immigrants to Canada.

The burgeoning economy of the fifties led to the increasing demands for immigrants to fill the needed places in industry; but the doors were not opened to ethnic minorities until 1960, when the federal government began lifting the discriminatory restrictions against people of non-white immigrants. From a mere handful of privileged South Asians and West Indians who arrived in the two decades after the Second World War, the numbers rose by 1977 to about one hundred thousand from Jamaica and Trinidad alone and exploded even more dramatically in the case of people from India and Pakistan (271,598) and Africa (54,485).

The impact of immigration on the schools of Toronto can only be properly appreciated when it is realized that the immigrant flow to Ontario outstrips that of any other province. In fact, in one peak year Metropolitan Toronto received close to sixty percent of all immigrant students. Most remarkable was the change in the statistical pattern for minorities. In 1951, 1961 and 1971, the percentages of the foreign born population were 31 percent, 42 percent, and 44 percent respectively. More recently, the number of students from ethnic minority backgrounds in the schools of the Toronto Board of Education was estimated at greater than half of the total school population. There are seventy ethnic groups or sub-groups with as many different languages and four hundred ethnic organizations in Toronto alone.

This diversity of immigrant settlers to Canada tended to compound the difficulties of coping with a population that was itself dichotomized between the Quebecois and the Francophone minorities of Alberta and Ontario on the one hand, and the Anglophones representing the rest of Canada, on the other hand. Thus, in 1963, the government of Mr. Lester Pearson established a Royal Commission on Bilingualism and Biculturalism whose recommendations were incorporated as the official policy of the Trudeau government's Multiculturalism within a Bilingual Framework.

Such a change in the political attitudes of the federal government must necessarily have drastic effects on the educational systems. However, it must be remembered that the British North America Act which virtually serves as the constitution of Canada gives the provincial governments exclusive jurisdiction over education and, therefore, the expansion and diversification in the ethnic composition of the student population necessarily presents new and unprecedented challenges to the administrators and faculties of the schools. In view of the statistics presented above, the burden of change would fall most heavily on one province — Ontario; the weight of that burden would be felt most by one city — Toronto.

Since 1960, the educators of Toronto have been faced with the difficulties never before imagined. There existed no concerted federal-provincial government agency to coordinate the accommodation of the new Canadian minorities. Teachers were never taught how to deal with a majority of children from Pakistan, India, Jamaica, Trinidad, Hong Kong, Sri Lanka, and

Bangladesh. How were they to equate the levels of academic preparation in a rural Indian village with that of an urban institution in the heart of Toronto? What kinds of tests could they use to index the levels of literacy or the academic aptitude of such atypical students? The consequence of the political change has been that the educators of Toronto have had to adapt their methods and instruments to match the needs of the students from an atypical population approaching one million.

The classroom teachers were trained in the traditional ways and like many of the school board officials remained wedded to the concepts of Anglo-conformity and the melting pot having had little guidance or experience to understand, assess and place, the new Canadian student, much more implement *the multicultural society which the new federal policies mandated.*

THE DESIGN OF THE STUDY

Throughout the latter half of the sixties and into the seventies, serious questions were being raised concerning the use of tests to label minority children as academically subnormal and to place them in special education classes with the consequent loss of normal preparation in the schools. Not unlike the sentiments expressed in the United States, there were many who believed that "many students drop out of school in despair or remain at school because it is compulsory but have accepted, along with their teachers, the mutual conclusion that they can achieve nothing worthwhile through this interlude".

The main purposes of our study were, therefore, to 1) examine and describe the current policies and practices in the counselling, testing, assessment and placement of recently immigrated students; 2) examine how policies and practices are applied to new Canadian students, with particular reference to specific groups, namely, West Indian, East Indian (including Pakistani) and Portuguese.

We were primarily concerned with the atypical student who would face the major hurdles of adjustment because of differences related to such variables as culture, colour, caste, religion, folkways, educational and socio-economic conditions in the country of origin. We were forced to make a decision to limit the study to certain specific ethnic minority immigrant groups that would best fit the purposes of our study realizing, at the same time, that we would have to rationalize our stance from time to time. Studying the educational conditions of minorities in Canada is not merely an academic research-oriented exercise; it is a political and volatile endeavour as well and we were reminded o the implications on several occasions as the team went about the task of garnering the data.

We chose to limit the subjects of the study to immigrant students from the West Indies, South Asia (India and Pakistan) and Portugal (including the Azores). Our examination of the immigration statistics indicated that these were the most numerous ethnic minority immigrants if we excluded persons from the United Kingdom and the United States. Furthermore, these three groups satisfied all the conditions of student atypicality (in terms of colour, culture, religion, etc.) and were, at the same time representative of newcomers from the Caribbean, Europe, and Asia.

SAMPLING PROCEDURES

The study was focussed upon the policies, trends, concepts, projections and practices as they relate to the testing, assessment, counselling and placement of ethnic monority students. In the absence of specific numbers and proportions of the various ethnic minorities in the boards and in individual schools, we were forced to depend upon available data gleaned from immigration sources and from such documents as the Toronto Board's *Every Student Survey* (1975) and, wherever possible, corroborative board estimates of the ethnic mix throughout their jurisdictions. To assure representativeness, school boards were categorized in terms of Small, Medium, and Large and according to degrees of low, medium or high concentrations of ethnic minority student population. The same procedure was used for identifying Public as well as Separate school boards. From our 3 × 3 matrix, we identified 44 school boards which fitted the criteria and 300 schools representing a 16 percent proportion in Metropolitan Toronto (about 140 schools) and an 8 percent sample from non-Metro (about 170 schools). However, since some schools and school boards declined to participate in the study, 245 schools comprising 34 school boards actually participated in the research.

ANALYSIS OF THE DATA

The data on which analysis could be carried out came from three sources: a) numerous interactions (personal, by telephone, and written) between the research team, and various groups and individuals during the planning and consultative phases of the study; b) the completed schedules from the structured interviews carried out at the board and school level; c) written documents obtained from the boards participating in the study.

The interview schedule contained 58 numbered questions, a professional data sheet, a student data sheet, and a post-interview assessment sheet to be filled in by the interviewer. For purposes of analysis, these latter were numbered questions 59, 60, and 61 respectively. There was a total of 279 schedules, 245 from school interviews and 34 from board interviews.

Essentially, the schedule examined four main aspects of the intake and review process for new students: The Placement Process (questions 1-7, 19-22, 28-30, 50-52); Testing (questions 8-18, 31-38); Counselling (questions 39-49); Special Programs (questions 23-27, 53).

It was decided that the data gathered should be broken down in various ways to indicate practices and procedures for different sets of boards and schools — for example, Metro and non-Metro systems. A list of possible comparisonf of groups was therefore compiled, which identified three levels of analysis — global, macro and mini. Various computer analyses were then conducted to ensure that the output of the computer reflected these various groupings, and enabled the desired comparisons to be made. Because of the immensity of the task, limited resources, and time pressures, later computer runs were streamlined and data on some of the less central issues such as details of which personnel are involved in testing and making final decisions (questions 36-38) were omitted.

Similarly, time and the immense quality of data gathered did not allow any analysis at all at the mini level, and only partial analysis of the variables of size and school level at the macro level.

DISCUSSION OF THE RESULTS

Our findings demonstrate some fundamental problems which remain unsolved in the various attempts to cope with the reception and placement of immigrant minority students. These problems stem from the obvious and significant descrepancies between the social, cultural, and economic backgrounds of immigrant minority students and that of the host country. Moreover, the differences in educational practices, in language, and (among a multiplicity of factors) in the assessment and methods employed in the teaching/learning process, all contribute to create the dilemma of adapting the Ontario educational system to a new immigrant clientele.

THE PROBLEM OF ASSESSMENT

The field data and documentary analysis underscore the problem of assessment as *difficult, elusive,* and *cumbersome.* The difficulty is increased when students arrive at school from the *Azores* or *Trinidad* or *India* with no recognizable documentation by which the principal or his aides can match levels of achievement with available programs. Experiences with minority students in Metropolitan Toronto have resulted in a policy whereby intelligence tests of all kinds *are discarded* (especially during the first two years) for *deciding initial entry into the school system.* It is interesting to emphasize, in this context, that boards with high ethnic concentrations tend to eschew the use of tests completely in the initial assessment of minority students. On the other hand, board data on the use of tests for initial placement for low and medium concentrations were at 38 and 22 percent respectively.

There is a growing body of evidence which would invalidate results obtained from tests of scholastic aptitude because they are based on meaningless comparisons with Canadian norms. As scholars like DeAvila and Bruner have so persuasively argued, tests are necessarily embedded within a cultural frame of reference, and can do nothing to distinguish between performance and capacity w tests are applied to individuals whose experiential background has been different from the norm group. Cole and Bruner as well, have shown that cultural deprivation is a redundant term in this context; the performance of ethnic minority immigrant students represent cultural differences — *not deficits.*

Yet despite the evidence, many educators still cling to the notion that standardized tests can perform an adequate sorting task by indicating the degree of the individual's atypical function.

An alternate trend in the use of tests in the province seems to adopt the position of the APA Society for the Psychological Study of social issues in its *"Guidelines for Testing Minority Group Children"* (Fishman et al.). Although critical of the general use of tests for minorities, advocates of this *alternative methodology* would stress training of teachers and counsellors in the problems of reliability and validity associated with minority group test results while modifying the structure of existing instruments as well as the procedures and test-taking situations. But such practices *retain the principle of the deficit model* or the cultural deprivation theory and the concomitant follow-up of compensatory education so as to help the minority student overcome what must be viewed *as deficiencies* within the educational and social system from which he came.

Attitudes reminiscent of Bloom, Carrol and Wolf could be discerned *when respondents were asked to suggest ways to overcome the educational problems of minority students*. Some responses to questions 55 and 56 of the interview schedule parallel the position held by adherents of environment measurement and its follow-up for enrichment so as to augment school performance. Respondents who favoured assimilation went from 2 percent to 5 percent to 21 percent as ethnic concentration in their school and board groups moved from low to medium to high. Moreover, 12 percent overall were in *favour of reception classes*. The specific responses within the assimilation category ranged from suggestions for a *"holding center", "culturalize them", to better screening of immigrants* and the *underlying notion that it is the duty of the immigrant to adopt Canadian ways, to join the melting pot, to assimilate into the dominant majority culture*.

Evidence in favour of Jane Mercer's pluralistic sociocultural perspective represents another trend in attitudes towards assessment. Some educators still believe that tests of intelligence (like the Stanford-Binet and the WISC) are valuable diagnostic tools having useful clinical value when viewed from a socioculturally pluralistic perspective. Thus, individual assessment could be made by comparing that individual's score with norms developed for his own sociocultural group. Mercer has espoused a system of assessment (a comparison between performance and capacity) which would help in placing minority students in special programs designed to prepare the individual to participate in the mainstream of the school and eventually in the mainstream of the society (see Samuda, 1975).

. Another interesting trend in the testing issue was demonstrated at more than one board and more particularly in one of the Metropolitan boards. To some extent, this trend seems to resemble the movement advocated by those psycholinguists who oppose the position taken by Bernstein and Bereiter. According to the latter view, minority children (and poor children in general) are impeded in their school performance because of their restricted use of language and particularly their difficulty in dealing with abstract concepts. Labov and Baratz have vigorously opposed such notions in demonstrating that norm-referenced standardized tests make normally intelligent minority children *look stupid*. Cole and Bruner have supported this view by showing that competence can be neither *situation blind nor culture blind*. In other words, Labov and his associates have shown that *"culturally different" students when tested appropriately for optimum performance, have the same grammatical competence as middle-class mainstream students, though it may be expressed* in different modes.

This trend in testing was instanced admirably in that one school board where the official in charge of placement *was himself a member of one of the largest minority groups* in the area. *He was able to adapt parts of achievement tests in the area of mathematics and reading to the accustomed style of the students;* he was able to *use familiar language and dialect, reduce anxiety to a minimum,* and thus *elicit a functional evaluation of the students in basic subjects.*

THE ROLE OF THE TEACHER

The second major factor perceived from the field data in particular was the predominant role of the classroom teacher in the design and use of tests, and in monitoring the placement of minority students in the absence of tests. Furthermore, of all the forms of assessment, *teacher-made tests were the most frequently used.* Even when initial placement is made *on the basis of age, it is the teacher who evaluates the student's progress; it is he or she who determines the content of the program and more often than not, activates the referral process.*

This responsibility *is often carried by the classroom teacher in the absence of definite, articulated policies for coping with the new Canadian ethnic minority. Board policy and institutional practices in a significant proportion of cases tend to place the reception, placement and programs for minority students under the rubric of Special Education,* thus tending to perpetuate the attitude that if a student is different (culturally), *he is therefore academically inferior.*

Our experience with interviewing board and school personnel revealed considerable variation in the awareness of, situations towards, and planning for, the accommodation of new Canadian students.

The *evidence points to the need for appropriate training or retraining for board officials as well as classroom teachers if multiculturalism in the Ontario schools is ever to become a province-wide reality.* The *importance of the role the classroom teacher plays also calls into question the programs of training at the various faculties of education. To what extent are the concepts, attitudes, and programs of the teacher-training establishments linked to the idea of multiculturalism? Do teacher trainees receive the appropriate exposure to the principles, definitions and issues concerned with the policy of cultural pluralism?*

Without training in the concepts of multiculturalism, the likelihood is that the attitudes of ethnocentrism, of Anglo-Canadian conformity and assimilation as the expected model for New Canadians will continue to exist. Nor can the attitudes, policies and practices change within the institutions unless there is commitment on the part of board officials and willingness on the part of teachers to become actively involved in re-training.

Re-training requires the deliberate act of repudiating the ethnocentric melting pot model and the acceptance of ethnic minority cultures as different rather than deficient. Such a stance *implies respect and a new mode of thinking.* As the central team of this research project can attest, *we were occasionally met with relative degrees of defensiveness on the part of respondents when questioned about the difference in testing and placement procedures and practices as they relate to mainstream and ethnic minority immigrant students.* A favourite response was: *"We treat them all alike",* thus emphasizing what was considered to be a *"democratic"* and *acceptable* mode. But such an attitude *might also imply deeply embedded notions of what some respondents* perceive education *ought to be as well as the absolute acceptance of an expected norm of behaviour matched to the Anglo-Canadian assimilationalist model.*

THE ROLE OF THE COUNSELLOR

Of all the aspects of the school's operation with which this project was concerned, the role of guidance and counselling has perhaps been the hardest to pin down. The fact is that guidance procedures seem to be very little in evidence when the reception and placement of New Canadian minorities are examined. We found, for example, that just over one-third of the 34 boards sampled (12) have an established policy requiring the ethnic minority student to be counselled during the process of placement. It should however be emphasized that most of the boards of Metropolitan Toronto, especially in the areas of high density minority student population, did require the involvement of guidance personnel throughout the placement and reassessment of the students. Only one-quarter of the boards outside Metro adhere to such a practice.

What we found curious was the fact that, of all the 128 documents analyzed, only 10 of the total had any direct or specific reference to guidance and counselling. We have speculated that the lack of counselling involvement in the reception and placement of ethnic minority immigrants stems from the fact that "immigrant" or "minority" education is generally perceived by the majority of board and school personnel as falling under the umbrella of special education, perhaps requiring the expertise of school psychology personnel and the special education consultant rather than the guidance counsellor. In other words, there seems to be an attitude among a large proportion of counsellors that the problems related to new Canadian minority students fall outside their province. Significantly, in this regard, for all but four Metro boards, the reception and placement of ethnic minorities were relegated to Special Education.

NEED FOR SYSTEMATIC PLANNING

We could find no formal cooperative structure throughout the province whereby ideas concerning the education of new Canadians are shared and the problems of testing, placement, and programs are articulated and tackled by the combined expertise of the various consultants, superintendents and their aides. No common data base exists and the methods of identifying the proportions of New Canadians within the various local jurisdictions differ from board to board. Although there does exist an organization of research officers of Metropolitan Toronto (and an organization of large Ontario boards), there seems to be no agreed upon process for sharing data and experiences as new policies, programs and teaching strategies are tried out. We were struck by the fact that each board seemed to be doing what it saw best with apparently little or no consultation among neighbouring jurisdictions.

The situation outside of Metro Toronto was even less cohesive. There appears to be little or no cooperation even between the large boards where ethnic minority immigrant students form a significant proportion of the population. Certain boards on the periphery of Metro Toronto are only now becoming actively engaged in developing multicultural programs and in formulating guidelines to deal with the reception, testing, placement and programs for ethnic minority students; moreover, certain boards on the boundaries of Metropolitan Toronto can only be described as hostile to the idea of this project. One board in particular bluntly stated its opposition to any form of participation while questioning the very need for the Ministry of Education to examine the issues concerning ethnic immigrant minorities.

The question that came to our minds on certain occasions was whether or not educators were indeed aware that multiculturalism was the Ontario government's policy. Somehow, the concepts of cultural pluralism do not seem to have been adequately communicated; we were struck by the apparent ad hoc arrangements in promulgating and implementing the government's policy. As we encountered the difficulties involved in collecting the data and, at times, in gaining permission to interview within certain jurisdictions, we realized that the issue is a much larger one than merely that of the school. What kinds of planning followed the adoption of a multicultural model? It must have been realized that the change in immigration policy would surely result in large numbers of Third World immigrants flocking to the industrial urban areas. It would have taken little imagination to have pictured the radical change in the population of Toronto that inevitably led to a drastic change in student composition.

The implementation of multi-ethnicity requires planning at the federal-provincial level, at the provincial-municipal level, and at the community level. It is not just the business of the teachers, or the school boards, but of the average citizen. Multiculturalism represents a change of values and a shift of attitudes from the melting pot model of acculturation. As Duncan Green has so succinctly expressed it, "In the centre of the city, we are Marshall McLuhan's global village with a vengeance ... What we are attempting to do then, in our new socialization, is to establish a concept that gives validity to other cultures and languages within a total framework as yet unconstructed" (in D'Oyley, Ed., 1977).

FURTHER RESEARCH

Clearly, this study has uncovered and brought into sharper focus many problems relating to the arrival and integration of New Canadian students into the Ontario school system. Because of the circumstances under which the study was conducted, only the beginnings have been made in investigating and coping with these problems.

A number of steps in dealing with these urgent problems are outlined in the recommendations. Included are several suggestions for further research; in particular, the team felt that the impact of this study has been greatly hindered by the inability to obtain and present first-hand data on the students themselves. Among possible ways of overcoming this deficiency, it could be possible to use the data already available and base some case studies upon them. Alternatively, because of the great need for a better and more comprehensive data base on New Canadian students, such studies might await the development of such a base.

RECOMMENDATIONS

We recommend:

1. That a planning structure be initiated immediately comprising representatives of the federal, provincial and municipal levels of government to coordinate the funding of projects and programs designed to implement policies of multiculturalism.

2. That the Ministry of Education take steps to initiate an organization of school boards (particularly within Metropolitan Toronto, and the bordering county boards) in order to facilitate the sharing of research findings, policies, programs, teaching strategies and resources for the promotion of multiculturalism and improvements to the education of ethnic minorities.

3. That a project be initiated by the Ministry of Education to establish a common data base of New Canadian students throughout the province.

4. That the Ministry of Education take steps to ensure that the curricula of all provincial teacher-training establishments include an acceptable program for multicultural education.

5. That incentives be provided to encourage school boards across the province to initiate and implement specific policies to facilitate programs and strategies for multicultural education and the provisions for the education of atypical ethnic minorities.

6. That the Ministry of Education institute an inter-board organization for the specific purpose of collecting, developing and trying out curricular strategies, resources and assessment instruments to augment and support the education of New Canadians.

7. That the Ministry encourage a system of recruitment of New Canadians for professional training as teachers, counsellors and administrators in areas of high density minority population.

8. That a data base on the individuals involved with testing and counselling of New Canadian students be established so as to ascertain their level of qualifications, professional experience, and knowledge of the types of New Canadians with whom they are working.

9. That a study focusing upon a series of case studies of different groups of New Canadian students be undertaken to point out the problems involved in assessment, placement, and monitoring of educational experiences; and suggesting guidelines for optimum treatment of the atypical student.

10. That the Ministry of Education fund a research project to investigate, collect, and describe assessment strategies leading to teaching/learning models of adaptive education as well as process-oriented methods for identifying differences in cognitive styles and processes among the various ethnic minority group students.

11. That counsellors involved with the assessment and placement of New Canadian students be required to undertake in-service training in the concepts, implications, and strategies relating to multicultural education.

12. That the Ministry of Education provide assistance in encouraging boards to participate in studies such as the present one so as to relieve researchers of the complex and prolonged negotiations involved in securing entry into the various jurisdictions.

13. That further analysis of the data contained in this study be commissioned by the Ministry of Education leading to more definitive distinctions in the different categories of students selected for this study.

14. That a study be conducted to determine the validity and reliability of standardized tests and other means of assessment presently being used to evaluate ethnic minority immigrant students across the Province of Ontario.

REFERENCES

ALLEYNE. M.H. "The Teaching of Bilingual Children. Intelligence and Attainment of Children in London, Wales and Trinidad Whose Mother Tongue is not English." Unpublished M. A. Dissertation, University of London, 1962.

ALLEYNE. M.H. "Research in the Effects of Bilingualism on Education." In Jones, J. (Ed.) *Linguistics and Language in a Multicultural Society*. London, England: Unwin, 1965.

ANDERSON. J.T. *The Education of the New Canadian*. Toronto: Dent, 1918.

ASHBY. B. ET AL. "The Abilities and Attainments of Immigrant Children." *Research in Education, 4*, pp. 73-80, 1970.

BARATZ. S. AND BARATZ. J. "Early Childhood Intervention. The Social Science Base of Institutional Racism." *Harvard Educational Review, 40*, pp. 29-50, 1970.

BECK. C. "Is Immigrant Education Only for Immigrants?" In Wolfgang, A. (Ed.) *Education of Immigrant Students: Issues and Answers*. Toronto: Ontario Institute for Studies in Education, 1975.

BELL. R. "The Grammar of English Spoken by Indian Immigrants in Smethwick." Unpublished M. A. Dissertation, University of Birmingham, England, 1966.

BERNARD. W.S. "The Integration of Immigrants in the United States." In Borrie, W. D. *The Cultural Integration of Immigrants*. Paris: UNESCO, 1959.

BHATNAGAR. J. *Immigrants at School*. London: Cornmarket Press, 1970.

BLOOM. L. *The Social Psychology of Race Relations*. London: Allen and Unwin, 1971.

BROWN. G.I. *Human Teaching for Human Learning: An Introduction to Confluent Education*. New York: Viking Press, 1971.

CASTILLO. G. *Left-Handed Teaching*. New York: Praeger Publishing, 1974.

CASTON. F. "Ethnic Studies: Out of the Melting Pot." *Scholastic Teacher, C*, pp. 8-11, April, 1972.

CLARK. K.B. "Desegregation: The Role of the Social Sciences." *Teachers College Record, 62*(1), October, 1960.

COLE. M. AND BRUNER. J. "Cultural Differences and Inference About Psychological Processes." *American Psychologist, 26*, pp. 867-876, 1971.

COLEMAN. J.S. ET AL. *Equality of Educational Opportunity*. Washington, D.C.: United States Government Printing Office, 1966.

DAS. J.P. "Cultural Deprivation and Cognitive Competence." In Ellis, N.R. (Ed.) *International Review of Research in Mental Retardation, 6*. New York: Academic Press, 1973.

Department of Manpower and Immigration. *Immigration Policy and Perspectives, 1*. Information Canada, 1974.

DYER. H. Educational Testing Service, 1971. Cited in L. Ruth, *How Tests Fail*. Berkeley, California: University of California Press, 1975.

EELS. K. ET AL. *Intelligence and Cultural Differences*. Chicago: University of Chicago Press, 1951.

EDELMAN. M.W. *The Rights of Children*. Reprint Series No. 9. Cambridge, Massachusetts: Harvard Educational Review, 1974.

EDSON. P. *East and West Meetings in Education for Integration*. London, England: Institute of Race Relations Newsletter, 1966.

FRIEDENBERG. Z.E. "Status and Role in Education." In Skolnick, J. and Elliot, C. (Eds.) *Crisis in American Institutions*. Boston: Little, Brown and Co., 1970.

Gendron Commission. *The Position of French Language in Quebec, 3*. The Ethnic Groups, Government of Quebec, 1972.

GINZBERG. E. *The Human Economy*. New York: McGraw-Hill Book Company, 1976.

GOLDMAN. R. AND TAYLOR. F. "Coloured Immigrant Children: A Survey of Research Studies and Literature on Their Educational Problems and Potential in the United States." *Journal of Educational Research, 9*, pp. 22-43, 1966.

GORDON. M. *Assimilation in American Life*: New York: Oxford University Press, 1964.

GORDON. M.L. "A Different View of the IQ-Achievement Gap." *Sociology of Education, 49*. January, 1976.

GREEN. A.G. *Immigration and the Post-War Canadian Economy*. Canada: Macmillan/ MacLean Hunter, 1976.

HALL. E.F. *The Silent Language*. New York: Doubleday and Company Inc., 1959.

HANDLIN. O. (ED.) *Children of the Uprooted*. New York: George Grosset and Dunlap, 1968.

HARBISON. F. AND MYERS. C. *Education, Manpower and Economic Growth: Strategies of Human Resource Development*. Toronto: McGraw-Hill Book Co., 1964.

HAWKINS, F. *Canada and Immigration: Public Policy and Public Concern.* Montreal and London: McGill-Queen's University Press, 1972.

HOUSTON, S.H. "A Re-examination of Some Assumptions About Language of the Disadvantaged Child." *Child Development, 41,* pp. 947-963, 1970.

JENSEN, A.R. "How Much Can We Boost IQ?" *Harvard Educational Review, 39.* Winter, 1969.

JONES, R.L. "Labels and Stigma in Special Education." *Exceptional Children, 38,* pp. 553-564, 1972.

JONES, R.L. "Student Attitudes and Motivations." In *Ohio State University Advisory Commission on Problems Facing the Columbus (Ohio) Public Schools (Ed.)* A Report to the Columbus Board of Education. Columbus: The Ohio State University, June, 1968.

KAWWA, T. "A Study of the Interaction Between Native and Immigrant Children in English Schools with Special Reference to Ethnic Prejudice." Unpublished Ph.D. Thesis, University of London, England: Institute of Education, 1965.

LEDERMAN, S. "Social Acceptance of Immigrants." *Race Today.* June, 1969.

LEITER, K.C. "Teachers' Use of Background Knowledge to Interpret Test Scores." *Sociology of Education, 49,* 1976.

LEWIS, E.G. "Immigrants, Their Language and Development." *Trends in Education, 19,* 1970.

LIGHT, R. AND SMITH, P. "Models of Intelligence." *Harvard Educational Review, 39,* Summer, 1969.

McFIE, J. AND THOMPSON, J. "Intellectual Abilities of Immigrant Children." *British Journal of Educational Psychology, 40,* pp. 348-351, 1970.

MERCER, J.R. "Institutionalized Anglocentrism: Labeling Mental Retardates in the Public Schools." In *Race, Change and Urban Society.* Orleans, P. and Russell, W. Jr. (Eds.) Urban Affairs Annual Review, 5. Los Angeles: Sage Publications, 1971.

MERTON, R.K. *Social Theory and Social Structure.* New York: The Free Press, 1957.

Ministry of Education. *English For Immigrants.* London, England: Her Majesty's Stationery Office, 1963.

PARK, R.E. AND BURGESS, E.W. *Introduction to the Science of Sociology.* Chicago: University of Chicago Press, 1921.

PONDER, E.G. *Orientation Classes for In-migrant Transient Children.* Second Report. ERIC Report No. ED 0022722, 1962.

REX, J. AND MOORE, R. *Race, Community and Conflict: A Study of Sparkbrook.* London, England: Oxford University Press, 1967.

ROGERS, M. "The Education of Children of Immigrants in Britain." *Journal of Negro Education, 51,* pp. 255-265, 1972.

ROHWER, W.D. JR. "Learning, Race and School Success." *Review of Educational Research, 41,* pp. 191-220, 1972.

ROSE, E. ET AL. *Colour and Citizenship.* London: Institute of Race Relations, 1969.

ROSENTHAL, R. AND JACOBSON, L. *Pygmalion in the Classroom.* New York: Rinehart and Winston, 1968.

RUFF, E. *Our Job as Counsellors.* American School Counsellor Association Newsletter, 5(3), 1968.

SAMUDA, R.J. *Psychological Testing of American Minorities: Issues and Consequences.* New York: Harper and Rów Publishers, 1975.

Scarborough Board of Education. *Meeting The Needs of Scarborough Immigrant Students: A Brief To The Minister of Manpower and Immigration,* 1977.

SCHULTZ, T.W. *The Economic Value of Education.* New York: Columbia University Press, 1973.

SEEMAN, M. "On the Meaning of Alienation." *American Sociological Review, 24(6),* pp. 670-677, 1959.

SILVERMAN, H. "Notes on Development and Research Directions with Reference to Canada's New Urban Black Students." In *Black Students in Urban Canada.* Special Issue of TESL Talk. January, 1976.

STINCHOMBE, A.L. "Environment: The Cumulation of Effects is Yet To Be Understood." *Harvard Educational Review, 39,* Summer, 1969.

TAYLOR, F. *Race, School and Community: A Study of Research and Literature on Education in Multiracial Britain.* London, England: National Council for Educational Research Publishing Company, 1974.

VERNON, P.E. *Intelligence and Cultural Environment.* London, England: Metheun Press, 1969.

VICK, M.I. *Realities and Fallacies of Reading Instruction for Ethnically Different Students: Cognitive and Affective Concerns.* ERIC Report No. ED 063087, 1971.

WALLWORK, J. "Language Teaching for Children from Immigrant Groups." *Education for Teaching, 90,* pp. 24-29, 1973.

WEINSTEIN. G. AND FANTINI. M. *Toward Humanistic Education: A Curriculum of Affect.* New York: Praeger Publishers, 1970.

WERNER. W. ET AL. *Whose Culture? Whose Heritage? Ethnicity Within Canadian Social Studies Curricula.* University of British Columbia, Faculty of Education: Center for the Study of Curriculum and Instruction, 1977.

WILLIAMS. J. "Immigrant Children: Schools' Role in Integration." Working Title for one Study, Which is Part of a Larger Study by Rex, J. (1966). *Race, Community and Conflict: A Study on Sparkbrook.* London: Oxford University Press, 1966.

ZIRKEL. P. "Spanish-Speaking Students and Standardized Tests." *Urban Review,* 5, pp. 32-40, 1972.

THE TRAINING AND USE OF INTERPRETER/TRANSLATORS IN THE EVALUATION OF LANGUAGE MINORITY STUDENTS

By Carol A. Fineman
Dade County Public Schools
Miami, Florida

Public Law 94-142 requires that students be evaluated in their native language or mode of communication; however the issue of labeling non-English and limited English speaking students as exceptional remains a serious one. There are no normed or validated tests available in many languages.

Translating tests developed in English into other languages may not remove language biases, it may serve to increase them (Oakland and Matuszek, 1977) especially as thorough norming of the translated test is unlikely. According to Sattler (1974), the studies which investigated translating test content or test instructions from English to Spanish, have indicated that such procedures are fraught with hazards. Sattler concludes that the need is for construction of tests in the native language with native cultural norms. This process is difficult and time consuming. It may not be considered practical for language groups infrequently found in this country's school.

In 1979, the State of Florida declared instrument validation and procedural guidelines to ensure non-biased evaluation of minority individuals a major statewide need. An influx of Haitian and Vietnamese students into the schools, along with smaller groups of Russians and other immigrants, compounded the evaluation dilemma already confronted when the hundreds of thousands of Cuban refugees raised the Dade County (Miami) population to one-third Hispanic. There were little or no guidelines available to determine appropriate non-biased diagnostic procedures for students from these language groups who might legitimately require exceptional student programs.

The EHA Title VI-B Project "Evaluating the non-English Speaking Handicapped" was funded to research existing evaluation instruments in languages other than English, validate these tests as well as additional translations where needed, and develop a procedural manual for distribution to utilize in evaluating non-English speaking handicapped students.

A review was made of ERIC, Tests in Print, The Educational Testing Service Test Collection Bulletins and other United States and foreign sources to determine what non-English evaluation instruments exist. School districts, universities and other sources were contacted to determine the availability of instruments and to obtain samples for review. Instruments in Spanish (normed on Puerto Rican, Cuban or Mexican-American populations), French, Vietnamese, Russian, Hebrew and other languages were researched.

The procedural manual (State of Florida, 1981) was developed for use by exceptional student administrators, school psychologists, educational diagnosticians and speech therapists. It's intent was to assist school districts in developing their most appropriate procedures for the evaluation of the non-English speaking handicapped and to provide information on material availability for specific diagnostic usages as well as recommendations for examiner selection, notification in home languages, test selection and interpretation. Based on needs assessments, a major need was seen to be suggestions for the proper utilization of personnel to assist psychologists and other evaluators when no tests are available in the native language of the student.

School districts reported that they had previously had bad experiences in utilizing personnel to translate tests for psychologists. In many cases the translator was found to be giving the student inaccurate translations of test material or was adding clues and explanations above and beyond standard wording. In few instances were the translation personnel given specific training in standardized test techniques. They were also rarely used to provide insight into cultural biasing factors which might be contained in the test materials. It was apparent that, without adequate selection and training procedures, the use of translation personnel could involve even more pitfalls than those found in translating the test materials themselves.

The following are recommended procedures for the selection, training and utilization of interpreter/translators which will serve to minimize the above problems while maximizing the retention of test validity.

SELECTION OF INTERPRETER/TRANSLATORS

A minimum of two interpreter/translators should be selected; even in the case of small populations of the language involved. Besides providing a back-up, this will aid in the training process as will be seen in the following section.

If there is a large local population of native speakers of the language the district will have the opportunity to identify persons who are college graduates or who might have had training in psychology or education. There might be current school system employees who would be willing to be trained for these duties.

The mere fact that the person is a native speaker of the language is not a guarantee that they are cognizant of cultural biasing factors. In selecting people with college backgrounds, the district must be aware that many of the people they will be considering have come from the upper strata of the countries involved. Inquiries should be made into the person's life experiences and awareness of cultural factors at all levels of society.

Selection is more difficult when there is only a small population of a particular language group in the community. The level of education available may be high school graduate or even less. In these cases, the district must take a lot of care to select persons who have had experience with children and who are able to recognize the purpose of the test procedures and exceptional student programming.

Whatever their educational background, the potential selectees should be as proficiently bilingual as possible. They will need to communicate with the examiner in English and to understand the test instruments in order to render correct translations. Language dominance testing must be used to make this determination. The person should score as being independent in English. In addition, some of the more difficult test questions should be discussed to determine if the person has the ability to comprehend the materials that will have to be translated.

The securing of applicants can be accomplished through newspaper advertisements, contacts with student's families, the school system bilingual department if available, refugee groups, or other sources. Cooperative agreements can be established on a regional basis for districts to share the services of personnel who may be highly qualified for providing this service.

If the school district cannot locate persons who are sufficiently bilingual and who meet other relevant criteria they should choose not to utilize interpreter/translators for testing purposes. The use of non-verbal tests along with observation and informal measures may be the most viable alternative.

TRAINING OF INTERPRETER/TRANSLATORS

Training needs may vary based on the person's background and experience. Whenever possible, two or more persons of the same language group should be trained at the same time.

The trainees should first take the tests that they will be later required to translate. This is intended for them to experience what the student will be facing as well as to give an opportunity to observe proper test administration.

Following the test administration the trainees discuss any aspects of the test that they felt were culturally biased towards them and the students who they would have to work with. The next step is to go over the test in more detail, pinpointing potentially biased items and items which may not translate appropriately into the language involved. Notes should also be kept of any changes in test wording which are recommended to alleviate these problems and the agreed upon translations for difficult terms.

The trainer next emphasizes the importance of standardized wording and procedures as well as the avoidance of non-verbal cues. The trainees are given the chance to administer tests to each other in English so that any difficulties they have with administration techniques can be corrected.

At this point the trainees of the same language translate to each other, correct inappropriate wording, and standardize their terminology so that they will be administering the tests in the same way to all students.

The trainees are then ready to practice interpreting for an English speaking examiner in a test situation. The importance of rapport with the student is emphasized as is the interpreter/translators role in establishing rapport. They will be the ones to make the introductions of the examiner to the child and explain the purpose of testing. The practice sessions should not be conducted with students who are being considered for exceptional student services. While one trainee is interpreting, another should be observing. After the test is completed, any alteration in accepted wording or procedures can be discussed and corrected.

THE UTILIZATION OF INTERPRETER/TRANSLATORS

The same small group of interpreter/translators should be used at all times. This will enable each person to develop a "feel" for the responses given by as many students as possible. The interpreter/translator can develop informal cultural and language norm information for comparing an individual student with others from the same or similar background.

The interpreter/translator can become a vital component of the assessment team and can function throughout the assessment process from screening through the placement conference. They may frequently be the only member of the assessment team who is a native speaker of the language involved and familiar with cultural and educational factors which are relevant for the student under consideration. Complete utilization of trained personnel can go far beyond direct test translation.

UTILIZATION IN SCREENING

Districts which receive a number of new entrants have the responsibility to screen students of all ages upon their arrival. Other districts may concentrate on pre-school age children who are entering school from families who speak a language other than English in the home. The trained interpreter/translator can assist in both situations. In screening of language minority students the emphasis should be placed on sensory and physical handicaps and severe retardation. Minor emotional or intellectual deficits may be related to cultural or situational causes and students who fail initial screening in these areas should be rescreened after a period of adjustment to their new environment.

Audiometric screening may utilize middle-ear impedance instruments which do not involve language but the interpreter/translator can assist by giving instructions to the student for screening with an audiometer.

Vision screening can utilize symbol charts. The interpreter/translator can provide screening staff with correct symbol labeling.

The interpreter/translator can obtain language development information for speech and language screening and can also perform cognitive screening through developmental scales. The cognitive screening of older entrants can also be performed by the interpreter/translator through adaptive behavior measures.

UTILIZATION IN
REFERRAL AND PARENT CONTACT

The interpreter/translator can be a vital support person to schools when they consider referring a language minority student for exceptional student services. This role is not one of testing assistance. It is one of "expert" in cultural and educational norms for the group involved. If the district uses visiting teachers and school social workers who do not speak the home language, the interpreter/translator can be a link with the student's family.

Every effort must be made to involve parents in the referral process. This is especially true as they may be primary informants. Among the information parents can provide are details about the student's language, educational, health and developmental history. The interpreter/translator can determine if the student has had the opportunity to develop the readiness skills at home which the school assumes for children of that age. Some cultures may not permit children to experience activities and levels of independence at the same ages.

Details about schooling in the country of origin are of major importance. Some countries deny education to children of families that have requested emigration. In other cases, no schooling, or very poor schooling, was available. Information about any special educational services the child may have received is important. If the student was appropriately served in regular educational programs in his native country, special education labeling should be considered here with much careful consideration.

The interpreter/translator can observe the child at home and in the community. Through their understanding of the culture and child rearing practices as well as the opportunity to work with a number of children over time they can give valuable input. One student may be doing poorly in school but is functioning as would be expected adaptively. Another may function at the same level at school and on tests but is also functioning at a lower developmental level at home and in the community. This information can best be obtained by a person who is also at home in the community involved.

Parents can also be a source of referrals but they are unlikely to refer a child who may be handicapped if they do not speak the language or understand the workings of the school system. The Dade-Monroe Child Find System has located many exceptional students who were being kept at home. Although the service area encompassing Miami and Key West has one-third Hispanic population, over half of Child Find cases were Hispanic.

When a community has a small population of a particular language group the interpreter/translator can assist child find efforts by preparing news releases for the language media, speaking to families, social groups and religious organizations and being available for discussion with families which have questions about the school system. These personnel can also assist with home visitations along with school social work staff.

UTILIZATION IN ASSESSMENT

Before an interpreted evaluation the examiner and interpreter/translator should become acquainted. The interpreter/translator for a particular language is likely to have to work with many different examiners throughout the service area. The examiner can be filled in on some basic cultural information about the student to be tested. The experienced interpreter/translator can also provide advance clues as to potential biasing factors, behavioral characteristics, and possible difficulties in test translation.

The examiner should be told of any changes in test wording that were agreed upon as part of the standard administration for the language group. Behavioral factors such as shyness or verbal passivity which may influence the student's scoring should be discussed in advance so that the examiner may take them into consideration in selecting test instruments that will be most appropriate for the student.

After the assessment has been completed, the interpreter/translator should present any noted areas of misunderstanding or item bias. The examiner is made aware of the interpreter/translators perceptions about the child. Did he or she seem as responsive as most children from similar background? Did he or she seem less able to communicate, reason or understand directions than would normally be expected? Did the child display emotional or behavioral problems that would not be expected? Conversely, were the emotional or behavioral observations what one might expect based on the child's culture or history?

Intelligence tests have the most significant impact on placement decisions as well as implications for the student's entire life. Possible biasing factors, besides those associated with language, include lack of exposure to the material, poor motivation, poor rapport and general unsuitability of the test used. The interpreter/translator can provide insight into all of these factors.

Trained personnel can avoid the use of words in directions or required responses that are not in the standard vocabulary of the student. Otherwise such words might be utilized due to direct translation of tests. Tests which have been translated into Spanish, for example, may not be normed at all or may not be normed on the same national or cultural group as the child being tested. When a minimum of two persons from the same background have agreed on the wording to be used, however, this should be considered a standardized practice and should not be changed for individual children.

When a child has entered school in this country and received all of his or her education in English it is appropriate to use achievement tests written in English. On the other hand, achievement levels of new entrants who have received all of their education in another language must be measured in that language. Appropriate achievement instruments may not be available and may have to be developed.

The interpreter/translator may perform the translation function in coordination with educators familiar with the subject matter needing assessment. Informal leveling tests can be developed. The interpreter/translator can suggest topics for reading level paragraphs and can note when systems and procedures for solving arithmetic problems differ from those used in this country.

It is also vital to have information on the previous grade placement of the student to compare with achievement level. Details of schooling such as age of first educational exposure and number of actual years in attendance can be obtained from the parents as part of the referral information.

When observational and informal measures are necessary, the examiner may wish to be accompanied by an interpreter/translator. They can follow the child through the school day including academic work, physical activities, peer interaction and response to authority. Specific concerns which were noted in the referral should be kept in mind. Some time should be left for the interpreter/translator to spend in conversation with the child. This will provide valuable information as to language skills and developmental level. Developed reading passages in the native language can be used at this time. In addition, the interpreter/translator can ask for the child's own reactions to the school situation and any problems that might be occurring.

The interpretation of test scores of minority children is a difficult task. The best assessment can be made when a variety of instruments is used that assess the child's functioning in a variety of situations. Ideally, the child's proficiency in language, health and developmental history, adaptive behavior and relation to peers must be assessed as well as test performance per se. The use of the interpreter/translator can help to provide as complete a picture of the child as is possible.

UTILIZATION IN
THE PLACEMENT PROCESS

Placement committees must be made up of a minimum of three persons. For student's who are not native speakers of English there should be at least one representative who speaks the native language of the parents and who can present culturally relevant information. The interpreter/translator can fulfill this role. It will be easy for this person to explain the assessment and placement process to the parents and to inform the committee of language and cultural factors that were noted. If other bilingual personnel are available this usage would not be necessary but could still be beneficial in cases which might be difficult to decide.

Parents should have the Individual Educational Program described to them in their own language and should be permitted to have input into the document. They also may have many questions about their child's school setting and handicapping condition.

UTILIZATION IN THE
PROVISION OF CULTURAL AWARENESS

Whenever there is an influx of new refugees into a community or even an established population of language minority families it is important that school personnel be aware of cultural factors which can impinge upon school performance. The interpreter/translator can fulfill a role of information giver that can avoid the unconscious perception in school personnel that differences are "handicaps". Cultural bias may enter whenever teachers and other school personnel are unaware of differences in opportunity to develop skills, attitudes towards authority, and educational systems.

Interpreter/translators can develop brochures about specific cultural factors, talk to parent and teacher groups, consult with school faculties and related agencies and respond to specific school needs. They can also assist in the development of curriculum changes which might be necessary to meet student needs.

All of the usages mentioned above rely on the designation of qualified personnel to fulfill the intended role and on the appropriate training of the interpreter/translator in each aspect of their job. With this in mind, interpreter/translators can enable school districts to provide the best possible services for the language minority handicapped.

REFERENCES

OAKLAND. T. (ED.) *Psychological and educational assessment of minority children.* New York, Brunner & Mazel, 1977.

OAKLAND. T. AND MATUSZEK. PAULA. Using tests in non-discriminatory assessment. *The School Psychology Digest,* 1977, *6,* 57-66.

SATTLER. E. (ED.) *The educator's dilemma: the adolescent with learning disabilities.* San Rafael, California, Academic Therapy, 1971.

State of Florida. *A resource manual for the development and evaluation of special programs for exceptional students. Vol. III-B. Evaluating the non-English speaking handicapped.* Tallahassee, Fla., Bureau of Education for Exceptional Students.

INTERCULTURAL COUNSELLING AND NONVERBAL BEHAVIOR

By Aaron Wolfgang
Department of Applied Psychology
The Ontario Institute
for Studies in Education and
The University of Toronto

INTRODUCTION

The United States is historically and presently an intercultural and interracial nation. There has been an almost constant flow of immigrants to the United States since its inception. Between World War II and 1972, over 14 million people have immigrated to the United States (Davis, 1974). Over the past two decades, in comparison to the host culture (white Anglo-Saxon), the flow of immigrants to the United States from nations with more diverse races, cultures and languages has been on the increase. The Government reported that in only ten short years from 1970 to 1980 there have been dramatic population shifts. Those of "Spanish origin" have increased 61%, the number of blacks, the nation's largest minority, increased by 17%, and lastly, the largest pecentage increase, 128%, was shown in the Asian and Pacific Islands category (Nelson, 1981). An even more dramatic population change has been reported on the more local levels. For instance, in South Florida, particularly in Dade County in 1950, there were 83% white, 13% black and 4% Hispanic out of a population of 495,000. By contrast, in 1980 only 44% of the population is white, 39% Hispanic and 15% black (Kelly, 1981).

Since the revolution 18 years ago, it has been estimated (Kurtines and Miranda, 1980) that over a half million Cuban-Americans reside in the greater Miami area (Dade County). Then too, recently about 125,000 more Cubans called Marielitos, who were said to be primarily convicts and psychiatric patients have landed in South Florida. No more than a decade ago it has been estimated that over 50,000 Haitians, mostly refugees, began arriving on the South Florida shores. Some 16,000 refugee children have been crowded into the classrooms of Dade County Public Schools (Kelly, 1981). In view of the faltering economic climate, competition for jobs and increased racial tensions, the socio-political situation is anything but stable. In this type of situation where immigrants from contrasting cultures, races and languages come in large numbers to urban centers and are seen as a threat to the existing socio-political balance of things, what often results is suspicion, unrest, and an unwelcome reception by those of the host culture.

Presented at "The Education of Ethnic Minority Immigrants Conference, December 13-16, 1981, Eden Roc Hotel, Miami Beach, Florida.

In immigrating to a foreign country it is normally the parents who make the decision. The children are powerless to do anything about it. They must come and stay as long as the parents stay whether they like it or not. They often find themselves in a helpless, unfriendly situation where they are not prepared to deal with the demands of the new school, peers, community and their parents. Within a short period of time these students are expected to speak English fluently, make new friends, learn new ways of behaving, and new learning and communicating styles. Such a situation with its demands for adaptation frequently results in a great deal of psychological stress for the students and their family.

One of the designated helpers in the school situation for the immigrant student from an ethnic minority background is the school counsellor. How prepared is the counsellor to help the students cope with the new demands of the school situation? Overall, in this paper the focus will be on issues dealing with factors that impede or facilitate communication between the school counsellor and the ethnic minority student in an urban school setting. An attempt will be made to look at the total communication process, with particular emphasis on the role and impact of nonverbal behavior and why it is important in an intercultural counselling situation. Also, how nonverbal behavior can be effectively used to facilitate the communication process, to match counsellor and students, and its relation to verbal behavior and culture will be discussed. Among other important issues to be dealt with will be the state of counsellor training, counsellor preparation, desirable qualities of an intercultural counsellor, and the state of research and theory in intercultural counselling. Intercultural counselling is defined in the broadest sense as a situation where the counsellor and client are of contrasting cultural backgrounds. In this paper the focus will be on the interaction in a school situation between a counsellor who is typically white, Anglo-Saxon and the client who comes from an ethnic minority group.

SOME HANDICAPS OF COUNSELLORS AND STUDENTS IN THE INTERCULTURAL COUNSELLING SITUATION

Counsellors and students are frequently not prepared for their encounter in the intercultural counselling situation (Wolfgang, 1975, 1981 a). The typical counsellor is probably white, middle-class, unilingual, unicultural, who is likely unaware of the minority students' learning and communication styles, nonverbal behaviors and values in specific social contexts. He/she most likely has no systematic training or preparation to help the ethnic minority students. In contrast, the ethnic minority students are probably lower to middle-class, bicultural, bilingual, poorly prepared like the counsellor for meeting the demands of the counselling situation. Both are often involuntarily put together in a very difficult sink or swim situation. Both must come to the realization that for the most part they are on their own and must rely on their own motivation and resources to make at least the initial encounter work. Sue (1977 b) shows how important the initial encounter is when considering that 50% of the ethnic minority clients don't return to the counsellor after the first session. In contrast, the rate of termination for Anglo-Saxon clients with Anglo-Saxon counsellors was only 30%. The onus is primarily on the intercultural counsellor, not on the client to make this initial encounter work.

Thus, the potential handicaps of counsellors attempting to help the ethnic minority students are many. It seems to me that just as the immigrant students undergo a great deal of stress in attempting to cope with their problems brought on by cultural conflicts, as well as a host of other factors, the intercultural counsellor may also be experiencing some stress in attempting to cope with the problems of being an intercultural counsellor. There are at least three main ways counsellors put in this situation can cope. Firstly, they can try to avoid dealing with ethnic minority students' personal, emotional and vocational problems by preoccupying themselves with administrative duties, that is, dealing with students only in a most perfunctory or superficial way. The counsellor may feel that it is up to the student to adjust and conform to the situation as soon as possible. This type of counsellor also prefers to associate with members of his/her own ethnic group and is suspicious of these "foreign" students with "foreign" values and "foreign" life styles. Such a counsellor would prefer that these students become Americanized as soon as possible, then their problems would be solved. Second, they can try to be like their ethnic minority students as much as possible, by trying to be a "buddy". They may even undermine the teachers or other counsellors and denounce their values and attitudes to the students. In this situation the counsellors can only alienate themselves from the staff of the school whose support may be needed to help the students. This type of counsellor may also be thought of as being "phony" by the ethnic minority students. Third, the counsellor can try to understand and see the value of the new American students' culture, lifestyle and values. This type of counsellor aspires to be culturally flexible, able to shift his/her frame of reference, accept cultural and racial differences and attempt to overcome ethnocentric tendencies. Also, this type of counsellor could see the strengths and weaknesses of the host culture and the culture of the ethnic minority students and advise the students on how to use the strengths of each to succeed in a wide variety of social situations. Intercultural counsellors can go through anyone or everyone of these stages or be fixed at one. It is hoped that most of them will aspire to be at stage three. Embodied in the third way of coping are some of the essential qualities of being an effective intercultural counsellor.

NONVERBAL BEHAVIOR, LANGUAGE AND CULTURE

The effective intercultural counsellor must be aware of the total communication process. He/she must be sensitized to the fact that communication occurs not only on the verbal, but also on the nonverbal level. Nonverbal behavior can be described as behavior that transcends written or spoken words (Harrison, 1974). The study of nonverbal behavior can be divided into 3 areas: proxemics, kinesics and paralinguistics. *Proxemics,* a word coined by Hall (1969), refers to how individuals use space in relation to one another or to objects in the environment.

How close individuals stand in relation to one another or arrange objects in the environment has been shown by Hall (1969) and others (Baxter, 1971; Aiello and Jones, 1971) to be culturally determined. Baxter (1971), in studying interpersonal spacing of different ethnic or groups in natural settings (The Zoo), found Mexican groups stood closest, blacks stood most distant and Anglos were intermediate. Aiello and Jones (1971) found that patterns of interpersonal spacing among ethnic groups are acquired early in life. In their study, first and second grade middle class white students maintained more interpersonal space on the play ground than lower class blacks and Puerto Ricans. Willis (1966) found that when whites spoke to blacks they maintained greater interpersonal distance than when whites spoke to other whites. In a study by Wolfgang (1980 a) it was shown that white Anglo-Saxons kept more social distance from West Indians than from white Anglo-Saxons displaying facial expressions reflecting the fundamental emotions. Social distance has also been shown to be a reflection of attitudes people have toward one another. Hall (1969) noted that interpersonal threat or uneasiness results in increased spatial distance. Several studies have shown that individuals will maintain greater social distance from those identified as having a social stigma, or marginal status in society than normal peers (Wolfgang, 1973 a; Wolfgang and Wolfgang, 1971).

The second area of nonverbal behavior is *kinesics*, a term coined by Birdwhistell (1970), that refers to patterns of body movement. The popular term for kinesics is "body language" which includes such behaviors as facial expressions, gestures, posture, head nods, etc. Birdwhistell (1970) maintains that body language is culturally determined and that although he has been searching for over 15 years he has found no gesture or body motion has the same social meaning in all cultures. Recently, Rosenthal and his collaborators (1979) in sampling about 2,300 people outside the continental United States, from 20 nations (e.g., Hong Kong, Mexico, Canada, etc.), found that individuals from nations that were most culturally and linguistically similar to the United States, (e.g. Canada, New Zealand, Australia, Britain, Ireland, etc.), did better on the PONS Test. This is a test that assesses an individual's ability to correctly identify various nonverbal signals shown in face, body, voice, or in combination of a female from the U.S. culture. However, the U.S. samples outperformed the English speaking samples from Britain, Canada, etc. on the nonverbal test. This seems to indicate that some of the non-verbal stimuli on the PONS Test were culture specific to the U.S.

Para Linguistics is the third nonverbal area of study. It refers to the extra-verbal elements that are associated with speech, e.g. tone of voice, pauses, hesitations, errors in speech, rate of speech, etc. Voice tone, like social distance, can be an indicator of attitude. For instance, it has been reported that in a simulated interracial interaction situation friendliness of voice tone of white was related to friendliness of behavior toward blacks (Weitz, 1972). Crystal (1975) in reviewing paralinguistic effects in cross-cultural studies notes that it is not always easy to see when someone from another culture is being upset, or embarrassed. In fact, it is a common reaction to misinterpret the para-language of people from other cultures as being rude, sarcastic or embarrassed by their tone of voice. For instance, Crystal (1975) notes that in some oriental languages giggling normally reflects embarrassment among adults, whereas in English it may relate to humour or be considered childish.

Nonverbal behavior can be characterized as operating normally at the unconscious or unawareness level (Argyle, 1975; Wolfgang, 1974). Unlike verbal behavior, it is difficult to manipulate or falsify since we have little direct training on how to use it effectively. Nonverbal behavior has a greater impact than words particularly in revealing emotions, attitudes, and expressing different degrees of warmth — coldness toward others (Gazda, 1973; Mehrabian, 1972). It also plays an important role in identifying the presence and intensity of anxiety (Waxer, 1977) and for communicating empathy, respect and genuineness in the counselling situation (Tepper and Haase, 1978). Nonverbal behavior can replace, modify, clarify and underscore speech. Unlike speech, however, it is more limited in conveying logical, sophisticated or creative ideas. It is more difficult to interpret nonverbal behavior because it is more ambiguous than speech; there is no common dictionary where you can look up the meaning of a particular gesture, posture, or frown without knowing the social context or culture in which this behavior occurred. Thus, nonverbal behavior is important because there is much room for misinterpretation of its meaning without, for example, knowing the cultural backgrounds of the people involved.

How is culture related to nonverbal behavior? Culture can be viewed as an organized body of rules concerning the ways in which individuals in a given population should communicate with each other, think about themselves and their environment and behave toward one another and objects in the environment (Levine, 1973, p. 4). The rules set down in a culture allow for individual differences and some flexibility in behavior. Cultures can be classified in terms of nonverbal behavior, e.g. contact vs. noncontact (Montagu, 1971), monochronic vs. polychronic or high context vs. low context cultures (Hall, 1976). People from monochronic, low context oriented cultures, like the U.S. and Canada, like to deal with only one thing at a time, and one person at a time. They tend not to be very involved with one another, don't expect much from others, resist self examination and their messages tend to be explicit with the words carrying most of the information. In contrast, polychronic, high context, oriented cultures such as Japan, middle eastern, Mediterranean and Latin American cultures people are more highly involved with one another, and are seldom alone. Interaction in these cultures may occur with several people at a time; people expect to be understood, individuality is minimized at the expense of the group and less information is contained in the verbal part of the message and more in the social context (Hall, 1976). Culture, like nonverbal behavior, is elusive, normally out of awareness, difficult to erase or control and has a potent influence in intercultural communication.

Montagu (1971) suggests that there may be *national, cultural* and *social class* differences in the ways nonverbal behaviors are expressed. Those who speak Anglo-Saxon derived languages would be more likely to come from a non-contact oriented culture than those speaking Latin derived languages. Thus, it would be expected that people from contact oriented cultures such as those from Latin America, Mexico, Puerto Rico, Italy, Portugal and Spain, would tend to touch each other more often, gesture more, and space themselves closer than

Anglo-Saxon British, Americans or Canadians. This behavior might lead to Anglo-Saxons being stereotyped as "cold", and "unemotional" (Montagu, 1971). In doing the research for the film "The Italian in Transition" (Wolfgang, 1973 b) Italian students and their parents complained when being interviewed that English Canadians appeared to be "cold" and "distant" people. Individuals interviewed from Portugal also felt that Anglo-Saxons tended to "lack warmth", were "closed mouthed", and "distant". Thus, people from different cultures practice nonverbal ethnocentrism. They believe that their nonverbal modes of expression are superior and universal and those from cultures different from their own are inferior and inappropriate when looked at from only their cultural perspective. These stereotypes can lead to misunderstanding and tension between groups with different orientations toward interpersonal communications. Montagu (1971) also suggests that the higher the person's social class the less tactile or contact behavior would be shown in interpersonal situations. This could also be another source of misunderstanding when people of different socio-economic classes interact.

By playing up the importance of nonverbal behavior I don't mean to minimize the importance of speech. It's just that our culture is so word oriented that we tend to forget that there are other important channels of expressive behavior that play an important role in human communication. Counsellors like others have been taught in school and in their training that the written and spoken word is supreme. As a result the impact of nonverbal behavior and its effects on others has been largely ignored.

NONVERBAL BEHAVIOR RESEARCH:
IMPLICATIONS FOR TRAINING AND
COUNSELLOR-CLIENT MATCHING

There is an important body of research in the area of nonverbal behavior that has some implications for training and for matching intercultural counsellors and their students. To answer the question of whether there were cultural differences in basic communication between and among blacks and whites both LaFrance and Mayo (1976) and Erickson (1979) studied listening and speaking behavior. LaFrance and Mayo (1976) discovered through intensive film analysis that gaze behavior among blacks was different than among whites, in that, for example, blacks while speaking tended to look at the listener continuously while whites looked intermittingly. Erickson (1979) took the research a step further by studying slow motion analysis of films dealing with listening and speaking behavior between blacks and whites in the interracial job interview and school counselling situation. He found that there were quite different styles of listening and speaking which could be related to cultural differences between blacks and whites in the timing of kinesic activity (e.g. eye contact, head nods). Erickson discusses how these differences put both groups at odds with one another since white counsellors or interviewers may look like they are talking down to blacks, and blacks may appear to be not listening or understanding the white speaker. This type of research has many implications for intercultural counselling. For instance, is there a basic difference in listening and speaking style between white Anglo-Saxon counsellors and Latin or "Hispanic" students? In a research study in Canada, it was discovered that black West Indians (adults and students) wer emore sensitive and accurate in reading the faces of white Anglo-Saxons displaying the fundamental emotions (e.g. happy, anger, sadness, etc.) than even West Indian faces. In contrast, Anglo-Saxon students made significantly more errors in identifying the fundamental emotions expressed on West Indian than white Anglo-Saxon faces. These faces were exposed on slides for only one second (Wolfgang, 1980 a). In another study, it was shown that West Indian adolescent students living in the West Indies showed more approach behavior toward significant others (e.g. mother, father, teacher, friend) than Canadian born students (Wolfgang and Weiss, 1980). Lastly, in a field study, it was shown that West Indian students were contact oriented among peers (Wolfgang, 1980 b) and used different nonverbal signals than Canadians for obtaining attention and making eye contact with authority figures (Wolfgang, 1979a). These basic differences in the use of eye contact and sensitivity to emotional expressions, etc., can add up to creating misunderstanding in the intercultural counselling situation if they are not understood by the counsellor or student.

It seems that we need more basic knowledge of how, for instance, the white Anglo-Saxon intercultural counsellors communicate (e.g. similarities in listening behavior, eye contact, etc.) and how their ethnic minority clients communicate in specific social situations. We also need to know how these similarities and differences manifest themselves in producing congruence or incongruence in the counsellor-student interaction. Collett (1971) devised a programme to train English students from Oxford to behave like Arab students on several nonverbal dimensions (e.g. eye contact, touching, social distance, smiling, etc.) at the appropriate moments during a conversation. In brief, he found that Arab students prefer (e.g., be friends, share flat) English students who behave most like themselves over those who continued to act like Englishmen. Dabbs (1969) based his experiments on the premise that individuals appear to communicate better when they are more similar to one another. Dabbs had an actor (confederate) interview two students. The actor was instructed to mimic the nonverbal behaviors (e.g., posture, personal mannerisms, gestures, etc.) of one and not the other. The one that was mimicked reported viewing the confederate as more like themselves, thought more like them, "identified" more with them, was more persuasive and evaluated them more favorably than the non-mimicked interviewees. This finding was consistent with Collett's results (1971). In a study by Josefowitz reported by Mall (1981) in The Los Angeles Times, she found executives hire and promote people who look and act like themselves. She concluded that people have a tendency to 'clone' one another. Rosenthal (1979) found when individuals were of a similar cultural and/or language group they could more accurately identify the non-verbal behaviors of a person from that cultural group than individuals from progressively more dissimilar cultural and/or linguistic groups. Then, too, Erickson (1979) as previously reported, showed that in school counselling and job interviews timing for nonverbal activity (e.g. head nods, eye contact) in listening and speaking behavior was similar among whites and among blacks but was dissimilar between whites and blacks.

In short, these studies suggest that individuals appear to like or are attracted to one another more when they show similar nonverbal behaviors. Also, the research indicates that individuals are better able to understand the nonverbal behaviors of those from a similar race, culture and linguistic group. These studies underscore the importance of similarity and timing of nonverbal behaviors for good interpersonal communication. It is important for intercultural counsellors to be aware of how differences in nonverbal behavior can obstruct or sabotage the intercultural encounter. However, we cannot look at nonverbal behavior per se as a simple homogeneous variable in attempting to match counsellors and clients. For example, Rokeach, Smith and Evans' (1960) research point up the importance of belief and value congruence over visible characteristics such as race. Thus, nonverbal behavior must be seen in the context of interacting with other variables such as verbal behavior, culture, personality, sex, socio-economic status, age, race, value orientation, and the social context. If we keep the complexity of the situation and these variables in mind we are unlikely to treat the training of intercultural counsellors in a simple minded way. The key is to see in what situation, with what type of problem these variables become important in the intercultural interaction.

On the basis of the research on nonverbal congruence and the models of belief and value congruence, it is important to look into the possibility of training counsellors to model or be aware of the crucial or critical nonverbal behaviors and value orientations of their clients in intercultural communication situations. For instance, can we train white Anglo-Saxon counsellors to be like Cubans or Haitians? Or train minority counsellors to be like their white Anglo-Saxon clients on certain critical dimensions similar to what Collett (1971) did? Or use the culture assimilator approach as developed by Fiedler, Mitchell and Triandis (1971)? The culture assimilator is a self administered programmed learning experience designed to expose members of one culture to such things as some basic concepts, attitudes, customs, role perceptions and values of another culture. There have been several assimilators developed (e.g., Arab, Thai, Hondouras, Greek, etc.) primarily for individuals working abroad. The authors report that the initial results are promising in that the programme has improved the effectiveness and satisfaction of those trained with this method. Perhaps nonverbal assimilators could also be developed. In using training approaches such as the ones mentioned one must be careful not to stereotype the clients into nice neat narrow cultural packages. Programs like this might be directed toward specific intercultural situations such as counselling. The trainer and user may have to continuously modify or adapt these approaches in being sensitive to such things as the client's culture, age, sex, personality, socioeconomic class, etc. Keeping these factors in mind these approaches seem like worthy areas of training and research.

The intercultural counsellor in using any approach might keep in mind Kluckholn and Murray's (1953) basic principle: that in some ways we are all alike (universal), share some common qualities with others (as culture) and in some ways we are like no other persons (individual-unique). In the intercultural counselling situation there are universal qualities that bind us together that transcend culture like the fundamental emotions (Eibl-Eibesfeldt, 1979; Izard,

1979), as well as having cultural and unique qualities. It is wise for the intercultural counsellor to keep these similarities and differences in mind to avoid undergeneralizations (cultural insensitivity) and overgeneralizations (stereotyping) about their clients. Research for the most part has ignored both universal and unique qualities of behavior and focused more on contrasting groups (Sundberg, 1981).

TIPS ON USING NONVERBAL BEHAVIOR

What are some specific ways nonverbal behavior can be utilized in the intercultural counselling situation? Nonverbal behavior can be used to help make a positive first impression. The importance of nonverbal behavior in establishing initial rapport is underscored by Waxer (1979) and in a book by Zunin and Zunin (1972). It is important to be aware of your nonverbal behavior particularly in greeting and parting. The smile is part of our innate equipment (Eibl-Eibesfeldt, 1979). All members of the human species are capable of expressing it. The smile I found is contagious; if you show it you will most likely receive it in return. It generates positive emotions and positive feeling if communicated in an honest and genuine manner. Several years ago in Jamaica the government had a campaign to encourage Jamaicans to use their smile more particularly to the tourists to make a positive first impression. Unless you have a positive attitude toward your client then it is unlikely that positive body language will show itself unless you are a good actor. Students who are bilingual are particularly sensitive to nonverbal behavior to make themselves understood and for understanding others. In the initial encounter the intercultural counsellor needs to be aware of such basics as listening and speaking behavior. He/she needs to check out if the basic communication styles are the same. That is, do the Latin or Haitian students show continuous eye contact while listening and vary their eye contact while speaking as white Anglo-Saxons appear to do. If not, then there might be misunderstanding right from the start. One also has to be cautious of how eye contact is maintained in relation to authority figures. Avoidance of direct eye contact in relation to authority figures as counsellors has been reported to be found in many West African cultures and practised by many black Americans (Johnson, 1971) Chicanos, native American and Puerto Ricans (Rosenfeld and Civikly, 1976). Teachers and principals have reprimanded ethnic minority students for not looking them in the eye when in fact the students thought they were showing them respect (Wolfgang, 1977). If the intercultural counsellor wants to avoid making gross errors in the initial encounter he/she might do well to check out their impressions with their new American students. Ask the students, for example, to role play how they would expect to be greeted. You might also try modelling and mirroring the listening and speaking behavior of your immigrant students and see how responsive they are. The intercultural counsellor could develop a catalogue of nonverbal behaviors to be used at the appropriate times with students of different cultural backgrounds. Likewise, the culturally competent counsellor could also make their clients aware of the basic communication styles of Anglo-white Americans in different situations (e.g. classroom, with peers, etc.) where common misunderstandings might occur. For instance, since the job market is so competitive the counsellor might make the ethnic minority students aware of the acceptable nonverbal behaviors in the job interview, such as be on time, dress neatly, smile appropriately, show good listening skills, show confidence, etc. (Wolfgang, 1978, 1981 b). Also it is important for the students to be aware of how their ethnic minority group is stereotyped by personnel managers when going for the job interview. For instance, West Indians were stereotyped as being "arrogant" and having a "chip" on their shoulders (Wolfgang, 1981 b). By knowing the stereotypes that exist students can work on overcoming them. It might also be fruitful for the intercultural counsellors to assess how students from different cultural groups stereotype them. If the stereotypes are negative it might color their first impressions toward the counsellor.

Other important considerations in the initial encounter are to practise patience. That is, allow the student whose first language is not English time to respond in the counselling situation. Americans frequently have problems dealing with silent time. We are time oriented and like things to move quickly and efficiently. Teachers of students with English as a second language have told me that one of their main problems is in interrupting their students and not giving them a chance to take time to think through their answers. Often times new American students who are just learning English lack self confidence and therefore hesitate to speak up.

If the intercultural counsellor wants to check out the power of nonverbal behavior and get in touch with their cultural norms in different situations then they might try out a few experiments. One is to go to the head of the line where a popular movie is playing while people have been lined up for an hour. Also, while in a movie house where there are rows and rows of empty seats sit next to someone in one of those empty rows. In a similar vein sit next to someone on an uncrowded beach as was done to me in southern Italy, or sit at someone's table in an uncrowded restaurant. Try walking up to a stranger and putting your hands on the person's arm while asking directions, or try to get someone's attention by using the paralinguistic expression, "psst, psst" as was done in Trinidad-Tobago, or clap your hands to get someone's attention as was done in Barbados and Jamaica (Wolfgang, 1979 a). Come three-quarters of an hour late for an appointment and don't offer any explanations. Bump into someone on the street and say "thank you" instead of "excuse me". When introduced to someone for the first time shake and then hold the person's hand for at least fifteen seconds. In meeting a man from Greece whom I hadn't seen for a long while, my hand was held for almost a minute after the handshake. This made me feel quite uncomfortable. Maybe he was doing an experiment with me. Notice the reactions of the people when doing your experiments. Are they amused, confused or annoyed with you?

It is important for the intercultural counsellor to experience other cultures with different forms of nonverbal expressions (Wolfgang, 1981 b). This can be done by visiting the homes of your ethnic minority students. Notice how they greet you, entertain you and say goodbye. How similar or different is it from what you are accustomed to? To be an effective intercultural counsellor it is important to be aware of the lifestyle of your students and their families, by participating in some of their community activities such as folk dance, films, food, sports, religious events, etc. To reflect the ethnic minority mix of the school the intercultural counsellor can decorate his/her office with posters showing scenes from different countries. Travel agencies and consulates would be happy to supply these materials. The office in which you greet students reflects your awareness and sensitivity regarding their cultural backgrounds. If you have a great many ethnic minority students from many different countries you might rotate your posters.

INTERCULTURAL COUNSELLING —
STATE OF THE ART

Up to this point the importance of nonverbal behavior in intercultural communication has been underscored. There are other important concerns that also need to be considered in intercultural counselling. For instance, what theoretical guidelines are there to follow to provide a framework for the intercultural counsellor? Does the research in this field help guide the counsellor in what approach or counselling style to use? Are there proper training facilities for intercultural counsellors?

Recently there has been a spate of books, government reports and journals devoting special issues to intercultural counselling, (e.g. Atkinson, Morten and Sue, 1979; Bedal, 1977; Levine and Padilla, 1980; Marsella and Pedersen, 1981; Pedersen, Draguns, Lonner and Trimble, 1981; Sue, 1977 (a); Sue 1981, and Samuda and Crawford, 1980). Most of these works were published in the United States. Overall, they deal with a variety of subjects ranging from counselling specific minority groups, research considerations, to training and models for intercultural counselling. The fact that these works were published within the past few years reflects the growing interest and pressing need for information in this field that for too long has been neglected.

Regarding the sophistication and utility of theories and models in intercultural counselling, the fact of the matter is there is no one broad sophisticated theoretical approach or model readily available to the intercultural counsellor to guide him/her in the intercultural counselling situation to deal with personal-emotional problems of students. To compound the matter even further, the more traditional well-developed theories tend to be blind to culture and to the social situation. These theories were developed from experiences with white Anglo-Saxon adults in a therapeutic one-to-one situation. They are quite ethnocentric in that their goals are based on white Anglo-Saxon middle-class values (e.g. talk out problems, come to individual decisions, etc.). These theories assume that their approach has universal qualities and can apply to any individual in any culture of any age, sex or social class.

In recent years, the authors of the books mentioned previously, and others, have attempted to counter the ethnocentric approach embedded in traditional counselling theories. They have pointed out how these approaches can have potential negative effects when counselling goals run counter to the values of the individuals they are supposed to help. Some writers have developed mini-models making specific suggestions on how to deal with a specific minority under certain specific conditions. There are a variety of writers who sensitize us to issues in counselling Chinese Americans (Sue, 1977 (b), 1981); American blacks (Vontress, 1981); Latinos (Ruiz and Padilla, 1979), and Asian Americans (Kitano and Matsushima, 1981). Although these writers have important things to say about intercultural counselling none of them have a research foundation on which to base their models and suggestions of how to counsel specific minority groups. In fact, we might even say that these writers unwittingly could lead us to stereotyping ethnic minorities by not allowing for individual differences.

In knowing the potential hazards in using the western based theories and models, what are intercultural counsellors to do for a framework to guide them? Assuming that intercultural counsellors have a working knowledge of theories of counselling and an appreciation for cultural differences, then one might suggest that they adopt an eclectic approach. This does not mean that counsellors should unsystematically adopt techniques or goals from several approaches without any rhyme or reason but rather that they should develop a consistent systematic personal approach (Hansen, Warner & Smith, 1980) that is tested and modified on a case-to-case basis. The intercultural counsellor, when using particular counselling strategies or techniques, ought to be sensitive to such things as the client's cultural background, sex, socioeconomic status, the life style, values, nonverbal behavior and relationships to family, peer groups and to authority figures.

The state of research in intercultural counselling can be summed up in a few words: fragmentary, disjointed, filled with many methodological problems and leaving many crucial questions unanswered (e.g., what is the relationship between cultural variables and outcome in intercultural counselling?). There doesn't seem to be anyone in the field of intercultural counselling that has a systematic research program. This includes those who talk and write about intercultural counselling strategies and techniques as well as those who propose models. The data base in this field is meagre and piecemeal. In fact, one would be hard put to find any body of research that deals with cultural variables in an ongoing intercultural counselling encounter. Most of the research comes from the United States and a trickle from Canada and Britain. What does the research accomplished thus far in this field suggest to the intercultural counsellor? Does it provide any guidelines?

There is a large body of research in the area of interracial counselling that deals with clients' preferences for the race of the counsellor. The body of knowledge in this area centers mainly around white middle-class counsellors and black students. Presently, there is little research that deals with effects of the Latin or West Indian counsellors on white Anglo-Saxon students. There are examples of studies that show that black students prefer black counsellors and undergo more self exploration with black counsellors (e.g., Banks, Berenson and Carkhuff, 1967). Atkinson and Maruyama and Matsui (1978) report Asian American clients prefer a more directive style of counselling than nondirective and find Asian American counsellors more credible and approachable than Caucasian counsellors. Haitians on the other hand responded well to client centered therapy for personal, vocational and social problems (Seligman, 1977). Then, too, there are studies that show the counsellors' race is not a significant variable. Some research showed it was the intrinsic human qualities of the counsellor that was more important than race (e.g., Backner, 1970). Two other studies showed that the degree of self exploration or counsellor preference was not affected by the race of the counsellor (Greene, 1974; Olivarez, 1975). These are but examples of the contradictory nature of the findings when we look at race per se as a simple homogeneous variable. Language compatability was shown to be a critical variable between white high school counsellors and their American black students. It was shown (Schumacher, Banikiotes and Banikiotes, 1972) that white high school counsellors could understand only 15% of the vocabulary words most commonly used by their black students and the black students could understand only 50% of the words frequently used by their counsellors. One wonders to what extent this condition exists in the American schools between immigrant West Indian students who speak Patois or Creole and their white counsellors. This would seem to be a worthy area of research.

What opportunities are available for the training of intercultural counsellors? In terms of the universities in the United States there are not any academic degree programs specifically designed to train counsellors in intercultural counselling skills (Pedersen, 1981). It seems that one of the main potential avenues of training is through in-service training programs. However, this is not a very consistent or common happening. Neither is there much happening in this area at professional meetings or conferences for intercultural counsellors. In fact, there are not very many well trained specialists in the area of intercultural counselling to train counsellors. This is an appalling state of affairs when considering the racial and cultural diversity of student bodies across the United States. Thus, overall, counsellors in this field are pretty much on their own to find avenues for receiving proper information and training in this field. Because of the general lack of research interest in this area we have no real way of fully assessing to what extent counsellors are hurting or helping ethnic minority students.

Considering the present state of affairs, what is the intercultural counsellor to do? Firstly, there are the books and articles listed that were previously mentioned in this paper that can sensitize the counsellor to ways of avoiding particular counselling approaches with particular clients that might be counter-productive. The counselling situation becomes more hazardous and difficult as the cultural, linguistic, nonverbal, socioeconomic and value differences between the counsellor and client increase. In this case counsellors must be sure to firstly, be aware of their own cultural values and nonverbal behaviors and how they could be productive or counter-productive with certain ethnic minority groups in the intercultural encounter. Then, the counsellors would be in a better position to understand the cultural values and nonverbal behaviors of their clients. Once the counsellor knows his/her communication styles from the initial greeting to parting and how these values and nonverbal behaviors operate, then the counsellor knows at least what the client is seeing and how these factors could overlap or run counter to the client's communication styles and values.

Initially, the task is to establish some synchrony and congruence between the counsellor and client. This is only possible if counsellors are willing to shift their cultural frame of reference, accept differences and overcome their ethnocentric tendencies (i.e., judge the client in terms of his/her standards). Of course, it would be ideal if the client was able to manifest these qualities. The importance of sharing similar frames of reference, sharing some similar cultural experiences and overcoming ethnocentrism for ease of intercultural communication is underscored by Szalay (1981) in his process model of intercultural communication.

What are some other ways the intercultural counsellor can help himself/herself be an effective intercultural communicator? Awareness that the field of intercultural counselling is a multidisciplinary one. There is no one discipline that holds a monopoly in this field. So it is important to be aware of some of the relevant works in the different disciplines. For example, Hall's models of culture in his books Beyond Culture (1976), The Hidden Dimension (1969) and The Silent Language (1959) are primary examples. In the field of intercultural communication The Samovar, Porter and Jain (1981) book on understanding intercultural communication is very readable for the beginner in this field. In the area of nonverbal behavior the book edited by Wolfgang (1979 b) brings together some of the latest thoughts of distinguished contributors who come from a variety of disciplines such as education, ethology, anthropology, psychology and psychiatry. They discuss issues and the intercultural aspects of nonverbal behavior in teaching, counselling and therapy. These are but a few examples of the interdisciplinary nature of this field.

Furthermore, the counsellor must keep a keen eye for courses, seminars, conferences, training programs, etc. when they do become available. For instance, The Society for Intercultural Education, Training and Research (SIETAR) has yearly conferences and continuous workshops as well as publications in the field of intercultural communications. They also have their own International Journal of Intercultural Relations. Other examples of journals that may have articles of interest to the intercultural counsellor are The International and Intercultural Communication Annual, Hispanic Journal of Behavioral Sciences, Journal of Cross-Cultural Psychology, Personnel and Guidance Journal, Journal of Counseling Psychology, and The School Guidance Worker.

The intercultural counsellor may need some help from the school boards, universities, the state and federal governments. They could help by providing training facilities, research, resource materials, and time off for professional development. The well trained and sensitive intercultural counsellor can develop preventative programs by offering special tips for teachers in dealing with the common problems of some of their ethnic minority students. The counsellor can also help create a positive atmosphere in the multicultural school by developing orientation programs, cultural appreciation courses and communication labs for the ethnic minority students to help them master their new environment and to feel positive about their cultural and/or racial identity.

CONCLUSION

The intercultural counsellor of the 80's must be a resourceful, risk-taking and imaginative person when considering the state of affairs in this field. I guess the same could be said for the ethnic minority students in coming to an urban school and community where the socio-political climate is far from optimal for fostering personal growth, self worth and academic achievement. What has been said about the role and impact of nonverbal behavior in intercultural counselling can be applied to teachers and educators in general who are in an intercultural environment. Although nonverbal behavior has been shown to be a very silent language it is also a very powerful language in intercultural communication. It is a language that educators must be aware of, sensitive to, and know how to use along with verbal language to be effective intercultural communicators in and outside of the school environment.

REFERENCES

AIELLO, J.R., JONES, S.E. Field study of the proxemic behavior of young school children in three subcultural groups. *Journal of Personality and Social Psychology,* 1971, *19,* 351-356.

ARGYLE, M. *Bodily Communication.* London: Methuen & Company Ltd., 1975.

ATKINSON, D.R., MORTEN, G. AND SUE, D.W. *Counselling American Minorities: A Cross-Cultural Perspective.* Dubuque: Wm. C. Brown Company, publishers, 1979.

ATKINSON, D., MARUYAMA, M. AND MATSUI, S. Effects of counselor race and counseling approach on Asian Americans' perceptions of counselor credibility and utility. *Journal of Counseling Psychology,* 1978, *5,* 76-83.

BACKNER, B.L. Counseling Black Students: Any Place for Whitey? *Journal of Higher Education,* 1970, *41,* 630-637.

BANKS, G., BERENSON, B.G. AND CARKHUFF, R. The effects of counsellor race and training upon counseling process with Negro clients in the initial interview. *Journal of Clinical Psychology,* 1967, *23,* 70-72.

BAXTER, J.C. Interpersonal spacing in natural settings. *Sociometry,* 1970, *33,* 444-456.

BEDAL, C.L. (ED.), Counselling in a Multicultural Society. *The School Guidance Worker,* 1977, *3,* 1-68.

BIRDWHISTELL, R.L. *Kinesics and context.* Philadelphia: University of Pennsylvania Press, 1970.

COLLETT, P. Training Englishmen in the Nonverbal Behavior of Arabs. *International Journal of Psychology,* 1971, *6,* 209-215.

CRYSTAL, D. *Paralinguistics.* In J. Benthall and T. Polhemus (Eds.), The Body as a Medium of Expression. New York: E. P. Dutton and Company, Inc., 1975.

DABBS, J.M., JR. Similarity of Gestures and Interpersonal Influence. Proceedings of *The 77th Annual Convention of The American Psychological Association,* 1969, *4,* 337-338.

DAVIS, K. The migrations of human populations. *Scientific American,* September 1974, 93-105.

EIBL-EIBESFELDT, I. *Universals in Human Expressive Behavior.* In A. Wolfgang (Ed.), Nonverbal Behavior: Applications and Cultural Implications. New York: Academic Press, 1979.

ERICKSON, F. *Some cultural sources of miscommunication of interracial interviews.* In A. Wolfgang (Ed.), Nonverbal Behavior: Applications and Cultural Implications. New York: Academic Press, 1979.

FIEDLER, F., MITCHELL, T. AND TRIANDIS, H. The cultural assimilator: An approach to cross-cultural training. *Journal of Applied Psychology,* 1971, *55,* 95-102.

GAZDA, G.M. *Human relations development: A manual for educators.* Boston: Allyn and Bacon, Inc., 1973.

GREENE, J.R. *Interactive effects of counsellor race and level of client-self exploration during the initial interview.* Unpublished doctoral dissertation, Georgia State University, 1974.

HALL, E.T. *Beyond Culture.* Garden City, New York: Doubleday and Company, Inc., 1976.

HALL, E.T. *The Hidden Dimension.* Garden City, New York: Doubleday and Company, Inc., 1969.

HALL, E.T. *The Silent Language.* Garden City, New York: Doubleday and Company, Inc., 1959.

HANSEN, J.C., WARNER, R.W. AND SMITH, E.J. (EDS.), *Group counselling: Theory and Process.* Second edition. Chicago: Rand McNally College Publishing Company, 1980.

HARRISON, R.P. *Beyond words: An introduction to nonverbal communication.* New Jersey: Prentice-Hall, 1974.

IZARD, C. *Facial Expression, Emotion and Motivation.* In A. Wolfgang (Ed.), Nonverbal Behavior: Applications and Cultural Implications. New York: Academic Press, 1979.

JOHNSON, K.R. Black kinesics: Some nonverbal communication patterns in the black culture. *The Florida FL Reporter,* 1971, 17-20, 57.

KELLY, J. Trouble in Paradise. *Time,* November 23, 1981, 28-41.

KITANO, H.L. AND MATSUSHIMA, N. *Counseling Asian Americans.* In P. Pedersen, J. Draguns, W. Lonner and J. Trimble (Eds.), Counselling Across Cultures, 1981.

KLUCKHOHN, C. AND MURRAY, H.A. (EDS.), *Personality in nature, society and culture.* New York: Alfred A. Knopf, 1953.

KURTINES, W.M., AND MIRANDA, L. Differences in self and family role perception among acculturating Cuban-American college students: Implications for etiology of family disruption among migrant groups. *International Journal of Intercultural Relations,* 1980, *4,* 167-184.

LAFRANCE, M., AND MAYO, C. Racial differences in gaze behavior during conversation. *Journal of Personality and Social Psychology,* 1976, *33,* 547-552.

LEVINE, R.A. *Culture, Behavior and Personality.* Chicago: Aldine Publishing Company, 1973.

MALL, J. About Women. *Los Angeles Times,* January 11, 1981, Part VII, p. 8.

MARSELLA, A.J. AND PEDERSEN, P. (EDS.), *Cross-cultural Counseling and Psychotherapy,* Toronto: Pergamon Press, 1981.

MEHRABIAN, A. *Nonverbal Behavior.* New York: Aldine-Atherton, 1972.

MONTAGU, A. *Touching.* New York: Harper and Row Publishers, 1971.

NELSON, B. Spanish-origin residents up 61%, blacks 17% in U.S. *Los Angeles Times,* February 24, 1981, p. 1, 16.

OLIVAREZ, C.L. *An analysis of the influence of race, sex, and skin pigmentation on student preference for potential counsellors.* Unpublished doctoral dissertation, Michigan State University, 1975.

PEDERSEN, P. *The intercultural training of mental health professionals.* Western Psychological Association meeting, Los Angeles, April, 1981.

PEDERSEN, P., DRAGUNS, J.G., LONNER, W.J. AND TRIMBLE, J.E. (EDS.), *Counseling Across Cultures.* The University of Hawaii Press, 1981.

ROKEACH, M., SMITH, P. AND EVANS, R.I. *Two kinds of prejudice or one?* In M. Rokeach (Ed.), The open and closed mind. New York: Basic Books, 1960.

ROSENFELD, L.B., AND CIVIKLY, J.M. *With words unspoken: The nonverbal experience.* New York: Holt, Rinehart and Winston, 1976.

ROSENTHAL, R., HALL, J.A., ARCHER, D., DIMATTEO, R.M., AND ROGERS, P.L. *Measuring sensitivity to nonverbal communication: The Pons Test.* In A. Wolfgang (Ed.), Nonverbal Behavior: Applications and Cultural Implications. New York: Academic Press, 1979.

RUIZ, R.A., AND PADILLO, A.M. *Counseling Latinos.* In D. Atkinson, G. Morten, and D. Sue (Eds.), Counseling American Minorities. Dubuque, Iowa: Wm. C. Brown Company Publishers, 1979.

SELIGMAN, L. Haitians: A neglected minority. *Personnel and Guidance Journal,* 1977, *55,* 409-411.

SAMOVAR, L.A., PORTER, R.E. AND JAIN, N.C. *Understanding Intercultural Communication.* Belmont, California: Wadsworth Publishing Company, 1981.

SAMUDA, R.J. AND CRAWFORD, D.H. *Testing, Assessment, Counselling and Placement of Ethnic Minority Students.* Toronto: Ontario Institute for Studies in Education, 1980.

SCHUMACHER, L.C., BANIKIOTES, P.G. AND BANIKIOTES, F.G. Language compatibility and minority group counselling. *Journal of Counseling Psychology,* 1972, *19,* 255-256.

SUE, D.W. *Cross-cultural counseling.* New York: Wiley and Sons, 1981.

SUE, D.W. (ED.), Counseling the culturally different. *Personnel and Guidance Journal,* 1977, *55,* 370-431 (a).

SUE, D.W. Counseling the culturally different: A conceptual analysis. *Personnel and Guidance Journal,* 1977, *55,* 422-425 (b).

SUNDBERG, N.D. *Research and research hypotheses about effectiveness in intercultural counseling.* In P. Pedersen, J. Draguns, W. Lonner, and J. Trimble (Eds.), Counselling Across Cultures. The University of Hawaii Press, 1981.

SZALAY, L.B. Intercultural Communication: A Process Model. *International Journal of Intercultural Relations,* 1981, *5,* 133-146.

TEPPER, D. AND HAASE, R. Verbal and nonverbal communication of facilitative conditions. *Journal of Counseling Psychology,* 1978, *25,* 35-44.

VONTRESS, C.E. *Racial and Ethnic Barriers in Counseling.* In P. Pedersen, J. Draguns, W. Lonner and J. Trimble (Eds.), Counseling Across Cultures, 1981, The University of Hawaii Press.

WAXER, P.H. *Therapist Training in Nonverbal Behavior: Toward a Curriculum.* In A. Wolfgang (Ed.), Nonverbal Behavior: Applications and Cultural Implications. New York: Academic Press, 1979.

WAXER, P.H. Nonverbal cues for anxiety: An Examination of Emotional Leakage. *Journal of Abnormal Psychology,* 197, *86,* 306-314.

WEITZ, S. Attitude, voice and behavior: A repressed affect model of interracial interaction. *Journal of Personality and Social Psychology,* 1972, *24,* 14-21.

WILLIS, F.N. Initial speaking distance as a function of speakers' relationship. *Psychonomic Science,* 1966, *5,* 221-222.

WOLFGANG, A. *Intercultural Counselling: The State of the Art.* Presented at The Invitational Symposium on Perspectives in Multiculturalism in Education. Queen's University, November 11, 1981 (a).

WOLFGANG, A. *Racial and ethnic minorities in the work place: The importance of nonverbal communication.* Presented at The Conference on Racial and Ethnic Minorities in the Work Place. Social Planning Council of Metropolitan Toronto, October 29-31, 1981 (b).

WOLFGANG. A. *The development of an inter-racial facial recognition test: Phase III. A comparison between new Canadian West-Indians and Canadians' sensitivity to inter-racial facial expressions and social distance.* Progress report: Department of Applied Psychology, The Ontario Institute for Studies in Education, 1980 (a).

WOLFGANG. A. *The West Indian student - A long way from home.* An audio-visual slide production, 1980, Toronto: Distributed by International Telefilm Enterprises Limited of Toronto, (b).

WOLFGANG. A. *The teacher and nonverbal behavior in the multicultural classroom.* In A. Wolfgang (Ed.), Nonverbal Behavior: Applications and Cultural Implications. New York: Academic Press, 1979 (a).

WOLFGANG. A. (ED.), *Nonverbal Behavior: Applications and Cultural Implications.* New York: Academic Press, 1979 (b).

WOLFGANG. A. *Expressing Yourself with Body Language.* The Educational ABC of Canadian Industry: Resource Book 78, 1978, 36-38.

WOLFGANG. A. The Silent Language in the Multicultural Classroom. *Theory into Practice,* 1977, *16*, 145-152.

WOLFGANG. A. *Basic issues and plausible answers in counselling new Canadians.* In A. Wolfgang (Ed.), Education of immigrant students: Issues and answers. Toronto: Symposium Series/5. The Ontario Institute for Studies in Education, 1975.

WOLFGANG. A. (producer), *Body language in the classroom.* Toronto: The Ontario Institute for Studies in Education, 1974. (film). Distributed by International Telefilms Enterprises Limited of Toronto and A.I.M.S. Instructional Media Services, Inc., Glendale, California.

WOLFGANG. A. Projected social distances as a measure of approach-avoidance behavior toward radiated figures. *Journal of Community Psychology,* 1973, *1,* 226-228 (a).

WOLFGANG. A. (producer), *The Italian in transition.* Toronto: The Ontario Institute for Studies in Education, 1973 (b). (film) Distributed by International Telefilms Enterprises Limited of Toronto.

WOLFGANG. A. AND WEISS. D.S. A focus of control and social distance comparison of Canadian and West Indian born students. *International Journal of Intercultural Relations,* 1980, *4,* 295-305.

WOLFGANG. A., AND WOLFGANG. J. Exploration of attitudes via physical interpersonal distance toward the obese, drug users, homosexuals, police and other marginal figures. *Journal of Clinical Psychology,* 1971, *27,* 510-512.

ZUNIN. L. AND ZUNIN. N. *Contact: The first four minutes.* Los Angeles: Nash Publishing, 1972.

COUNSELLING OF ETHNIC MINORITIES

By R. Chodzinski, Ph.D. and
R. J. Samuda, Ph.D.

This paper concerns itself with some of the difficulties encountered by school counsellors who provide services within a multi-cultural setting. Furthermore, some strategies are proposed which might help alleviate the pressures often associated with these problems.

Basically there are three specific areas of concern. They can be categorized as concerns related to Training, Personal Development, and Direct Services (Pederson 1981; Sue 1981).

TRAINING

School counsellors have traditionally been trained to deliver services based on a model which encourages a primarily WASP perspective. Although accpetance, understanding, empathy and expressed awareness of individual uniqueness are the trademarks of the effective counsellor (Rogers 1951, Wrenn 1962), many school counsellors find it difficult to apply these traits and skills within an atmosphere of cultural and social diversity (Samuda 1980). Some counsellor educators have suggested that the major problem for counsellors of minority group students is that there are no specific theoretical guidelines or models to follow. Wolfgang (1975) writes that the major problem is that counsellors do not have the benefit of theoretical guidelines to follow because most if not all counselling theories assume that the counsellor and student are of the same cultural orientation."

Sue (1977) agrees that counsellors must develop a sensitivity toward cultural and ethnic differences and Samuda and Crawford (1980) suggest that counsellors and teachers who are faced with challenges of working with people who are culturally different must recognize the fact, be sensitive to such needs as are unique to it and keep open many lines of communication." (p. 46) Trainers of school counsellors must tune in to the growing demand for training within a multicultural setting and must provide a concerted effort to liberate what Wrenn (1962) calls the encapsulated counsellor. Johnston and Vestemark (1970) described the encapsulated counsellor as one who assumes that their own dominant or majority group bias with respect to counselling methodology can be generalized to other cultures. As I see it, perhaps more important is that encapsulated counsellors will tend to demonstrate an insensitivity toward cultural diversity, different needs, and different culturally acceptable ways of accomplishing goals, thereby promoting advocacy of a predominant cultural norm and thereby demonstrating rejection of the cultural heritage and experience of the minority group student.

Pederson (1981) and Wolfgang (1975, 1980), argue that there is a paucity of counsellor training programs which specifically train counsellors to work within the multicultural setting. Future programs must focus on concerns which have been identified as crucial to the success of the inter cultural experience. For instance, language compatability between counsellor and client has been identified as instrumental to the success of the intercultural counselling relationship. In this regard Wilson and Calhoun (1974) have shown that dialect can cause difficulties between counsellor and client. Samuda (1975) has shown that differences in usage of English language can cause counsellors to misinterpret responses to test questions and therefore lower scores. Consequently, minority group children are often disadvantaged with respect to achieving satisfactory scores on tests such as IQ indicators, attitude or self report scales, or career related inventories. Wolfgang's (1980) research in counsellor training demonstrates the need to stress differences in communication styles, nonverbal behaviours, body language, and response behaviours. He has shown for instance that black West Indian students were more perceptive in interpreting facial expressions of white Anglo Saxons than of other culturally defined groups, and that white Anglo Saxons made significantly more errors in perceiving and interpreting emotional facial gestures of West Indian students. The implications for counsellor trainees is simply that they must be taught to appreciate the importance of identifying, and understanding the significance and value of culturally different expressive behaviours such as social distance, eye contact, recognition gestures, body movements and furthermore, must be shown how to interpret those behaviours within the context of the counselling relationship.

Differences in cultural background, history, experience and social condition are primary focus points for future counsellor training programs. For instance the current influx of Haitian and Cuban refugees to Southern Florida communities poses great problems for school counsellors. As Miner (1981) points out, understanding the Haitians needs, goes beyond a language barrier. Counsellors must learn to understand the mind set of the Haitian refugee. He argues that they do not understand freedom as we know it. "The permissive way many of our children are raised, lawlessness in our cities, our apparent lack of discipline and formality, are all frightening to people whose only experience has been in countries where these freedoms are not tolerated." Counsellors must learn to deal with "culture shock." Another interesting phenomenon particular to the Haitian refugee client is their acceptance and belief in the influence of voodoo and their reliance in the power of faith healers called Houngan or Mambo. (Rothman 1981) Majority group counsellors are required to understand and respect these cultural differences and yet provide traditional services to these people. Counsellors therefore will require training in new methods of communicating empathy and understanding within a multicultural context. We must learn to listen to the culturally different client. Counsellor educators must focus on teaching counsellors to learn how to not only listen to what is being said but to listen to what has not been verbally expressed. Counsellor trainees and those currently in the field, must learn to listen to the contextuality of the clients words and behaviours. Counsellors can do this by taking the time to learn about the customs, and values, of the cultural background of the student. Counsellors would benefit greatly from interacting with parents and community leaders, attending community and cultural functions and by familiarizing themselves with the problems and difficulties encountered by the student from a culturally different background (Sue 1981).

In the past, teacher and (counsellor) have not been prepared for the reality of cultural diversity (Washington, 1981). Evidence suggests that this is still the case (Samuda & Crawford 1980).

Multiculturalism will not go away; it is a fact and reality of global existence. If school counsellors are to be effective at all; they must be trained in a manner which prepares them to meet the demands and needs of the diversity of the human experience. Counsellors must be exposed to the principles, definitions and issues concerned with the policies of cultural pluralism.

DIRECT SERVICE

There are many functions that the counsellor must provide within the context of direct service. These include, educational testing and counselling, personal and social counselling, vocational guidance and counselling and community service assistance. These services are often difficult to provide within the context of a dominant cultural setting however, when attempting to provide these services within the context of the multicultural milieu counsellors are often confronted with a plethora of barriers. Aside from the personal biases such as racism, bigotry and stereotypic attitudes which are difficult to modify and severely hamper the climate for social change Elliston (1977b), Head (1975) counsellors are faced with external pressures. The lack of educational support systems; the lack of community acceptance of incoming or resident minority groups; too few receptive teachers, inadequate second or third language training facilities, unorganized intake procedures, language and social barriers, public racial discrimination practises, lack of social assistance funding, poor health care, resistance to dominant culture life style and culture specific differences, are just a few of the barriers to cross cultural counselling. However, aside from the difficulties outlined above, there are often factors which require attention by counsellors who provide direct services within a pluralistic setting. The area of educational testing for instance, is fraught with difficulties and pit falls. Mercer (1971) and Samuda (1975) have best described the need for adopting a cautionary approach to the use of tests with minority group children. They have suggested that if and when tests are used that interpretations be made only within the context of a "pluralistic, sociocultural perspective." The point is made that norms should be developed for each distinct sociocultural group within the ethnic group (Samuda 1975). Additionally they support the position that description and prescription techniques based on data from tests which are more culture and language specific be employed to ensure equitable and appropriate application of educational programs.

Although much has been written about the reliability and validity concerns of culturally biased tests (   ) (   ) and the use and misuse of tests within a culturally mixed society (   ) several points bear repeating. Perhaps the most important is that counsellors must recognize the limitations with respect to language facility and linguistic differences. Students, whose first language is not English and who have not been acculturated within the dominant society are likely to be disadvantaged with respect to test results. Lowered test results generally precipitate false interpretations, which often result in inappropriate placements thereby effectively limiting the potential educative expeience of the minority child. Every effort must be made to avoid this sort of *intellectual rape*. Students, particularly immigrant minority students whose language is not of the predominant culture, deserve a more sensitive approach to placement within our schools than is presently taking place. Because culturally different groups do not respond as well on middle class tests such as the WISC-P or the Slingerland it *can not* and *must not* be inferred that these students are less bright. It simply means that we have not *fairly* assessed the students capabilities.

Writers such as Labov (1971), Mercer (1971), Samuda (1975) and Scarr (1977) have helped to dissuade counsellors from using tests inappropriately, however, the Coleman studies (1966) and the Samuda and Crawford Studies (1980) demonstrated that more vigilance is required in this regard.

Although testing in the students primary language can alleviate some of the difficulties, questions, which are predominantly culturally value laden, are inappropriate, and therefore hinder the students chances of success. An approach which promotes competency testing, skill proficiency and incorporates a reasonable acculturation process would be more beneficial. The training of bilingual and bicultural counsellors might facilitate more equitable services to minority group children and might ensure that linguistic and cultural criteria be employed when student competencies are evaluated.

VOCATIONAL AND PERSONAL COUNSELLING

The delivery of vocational and personal counselling services to minority group children also poses some difficulties. Counsellors must be aware that cultural differences may be expressed in different career aspirations and career goals. Counsellors must be sensitive to these differences and offer appropriate counselling assistance. Even though preferences toward career choice may be different, for certain minority groups; (and this issue has yet to receive the attention it deserves), there are barriers which effectively limit the ability of some minority group children to realize their career goals. For instance, Santigo and Feinburg (1981) report that Hispanics aged 14-19 were twice as likely as whites not to complete high school," page 294. A study by Levitan (1980) showed that a great percentage of Hispanic immigrants are under employed or unemployed. With respect to Cubans it is reported "that this group has experienced a noticeable downward occupational mobility among those who were at the top of the occupational ladder," page 14. The Santigo and Feinburg (1981) study also reported that 80% of the migrant children in the United States are Hispanic and that the majority of these children live in households that earn less than $3000.00 per year, page 294. The implication for school counsellors are many. As Elliston (1977) has argued, counsellors must be aware and respond to the effects of cultural racism on general performance, on vocational decision and on the realization of selfhood.

Minority group children must be provided with equal opportunities to develop vocational maturity, and vocational self-concept. Students should be exposed to vocational experiences, and career development programs. Job opportunities, must be presented to students, and attempts to develop this vocational potential through skill development, and workstudy programs must be encouraged at the school level. School counsellors must become involved with community agencies, develop out reach programs, develop liaison activities with local minority group leaders and be prepared to assist students in asserting their rights and preferences with respect to implementing long term career goals. Additionally counsellors should encourage in-service training of bilingual volunteers to assist them in planning and implementing vocational development programs. More school counsellors with bilingual and bicultural backgrounds are needed. Therefore majority group counsellors should encourage and support the training of additional professionals.

As with vocational counselling the counsellor has the responsibility of providing personal-social counselling to minority group children. Barriers to effective cross cultural counselling have been itemized by Belkin (1980), Elliston (1977), Padilla Ruiz and Alverez (1975) and Sue and Sue (1977). Essentially, they are defined within the context of language-values, customs, expectations and aspirations. Linguistic patterns that are unfamiliar to the student or counsellor can promote inappropriate message statements and can cause misconceptions, Taylor (1974), Sue and Sue (1977). Class affiliation and sociometric status have been shown to be instrumental barriers to effective cross cultural counselling (Hollingshead and Redlich, 1958). Race, sex and colour of the counsellor have also been shown to be important determinants of effective counselling within a multicultural context. Nonverbal behaviour can greatly effect the cross cultural counselling experience, Wolfgang (1975). Despite the barrier, the so-called dominant group school counsellors are expected to continue providing support services. Minority group students, like any other students, have needs with respect to self-esteem building, personal development, behaviour management, educational counselling as well as variety of other physiological, social, or psychological needs. Counsellors must recognize that differences exist within a cultural mix and therefore must address the demands and needs arising from the pressure of culturally different children (Samuda and Crawford, 1980). Counsellors can assist students through personal counselling to help them through the acclimatization process. They can assist students to preserve and value their own cultural values and heritages. Additionally counsellors can assist students in determining which traditional values may not be appropriate within a new cultural experience. Counsellors must assist minority group students in achieving social acceptability and developing positive self-concepts. Counsellors must discover the experiences which give rise to self-defeating motives and then attempt to ameliorate the effects of such negative factors. Peer counsellors, particularly those of "similar cultural background" to the student clients should be trained. Volunteer counsellors, business and community leaders of similar backgrounds and cultural experiences can be effective *partners* in the counselling process. Group counselling activities which provide opportunities for positive interaction between majority group and culturally different students can be positive and rewarding experiences (Chodzinski, 1979). Counselling activities and strategies which promote and perceive the dignity, liberty and integrity of minority group students must be pursued with vigour. Counsellors can encourage other staff members to be more sensitive to the needs of minority group children thereby helping to improve acceptance and understanding of diversity.

PERSONAL DEVELOPMENT

The last issue which I wish to raise is perhaps the most important. It deals with the acceptance of multiculturalism as a philosophy and policy. Many counsellors of minority group children are faced with resolving fundamental questions pertaining to how they as individuals perceive the multicultural experience. More specifically, they must confront themselves with questions about their own prejudices, biases, and stereotyped attitudes with respect to the acceptance, understanding and tolerance of peoples considered as outside the majority group population. As I see it, at the foundation of counselling is self-knowledge. Along with self-knowledge is the willingness to accept ourselves as we are and to be reasonably at peace with ourselves and our environment. Acceptance of others and other environments cannot occur without the precondition of acceptance of self. Counsellors must continually work toward this fundamental principle. Furthermore, counsellors must employ basic traits and skills such as empathy, positive regard for others, understanding, listening, trust and honesty to ensure that the rights and privileges of a democratic society are extended to all groups. Cultural diversity invites creativity and sensitivity. Counsellors must make every effort to demonstrate acceptance and respect for cultural differences. As Samuda and Crawford (1980) have pointed out, avoidance of the recognition of differences, pretending that they do not exist, generates and perpetuates an insensitivity to and distrust of diversity. Human differences must be perceived not as threats to the dominant culture but as symbols of the diversity and richness of the human experience. Shiman (1981) makes the point:

> that we must deal with the tensions that emerge as we try to promote a common civic culture, encourage children's self-esteem with respect to their own ethnic group, and foster intercultural understanding and tolerance. The dynamics created as we try to achieve these potentially conflicting goals is a source of great strength and enormous growth. (page 39)

We can accomplish these goals by employing strategies which are designed to accommodate ethnic and minority differences and which reflect the constant changes in the social fabric. Those activities which promote and develop interactive experiences and enhance self-understanding through awareness of personal abilities, competencies, strengths, personal characteristics, interests and values will be most beneficial in this regard.

Counsellors who provide direct services to minority group children must not interpret diversity and pluralism as threats or assaults on the dominant culture rather they should view multiculturalism as an opportunity to expand horizons and experience the richness of the human experience. Acceptance and tolerance of others lies at the root of the helping professions. Ethnic minority cultures must be viewed as different not deficient (Samuda and Crawford 1980) and accordingly, must be afforded the same rights and privileges afforded every other citizen. Counsellors, if they are to be effective at all must first resolve the fundamental question of how they view the multicultural mosaic.

SUMMARY

The issues relative to multiculturalism in education and particularly those that focus on the role of the counsellor within the multicultural setting, speak to the core of what it is to be   counsellor. It is encumbant upon counsellors that they engage in soul searching and reflect on the ethics and professional codes which govern our behaviour. The American Psychological Association and the Canadian Guidance and Counselling Association recognize that cultural differences and minority rights are important considerations for practising counsellors. It has been reported that by 1990 Hispanics will be the largest minority group in American schools (Santigo and Feinburg 1981), therefore the needs of this group should be of *primary interest* to school counsellors. Since it has been shown that disadvantaged groups are susceptible to stresses that detract from good mental health (Canino 1980), school counsellors must ensure that schools do not contribute to that stress. Furthermore, as Santigo and Feinburg (1981) have so succinctly pointed out that improvement in the condition of Hispanics in the United States will depend to a great extent on a change in attitude of the American public toward Hispanics. School counsellors can help facilitate attitudinal change on the part of majority group children by expending efforts to ensure that diversity and the richness of difference is respected and honoured and by promoting experiences that promote the acquisition of positive concepts of racial diversity. As Morris (1981) writes, unless the young have positive experiences they can become victims of indirect influences which can translate into rigid prejudices," page 287. Counsellors can not undo the harm that has already been done and we know that attitudes and goodwill cannot replace the pain of past prejudices, eliminate societal ills, change socio-economic differences, reduce class distinctions, eradicate colour barriers, reduce suspicions, or produce favourable advantages for the disadvantaged. All that can be hoped is that positive interactive expeiences foster positive growth and promote mutual understanding of self and others.

School counsellors can become actively involved in encouraging school boards to ensure quality education for all groups. They can promote the training and use of bilingual, bicultural counsellors, and they can pursue in-service programs that promote understanding of culturally different values and customs. Counsellors can become more sensitive to the misuse of standardized tests, promote evaluative procedures more compatible with language and cultural differences, provide opportunities for minority and minority group children to positively interact, acknowledge differences in career preferences, and aspirations and provide services accordingly and promote self-development activities that enhance self-esteem. Counsellors must continue to preserve the basic values of dignity, liberty, and integrity of the persons for whom or on whose behalf services are performed.

REFERENCES

BELKIN, G.S. *An introduction to counseling.* Dubuque, Iowa. W.C. Brown Co. Ltd., 1980.

CANINO, I. The Puerto Rican child in New York city: Stress and mental health. Monograph #4. Bronx, N.Y: Hispanic Research Centre, 1980.

CHODZINSKI, R.T. Towards an understanding of self-concept. Unpublished manuscript presented to the Saskatchewan Teachers' Federation Professional Development Conference, Saskatoon, November, 1979.

ELLISTON, I. Social and vocational adjustment in a multicultural society: Implications for a school counsellor. *School Guidance Worker,* Jan./Feb., 1977, *32* (3), 6-13.

HOLLINGSHEAD, A.B. AND REDLICH, F.C. *Social class and mental health.* New York: John Wiley & Sons Inc., 1958.

IJAZ, M.A. AND IJAZ, I.H. Changing racial attitudes. *The History and Social Science Teacher,* 1981, *17* (1), 21-29.

JOHNSTON, D.E. AND VERSTERMARK, J.J. *Barriers and hazards in counseling.* Boston: Houghton Mifflin Co., 1970.

LABOV, W. Academic ignorance and black intelligence. *The Atlantic Monthly,* 1971, 59-67.

LEVITAN, A.T. Hispanics in Dade county, characteristics and needs. Office of the County Manager, Spring, 1980.

MERCER, J. Institutionalized anglocentrism: labelling mental retardates in the public schools. In P. Orleans and W. Russell (Eds.) *Race, Change and Urban Society.* Los Angeles: Sage Publications, 1971.

MINOR, C. Understanding the Haitians: Need goes beyond a language barrier. *Miami Herald,* Miami, Florida, Sept., 1981.

MORRIS, J.B. Indirect influences on children's racial attitudes. *Educational Leadership,* January, 1981, 286-287.

PADILLA, W.M., RUIZ, R.A. AND ALVEREZ, R. Community mental health services for the Spanish speaking/surnamed population. *American Psychologist,* 1975, *30,* 892-905.

PEDERSEN, P., DRAGUNS, J.G., LONNER, W.J., TREMBLE, J.E. (EDS.). *Counseling across cultures.* The University of Hawaii Press, 1981.

ROGERS, C.R. *Client-centred therapy.* Boston: Houghton Mifflin, 1951.

ROTHMAN, S. Haitian Aliens. *The Independent Professional,* September, 1981.

SAMUDA, R.J. *Psychological testing of American minorities:Issues and consequences.* New York:Harper and Row, 1975.

SAMUDA, R.J. AND CRAWFORD, D.H. *Testing, assessment, counselling and placement of ethnic minority students:Current methods in Ontario.* Toronto: Ministry of Education, 1980.

SANTIGO, R.L. AND FEINBURG, P.C. The status of education for Hispanics. *Educational Leadership,* January, 1981, 292-297.

SCARR, S. Testing minority children: why, how, and with what effects? *Proceedings of the National Conference on Testing: Major Issues.* Richard Bossone and Max Weiner (Eds.) New York: The Graduate School and University Centre of the City University of New York, 1977.

SHIMAN, D.A. Confronting prejudice in the schools. *The Education Digest,* March, 1981, 38-41.

SUE, D.W. Counseling the culturally different: A conceptual analysis. *Personnel and Guidance Journal,* 1977, *55,* 422-425.

SUE, D.W. *Cross cultural counseling.* New York: Wiley and Sons, 1981.

SUE, D.W. AND SUE, S. Barriers to effective cross-cultural counselling. *Journal of Counselling Psychology,* 1977, *24.*

TAYLOR, F. *Race, school and community.* London, England: National Foundation of Educational Research Publishing Co., 1974.

WASHINGTON, V. Impact of antiracism/multicultural education training on elementary teacher attitudes and classroom behaviour. *The Elementary School Journal,* 1981, *81* (3), 186-191.

WILSON, W. AND CALHOUN, J.F. Behaviour therapy and the minority client. *Psychotherapy: Theory Research and Practice,* 1974, *11* (4), 317-325.

WOLFGANG, A. (ED.). *Education of immigrant students: Issues and answers.* Toronto: Ontario Institute for Studies in Education, 1975.

WOLFGANG, A. The development of an inter-racial facial recognition test: Phase III a comparison between new Canadian West-Indians and Canadians sensitivity to inter-racial facial expressions and social distance. Progress report: Department of Applied Psychology, The Ontario Institute for Studies in Education, 1980.

WRENN, C.G. The culturally encapsulated counselor. *Harvard Educational Review,* 1962, *32* (4), 444-449.

COUNSELING THE
ETHNIC MINORITY IMMIGRANT:
A SECOND LOOK

By Jethro W. Toomer, Ph.D.

The phrase "Ethnic Minority Immigrant" creates many different images in the minds of different people. Given this confusion and the confusion that still exists among sociologists and anthropologists regarding a definition of terms, it appears only proper to begin a discussion of the ethnic minority immigrant with an attempt to define the terms involved.

Historically, sociologists have used at least three different kinds of definitions of the term "minority group". The oldest is called a descriptive or trait definition (Young, 1932). For Young, minority groups are those individuals that American society distinguishes according to their race (biological features) or their ethnicity (national origin). A second definition is provided by Wirth (1945), Wirth defines a minority as a group of people, who because of their physical or cultural characteristics, are singled out from others in the society in which they live, for differential or unequal treatment, and who, therefore, regard theirselves as objects of collective discrimination. This particular orientation suggests that minority status is determined not by race or national origin alone, but by any physical or cultural trait. Here the notion of group consciousness is introduced. Third, the definition points to the fact that minority groups are those groups that are subject to discrimination, differential and unequal treatment in society. A third definition by Schermerhorn (1970), defines minority groups, not according to specific group traits or consequences of those traits (prejudice or discrimination) but on the basis of the variation of three important aspects of social groups: Size, power and a third aspect called ethnicity. Schermerhorn defines ethnic minority groups as those ethnic groups that form less than one-half the population of their society and are subordinate with regard to the distribution of power in that society. Ethnic group is defined by Schermerhorn to mean groups that possess any trait, cultural or physical that serves as a symbol of the group's distinctiveness.

While many theorists deal with the words "ethnic", "racial", "minority" in varying ways, these labels fail in many ways to encompass the entire range of groups that may be defined as minorities. The more appropriate typology suggests we look at minority groups as being of three basic types. There is the physical minority group that varies from social norms in terms of appearance, such as Blacks, the handicapped, the aged, Asians, etc. There is the cognitive group that varies from social norms in terms of beliefs, such as Jews, Irish Catholics, various religious sects, social communes, etc. and there is the behavioral minority group that varies from social norms in conduct such as homosexuals (Newman, 1973).

Regardless of the particular approach taken by a particular theorist, certain characteristics stand out. First, minority status in the U.S.A. is determined by race, national origin as well as by physical traits. Secondly, those identified by the larger society as minority are aware of the way in which they are defined and treated by the larger society, i.e., a sort of group consciousness, thirdly, members of a minority group are subject to discrimination as well as differential and unequal treatment in society, both as individuals and members of a group, and fourth, having direct relationship to the subject as hand, the ethnic minority immigrant is at variance with the social norms of larger American society and is categorized as belonging to a minority group in terms of the physical, cognitive as well as behavioral aspects.

THE IMMIGRATION MYTH

Historically a myth has been perpetrated, which indicates that the United States of America welcomes all immigrants to it's shores and that the immigrant, once learning certain cultural mores, mastering the language and securing gainful employment is assimilated into the larger American society and lives happily ever after. Closer examination of that history, however, reveals that this is true only to the degree to which, immigrants coming to America approximate certain American "high" status variables. The closer the approximation to such variables as speaking fluent English, caucasian features, christian religion, being well educated (professional occupation), adherence to "christian moral code of ethics" the easier was the process of assimilation, and the more positive their reception on the part of the larger white American society. The farther removed the immigrant happened to be from the "high status variables", the more difficult the transition. The ethnic minority immigrant is distinguishable from the dominant group by reasons of differences of physiognomy and are regarded an inherently different and not belonging. They may speak a different language, have different customs, both social and religious, and may not necessarily, come with a history of participation in a high status profession. Add to this the fact that the immigrant may have entered the country illegally, at a period in American life characterized by high inflation, government cutbacks, dwindling resources and ultra-conservative atmosphere, and the plight of the ethnic minority immigrant becomes crystalized.

ADAPTATION OF THE ETHNIC MINORITY IMMIGRANT

Immigrants from all parts of the world have come to America. The goal of society was to "Americanize" the immigrants and to assimilate them into the larger society. The process of leaving one's native land in search of a better life, causes both exhiliration and pain. Confronting the realities of living in a new country always arouses feelings of sadness and disorientation. Namias (1978), Sowell (1978), and other writers suggest that dislocation, especially in the case of immigration places individuals in the midst of a crises, and the reactions expressed are described as similar to that of "grief". Fried (1977) described the process of dislocation evolving into feelings of pain, loss, a sense of helplessness, direct and displaced anger, and idealizations of the lost place. Oberg (1972) uses the term "culture-shock" to describe the anxiety, sense of loss and despair, experienced by immigrants arriving in a new country. Oberg proposed the following stages in the process of culture-shock experienced by a new immigrant. Stage one: One feels euphoria about the new culture. Stage two: Normal daily activities seem more like crises. As a result, immigrants direct feelings of hostility towards those around them. This is a period of psychological transition from back home values to host home values, when failure to succeed can lead to extreme dissatisfaction with the host culture. Stage three: Persons begin to understand the host culture and feel more in touch with themselves. Stage four: The host is viewed as offering both positive and negative alternatives. Freese (1977), Bowlby (1961) propose that the transition from one culture to another experienced by an immigrant involves a grieving process the immigrant experiences numbness, shock and disbelief. They come face to face with the fact that they actually left and they are no longer going to see familiar faces and sights. This sense of estrangement is heightened by the foreignness of the new environment. For the ethnic minority immigrant, this process causes one to assume a minority status in a majority culture, wherein one once was a member of the majority culture. Questions such as "Why did I ever come here?" "Why don't they like newcomers?" are frequent. The enthusiasm with which they came is slowly tempered by hardship, disappointment, discrimination, and in many instances, poverty. The first stage slowly evolves into the second stage, which is characterized by feelings of pain, despair and disorganization. Homesickness sets in as persons experience their emotional losses. In many instances, individuals who previously had criticized their homeland as not offering enough, tend now to idealize the homeland. Defense mechanisms, such as displacement, projection, and reaction formation, tend to be used most frequently. Feelings of confusion, loneliness and a sense of isolation are common. The social isolation is further aggravated by difficulty in speaking the language. It is during this stage that the displaced immigrant begins to sense deeply the loss of familial and support networks. The shock of adapting to a different standard of living must also be encountered. During phase three, the immigrant faces reality as expressed in the notion, "I guess we are here to stay". There is a resolution to reorganize one's life, start anew and build new relationships. It appears as if during this stage the immigrant ceases to grieve over losses and begins to accept a new role in a new environment. This grieving process may continue or recur many years after the departure of the immigrant. The pain of leaving one's homeland, siblings and other family members often remains with the immigrant until his death.

Evidence suggests that the aforementioned stages are experienced by most immigrants, who, for the most part, enter the country with its blessings. Consider then the plight of the ethnic minority immigrant. If this is the plight of the immigrant, who comes to America well received, then it does not take a great deal of imagination to understand the plight of the ethnic minority immigrant who, fleeing oppression, and under conditions of duress, or force, have come to a country that has greeted them with anything but open arms. The ethnic minority immigrant does not have to wait for the advent of stages to experience the feeling of pain, despair and disorganization. The numbness, shock, and disbelief, are experienced almost immediately, upon learning that they are unwelcomed and unwanted.

The role of the immigrant and the process of immigration simulate mixed and varied responses at unpredictable periods of time. Bowlby (1961) provides a framework for understanding personal loss and grief as a result of immigration. Comparative theoreticla models, on the process of culture shock (Oberg, 1972), adjustment (Foster, 1965) and bilingual/bicultural adaptation (Triandis, 1980) all focus on the trauma, feelings of loss and isolation characterized by the immigrant. The assumption of these writers, however, has been that the immigrants would be welcome and would be Americanized and assimilated into the larger culture. Arredoendo-Dowd (1978) Namias (1979), and Sowell (1978), are theorists who describe in detail the feelings of exhiliration and pain experienced almost simultaneously by the immigrant. Whether leaving was voluntary and anticipated, forced and anticipated, or unexpected, there is a period of settlement to be faced by all. Fried (1977) described the feelings of sadness and disorientation as well as grief experienced by immigrants. Toffler (1970) and Packard (1969) describe the sense of loss, helplessness, direct and displaced anger, and idealizations of the former homeland as reactions by immigrants upon arrival in a new country.

The ethnic minority immigrant experiences the above reactions, only they are magnified ten-fold. As indicated, in addition to the usual reactions of the "welcomed" immigrant, the ethnic minority immigrant by virtue of ethnic background, skin color, religion, cultural norms, finds himself often unwelcomed and unwanted in a country which, up to very recently, ahd professed an "open door policy" with regard to immigrants. Although heavily influenced by political considerations, at this writing (Miami) Dade County in southern Florida has experienced a major face-lift, by virtue of an almost tota open door policy, with regard to the influx of Cuban immigrants who came with not only government support, but government financing. The ethnic minority immigrant of past years and in the 1980s finds himself experiencing the racism, and discrimination accorded to native born Black Americans. In addition, the ethnic minority immigrant of the 80's finds an already unwelcomed attitude rendered even more calloused by the resurgence of political conservatism during a time when resources are scarce and deep cuts in government support in the area of health and human services are being experienced.

The aforementioned reactions, i.e., sense of loss, grief, isolation, culture shock, anger, lead to utilization of defense mechanisms such as displacement, rejection and reaction formation to allay anxiety, stress and trauma by ethnic minority immigrants. Other modes of adaptation, however, are adopted. For the ethnic minority immigrant who is able through his own resources to move closer, even if only on the peripheral, to a point of functioning in the larger American society uses a number of psychological defenses. First, depending upon certain personality variables the individual, in an attempt to adapt to the larger American society, may experience a form of what has been called, "identity difusion" where there is an inner experience of internal sense of devaluation. A second reaction is termed a defensive narrowness (DeVos, 1978). Here intellectual processes are not developed as a means of coping with the external world. A sense of self remains defined by maintaining barriers against possible enrichening experiences from the larger culture. A third reaction consists of a more flexible maintenance of an identity by emphasizing thought over feeling. The ethnic minority immigrant may become embittered and cut himself off from his inner feelings in his relations to others. They may become rigid, cold-blooded, lacking in compassion, calculating and expediential in their relationships. Their actions, social lives, contact and relations with people, all become highly instrumentalized. Their ethnic identities may be either discarded or manipulated, depending upon the circumstances. These individuals, however, still experience feelings of self-devaluation and self-disparagement. While perceived by others as socially mobile and ruthless, these individuals manage to attain social and intellectual competence at the expense of their affective lives.

The process of adaptation may be further complicated by the fact that the ethnic minority immigrant must also make the transition from that of being a member of the majority group in his homeland to that of a minority group member in his new country.

COUNSELING THE ETHNIC MINORITY IMMIGRANT

Mental health professionals have concluded that racial or ethnic factors may act as impediments to counseling. (Attneave, 1972; Sue, 1975; Vontress, 1971.) In order to effectively counsel the minority ethnic immigrant, counselors must understand cultural differences between the minority and majority groups. Sue (1976) noted that most theories of counseling have characteristics of the white middle class society. For example, culture bound traits of counseling dictate an individual orientation characterized by such factors as verbal emotional behavior expressiveness, openness and intimacy, obtaining insight, spontaniety, etc. Classbound factors emphasize a linear concept of time and punctuality and the seeking of long-range goals and solutions. In addition, use of standard English is characteristic fo western counseling approaches. Ethnic minority immigrants may come from a culture or society that believes in restraint of strong feeling, where insight is not highly valued, where a clear distinction between physical and mental health is not made, and which does not utilize English, as the primary language. Inaccurate interpretations to these cultural variables given by "white" counselors, may lead to potential misunderstanding that destroys rapport. Wrenn (1962) discusses the "culturally encapsulated counselor" who disregards cultural variations in favor of applying some mistaken universal notion of technique oriented truth. In that groups and individuals differ, the blind application of some technique to all situations, and all populations, is totally inappropriate. Approaches consistent with the life experiences, the values and needs of the counselee are required. In this sense, as Wrenn points out, equal treatment in counseling, may be discriminatory treatment, as it relates to the ethnic minority immigrant.

It is therefore of the utmost importance for counselors to be aware of group and individual differences, when working with racial or ethnic minorities as well as ethnic minority immigrants. The culturally competent counselor must be able to relate to minority group experiences, and must have knowledge of cultural and class factors. Relative to the ethnic minority immigrant, the counselor must be aware of the individuals background, the situational variables surrounding the persons immigration as well as experiences encountered as part of that process. The counselor must also recognize that counseling individuals from different cultures dictates not the same approach, but a different approach, consistent with the client's lifestyle. In other words the counselor must look systematically at racial and ethnic differences as they relate to the counselor's own approach and value system as well as the various schools of thought in counseling. Failure to do this, will result in an ineffective counseling process as it relates to the ethnic minority immigrant and a process that will lead to further alienation of the client and an increase in statistics which show that minority clients tend to underutilize mental health services or prematurely terminate after an initial contact. (Padilla, Ruiz and Alvarez, 1975; Sue and Kirk, 1975). The counselors lack of adherence to cultural differences will result in the continued implementation of a counseling process, inconsistent with the life experiences of his clientele.

IMPLICATIONS FOR COUNSELORS

Sue (1975) lists four major variables that all counselors must be aware of and have information regarding in order to effectively counsel culturally different individuals. They are: (1) cultural values, (2) class values, (3) language factors, (4) unique and common experiences (oppression). Knowledge of the four variables will enable the counselor working with the culturally different client to implement appropriate counseling processes that are consistent with the client's and to develop appropriate goals for the client.

Many ethnic minority immigrants entering the U.S. come from cultures where the family is traditionally extended. Godparents are very important and are generally treated as part of the natural family. Parents often have a very strong voice in the childs selection of a mate and child's choice of a career. Accepting guidance from authority figures on social and vocational matters is common. In Haiti, for example, legal marriage is encouraged but common-law relationships are frequent. A distinction is made between placage and concubinage. Placage is a stable form of common-law marriage that carries a stigma, while concubinage does not carry social approval (Rey, 1970).

While many ethnic minority immigrants are Black and share a heritage with

Afro-Americans that extends back to pre-slavery, the groups do not mix socially and the relationship is often characterized by mistrust. All immigrants to a particular country almost always identify with the majority (white) culture regardless of skin color. Often coming from a position in the majority culture, the ethnic minority immigrants have little insight into racial prejudice with which Afro-Americans have had to contend. Many times immigrants come from cultures where upper classes are inhabited by lighter skinned Blacks with lighter skin regarded as more prestigious than dark skin. Consequently, some ethnic minority immigrants feel negatively toward dark skinned American Blacks who lack comparable symbols of status valued in their homeland (Rey, 1970; Leyburn, 1955). Most cultures value education because of the social prestige and upward mobility it conveys. For example, Haitians generally view themselves as good business people. Medicine, however, is nationally regarded as the most desirable and prestigious occupation. In many African cultures a career in politics is highly desirable and prestigious.

Knowledge of this kind of information can help the counselor increase his understanding of a particular group in terms of providing assistance, for example, in meeting the clients vocational needs (broaden knowledge of careers and choice processes) and social needs (isolation, difficulty in interpersonal skills).

Lack of understanding of the aforementioned variables will lead to the counselor's establishing an inappropriate counseling process that is antagonistic to the client's lifestyle and will lead to the establishment of inappropriate goals for the client.

Counselors, educators and psychologists working with immigrants must understand the many forms of loss and reactions to loss which may be exhibited by the ethnic minority immigrant. The counseling process should identify the need for, and facilitate the process of grieving, so that the ethnic minority immigrant is not overwhelmed by the experience. The counselor should also keep in mind that there is no certainty as to when the feelings of grief, or loss will occur. In many instances, the feelings of loss and grief may be delayed for years afterward, when one would have anticipated the achievement of some measure of assimilation on the part of the immigrant. Coupled with this, is a necessity for the counselor to recognize that the manifestation of loss, grief and other reactions associated with the process of immigration, may appear in ways so subtle as to be misunderstood. The immigrant experience is different for each ethnic minority immigrant, and by recognizing grieving stages such as that of Bowlby (1961) can the counselor suggest approaches for resolving personal trauma. It is of the utmost importance that counselors keep in mind, that only when basic survival needs are met, is there an energy reserve for demanding and pursuing higher level needs (Grier and Cobbs, 1968). The dilemma for the ethnic minority immigrant, however, is often the clash between higher level and lower level needs. Filling one's need for belongingness, one's need for self esteem, for example, requires some difficult choices, especially when one has a foothold in two conflicting value systems and desires membership in both.

SUMMARY

The plight of the ethnic minority immigrant exposes as a myth the historical notion that the United States of America welcomes immigrants to its shores with open arms, and once, having learned certain cultural mores, mastered the language, and secured gainful employment, is assimilated into the larger American society to live happily ever after.

Because of the discrepancy and the lack of approximation of ethnic minority immigrants to certain American high status variables (i.e., caucasian features, christian religion, well educated, etc.) the ethnic minority immigrant experiences grief, a sense of loss, and anger. The ethnic minority immigrant of 1980's experiences the same hostility, discrimination, and rejection as his counterpart of previous years. In the 1980's the rejection, hostility and discrimination are manifested against a backdrop of an increasing conservatism, eroding of government support, runaway inflation, unemployment and dwindling resources.

Needed to help the ethnic minority immigrant are culturally competent counselors, who understand cultural differences between minority and majority groups. These counselors must be able to relate to the experiences, culture, and class factors of the ethnic minority immigrant. Second, the counselors must understand that counseling individuals of different cultures requires not the same approach, but a differential approach, consistent with the client's lifestyle. Third, the counselor must systematically look at race and ethnic differences as they relate to the counselors own approach in values and the various schools of counseling.

Failure to recognize the importance of the above variables will create barriers to effective counseling, that will lead to the alienation and inability to establish client rapport and premature termination as a client in the helping process.

REFERENCES

ARREDONDO-DOWD, P. Psychological education and the foreign born adolescent. Unpublished doctoral dissertation, Boston University, 1978.

ATTREAVE, C. Mental Health of American Indians. Paper presented at 80th Annual Convention of American Psychological Association, Hawaii, August, 1972.

BOWLBY, J. Processes of Mourning. *International Journal of Psychoanalysis,* Vol. XLII, 1961.

DEVOS, G. Ethnic Adaptation and Minority Status. *Journal of Cross-Cultural Psychology.* Western Washington University Press, Vol. II, No. 1, March, 1980.

FOSTER, R.J. *Examples of Cross-cultural problems encountered by Americans working overseas: An instructors handbook.* Alexandria, Va.: Human Resources Research Office, 1965.

FREESE, A. *Help for Your Grief.* New York: Schoker, 1977.

FRIED, M. Grieving for a lost home. In A. Monet and R. Lazarus (Eds.) *Stress and Coping.* New York: Columbia University Press, 1977.

GRIER, W. AND COBBS, P.M. *Black Rage.* New York: Basic Books, Inc., 1968.

LEYBURN, J.G. *The Haitian People.* New Haven, Ct.: Yale University Press, 1955.

NAMOIS, J. *First Generation.* Boston: Beacon Press, 1978.

NEWMAN, WILLIAM M. *American Pluralism.* New York: Harper & Row, 1973.

OBERG, K. Culture shock and the problem of adjustment to new cultural environments. In D. Hooper (Ed.) *Readings in Intercultural Communications.* Pittsburgh: Intercultural Communications Network of Regional Council for International Education, 1972.

PADILLA, A.M., RUIZ, R.A., AND ALVAREZ, R. Community mental health services for the Spanish speaking surnamed population, *American Psychologist,* 30, 1975.

REY, K.N. *The Haitian Family.* New York: Community Service Society, 1970.

SCHERMERHORN, RICHARD. *Comparative Ethnic Relations.* New York: Random House, 1970.

SOWELL, T. (ED.) *American Ethnic Groups.* The Urban Institute, 1978.

SUE, D.W. Asian Americans: Social-psychological forces affecting their life styles. In S. Picon & R. Campbell (Eds.) *Career Behavior of Special Groups.* Ohio: Charles Merrill, 1975.

SUE, D.W. Barriers to effective cross-cultural counseling. Paper presented at East-West Center, Honolulu, Hawaii, August, 1976.

SUE, D.W. AND KIRK, B.A. Asian-Americans: Use of counseling and psychiatric services on a college campus. *Journal of Counseling Psychology,* 22, 1975.

TOFFLER, A. *Future Shock.* New York: Random House, 1970.

TRIANDIS, H.C. A theoretical framework for the study of bilingual-bicultural adaptation. *International Review of Applied Psychology.* Beverly Hills: Sage Publications, Vol. 29, 1971.

VONTRESS, C.E. Racial differences: Impediments to rapport. *Journal of Counseling Psychology,* 18, 1971.

WIRTH, LOUIS. Problem of minority groups, in Ralph Linton (Ed.) *Science of Man in the World Crisis.* New York: Columbia University Press, 1945.

WRENN, G. The culturally encapsulated counselor. *Harvard Educational Review,* 32, 1962.

YOUNG, DONALD. *American Minority Peoples.* New York: Harper & Row, 1932.

COMPARATIVE STUDIES
OF COGNITIVE STYLES

By J. W. Berry
Queen's University
Kingston, Canada

INTRODUCTION

It is obvious to any traveller that cultures and individuals differ from place to place; these differences have been the stuff of tales of exploration and of anthropology, and need no elaborate documentation here. The general position taken in this paper is that these differences arise because peoples around the world develop cultural and psychological characteristics which help them to adapt to the kinds of problems which they frequently encounter. These characteristics serve people well when they remain in the place where they developed; however, when individuals migrate to other settings, and meet other kinds of problems, there may be a miss-match between the individual and the requirements of living in the new place.

This paper is concerned with one kind of behavior, the "cognitive" (or intellectual) functions, and to some extent it ignores other important features of human development, such as emotional and social life. It asks the question "What do we know about cognitive variation across cultures, and about the sources of this variation?" Now, for some of you, this may be a dangerous, even a subversive, question; but set in the context of the issue of human adaptation, it becomes a small but natural part of our attempts in the social and behavioral sciences to understand the nature and function of human variation.

The *way* in which we understand cognitive behavior is an important element in our approach. If one accepts uncritically the notion of "general intelligence", then serious problems arise when we work cross-culturally. However, if one moves away from such a rigidly quantitative approach, to the more qualitative notion of "cognitive styles", then many of the problems disappear (Berry and Dasen, 1974).

The effects of ecological and cultural factors on the development of cognitive styles will be examined, using as an example the Field Dependent-Field Independent cognitive style (FD-FID) of the late Hy Witkin (Witkin and Goodenough, 1981), and the eco-cultural model of Berry (1976). The effects of cultural change on these styles will also be considered. Experiences both prior to migration, and after, are known to alter the behavior of individuals. What do we know about the effect of "Westernizing" influences in the various countries of origin, and of acculturation in host countries, on the cognitive styles of migrants? (Berry, 1981)

A final issue to be addressed is that of the educational implications of these observations and arguments. If people develop differently in their cultures of origin, and if these differences persist to some extent over their life span in the new culture, what needs to be done to the educational and other social systems of host countries in order to meet the needs of immigrants?

CULTURE AND COGNITION

In current work on cognition cross-culturally, three general positions may be discerned. All three share an interest in describing and interpreting the *cognitive performance,* the *cultural context* of that performance, and the *relationships* which may exist between them. They differ in a number of ways, which are illustrated in Figure 1.

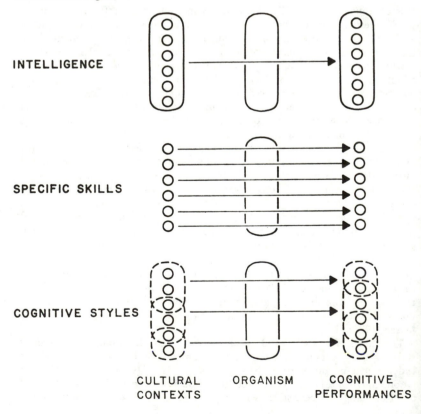

The conventional approach has been to take a **standard** test of general ability or "intelligence" and to administer it to all and sundry. Usually the only modification to the test has been its translation, or to make some minor variation in content. Two assumptions are typically made: one is that the cultural life of the test developer and the cultural life of the test taker differ in only one important respect, that of language. The other is that the cognitive abilities which are characteristic of the cultural life of the test developer and those of the test taken differ in only one respect, that of *level* of development.

These two assumptions are illustrated in the upper portion of Figure 1. First, elements in the cultural context are treated more or less as a unit (solid boundary around elements on the left), and, second, the cognitive abilities are assumed to be a single package (solid boundary on right). Test scores are then usually interpreted in terms of populations having bigger or smaller packages. For example, Vernon (1979, p. 7) has noted that it is commonly assumed that ingelligence is a "homogeneous entity or mental power that, like height or weight, can vary in amount or in rate of growth or decline ..." His own empirical work (Vernon, 1969) illustrates these assumptions.

With respect to the first assumption, it is clear to me that cultural differences have not been taken seriously in the debate on population differences in intelligence. And with respect to the second assumption, little attempt has been made to find out what (perhaps different) cognitive abilities are actually in place in various groups, and how they are structured. Given these two errors of omission, the great logical error of commission is then performed: if the cultures are not really different, if the abilities are not really different, then the differences in test performance must be due to different levels of development. However, from the point of view of cultural relativism, if cultural differences are real and large, and if abilities develop differentially in adaptation to these differing contexts, then differences in test performance cannot logically be claimed to be differences in levels or amount of development.

An alternative to this approach is that taken by workers in "cognitive anthropology" (e.g., Cole et al., 1971). From their perspective, a single feature of the context (such as a specific role or a particular experience) is linked to a single performance (such as performance on a categorization task, or accuracy on a test of quantity estimation); this approach is illustrated in the mid portion of Figure 1. They contrast their "notion of culture-specific skills" with general ability theory (Cole et al., 1971, p. xiii), which often asserts that in some cultures, cognitive development is pushed further than in some other cultures (i.e. that levels or amount of intelligence differs). Assuming that cognitive processes are universal (Cole et al., p. 214; Cole and Scribner, 1974, p. 193), they argue that "cultural differences in cognition reside more in the situations to which particular cognitive processes are applied, than in the existence of a process in one cultural group and its absence in another" (Cole et al., 1971, p. 233). This emphasis on the particular, and culturally relative, nature of cognitive skills has meant that Cole and his co-workers do not search for *patterns* in their data. Generally, they appear unconcerned whether performance 1 is related to performance 2, or whether cultural element 1 tends to be experienced along with cultural element 2 in their sample. Unlike intelligence testers, they do not assume any universal pattern or structure in their skill data; indeed they seem uninterested a question. Similarly, they also seem uninterested in how the numerous cultural elements may be organized in a cultural system in which the individual develops.

The two approaches to understanding the relationships between culture and cognition thus far considered have differed in their acceptance of cultural relativism and in their concern for systematic relationships. The approach taken by *intelligence* testers ignored cultural relativism but assumed a universal structure in relationships; the approach taken by those interested in *specific skills* assumed the position of cultural relativism, but ignored systematic relationships. The approach taken by researchers into cognitive styles also assumes the position of cultural relativism, but in addition, searches for systematic relationships among abilities, among elements of the cultural context, and between patterns of contexts and abilities (see lower part of Figure 1).

One basis for this approach is in the work of Ferguson (1954, 1956) who argued that "cultural factors prescribe what shall be learned and at what age; consequently different cultural environments lead to the development of different patterns of ability" (1956, p. 121). Further, he argued that through overlearning and transfer, cognitive abilities become stabilized for individuals in a particular culture. Both cultural relativism and systematic relationships are thus implicated in this approach, and these have been adopted in much of the work on cognitive style.

A recent review of the research on various cognitive styles (Goldstein and Backman, 1978) makes it clear that while sharing a general approach, there are many important differences among the numerous research traditions. This need not be a problem here, for only one has received any substantial treatment in the cross-cultural field, that of field dependence-field independence (Witkin et al., 1962; Witkin and Goodenough, 1981).

This particular cognitive style includes not only cognitive (intellectual or perceptual), but also some social and emotional characteristics; this makes it a particularly useful approach to understanding the individual as a whole. The central feature of this style is the "extent of autonomous functioning" (Witkin, Goodenough and Oltman, 1979); that is, whether an individual characteristically relies on the external environment as a given, in contrast to working on it, is the key dimension along which individuals may be placed. As the name suggests, those who tend to accept or rely upon the external environment are relatively more Field Dependent (FD), while those who tend to work on it are relatively more Field Independent (FID). The construct is a dimension, the poles of which are defined by the two terms, FD-FID; individuals have a characteristic "place" on this dimension, reflecting their usual degree of autonomy (Witkin and Goodenough, 1981). However, individuals are not "fixed" into this usual place, since relatively more field-independent people may shift to a more field-dependent approach as the situation warrants; this "mobility" of cognitive style is an important feature of the style. Moreover, specific training has also been shown to affect one's usual style or approach.

This most recent conceptualization, which draws together perceptual, cognitive and social characteristics, is much broader than the original use of the term by Witkin et al., (1962). Over the course of research the field-dependent-independent dimension has referred to a series of components which has evolved as the research programme advanced. Initially it included only the contrasting ways in which individuals establish the upright in tests involving tilted frames or tilted rooms; more field-dependent people tended to rely upon the external frame, while more field independent persons tended to rely upon internal standards. Later on it came to include, as well, the tendency to separate or disembed a small item from a larger context; more field-dependent individuals had difficulty in overcoming the embedding context, while those more field-independent found it easier to overcome the influence of the organized complex. Later still, the dimension grew to include the articulated-vs-global field approach. Here, cognitive tasks were presented whose solution depended upon taking an essential element out of the context in which it was presented, and on restructuring the problem material so that the element became used in a different context; more field-dependent persons were less likely to restructure (and hence not solve) the problem, whereas more field-independent persons did restructure and more often arrived at a correct solution. Most recently the whole area of autonomy in social behavior and interpersonal competencies has come to be included in the FD-FID cognitive style as well; those who are more field-dependent tend to accept social influence more, and to be more competent in social relations, while those more field-independent tend to be more independent of social influence, and to exhibit less social competence.

The current conceptualization of the field dependent-field independent cognitive style, which we employ in this study, is that arrived at by Witkin and Goodenough (1981): autonomy of external referents in perceptual and social behavior. It has two indicators or components which are termed "restructuring skills" and "limited interpersonal competencies". The field dependent-independent cognitive style is thus a pervasive dimension of individual functioning, showing itself in the perceptual, intellectual, personality and social domains (Witkin and Goodenough, 1981), and it tends to be relatively stable over time and across situations. It "involves individual differences in process rather than content variables; that is to say, it refers to individual differences in the 'how' rather than the 'what' of behavior" (Witkin and Goodenough, 1981, p. 57). Since it refers to the 'how' of one's behavior, the field dependence-independence construct avoids some of the difficulties of the "ability" approach, where the focus is on the "how much"; this is particularly important in our use of the dimension cross-culturally.

Individual and group differences in the FD-FID cognitive style have been traced to two broad categories of influence: eco-cultural and acculturational. In the first, a cognitive style is viewed as a way of behaving which helps individuals and groups to cope with (adapt to) prevailing problems in their immediate environment. In the second, the style which has developed under these traditional conditions becomes altered to respond to new cultural influences; for the immigrant these typically are initial "Westernization" while still at home (e.g. by education, telecommunications), and the whole set of new influences which innundate him on arrival in the new setting. The reason for distinguishing these two broad sets of influences is that what may be adaptive in the traditional setting may not be adaptive in the new one.

What do we know about these two types of influence? In Table 1 are outlined some of the important influences: beginning with the ecological variables, an ecological approach asserts that interactions between an organism (in pursuing satisfaction of its primary needs) and its habitat will generate characteristic patterns of economic, demographic, sociocultural, and biological adaptations. The relationships in such a system are probabilistic, rather than guaranteed productions. One pervasive set of adaptations has been that of the "nomadic style", and incorporates a nomadic settlement pattern, a low concentration of population, and a hunting and gathering subsistence base. An adaptation in sharp contrast to this may be termed a "sedentary style", and includes a sedentary settlement pattern, a higher population concentration, and an agricultural economic base. Other subsistence activities, such as herding and fishing, have variable relationships to these demographic elements (see Berry, 1976, p. 119). This basic contrast in settlement style is evident in much of the background literature of studies of cultural ecology.

Table 1 -   Variables Influencing the Development of
Field Dependent-Field Independent Cognitive Style

Influence	Prediction of Cognitive Style	
	Field Independent ⟷ Field Dependent	
Ecological		
Subsistence pattern	hunting, gathering	agricultural
Settlement pattern	nomadic	sedentary
Population density	low	high
Cultural		
Stratification	low ("loose")	high ("tight")
Family type	nuclear	extended
Socialization emphases	assertion	compliance
Acculturation		
Western education	high	low
Wage employment	high	low
Telecommunications	high	low

In adaptation to these contrasting settlement styles are a set of cultural variables. In those societies with a nomadic style, there are likely to be relatively low levels of role diversity and sociocultural stratification; these have been termed "loose" by Pelto (1968). In contrast, those societies with a sedentary style are likely to have higher levels of role diversity and stratification; these have been termed "tight" by Pelto. Also lying along the dimension are the characteristic socialization practices examined by Barry, Child, and Bacon (1959). In their classical analysis, they were able to demonstrate that societies with a nomadic style tended to foster "assertion" during child rearing, whereas those with a sedentary style tended to foster "compliance".

The importance of these contrasting socialization emphases is that Witkin et al. (1962) have shown such emphases to be systematically related to the development of cognitive style among individuals within Western society. In the Western studies reviewed by Witkin and Goodenough (1981), socialization practices that emphasize strict rules and overprotection (cf. "compliance") tend to foster field dependence. In contrast, those practices that encourage separation from parental control (cf. "assertion") tend to foster the development of higher levels of field independence. In the cross-cultural studies reviewed by Witkin and Berry (1975) a similar relationship was evident. But, in addition, there is strong evidence that differences in the broader societal pressures emanating from tight and loose structures may reinforce such specific socialization emphases.

A final set of variables (in Table 1) deals with the impact of other cultures on both the traditional culture and individuals in it. These acculturative influences include education (very often of a Western type), a shift from traditional economic activity to wage employment, and an increase in settlement size and population density (urbanization). It is considered that both education and wage employment often encourage the analytic activity included in the field-independent cognitive style. Thus, an increase is likely in field-independence with increasing acculturation. However, in some cases there is a persistence of the traditionally-adaptive cognitive style for many generations during acculturation (Berry, 1981).

Both the ecological and cultural factors found among subsistence-level peoples are predictive of greater FD among agriculturalists and greater FID among hunters and gatherers. The evidence presented by Berry (1976), and the bulk of the evidence reviewed by Witkin and Berry (1975) support this generalization. Whether analyzed at the sample or individual level, ecocultural adaptation clearly accounts for a high proportion of group and individual differences in cognitive style development. In other words, samples that were nomadic and hunting and gathering in subsistence pattern were relatively FID in contrast to the sedentary agriculturalists. Influences stemming from acculturation also contribute to the distribution of scores on these tests. In all cases, though, acculturation (mainly through a form of Westernization) is less strongly related than is ecocultural adaptation.

In the outline of the concept of cognitive style, mention was made of "social autonomy" being theoretically related to "restructuring" within the FID cognitive style, and of "interpersonal competencies" being related to the FD end of the dimension. Social behaviors may also thus be included within the framework. More specifically, it may be predicted that individuals who grow up in a tight, stratified, and densely populated society, such as those often found in agriculturally based groups, will be more sensitive to group needs and more responsive to group requirements. In contrast, those developing in loose social units might be expected to be more independent of authority and less conforming to group pressure. A first examination (Berry, 1967) of this prediction contrasted samples from two cultures on a conformity task. This involved a situation where individuals are requested to judge the length of a line in the face of a false social norm. Differences between the two groups were as expected: in the tight samples, judgments were significantly closer to the suggested group norm than in the loose samples. At this group level of analysis, there was correspondence between the two behavioral domains that are theoretically related in the FD-FID cognitive style (Berry, 1979).

In summary, it should be clear that *individuals* are different from one another in cognitive style; to the extent that ecological and cultural factors play a communal role, we may also say that *groups* are likely to differ in cognitive style as well. Acculturational influences may work, both before and after immigration, to reduce these large cultural variations; however, cultural groups do tend to persist in traditional patterns of behavior in their new home (see Berry 1981 for an overview of patterns of acculturation). Host societies are thus likely to encounter nearly the full range of these cross-cultural differences among immigrant peoples. What does this mean for the educational process?

IMPLICATIONS FOR EDUCATION

In plural societies, institutions must increasingly "open up" to accommodate the broadening variety of clients. In some countries (for example Canada and Australia) there are official national policies of *multiculturalism,* which recognize cultural diversity to be a resource rather than a problem, and which encourage the maintenance and development of numerous cultural tradit ions within the framework of the larger society. For schools, this policy and ideology raises many questions, some of which are now receiving substantial attention (Samuda, Berry and Laferriere, 1981). One of these issues is how to work with such a variety of culturally-based cognitive styles in an educational system.

A major review of the educational implications of the FD-FID cognitive style was completed in 1977 by Witkin and his colleagues. The review is an extremely valuable source, and this section follows its structure closely. In that review Witkin et al. (1977) examined four major questions: how students learn, how teachers teach, how students and teachers interact, and the role of cognitive style in career differentiation.

Student learning styles are known to vary in relation to cognitive style. First, relatively FD students tend to be better than FID students at learning and remembering social material. There is no known difference in sheer learning ability or memory; however, the relevance of social materials to FD students give them the edge in this domain. Second, reflecting their external orientation

FD students are likely to learn better with external reinforcements, while FID students tend to learn better under conditions of intrinsic motivation. And third, FID students have been shown to learn better than FD students when the material lacks organization; however, the level of learning does not differ when the materials are already structured. All three differences in learning styles are directly predicted by the known orientations of students with differing cognitive styles. A foreknowledge of the likely style of individuals or groups of students, then, will be useful in the choice and presentation of educational materials.

Turning to the second area, that of teaching style, Witkin et al. (1977) have shown that relatively FID teachers are more likely to assume the responsibility for directing the teaching situation, while FD teachers favor teaching situations that allow interaction with students. Furthermore, FID teachers, but not FD ones, "feel that informing the student when a response was incorrect and, in addition, telling him why it was incorrect, was effective in enhancing student learning" (p. 29). Thus, the cognitive style of the teacher is also important, and this raises the question: what happens during student teacher *interactions*, when there is a stylistic match or mismatch between them?

A few answers have been indicated by Witkin et al. (1977). When the cognitive styles of students and teachers are matched, they view each other more positively than when they are not matched; this differential evaluation includes views about personal and about intellectual characteristics. Moreover, when cognitive styles are matched, evaluations of student performance are higher than when they are mismatched. This latter finding may not indicate bias but simply better actual performance (of both teaching and learning) when cognitive styles are similar.

Finally, Witkin et al. (1977) have brought together substantial evidence that a student's cognitive style is an important factor in career paths; thus, it is not only general ability which is operating here, but also the profile or organization of these abilities which is important (see Figure 1). With respect to vocational interests, relatively FID students tend to prefer positions where analysis is required, but social relations are not; in contrast FD students tend to prefer a job with a "people emphasis". Actual vocational choices are also related to cognitive style: in the academic setting, relatively FD students tend to specialize in the humanities, languages, clinical psychology, nursing and social or human services; FID students tend to choose the sciences, mathematics, engineering and experimental psychology. Despite these general orientations, overall achievement is not related to cognitive style. Thus, there is evidence for better performance in the "appropriate" special area, but across the board, it is not possible to claim that one is, for example, a better linguist than another is an engineer.

In addition to these observations about teaching and learning, similar arguments may be made in other educational spheres. In the design of school programs and the development of curriculum, it should be possible to make the material relevant to student interests, and to "pitch" the material in the appropriate way. And in the areas of testing, selection, guidance and counseling, an appreciation of stylistic differences, and their possible cultural roots, should permit a more sensitive, less rigid and less quantitative approach to student needs in a culturally plural system.

In summary, then, there are clear and documented implications of the cognitive styles of individuals in the educational process. While large individual differences are normally present in all cultural or ethnic groups, it is true to say on the basis of the section on cultural influences, that we are likely to find more FD persons from those societies which are traditionally tight agricultural groups than in looser social structures. Similarly, based upon acculturational influences, we are likely to find more FID persons in those societies which have been more exposed to "Westernization" than those which were more traditional before emigration.

Armed with these general relationships, it should be possible to provide educational services which take the students' (and their families') cognitive style into account, rather than attempt to treat all as if they were identical culturally and psychologically. To ignore these stylistic differences is to court the incorrect (and unjust) interpretations which have stemmed from unilinear "general intelligence" position — that differences are deficits, rather than qualitative variations which can enrich a school, a community and a nation.

REFERENCES

BARRY, H., CHILD, I., AND BACON, M. Relation of child training to subsustence economy. *American Anthropologist* 1959, *61*, 51-63.

BERRY, J.W. Independence and conformity in subsistence-level societies. *Journal of Personality and Social Psychology*, 1967, *7*, 415-418.

BERRY, J.W. *Human Ecology and Cognitive Style: Comparative Studies of Cultural and Psychological Adaptation.* New York: Sage-Halsted, 1976.

BERRY, J.W. A cultural ecology of social behavior. In L. Berkowitz (Ed.) *Advances in Experimental Social Psychology*, Vol. 12, New York: Academic Press, 1979.

BERRY, J.W. Acculturation: A Comparative analysis of alternative forms. Paper presented at conference, "The Comparative Acculturation of Ethnic Minority Immigrants". CUME, Florida International University, June 1981.

BERRY, J.W. AND DASEN, P.R. (EDS.). *Culture and Cognition.* London: Methuen, 1974.

COLE, M. ET AL. *The Cultural Context of Learning and Thinking.* New York: Basic Books, 1971.

COLE, M. AND SCRIBNER, S. *Culture and Thought.* New York: Wiley, 1974.

FERGUSON, G.A. On learning and human ability. *Canadian Journal of Psychology*, 1954, *8*, 95-112.

FERGUSON, G.A. On transfer and the abilities of man. *Canadian Journal of Psychology*, 1956, *10*, 121-131.

GOLDSTEIN, K. AND BACKMAN, S. *Cognitive Style: Five Approaches and Relevant Research.* New York: Wiley, 1978.

PELTO, P. The difference between tight and loose societies. *Transaction*, 1968, April, 37-40.

SAMUDA, R., BERRY, J.W. AND LAFERRIERE, M. *Perspectives on Multiculturalism in Education: An Invitational Symposium.* Kingston, Ontario, 1981.

VERNON, P.E. *Intelligence and Cultural Environment.* London: Methuen, 1969.

VERNON, P.E. *Intelligence: Heredity and Environment.* San Francisco: Freeman, 1979.

WITKIN, H.A. AND BERRY, J.W. Psychological differentiation in cross-cultural perspective. *Journal of Cross-Cultural Psychology.* 1975, *6*, 4-87.

WITKIN, H.A., DYK, R.B., FATERSON, H.F., GOODENOUGH, D.R. AND KARP, S. *Psychological Differentiation.* New York: Wiley, 1962.

WITKIN, H.A. AND GOODENOUGH, D.R. *Cognitive Styles: Essence and Origins.* New York: International Universities Press, 1981.

WITKIN, H.A., GOODENOUGH, D.R. AND OLTMAN, P.K. Psychological differentiation current status. *Journal of Personality and Social Psychology*, 1979, *37*, 1127-1145.

WITKIN, H.A., MOORE, C.A., GOODENOUGH, D.R. AND COX, P.W. Field-dependent and field-independent cognitive styles and their educational implications. *Review of Educational Research*, 1977, *47*, 1-64.

APPRENTICESHIP IN
MULTICULTURAL LIVING

By M. Ahmed Ijaz
and I. Helene Ijaz

> A truly pluralistic society where all peoples (men and women) of the world would
> be viewed and appreciated for being different, for contributing, and for being equal
> is not reserved for the millenium. It is an achievable goal with this generation. The
> challenge lies in bringing it about or causing it to happen (W. L. Smith, 1977:40).

Is a truly pluralistic and multicultural society such as that envisaged by Smith
(1977) a utopia or a realistic goal? Are we setting our aspiration too high in
seeking to create an awareness among our fellow-men that our ways of life, our
values, customs, and traditions, all that seems so familiar to them and to us, so
natural, and almost inevitable, represents only a fraction of the whole human
experience, that there are many people in this world who live in different
circumstances, with different values, and different styles of life? Is it an
unrealistic objective to bring about not only tolerance toward and acceptance of
all races and cultures, but also the recognition that the diversity of cultures
constitutes the very essence of the human experience? Are we striving for the
impossible in seeking to foster empathy, a sense of fellow feeling, for those who
values, behaviours and ways of life differ from our own, a feeling of shared
identity and a belief in what Murdock (1945) has termed "the psychic unity of
mankind."

> the assumption that all peoples ... irrespective of differences in geography and
> physique, are essentially alike in their basic psychological equipment and
> mechanism, and that cultural differences between them reflect only the different
> responses of essentially similar organisms to unlike stimuli or conditions
> (Murdock, 1945:125).

Our effort is essentially an educational one. The processes it involves are changes
in social structure as well as changes in attitudes, perception and thinking.
Ideally, these processes will result in the transformation of a society in which the
acceptability of life styles, values, and behaviours of ethnic minority groups is
measured by the degree to which they conform to those of the prevailing
majority group into a truly multicultural society in which behavioural patterns
of all cultural groups are regarded as equally acceptable and are, indeed, valued
because of their diversity.

Traditionally, the prime responsibility for educational measures has fallen to
the school. However, while it has unquestionably been viewed as the function of

the school to provide instruction in the three R's and at least a smattering of knowledge in such fields as science, geography and history, it has not been considered its responsibility to develop positive interethnic attitudes nor to attempt to change existing ones. Schools have had little experience in this area, and where attempts have been made to promote positive intergroup attitudes by educational measures in schools, the results have proved singularly unimpressive.

The problem partly derives from the fact that negative ethnic attitudes are often not recognized or acknowledged unless they have resulted in open violence and, at that stage, they are almost beyond remedy. On the other hand, actions of open violence may remain dormant for a considerable period of time, particularly in the presence of a minority group that "knows its place." New immigrants are especially vulnerable in that respect. They often tend to eagerly comply with the norms of the host culture in order to participate in its social and economic trappings. Many new immigrants consider prejudice, social abuse, and even exploitation by members of the host culture as inevitable consequences of immigration and tacitly accept them in the hope for a better future.

In school children ethnic prejudice, even where it manifests itself in name-calling and the occasional act of violence, is often not taken seriously. It is frequently interpreted as merely "kids' squabble" because it is assumed that children of different races and cultures "naturally" play together, mix with one another, and get along well. While hard data could sometimes provide evidence to the contrary, many school administrators are reluctant to undertake empirical investigations on the ethnic attitudes of students in their schools. Attitudes are developed in the home, so they claim, or by society at large, and attitude change is a territory that is beyond the responsibilities of the school. Efforts to purposely teach tolerance toward and understanding of other races and cultures frequently stem from the personal commitment of individual teachers rather than from systematic large scale attempts by school boards to teach multiculturalism. While in recent years a variety of teaching materials has been developed to assist teachers in their effort to teach multiculturalism, to date it is not clear exactly what pedagogical measures are conducive to the development of positive intergroup attitudes.

Empirical evidence regarding the effect of instruction on the development of positive ethnic attitudes is contradictory and inconclusive. Hayes and Conklin (1953) noted very little effect on the ethnic attitudes of eighth-grade students as a result of academic instruction about prejudice, and McNeil (1960), in a similar study with high school seniors, established an increase in prejudice. Kraus (1960) and Elrod (1968) found the use of movies in a course with high school students ineffective. Katz (1955) found that information about Jews only resulted in a decrease in anti-Semitism when it was linked with direct discussion about anti-Semitism. By contrast, instructional programs that focused on cultural similarities (e.g. Litcher and Johnson, 1969; Kehoe and Hood, 1978; Salyachivin, 1972, 1973) have been found to be more successful in promoting positive intergroup attitudes. Litcher and Johnson (1969) in a study with second-grade white Mid-western children with little previous exposure to Blacks found that the use of a multi-ethnic rader which contained interracial stories brought about more favourable attitudes toward Blacks. Teachers were instructed not to initiate or "encourage" discussion with regard to racial or ethnic differences. A study by Salyachivin (1972) in Toronto, Canada, with fifth- and sixth-graders and a later replication by the same investigator (Salyachivin, 1973) with grade eight and eleven students in British Colombia found that stressing similarities, both positive and negative, between the pupils' own culture and the target culture produced more positive attitudes toward the target culture. Similarly, a study by Kehoe and Hood (1978) with grade five and grade six students in British Colombia was successful in achieving attitudinal change. Over a period of eleven weeks, the children viewed films and were involved in a variety of activities accentuating positive similarities between the cultures of various ethnic groups in Canada. Activities involved discussions, singing, painting and role playing.

In several studies role playing has been found to be successful as a strategy for reducing racial prejudice. Gray and Ashmore (1975) had subjects read brief descriptions of three newspaper articles documenting the suffering of a minority group. The subjects were then asked to write an essay in favour of strong public and private efforts to create opportunities for minorities. Breckheimer and Nelson (1976) asked subjects to act out causes of discrimination and ways of promoting better interracial cooperation. Kehoe and Rogers (1978) used a role exchange test in principle testing discussions in order to induce self-insight. Acts of discrimination against members of minority groups were shown and students were subsequently asked whether they would be willing to exchange places with the most disadvantaged person in the situation. According to Kehoe (1980:37)

> role playing a previously unacceptable position increases its acceptability ... if a subject voluntarily chooses to undertake the action opposed to his beliefs, the resultant attitude change can be even greater.

Role playing activities essentially involve a vicarious experience approach. In all of the above studies involving role playing (Breckheimer and Nelson, 1976; Gray and Ashmore, 1975; Kehoe and Rogers, 1978) members of minority groups were shown in the role of victims. Kehoe (1979:4) cautions that vicarious identification with victims may produce results opposite to the ones desired:

> If the attitudes towards the minority group are already extremely negative, the showing of cruelty against that minority group may permit vicarious identification with the assailant not the victim.

By contrast, vicarious identification with a person of another culture in a situation typical to that culture may represent a highly sensitive means of apprending differential social and moral norms and behavioural patterns, i.e. what Triandis (1972) has defined as a people's "subjective culture." Acting out the role of a member of another culture in an environment particular to that culture not only provides a new perspective, opens up new insights into unfamiliar situations and experiences, but also fosters the development of empathy for the person represented.

According to Triandis (1975), intercultural conflict is largely based on a lack of understanding of each other's subjective cultures. Triandis defines "subjective culture" as a cultural group's "characteristic way of perceiving the man-made part of its environment ... The perception of rules and the group's norms, roles and values are aspects of the subjective culture" (1972:4). He argues that "cultures differ in the amount of differentiation that characterizes them" (p. 45). This differentiation may vary among and within modes of exchange, and in the concept of time. Persons who come from societies with different levels of differentiation will have difficulty communicating with each other because they are likely to make wrong isomorphic attributions. According to Triandis (1975:41) "isomorphic attributions" correspond to the idea "If I had been raised in that culture and had the kinds of experiences that he has had, I would do exactly what he did."

Triandis (1975) suggested the use of cultural programs that place a prime focus on the imparting of information regarding the nature and strength of the connections between norms, role structures and role perceptions, the expression of general intentions, common self-concepts, the evaluation of certain kinds of behaviours, common differentiations among types of people within and between modes of exchange, as well as across time and space, in the other culture. Triandis and his associates developed the so-called "cultural assimilator", a programmed technique of cultural training in the subjective culture, which is designed to improve isomorphic attributions toward a particular cultural group. By means of this technique, the learner is gradually guided toward an understanding of given situations in the target culture from the viewpoint of members of that culture. Instruction essentially involves the imparting of knowledge about differential situations in the target culture and an analysis of the norms underlying behavioural patterns in those situations. Triandis and his associates found that in adults such training produced not only a greater understanding of the target culture, but also an improvement in intergroup relations and greater success in intergroup activities.

Triandis' method constitutes a highly cognitive approach to attitudinal change although one of its essential components is the attempt to achieve vicarious identification with members of the target culture. While such a method may be effective with adults, the findings of Hayes and Conklin (1953) and McNeil (1960) have shown that a focus on knowledge and understanding alone is little successful in reducing prejudice in school children. The findings of Litcher and Johnson (1969), Kehoe and Hood (1978) and Salyachivin (1972, 1973) suggest that while even with elementary school children information about the target culture may constitute an important component of an educational approach for developing positive intergroup attitudes, it is essential that such information be organized around cross-cultural similarities.

When information about another culture is provided, intercultural differences often tend to become accentuated more than similarities. Such a strategy may result not so much from the ethnocentrism of the person providing the information or from his unfavourable attitudes toward members of the target culture as from the fact that by the human conceptual system contrasts are perceived as being more salient than similarities (Rosch, Mervis, Gray, Johnson and Boyes-Braem, 1976). Consequently, a person's informative reporting about the life style, customs, traditions and behavioural patterns of members of another culture will often unintentionally highlight aspects in which the cultures differ rather than those where they are similar, unless a conscious effort is made to accentuate the similar. On the other hand, the perception of such differences by the recipients of the information is likely to foster prejudice rather than tolerance and acceptance.

According to Newcomb (1950), people often tend to associate being different with being bad. Such associations appear to derive from a need for psychological consistency or balance. Differences are felt to create dissonance and, for this reason, are associated with badness. By contrast, the perception of similarity provides psychological balance and is more likely to produce associations of goodness and acceptability.

Similarities between cultures exist predominantly in the basic human needs, values, feelings, and emotions which underlie the surface structure of social and behavioural patterns. Basic human needs such as the need for food, clothing, shelter, and health-care are the same across cultures. Similarly, feelings such as love and hatred, happiness and sorrow, joy and anger, are universal among humans. Many social conventions are also similar cross-culturally, e.g. greetings, courtship, marriage, the valuing of kinship ties, religious rituals, and funeral rites. While such basic human needs and values are shared across all cultures, cultures differ in their interpretation and expression.

An educational approach structured around cross-cultural similarities will have to consciously trace and highlight such basic intercultural links if prejudice toward a particular culture is to be overcome. The reduction or elimination of prejudice is an inevitable prerequisite if understanding of and empathy for members of that culture are to be developed. Approaches such as the consistency approach and role exchange test advocated by Kehoe (1979) and Kehoe and Rodgers (1978) which are designed to break down prejudice by inducing self-insight, may be successful with older students, but it is doubtful that methods involving such abstract reasoning will be very effective with elementary school children. Students at the elementary school level will also find it more difficult than older students to independently draw inferences from differential cultural and behavioural patterns regarding underlying universal values and norms, and they will require help and guidance in developing this ability. With them a non-rationalistic and highly experiential approach with a strong appeal to the senses, the emotions and the imagination may be more effective in attacking such an irrational phenomenon as prejudice. In younger students the most fruitful learning experiences usually occur through *doing* and experiencing things themselves. Activities that provide an opportunity for active personal involvement, intellectual, physical, and emotional, are most likely to result in successful learning. Such activities will also produce the greatest motivation and thereby a high level of energy and effort which, in turn, will enhance learning ability.

Activities that are highly charged in terms of vicarious identification may be particularly effective in effacing existing emotional and social barriers. Acting out the part of a person in a different culture in a situation typical to that culture, trying to sense and express his or her feelings, emotions, and thoughts in that situation, and determining appropriate action plans provides shared participation in the other culture which is second only to actually being placed in that situation oneself. Genuine vicarious identification with a person in another culture not only requires intuition and role reasoning skill, but also empathy, i.e. the ability to project one's personality entirely into that of the person represented, not only to understand his or her viewpoint of the situation, but to adopt it and to act in accordance with it. Indeed, the development of empathy for members of another culture may constitute the key factor to intercultural understanding.

Four major components have been identified that are essential for a successful educational program at the elementary school level which is to bring about positive attitudes toward members of a different cultural or racial group: (1) information about the target culture; (2) a focus on intercultural similarities and basic human values; (3) activities providing active personal involvement, intellectual, emotional, and physical; and (4) opportunities for vicarious identification with members of the target culture. An instructional program containing these four components will address all levels of the students' personalities and thus shape their attitudes through a variety of channels, rational, emotional, affective, and physical. By emphasizing universal human needs and values as the basis of cultural diversity and by providing meaningful opportunities to students to vicariously experience differential expressions and interpretations of such basic human needs and values, schools may effectively contribute to a feeling of shared identity among members of all races and cultures.

That such educational programs can also change existing intergroup attitudes among students in a positive direction becomes evidenced by a recent study we undertook in Toronto, Canada. An empirical investigation of racial attitudes of 170 white fifth- and sixth-graders had revealed a high degree of racial prejudice toward East Indians. A program was introduced which focused on a cross-cultural comparison of norms, values, role structures and behavioural patterns with special emphasis on the East Indian and North American cultures. Cross-cultural similarities were accentuated and differences between cultures were interpreted as being essentially differential expressions of similar human values. It was attempted to achieve an understanding of the above concepts through the medium of the arts: drama, music, folk-dance, and crafts. An artist/teacher from India was hired to implement the program in two grade five and two grade six classes which had participated in the previous attitudinal study. Six grade five and an equal number of grade six classes which had also taken part in that study served as the control group.

The instructor sought to elucidate moral and social values prevailing in India by describing and interpreting typical behavioural patterns in a variety of situations. The children were immersed into situations that are typical of the East Indian culture, and through role-playing they were encouraged to identify with members of that culture in those situations. Finally, the situations described and the values reflected in them were related to similar situations and values in the students' own culture.

Folk dances as a form of communal celebrations in India and other parts of the world were learned and compared. It was shown that although such dances may differ across cultures, the feelings and emotions expressed by them are universal and shared by all peoples: the joy and happiness felt at a wedding, at the birth of a child, and on other joyous occasions; the grief and sorrow experienced at the loss of a beloved person, or the misery and hardship resulting from natural and other disasters. Indian folk dances are characterized by a distinct language of symbolic hand gestures and motions which are highly expressive in terms of social and religious behaviour. The meaning of such gestures and motions was elucidated and related to similar behavioural patterns in everyday life. For example, the instructor explained that a dancer's tightly folded hands and her reverential bowing motions at the beginning of a dance express her respect for her teachers and the deity. She then showed that forms of greeting in everyday life are characterized by similar behavioural patterns. Religious rituals reflected in the dances such as the lighting of candles at Divali, the Hindu festival of light, were related to similar customs and traditions in other cultures, for instance, the Jewish festival of 'Hanukka' and the Swedish festival of St. Lucia. Thanksgiving dances in India and North America were compared and interpreted in terms of differential geographic and climatic conditions. Similarly, it was shown how work dances in different countries reflect typical activities in and social prescriptions for certain occupations and social classes.

Dances served as an objective as well as a medium of instruction. They provided starting-points for discussion and a variety of other activities such as drama, story-telling, toy-making and crafts. Of special appeal to the students was a comparison of children's games and toys in India, North America, and other parts of the world. The emphasis was always on similarities rather than on differences between cultures.*

A wealth of information was provided about the East Indian culture. By acting out the roles of members of the East Indian culture in a variety of situations, the students were led to identify with them and to understand and empathize with their actions and patterns of behaviour. Finally, by relating East Indian behavioural patterns, customs and traditions to modes of conduct in North America and in other parts of the world in similar situations, it was attempted to reduce the notion of foreigness and "strangeness" the children may have attached to the East Indian culture.

The program which was introduced as part of the Social Studies curriculum consisted of nine seventy-minute sessions spread, at weekly intervals, over a period of nine weeks. The students greatly enjoyed the program and it generated active participation by all those involved in it. It stimulated interest in other cultures and the East Indian culture in particular, and it lead to various kinds of follow-up work in social studies, language arts, art and crafts, and music.

The effect of the program on students' racial attitudes toward East Indians was evaluated by means of a Semantic Differential Measure, the Bogardus Social Distance Scale, and a student evaluation sheet. The results revealed significantly improved attitudes toward East Indians in all students who had participated in the program. A follow-up study showed that the effects of the program were maintained three months after its conclusion (Ijaz, 1980).

*Note: A detailed description of the program may be found in Ijaz and Ijaz (1981).

Evidently, the program was so successful in changing the students' racial attitudes because it represented a realistic and emotionally intensive experience in multicultural living. It provided an apprenticeship in multicultural living. It provided an apprenticeship in East Indian living rather than academic instruction *about* life in South East Asia. Through its focus on similarities between cultures the program succeeded in creating greater tolerance toward and acceptance of cultural differences which so often constitute the sources of ethnic prejudice.

More such multicultural programs need to be introduced into our schools. In a pluralistic society such as ours schools can no longer afford to ignore the cultural heritage and values of large numbers of minority group members. The retaining of what Brown (1976) has called a "monocultural perspective" in terms of historical and social events and issues can only lead to an undermining of the feeling of self-worth of minority group members, a devaluation and disintegration of their cultures, and increasing social tensions between members of the majority and minority groups. Training and retraining in the concept of multiculturalism will be required on the part of teachers and administrators as well as of all of us. "Retraining requires the deliberate act of repudiating the ethnocentric melting pot model and the acceptance of ethnic minority cultures as different rather than deficient" (Samuda, 1980:241). In a multicultural society such as ours, cultural diversity is a reality and, in a way, a necessity for the smooth interaction of all members of society. Only an effective apprenticeship in multicultural living can help develop in our children a feeling of shared identity with those whose values and ways of life are different.

REFERENCES

BRECKHEIMER, STEVEN E. AND NELSON, ROSEMARY. Group Methods for Reducing Racial Prejudice and Discrimination, *Psychological Reports,* 1976, *39,* 1259-1268.

BROWN, JAMES A. Intercultural Understanding, *McGill Journal of Education,* 11, 2, 1976, 190-197.

ELROD, W. The Effect of Persuasive Communication in Interracial Attitudes, *Contemporary Education,* 1968, *39,* 148-151.

GRAY, DAVID B. AND ASHMORE, D. Comparing the Effects of Informational, Role-playing and Value-discrepancy Treatments of Racial Attitude, *Journal of Applied Social Psychology,* 1975, *5,* 3, 262-281.

HAYES, M.L. AND CONKLIN, M.E. Intergroup Attitudes and Experimental Change, *Journal of Experimenal Education,* 1953, *22,* 19-36.

IJAZ, M.A. Ethnic Attitudes of Elementary School Children Toward Blacks and East Indians and the Effect of a Cultural Program on these Attitudes, Unpublished Doctoral Dissertation, University of Toronto, 1980.

———— AND IJAZ, I.H. A Cultural Program for Changing Racial Attitudes, *The History and Social Science Teacher, 17,* 1, 1981, forthcoming.

KATZ, I. *Conflict and Harmony in an Adolescent Interracial Group.* New York: University Press, 1955.

KEHOE, JOHN. Ethnic Prejudice and the Role of the School, A collection of published and unpublished papers, 1980.

———— Effective Tools for Combating Racism in the Schools, Keynote Speech, Third Annual Human Rights and Civil Liberties Institute, Toronto, March, 1979.

———— AND HOOD, BETTY. An Evaluation of an Anti-Prejudice Film Program, Unpublished paper, University of British Columbia, 1979.

———— AND ROGERS, TODD W. The Effect of Principle Testing Discussions on Student Attitudes Toward Selected Groups Subjected to Discrimination, *Canadian Journal of Education, 3,* 4, 1978.

KRAUS, S. Modifying Prejudice: Attitude Change as Function of the Race of the Communicator, *Audiovisual Communication Review,* 1960, *10,* 12-22.

MCNEIL, J.D. Changes in Ethnic Reaction Tendencies During High School, *Journal of Educational Research,* 1960, *53,* 199-200.

MURDOCK, G.P. The Common Denominator of Cultures, in R. Linton (Ed.), *The Science of Man in the World Crises,* New York: Colombia University Press, 1945.

NEWCOMB, T.M. *Social Psychology,* New York: Dryden Press, 1950.

ROSCH, E., MERVIS, C.B., GRAY, W., JOHNSON, D. AND BOYES-BRAEM, P. Basic Objects in Natural Categories, *Cognitive Psychology, 8,* 3, 1976, 382-439.

————, Strategies for International Understanding, cited in John Kehoe, Accentuate the Similar, *Edge,* 1973, *1,* 1, 9-10.

SAMUDA, RONALD J. AND D.J. CRAWFORD. *Testing, Assessment, Counselling and Placement of Ethnic Minority Students:* Current methods in Ontario. Ministry of Education, Ontario, 1980.

SMITH, W.L. Why Different Education for Different Groups? in C. A. Grant (Ed.), *Multicultural Education: Commitments, Issues, and Applications,* Washington: Association for Supervision and Curriculum Development, 1977.

TRIANDIS, H.C. Culture Training, Cognitive Complexity and Interpersonal Attitudes, in Brislin, R. W., Bochner, S., and Lorner, W. J. (Eds.) *Cross-cultural Perspectives on Learning,* New York: John Wiley and Sons, 1975.

————, VASSILIOU, V., TANAKA, Y., AND SHANMUGAN, A.V. *The Analysis of Subjective Culture,* New York: John Wiley and Sons, 1972.

LANGUAGE IN THE EDUCATION
OF ETHNIC MINORITY IMMIGRANTS

By Wallace E. Lambert
and Donald M. Taylor
McGill University

When there are policy decisions to be made about education for children from immigrant families, it would be inappropriate, in our way of thinking, to let language considerations play the dominant role, even in the case where the immigrant youngster has a home language different from that of the school and of the host nation. Rather than emphasizing language, education itself should be kept clearly in the center of focus, we believe. And the education offered should be deep and comprehensive because the children and families involved have enough problems of catching up and integrating without being short-changed with a superficial or non-relevant program of education. To water down or unduly stretch out the education offered would increase the immigrant student's handicaps in trying to cope, belong and succeed in a new land.

With attention focused squarely on how to provide ethnic minority students a comprehensive, even better-than-average, education, policy makers must then broaden their perspective os that they can deal effectively not just with language issues but also with the social contexts in which languages are embedded. In other words, those in responsible positions have to be sensitive to a) the psychological realities of language — realizing that languages are always intimately linked with peoples' identities and social skills and with their feelings of security and confidence, and b) the social realities — realizing that language programs have serious implications not only for a particular target group, like immigrant ethnic pupils, but for all other groups who share the same social environment and who interact with those in the target group. It is at this point that educational policy makers can ask themselves a set of critical questions about the language competencies of immigrant ethnic pupils. In the USA, the questions would likely take this form: Is there any hope for immigrant ethnic children who are essentially monolingual in a language other than English? Do children who are nearly bilingual in that language and English suffer confusion and divided loyalties? Can anything be done for those who have only a rudimentary mix of parts of the two languages, to the extent that they are actually hampered in their verbal potential across the board?

---

*Paper presented at the conference on The Education of Ethnic Minority Immigrants, December 13-16, 1981, Miami, Florida, sponsored by The Center for Urban and Minority Education and The South Atlantic Bilingual Education Service Center.

In each instance policy decisions are complex and there are no simp͏ answers. Take the case of essentially monolingual non-English-speak͏ children. Should one try to help by immersing them in English so that t͏ can catch up? At first glance, the obvious answer would be "Yes" "Proceed with full speed!" But such an apparently constructive decision is n͏ without its costs. Immersion or submersion in English in this instance represents an abrupt switch-off of a linguistic system that is simultaneously the child's "home" language, with all that that implies, and his/her "conceptual" language — the linguistic code that has functioned from infancy on to form, maintain, and elaborate thoughts and ideas. It is also a culturally significant language — be it Albanian, Basque, Chinese — and to wash it out of that child's mind, through disuse, through swamping by English, or through social disrespect in any form, is to reduce by one an American adult-to-be who could have linguistic and cultural command of a significant foreign language. It may also produce culturally frustrated and disappointed adults who might well feel that, in becoming Americanized, they were induced to eradicate an important part of themselves.

Consider next the subgroup of children who are either already close to being bilingual or potentially so in the home language and English. How much should English language training be emphasized in these instances? The same considerations mentioned above hold again, and perhaps with even more force, because real opportunities could be missed in this case to help children become comfortably at ease with two precious languages.

What typically happens in such considerations, just when the argument for the value of bilingualism starts to make sense, is that policy makers are prone to shift the thrust to another related issue: they begin to worry about divided allegiances and about biliguality itself which is seen as a clear signal of mixed-up allegiances. The really important question, however, is whether such worries and suspicions are justified in light of what is now known about bilinguals and bilingualism.

Consider also the subgroup of ethnic immigrant children who become trapped between the language of home and the language of the new nation, trapped in the sense that they are grossly handicapped in dealing with any form of written or spoken language. This subgroup which is sometimes referred to as "semi-lingual" (Skutnabb-Kangas & Toukomaa, 1976) or as "in a psycholinguistic limbo" (Lambert, 1981) must be treated with special care because they are less likely to respond to any form of remedial language program, even those that immerse or submerse them in English. Protracted language rehabilitation or catch up programs can also put such children hopelessly behind in the academic content subjects that are appropriate for their age. And these basic academic content subjects are just what these children want and need most. They are also just what these frustrated children would grasp best if language did not get in the way.

Finally, to be effective, policy makers would have to broaden their perspective one step further. While keeping the aims of education in the center focus and then taking into consideration the language competencies and weaknesses of ethnic immigrant pupils, policy makers must then adjust their perspective to include the host nation peers of the immigrant youngsters. The English-speaking white and black mainstream students are not passive onlookers to the struggles of ethnic immigrants. Indeed their reactions determine the ultimate success or failure of the struggles. They function as representatives of the host nation's major reference groups and they are taken as positive or negative models by the immigrant child. Should these mainstream models become suspicious or negative, or should they feel relatively neglected because of the attention shown to immigrants, no educational program for ethnic immigrants could work. How to involve the mainstream child and to solicit his/her support in any program for immigrants becomes the critical question. And since the mainstream students most likely to be negative are those who have not been given the opportunity to be fully integrated nor adequately educated themselves — *like the blacks in most urban areas of the USA* — these already neglected mainstream minority groups become the most critical element of all in the puzzle of policy decisions about immigrants.

The complex issue of helping ethnic immigrant children become educated, regardless of the language problems involved, ends up being the least of our worries. This is so because we have, we believe, some cogent and persuasive research information to present that can help ethnic immigrant children become both well educated and comfortably Americanized. Similarly, we have solid suggestions for the English-speaking American mainstreamers. However, were these suggestions to be put into practice in communities, and were they to become promising and exciting educational alternatives for the immigrant and the established mainstreamer, they could at the same time be seen as threatening and disheartening for the neglected mainstream minorities. We deal with this matter in the final section of the paper.

Our purpose here is to offer suggestions for a new and different form of bilingual education for ethnic minority immigrant children, one that puts the main emphasis on education at the same time as it broadens the scope of what is meant by "bilingual education" to include majority or mainstream young people as well as ethnolinguistic minority groups. Bilingual education, however, cannot be divorced from its psychological and social consequences. We offer first an overview of bilingual education. In the following sections we focus on psychological and social factors separately. The suggestions to follow are not meant for policy makers only, but for educators, teachers, parents and pupils as well.

BILINGUAL EDUCATION:
SOCIAL-PSYCHOLOGICAL CONSIDERATIONS

Let us illustrate our argument with examples from comparable Canadian experiences that were directed at making society fairer for both of Canada's two "founding peoples" — French speaking and English speaking Canadians. Although Canadian in content, these examples are pertinent to American society because similar social processes run their courses in both settings. In Canada these are more visible because of socio-political movements towards independence or separation on the part of the French Canadians. Although there are many Canadian/American parallels, there are still important differences. For instance, Canada's constitution has clear provisions for the protection of the language and culture of both French- and English-speaking subgroups, and although the government has a policy favoring multiculturalism, it does not provide extended support for education being conducted in any of the numerous other home languages spoken in Canada. Since World War II, non-English speaking immigrants make up a sizeable proportion of Canada's population. To its great credit, the USA has federal laws requiring educational help — involving teaching via the home language of pupils — for all non-English speaking ethnic groups who, it is recognized, are placed at a disadvantage in schools and in occupations that presume native competence in English. *However, the USA shows no signs of recognizing or appreciating the de facto bilingual character of contemporary America which has nearly as many families with Spanish as the home language as there are people in the total population of Canada.* And the English-Spanish bilingual character of contemporary America is only one strain, for there are various other equally vital ethnolinguistic groups, each contributing to a fascinating multicultural American society. There is, then, much more to be done to capitalize on this ethnolinguistic richness in both America and Canada.

French-speaking Canadians have had a long history of finding themselves second-class citizens in a social world which has reinforced Anglo-American values and the English language. The second-class status showed itself in the form of French-speaking Canadians playing subordinate roles to English Canadians, the dominant subgroup in Canadian society, comparable to the English-speaking white mainstreamer in America. Not only have French Canadians been grossly underrepresented in the upper levels of Canada-wide status hierarchies, but even in the Province of Quebec, where they constitute some 80 percent of the population, French Canadians have not, relative to English Canadians, made it occupationally or economically, and their style of life has been ignored, ridiculed and blamed as the cause of their social and economic position. The trouble is that this type of thinking becomes contagious and over time even members of the marked minority group begin to believe they are inferior in some sense and blame themselves for their inferiority (see Lambert, 1967). It takes much reflection in frustrating situations of this sort to see through the sophistry and realize that one's ethnic or social-class group is in no way inherently inferior, but simply that those with the power advantages have learned well how to keep the advantages and that their social-class cushion makes keeping power relatively easy for them. Stereotyping or otherwise marking minority groups — people they really know very little about — becomes an effective way for the majority group to keep others out of the power sphere.

As social psychologists, we began to study this state of affairs in Canada some 25 years ago just as two extreme solutions to the "French Canadian problem" were coming into vogue: 1) French Canadians should pull up their socks and compete — meaning they should master English and Anglo-American ways — while toning down their French Canadian-ness; 2) French Canadians should pull apart or separate — meaning they should form a new independent nation where they could be masters of their own fate and where the French Canadian language and culture could be protected. Both alternatives worried us because one meant giving up a style of life that was precious, and the other meant closing a society through separation, "closing" in the sense that Karl Popper (1966) uses the term in describing socio-political attempts to create a conflict-free subworld where the "good old ways" will be protected. Instead we viewed the French Canadian way of life as something valuable for Canada as a whole — a nation whose potential and fascination rest in its multicultural/multilingual makeup — whether or not it was appreciated as such by the majority of English or French Canadians.

So we became interested in reducing if possible the ignorance of French Canadian-ness and in enhancing an appreciation for it among Anglo-Canadian children. This then became the guiding purpose for the research initiated at McGill on "early immersion" schooling (see Lambert & Tucker, 1972; Swain, 1974; Genesee, 1978-79) wherein English speaking children, with no French language experience in their homes and little if any in their communities, entered public school kindergarten or grade 1 classes that are conducted by a monolingual French speaking teacher. This "early immersion" or "home-to-school language-switch" program, as we call it, is kept exclusively French through grade 2 and only at grade 2 or 3 is English introduced, in the form of a language arts program, for one period a day. By grade 4 particular subject matters are taught in English (by a separate English speaking teacher) so that by grades 5 and 6 some 60% of instruction is in English (see Lambert, 1979).

The concept of immersion schooling was based on a very important and fundamental premise, that people learn a second or third language in the same way they learn their first, and that language is best learned in contexts where the person is socially stimulated to learn the language and is exposed to it in its natural form.

The consistent findings from 15 years of careful research on children in immersion programs permit several conclusions which bear not only on the linguistic consequences of these programs but the psychological and social consequences as well. 1) Immersion pupils are taken along by *monolingual* teachers to a level of functional bilingualism that could not be duplicated in any other fashion short of living and being schooled in a foreign setting. Furthermore, pupils arrive at that level of competence 2) without detriment to home-language skill development; 3) without falling behind in the all-important content areas of the curriculum, indicating that the incidental acquisition of French does not distract the students from learning new and complex ideas; 4) without any form of mental confusion or loss of normal cognitive growth; and 5) without a loss of identity or appreciation for their own ethnicity. Most important of all in the present context, 6) they also develop a deeper appreciation for French Canadians and a more balanced outlook towards them by having learned about them and their culture through their teachers and through their developing skill with the language of French Canadians.

What is exciting about this program, over and above its educational and cognitive impact, is that it opens children's minds to an otherwise foreign and possibly threatening outgroup. It also provides certain socio-political insights that monolingual mainstreamers would likely never have. For example, the immersion children come to the realization that peaceful democratic coexistence among members of distinctive ethnolinguistic groups calls for something more than simply learning one another's languages (see Blake, Lambert, Sidoti, & Wolfe, 1981; Cziko, Lambert, Sidoti, & Tucker, 1979). Having learned the other language well and having learned to appreciate the other cultural group, children with immersion experience, compared to controls, realize that effective and peaceful coexistence calls as well for opportunities for both ethnic groups of young people to interact socially on an equitable basis. This is a very sophisticated insight.

Thus a new approach to bilingual education is now available, and since it works as well in other parts of Canada where few if any French Canadians are encountered in social life (see Swain, 1974), it, or some variation of it, can be expected to work equally well in the USA. In fact, there are currently some ten or more communities in the USA where comparable early immersion programs for mainstream English-speaking children are underway (in Spanish, French and German, so far), and from all available accounts they are working splendidly (see Cohen, 1976; Samuels & Griffore, 1979; Montgomery County Public Schools, 1976; Derrick, 1980; Grittner, 1981; O'Connell, 1981; Sidoti, 1981). Part of the reason for their success is that school administrators and principals, after an initial period of skepticism and wariness, become extremely pleased and proud of the outcomes. Furthermore, the costs of the programs are surprisingly low, compared to second-language-teaching programs, because the regular teachers' salaries go to the new "foreign speaking" teachers.

But what really counts as success is the pride and progress reflected by teachers, parents and pupils. For example, Frank Grittner, the supervisor of Second Language Education for the State of Wisconsin has collected data on third grade English-speaking children (few with German ethnic backgrounds) in a German immersion program where they were taught thorough German for three years. That particular immersion program was related to a plan for desegration and thus some 40% of the pupils involved are black. At the end of grade 3, 100 percent of the German immersion pupils scored in the average to above average range on the Metropolitan Achievement Test for Reading (in English) compared to 70 percent for Milwaukee schools in general and 77 percent for U.S. norm groups. Likewise for Mathematics Test scores (also tested through English) the respective averages were 92, 71 and 77 percent. Similar outcomes are available for English-speaking American children in a French immersion program in Holliston, Massachusetts as of the end of grade 2 (O'Connell, 1981). In New York City where an interesting program of partial immersion in Spanish for English-speaking pupils has been tried out, the end-of-year parental responses and evaluations are extremely favorable. What characterizes the parents' reaction is the delight they show that their children are learning about Spanish-speaking people and developing an appreciation for them at the same time as they acquire the basics of the language. They are pleased not for "instrumental" reasons but for "integrative" ones, i.e., inter-group harmony is initiated, not that their children can profit in the business world by knowing Spanish (Sidoti, 1981).

Furthermore, there is strong evidence to show that monolingual Anglo-Canadian children can handle easily a "double immersion" program wherein French and Hebrew, for example, are used in separate streams, as the languages of instruction for Jewish youngsters in Montreal (see Genesee & Lambert, 1979). The striking success of double-immersion programs, incidentally, gives second thoughts to Canadian policy makers who promote multiculturalism but stop short of providing at least some instruction via the home language. The point is that ethnic monirities in Canada might easily handle and enjoy education that is trilingual — French, English and home language — just as these Jewish children handle and enjoy education that is French, Hebrew and English.

The variants of the immersion program that might be particularly relevant when applied in the USA are limited only by one's imagination. For instance, the New York City variant is a partial immersion program that can be increased in time devoted and in scope to satisfy large numbers of pupils with a variety of language options (see Sidoti, 1981). Then there is an extremely interesting "Language to Share" program (Thomas, 1980) wherein ethnic minority adolescents are trained to be junior teachers of their home language to pupils two or three years younger than themselves. Similarly, there are possibilities for "language exchange" programs (Lambert, 1978b) wherein anglophone pupils who are interested in learning a particular foreign language are paired up by a master teacher with a pupil who has that foreign language as his/her home language and who exchanges two or so hours per week in teaching it informally while receiving English instruction in return.

What this all means is that there is now available an effective means of developing a functionally bilingual citizenry. The evidence, both scientific and anecdotal, is so consistent that our concern is not that such programs will not be implemented, but rather that they will be instigated without careful consideration to the psychological and social consequences. It is to these issues that we now turn our attention.

PSYCHOLOGICAL IMPLICATIONS
OF LANGUAGE PROGRAMS

Our analysis begins by noting which segments of society were given major attention in the immersion experiments: it was the English-speaking Canadian and the English-speaking American mainstreamers — the segments that are most secure in their ethnic and linguistic identity, but the ones most in need of knowledge about and sensitivity towards other ethnic and linguistic groups. To the extent that mainstream children are sensitized to and educated in another language and culture, the better the chances are of developing a fairer, more equitable society. The better too are the chances of improving the self-views of ethnolinguistic minority children who are heartened and complimented when they realize that mainstream children are making sincere gestures to learn about them, their language, and ways of life.

We have referred to this process of developing bilingual and bicultural skills among English speaking Canadians or American children as an "additive" form of bilingualism, implying that these children, with no fear of ethnic/linguistic erosion, can add one or more foreign languages to their accumulating skills, and profit immensely from the experience, cognitively, socially and even economically (see Lambert, 1978a). Most mainstream parents, incidentally, are aware of these advantages and are surprisingly eager and anxious to have their children enroll in immersion programs or variants thereof. They want something more for their children than the traditional foreign language programs that they followed a generation ago which failed to develop either language competence or cultural sensitivity.

However, we draw a very sharp contrast between the "additive" form of bilingualism described above and the "subtractive" form which constitutes a totally different psychological and social reality, having different outcomes, different potential hazards and different means-to-ends demands. The hyphenated American child, like the French-Canadian child, embarks on a "subtractive" bilingual route as soon as he/she enters a school where a high prestige, socially powerful, dominant language like English is introduced as the exclusive language of instruction. Perceptive members of ethnolinguistic minority groups have good grounds for worry and concern about the steam-roller effect of a powerful dominant language; it can make foreign home languages and cultures seem "homely" in contrast, ghosts in the closet to be eradicated and suppressed. The effects of this subtractive aspect of bilingualism among Francophone university students in Quebec has been carefully studied by Taylor, Meynard and Rheault (1977). Two findings from that study help illustrate our main point. First, it was found that feelings of threat to one's ethnic identity function as a *negative* motivation in the second-language learning process. Second, it turned out that those Francophones who were least fluent in English were those who felt their cultural identity to be most threatened.

But just as French is too precious to be subtracted out of Canadian society, so too are the multitude of "foreign" languages and cultures extant in America too precious to be eradicated from that society. Even more devastating is the cognitive risk children run when their basic conceptual language — the linguistic system that has been used to form and express thoughts and ideas from infancy on — is abruptly put aside and suppressed so as not to interfere with the new school language.

A major responsibility of educational policy makers then becomes one of transforming subtractive forms of bilingualism into additive ones for the benefit of both the ethnolinguistic minority groups involved as well as the mainstreamers. Community experiments that attempt to implement such transformations, although few in number so far, are now underway (see Lambert, 1978; Lambert, 1981; Kessler & Quinn, 1980; Troike, 1978; Tucker, 1980). Basically these new experimental programs call for schooling to be conducted in the likely-to-be neglected home language of the ethnolinguistic minority child, starting at kindergarten or grade one. The programs continue until it is certain that that language is strongly rooted and able to flourish on its own and that the children themselves get rooted and oriented as to their ethnic identity. The programs of course provide a concurrent strand of English language instruction, in the form of ESL or English immersion, with a separate teacher, for part of the day, but the dual-track program involving home language instruction is kept up for the first three or four years of primary education. It is only then that a switch to a mainly English language program can safely take place.

In practice, it is no simple matter to get these programs started or to maintain them, because the immigrant parents have first to be convinced that there is any merit at all in having home-language instruction. With patience and tact these basic advantages can be presented, and once the originally skeptical parents see the outcomes, they become the best future salespersons for other parents. But the starting is difficult.

Richard Tucker recently evaluated a number of such community-based studies and came to the conclusion that there is "a cumulative and positive impact of bilingual education on all youngsters when they are allowed to remain in bilingual programs for a period of time greater than two or three or even five years and when there is an active attempt to provide nurturance and sustenance of their mother tongue in addition to introducing teaching via the language of wider communication" (1980, pp. 5-6). This is the best way that we can see for the American society to help salvage minority languages and cultures and to help develop a new generation of children who could be happy to be *both* American *and* Hispanic, Haitian, Portuguese, Navajo, Ukranian, or whatever. But note the two essential ingredients of the suggested plan: 1) at the same time as the needs of the ethnic minority child are being catered to, the mainstream child is simultaneously developing skills in and an appreciation for at least one of these other languages and its associated culture; and 2) no time is taken from the all-important task of developing competence in the critical content subjects that make up a solid and demanding educational curriculum. The incidental learning of language and learning about another culture need not and should not get in the way of providing a thorough education in science, math, creative language arts, etc. Immigrant ethnic groups need such education as much as anyone else. Educational policy makers must not be distracted by the current confusion in America about bilingual education from their responsibility to produce a valuable curriculum that permits both minority and mainstream children to actualize their full potentials while contributing to a new, ethnically rich society.

SOCIAL IMPLICATIONS
OF LANGUAGE PROGRAMS

It would be naive to assume that members of different ethnolinguistic groups would be interested in learning a second language for the same reasons. The distinction between additive and subtractive bilingualism discussed above points to particular motivational differences that can have important consequences. It would be equally naive to assume that educational programs targeted for one group effect only that group. Any attention given one group will have both direct and indirect implications for all other social groups in the same setting and for intergroup relations that develop. Thus, when a second language program is implemented for English-speaking white students, the effects would certainly be felt among members of the immigrant and black communities. If the second language introduced in such a program was one spoken by many immigrants, it could easily appear that English-speaking white students were being given preferential "access" to that community, and more generally that they were in a position to "add" a skill that could make a powerful group even more powerful. Similarly, giving immigrant children special educational attention, like providing them with instruction in their home language as well as English, would have an impact on other groups. The immigrant group could be perceived as being given advantages that allow them to become rapidly competitive, thus threatening strategic and well established power relations.

THE NEGLECTED GROUP:
BLACK AMERICANS

If the intergroup implications of language programs are important for the English-speaking white and ethnic immigrant groups, they are critical for the English-speaking black community. Blacks already have many deep reasons for feeling neglected and exploited in the American society and these feelings can be very easily exacerbated by the educational solutions suggested so far. Whether the setting is Chicago, Detroit, Boston, New York, Dade County in Florida or elsewhere, one can easily imagine that black families will be upset because special attention is being directed towards new immigrant as well as white establishment children, giving them, in the long run, more advantages over black children. We cannot expect black children in Dade County, for example, to learn Spanish, Haitian, Creole and/or French with necessarily the same aims in mind as the white English-speaking American child. Accommodating to an immigrant group by learning their language could be seen by blacks as a new type of humiliation. American blacks have difficulty identifying themselves as American if they have to rely on the white American's definition of "American", and the personal and social advantages of becoming bilingual, that are so attractive to English-speaking white Americans may be unimportant and irrelevant for blacks. For them becoming bilingual in Spanish might mean that a new Spanish-speaking immigrant elite group could use blacks as their hewers of wood just as white elites have traditionally done. Blacks can be humiliated further if their children are surpassed in educational and occupational competitions by total newcomers to America who succeed because of special educational attention they receive.

Blacks in America have much experience in various national and local attempts to improve their educational and occupational achievement. Desegregated schooling and Head Start programs are notorious examples. The research evidence on desegregated schooling shows that black children suffer badly from low self-esteem and inferiority, and that their self-esteem is lowered, not raised, by desegregated school contacts with whites. Such psychological damage should not be surprising given that to date school environments have been largely defined by white habits and values. Similarly, desegregation makes white children's attitudes towards blacks less, not more, positive (see Stephan, 1978). Thus, the prospects of wider desegregation that includes ethnic immigrants are not promising for blacks because their self-esteem could be further debased by any signs of relative success on the part of immigrant children, and they might become the target of negative attitudes from a new source, namely ethnic immigrants themselves.

Bleak as the prospects of desegregated schooling are for black pupils' self-esteem and the prejudice directed against them, integrated schooling nonetheless does improve the academic achievement of blacks (see Stephan, 1978). This important fact is a hopeful one to build on in any new suggestions for Ameria's multi-ethnic educational system. There are also hopeful messages in the work of Elizabeth Cohen (1979) which demonstrates that the self-esteem and academic achievement of black students can both be ameliorated when administrative hierarchies in the school system permit an equitable representation of black personnel in the teaching and administration of school programs. Black pupils clearly recognize equities and inequities in academic power systems and, most important of all, their self-feelings and their academic performance reflect these critical background features.

What suggestions, then, can we make for the education of black American children that can be effectively integrated with the plans suggested above for immigrant ethnic and white English-speaking mainstream Americans? This final section is our attempt to provide a structure for a viable solution. The suggested solution presupposes, first, that language issues are kept secondary to the main interest of providing comprehensive educational preparation for all pupils to ensure that they are given equal chances to cope in the highly technical society they all are to enter. (An illustration of this type of educational preparation is given in a paper for the World Bank by Lambert & Sidoti, 1981). It is also presumed that all participating social groups desire a solution, that is, that all groups want a resolution of social conflict, even though conflict itself is required for the solution, and that no one group will impose a one-way resolution on all participants.

A MULTI-GROUP PLAN

In the post-1980's period, integrated schools in America will be mixed three ways, with white English-speaking mainstreamers, black mainstreamers, and immigrant ethnics. Meeting the educational needs of any one particular group through innovative programs is itself a major challenge; it is more problematic to implement programs in such a way that no one group is, or feels, unjustly treated in the process. Here we shift attention from meeting the individual needs of particular communities to simultaneously meeting the needs of various groups in an effective but fair manner for all concerned.

The English-speaking white, black and ethnic immigrant groups we are concerned with here are socially separate collectivities in important respects, and each has contriuted to the rich, multi-ethnic social system that Ameria has become. At the same time, however, these separate social groups share membership in a common social environment and they are all essential members of a particular state and a common nation. As a consequence the unique needs of each group are formulated within the context of this shared social system. There are, therefore, certain fundamental needs, values, and aspirations that all individuals share as citizens of, for example, their community, Miami, the State of Florida and the United States of America. The central concern here is with the education of children from diversified ethnic and linguistic backgrounds and with the task of preparing them for full participation in the social, economic and political life of American communities. The concrete question we arrive at then is: What are the agreed upon aims of education that all members of all three of these groups share? Presumably, a facility in English for their children would constitute one aim shared by all parents, as would an adequate academic preparation to cope successfully in a highly technical society (no matter how that idea would be expressed). But how should "a facility in English" be defined concretely, and who should define it? Usually, such pervasive, shared aims are defined by the most powerful group in the society, and this makes most shared aims impositions on the less powerful group or groups. To be left out of the definition process leaves members of these other groups provisionally committed at best to such aims. "Facility in English" and "adequate academic preparation" then must become shared aims in another sense. Sharing requires that members of all groups involved agree through collaboration on what the realities of American life are nowadays, and through free participation of all groups — conflictual as this may be — what in concrete terms is meant by "facility in English" and "adequate academic preparation".

Beyond the shared aims, each community also has a set of unique needs which are equally relevant and important for each participating group. The responsibility of each community then is to describe what its particular needs are and how these are related to that group's perspective of the shared needs. For the English-speaking white community in the USA, this may require no special attention to the shared aim of "facility in English", but they may well want to safeguard the "adequate academic preparation" and also place special emphasis on the development of bilingual skills for their children. The ethnic immigrant community may place great stress on the need for help in attaining excellence in the shared aim of English language skill and relate it to adequate academic preparation at the same time as they explore for themselves the importance, or not, of keeping the mother tongue vibrant. The black community may also perceive the need to direct resource attention to the shared aim of English language skills and particularly to adequate academic preparation which, they may argue, has not been provided in the past. Thus they might bargain for a greater share of resources to make up for past shortcomings. The particular aims of the black community might include special attention to black English as a formal element in the general curriculum, and then a share in second language learning for their own children.

It should be made clear that these illustrative examples are not the actual unique aims or needs of any of the three communities. The decisions and choices are to be made by the three communities in concert, in the case of defining shared aims, and for each community by itself, in the case of defining unique needs. The essential feature of the proposal is that each community's special needs are considered and no group is slighted in terms of the resources allocated, what differs is the nature of the resources, the needs to be satisfied by resource allocations, and the nature of these needs as determined by the communities themselves.

In conclusion, we ask ourselves who is to take the initiative so that all parties to this community-based problem can congregate in order to compete equitably and ultimately collaborate on a program of shared and unique educational goals? Policy makers in responsible positions who do not facilitate such a congregation would be signalling their disagreement with the proposals offered here. And what else can we say to those who may still maintain that white or black English-speaking mainstreamers are irrelevant to the central issue, which is educating immigrant ethnic minority children? We have argued here that quality education for children need not be jeopardized because it is made bilingual and bicultural. Instead we are persuaded by an accumulation of recent psycholinguistic research that all children can be helped to develop high level skills in two languages and two cultures at the same time as they achieve at or above normal standards in the educational demands made on them. Children who become functionally bilingual and bicultural in this fashion constitute, we believe, a new breed of young Americans particularly well equipped to cope in and contribute to the fascinating multi-cultural society America is becoming. Our only concern is in the implementation of language-enriched educational programs because the implementation requires that policy makers be sensitive to the psychological and the social realities of language for all groups in the society — the ethnic immigrant, the mainstream white English-speaking and the mainstream black English-speaking.

REFERENCES

BLAKE, L., LAMBERT, W.E., SIDOTI, N., AND WOLFE, D. Students' views of intergroup tensions in Quebec: The effects of language immersion experience. *Canadian Journal of Behavioural Science*, 1981, *13*, 144-160.

COHEN, A. The case for partial or total immersion education. In A. Simoes, Jr. (Ed.), *The bilingual child*. N.Y.: Academic Press, 1976.

COHEN, E. Design and redesign of the desegregated school: Problems of status, power and conflict. In E. Aronson (Ed.), *Desegregation, past, present and future*. N.Y.: Plenum, 1979.

CZIKO, G., LAMBERT, W.E., SIDOTI, N., AND TUCKER, G.R. Graduates of early immersion: Retrospective views of grade 11 students and their parents. In R. St. Clair & H. Giles (Eds.), *The social and psychological contexts of language*. Erlbaum Associates Inc., 1980.

DERRICK, W.J. Personal communication, 1980.

GENESEE, F. Scholastic effects of French immersion: An overview after ten years. *Interchange*, 1978-79, *9*, 20-29.

GENESEE, F., AND LAMBERT, W.E. *An experiment in trilingual education: Report 6*. Mimeo, McGill University, Psychology Department, 1979.

GRITTNER, F. Personal communication, 1981.

KESSLER, C., AND QUINN, M. *Bilingualism and science problem-solving ability*. Unpublished paper presented at the 14th Annual International Convention of Teachers of English to Speakers of Other Languages, San Francisco, 1980.

LAMBERT, W.E. The social psychology of bilingualism. *Journal of Social Issues*, 1967, *23*, 91-109.

LAMBERT, W.E. Some cognitive and sociocultural consequences of being bilingual. In J. E. Alatis (Ed.), *International dimensions of bilingual education*. Washington, D.C.: Georgetown University Press, 1978. (a)

LAMBERT, W.E. An alternative to the foreign language teaching profession. *Interchange*, 1978, *9*, 95-108. (b)

LAMBERT, W.E. *A Canadian experiment in the development of bilingual competence: The home-to-school language switch program*. Mimeo, McGill University, Psychology Department, 1979.

LAMBERT, W.E. Bilingualism and language acquisition. *Annals of the New York Academy of Sciences*, in press, 1981.

LAMBERT, W.E., AND TUCKER, G.R. *Bilingual education of children: The St. Lambert experiment*. Rowley, Mass.: Newbury House, 1972.

LAMBERT, W.E., AND SIDOTI, N. *The selection of appropriate languages of instruction and the use of radio for education in less developed countries*. Unpublished manuscript, Washington, D.C.: The World Bank, Department of Education, 1981.

Montgomery County Public Schools, Maryland, 1976. *End of the second year report on the French language immersion program at Four Corners*.

O'CONNELL, J. Personal communication, 1981.

POPPER, K.R. *The open society and its enemies*. Volumes 1 & 2, London: Routledge & Kegan Paul, 1966.

SAMUELS, D.D., AND GRIFFORE, R.J. The Plattsburgh French language immersion program: Its influence on intelligence and self-esteem. *Language Learning*, 1979, *29*, 45-52.

SIDOTI, N. Personal communication, 1981.

SKUTNABB-KANGAS, R., AND TOUKOMAA, P. *Teaching migrant children's mother tongue and learning the language of the host country in the context of socio-cultural situation of the migrant family*. The Finnish National Commission for UNESCO: Helsinki, 1976.

STEPHAN, W.G. School desegregation: An evaluation of predictions made in Brown University Board of Education. *Psychological Bulletin*, 1978, *85*, 217-238.

SWAIN, M. French immersion programs across Canada. *The Canadian Modern Language Review*, 1974, *31*, 117-128.

TAYLOR, D.M., MEYNARD, R., AND RHEAULT, E. Threat to ethnic identity and second-language learning. In H. Giles (Ed.), *Language ethnicity and intergroup relations*. London: Academic Press, 1977.

THOMAS, S. *A language to share*. Newton, Mass.: Educational Development Center, Inc., 1980.

TROIKE, R.C. Research evidence for the effectiveness of bilingual education. *NABE Journal*, 1978, *3*, 13-24.

TUCKER, G.R. *Comments on proposed rules for nondiscrimination under programs receiving federal financial assistance through the Education Department*. Washington, D.C.: Center for Applied Linguistics, 1980.

PART FOUR
PROGRAMS AND
CURRICULAR STRATEGIES

ETHNICITY AND CURRICULUM REFORM

By James A. Banks
Professor of Education
and Kellog Fellow
University of Washington
Seattle, Washington

ASSIMILATION AND EDUCATION

The school curriculum within a society, like other institutions within a social system, reflects its dominant ideologies, beliefs, and goals. Historically, the common school curriculum in the United States has been dominated by the pervasive assimilationist forces in American life, largely because the assimilation of millions of immigrants and indigenous ethnic groups has been a major national goal. Social science within the United States, which serves as the basic foundation of the school curriculum, has also been assimilationist oriented since American social science began to mature. When established social scientists began to seriously study race relations in the 1940s and 1950s — notably Robert E. Park and the "Chicago school" — they predicted that total assimilation would, and should, be the ultimate fate for ethnic groups in the United States. They developed elaborate typologies and models which described this inevitable process of assimilation. Park described the cycle as *competition, conflict, accommodation, and assimilation.*[1]

The assimilationist ideology,* called the "liberal expectancy" by Milton M. Gordon,[2] maintains that ethnicity and ethnic attachments are fleeting and temporary within an increasingly modernized world. Ethnicity, argues the assimilationist, wanes or disappears under the impact of modernization and industrialization. The modernized state is universalistic rather than characterized by ethnic allegiances and attachments.

---

*I am using *assimilationist ideology* and *pluralist ideology* as ideal type concepts in the Weberian sense. These ideologies may be conceptualized as existing on a continuum and are useful in describing and classifying major theories and movements related to ethnicity and pluralism in the United States. For a further discussion of these ideologies see James A. Banks, *Multiethnic Education: Theory and Practice* (Boston: Allyn & Bacon, 1981), pp. 61-74. Other social scientists have also structured typologies related to ethnicity and pluralism in the United States. See Milton M. Gordon, "Assimilation in American Life: Theory and Reality," reprinted in *Minority Responses,* edited by Minako Jurokawa (New York: Random House, 1970), pp. 87-94; and John Higham, "Integration vs. Pluralism: Another American Dilemma," *The Center Magazine* 7 (July/August 1974): 67-73.

The assimilationist believes that ethnic identities and attachments are rather dysfunctional within a modernized state. The ethnic group promotes group rights over the rights of the individual. Consequently, the individual must be freed in order to have choices within society. The assimilationist views ethnicity as a force that is inimical to the goals of a democratic society. Ethnicity, argues the assimilationist, promotes divisions, exhumes ethnic conflicts, and leads to the Balkanization of society.[3] Consequently, the best way to promote the goals of American society and to develop commitments to the ideals of American democracy is to promote the full socialization of all individuals and groups into the universalistic culture. The primary goal of the common schools, like other publicly supported institutions, should be to socialize individuals into the national universal culture and to enable them to function more successfully within it. At best, the school should take a position of "benign neutrality" in matters related to the ethnic attachments and identities of students.

THE NEW PLURALISM

In the 1960s, Afro-Americans began a fight for their civil rights that was unprecedented in their history. Other non-White ethnic groups, who were made acutely aware of their ethnic status by the Black revolt and were encouraged by what they perceived as the benefits gained by Afro-Americans, also began to make unprecedented demands upon American social and political institutions. These groups demanded more control of their communities, more ethnic teachers for their youths, and new interpretations of American history and culture that would more accurately and sensitively describe their experiences in the United States. Ethnic minority groups began to seriously question both the societal goals and the dominant assimilationist ideology within American society.

The assimilationist ideology and the practices associated with it were strongly attacked by ethnic minority intellectuals, researchers, and social activists.[4] Traditionally, most ethnic minority intellectuals and social activists have supported assimilationist policies and regarded acculturation as a requisite for full societal participation.[5] Minority writers and researchers in the United States attacked the assimilationist ideology for several reasons. They saw it as a weapon of the "oppressor" that was designed to destroy the cultures of ethnic groups and to make their members personally ineffective and politically powerless. These writers also saw it as a racist ideology to justify damaging school and societal practices that victimized minority group children.

Many minorities also lost faith in the assimilationist position because they had become very disillusioned with what they perceived as its unfulfilled promises. The rise of ethnic awareness and ethnic pride also contributed to the rejection of the assimilationist ideology by many ethnic minorities in the 1960s. Minority leaders and writers searched for an alternative ideology and endorsed some version of cultural pluralism. They viewed the cultural pluralist ideology as highly consistent with the liberation of oppressed and victimized ethnic groups.

The ethnic protest movements that emerged among non-White ethnic groups stimulated the rise of the ethnic revitalization movements among White ethnic groups, such as Polish Americans, Italian Americans, and Jewish Americans. These groups also demanded that educational and social policy reflect ethnic pluralism and that ethnic studies programs focus on their particular ethnic heritages.[6] In some communities White ethnic groups and non-White ethnic minorities aggressively competed for limited resources allocated for ethnic studies programs. The rise of the ethnic revitalization movements in the 1960s and 1970s, especially among White ethnic groups, became known as the "new pluralism."[7]

SCHOOL REFORM AND PLURALISM

School districts throughout the United States, stimulated by the ethnic revitalization movements and supported by private and public agencies, implemented a wide variety of curricular reforms related to ethnic pluralism in the 1960s and 1970s.[8] Many of these efforts lacked clear goals and objectives and were based on questionable assumptions about the nature of ethnic pluralism in American society, the type of curriculum that is most consistent with a pluralistic democratic nation-state, and about the ethnic characteristics of individuals. We need to question some of the pervasive assumptions and school practices related to ethnicity and to formulate more reflective goals for school reform in the 1980s.

Neither the assimilationist nor the cultural pluralist ideology, in their ideal forms, can effectively guide curriculum reform in a democratic pluralistic nation. Programs based primarily on assimilationist assumptions violate the ethnic identities of students. Curricular practices which reflect a strong notion of ethnic pluralism in the United States exaggerate the importance of the ethnic group in the socialization of American youths and give inadequate attention to the universal American values that influence the youths' behavior.

Ethnic identity is important to many Americans and is the major source of identity for others. Ethnicity also exerts a strong influence on the socialization of many Americans. However, acculturation has taken place both within and across ethnic groups in the United States to widely varying degrees. Even when Afro-American children are socialized primarily within Black communities, they inculcate many mainstream American values from the mass media, professional workers in the Black community, and from institutions such as the schools. However, they are often unable to actualize many of their values, hopes, and aspirations because of limited resources. Their expressions of mainstream American values, therefore, may take unique forms. Research by Valentine indicates that many of the values of Afro-American youths are similar to those of middle class Whites.[9]

While ethnic minorities share many cultural characteristics with other Americans, there are some significant differences between the American universal society and the various ethnic subsocieties.[10] Although members of ethnic minority groups often attain high levels of acculturation, they frequently form ethnic groups and institutions and limit many of their activities to the ethnic community, which has many unique values, communication modes, life styles, norms, and institutions.

CULTURAL ASSIMILATION, STRUCTURAL PLURALISM, AND MULTIPLE ACCULTURATION

Gordon believes that two concepts, *cultural assimilation* and *structural pluralism,* can best describe the nature of ethnic group life in the United States.[11] According to Gordon, ethnic groups in the United States have experienced high levels of cultural assimilation but the nation is characterized by structural pluralism. In other words, although many ethnic group *individuals* are highly culturally assimilated, American ethnic groups have separate ethnic subsocieties, such as Cuban social clubs, Chicano theaters, and Jewish religious institutions.

While Gordon's notion of structural pluralism is helpful and deals more adequately with the complexity of ethnic diversity in modern American society that concepts such as Anglo-conformity and melting pot, I believe that *multiple acculturation* more accurately describes how the universal American culture was and is forming the concept of cultural assimilation. The White Anglo-Saxon Protestant culture was changed in America as were the cultures of Africans and of Asian immigrants. African cultures and Asian cultures influenced and changed the WASP culture as the WASP culture influenced and modified African and Asian cultures. What we experienced in American, and still are experiencing, is multiple acculturation — not a kind of unidirectional type of cultural assimilation whereby the Black culture was influenced by the WASP culture but not the other way around.

The general or universal culture in the United States resulted from this series of multiple acculturations. This culture is still in the process of formation and change. The universal American culture is not just a WASP culture; it contains important elements of the wide variety of ethnic cultures that are and/or were part of American society. Those ethnic cultural elements that became universalized and part of the general American culture have been reinterpreted and mediated by the unique social, economic, and political experience in the United States. It is inaccurate and misleading to refer to the universal American culture as a WASP culture.[12] This notion of American culture has been and is often perpetuated in the school curriculum.

THE MULTIETHNIC IDEOLOGY AND CURRICULUM REFORM

The structural pluralistic and multiple acculturation nature of American society suggests that a *multiethnic ideology* should guide curriculum reform in the nation's schools. A sound curriculum must reflect the reality that the sociocultural and psychological environments of students consist of their own ethnic subsociety and the universal American society, as well as other ethnic subsocieties. While these cultural environments share many characteristics, each constitutes unique wholes, and has systems of distinctive values, norms, languages, and institutions. Each also exerts a cogent influence on the socialization of youths and requires a distinct set of skills to function successfully within it. An individual may be able to function effectively within his or her ethnic community, and poorly within the universal American culture and other ethnic subsocieties. The converse may also be true.

Conceptualizing the sociocultural and psychosocial environment of ethnic youths as multicultural is an ideal-type notion. In reality, these cultural environments are not as distinct as is often asserted by cultural pluralists and they share many characteristics. Also, many ethnic youths — especially those who are upward mobile — have few or no ethnic cultural characteristics and are socialized and function primarily within the universal American culture. Many Afro-American and Mexican-American youths are as Anglo-American as many English-Americans. However, the socialization of many youths is highly restricted to their ethnic communities and they are to a large extent monocultural.[13] The influence of the universal American culture on these kinds of ethnic students is often indirect, such as through the mass media, movies, and textbooks.

Ideal-type constructs can help us to conceptualize a problem, even though they are not totally consistent with reality. By viewing the sociocultural and psychosocial environment of ethnic youths as multicultural, we can formulate a philosophically sound position regarding the goals of pluralistic education. However, we should keep in mind the limitations of our conceptual framework.

TEACHING CROSS-CULTURAL COMPETENCY SKILLS

A major goal of the multiethnic curriculum should be to help students develop *cross-cultural competency,* which consists of the attitudes, knowledge, skills, and abilities needed to function within their own ethnic culture, the universal American culture, and within and across other ethnic cultures both in this nation and in other societies.[13] American students should have the cross-cultural literacy and skills needed to function effectively not only within our national borders but within other nations as well.

When helping youths to develop the skills and attitudes needed to function successfully within and across different ethnic cultures and within the universal American culture, we should not violate their ethnic cultures in the process or force them to undergo self-alienation. Ethnic youths should not be forced to reject their ethnic identities and experiences, as frequently happens, in order to function within cultures that are, in many ways, alien to them. Self-denial and self-rejection is too big a price to pay for economic, political, and social mobility.

David Apter argues convincingly that individuals within highly modernized societies — despite assimilationist beliefs to the contrary — psychologically need strong ethnic attachments and will hold on to them.[14] The assimilationist insists that ethnic attachments are fleeting and disappear within a modernized democratic state; Apter argues that this is not and cannot be the case. As he points out, individuals are quite capable of multiple identities and of functioning effectively within their own ethnic communities as well as within the universal culture. They can have both ethnic allegiances and allegiances to the national democratic culture. Nathan Glazer, extending Apter's argument, suggests that the school should help youths to become *universalized primordialists* — individuals who are able to function effectively within their own ethnic cultures as well as within the shared national culture.[15]

It is necessary but not sufficient for the school to help ethnic youths to acquire the skills they need to attain social, economic, and political mobility and to function successfully within the universal national culture. The school should also help them attain the skills, attitudes, and political efficacy needed to effectively participate in the reformation of the social, economic, and political systems. We will perpetuate the status quo if we merely acculturate students so that they will conform to mainstream norms and values. They need to acquire both the skills and the commitment needed to engage in effective social and political action needed to reform our society to help close the gap between our democratic ideals and societal realities.

AN INTERDISCIPLINARY CONCEPTUAL CURRICULUM

A curriculum that reflects a multiethnic ideology focuses on higher levels of knowledge and helps students understand the complex nature of ethnicity in contemporary society. In many ethnic studies units, activities, and programs, emphasis is placed on factual learning and the deeds of ethnic heroes. These types of experiences use ethnic content but what Larry Cuban has called "white instruction," or traditional teaching methods.[16] Isolated facts about Jose Marti do not stimulate the intellect or increase students' intellectual abilities any more than discrete facts about Thomas Jefferson or Betsy Ross. The emphasis in sound multiethnic programs must be on *concept attainment, value analysis, decision making,* and *social action.* Facts should only be used to help students to attain higher level concepts and skills.

Concepts taught in the multiethnic curriculum should be selected from several disciplines and, when appropriate, viewed from the perspectives of such disciplines and areas as the various social sciences, art, music, literature, physical education, communication, the sciences, and mathematics.[17] It is necessary for students to view ethnic events and situations from the perspectives of several disciplines because any one discipline gives them only a partial understanding of problems related to ethnicity. When students study the concept of culture, they can attain a global perspective of ethnic cultures by viewing them from the perspective of the various social sciences and by examining how they are expressed in literature, music, dance, art, communication, and foods. The other curriculum areas, such as science and mathematics, can also be included in an inter-disciplinary study of ethnic cultures.

Concepts such as *culture* can be used to organize units and activities related to ethnicity that are interdisciplinary. Other concepts, such as *communication* and *interdependence,* can also be analyzed and studied from an interdisciplinary perspective (see Figure 1). It is neither possible nor desirable to teach each concept in the curriculum from the perspectives of several disciplines and curricular areas. Such an attempt would result in artificial relationships and

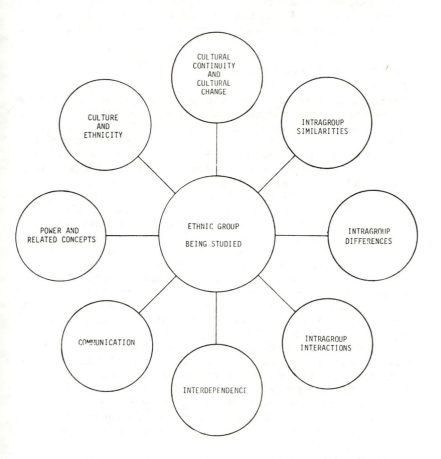

superficial learnings by students. However, the many excellent opportunities that exist within the curriculum for teaching concepts from an interdisciplinary perspective should be fully explored and used.

Interdisciplinary teaching requires the strong cooperation of teachers in the various content areas. Team teaching will often be necessary, especially at the high school level, to organize and implement interdisciplinary units and lessons.

TEACHING MULTIETHNIC PERSPECTIVES

The multiethnic curriculum should also help students to view historical and contemporary events from diverse ethnic perspectives and points of view. Most school courses are currently taught primarily from Anglo-American perspectives and points of view.[18] These types of courses and experiences are based on what I call the *Anglo-American Centric Model* or Moel A (see Figure 2). Ethnic studies, as a process of curriculum reform, can and often does proceed form Model A to Model B, the *Ethnic Additive Model.* In courses and experiences based on Model B, ethnic content is an additive to the major curriculum thrust, which remains Anglo-American dominated. Many school districts that have attempted ethnic modification of the curriculum have implemented Model B types of changes. Black Studies courses, Chicano Studies courses, and special units on ethnic groups in the elementary grades are examples of Model B types of curricular experiences.

However, I suggest that curriculum reform proceed directly from Model A to Model C, the *Multiethnic Model.* In courses and experiences based on Model C, the students study events and situations from several ethnic points of view. Anglo-American perspectives form only one group among several, and are in no way superior or inferior to other ethnic perspectives.

I view Model D (the *Multinational Model*) types of courses and programs as the ultimate goal of curriculum reform. In this curriculum model, which links multiethnic and global education, students study events and situations from the perspectives of ethnic groups in various nations. Since we live in a global society, students need to learn how to become effective citizens of the world community. They are unlikely to learn this if they study historical and contemporary events and situations only or primarily from the perspectives of ethnic cultures within their own nation-state.

When studying a historical period such as the American Colonial era, in a course organized on the Multiethnic Model (Model C), the inquiry would not end when the students had studied the English colonies in North America from the perspectives of Anglo-American historians, as is usually the case. Conceptualizing the Colonial period as only the study of the English colonies is limiting and Anglo-centric. Long before the English were successful in settling Jamestown, the Spaniards had established colonies in Florida and New Mexico and the French had established one in Louisiana.

When the Spanish and the French colonies are studied in addition to the English colonies, the students are able to see that during this period the region that became the United States was highly multiethnic. Not only were many different European nationality groups in North **America** during the Colonial period, but there were many different groups of Indians and Blacks as well. To gain a full understanding of the period, students must view it from the perspectives of the English, Spanish, and French colonists, and from the points of view of the many different groups of Indians and Blacks. The era of colonization had very different meanings for the Pueblo Indians and the Spanish colonists, the Black slaves, the free Blacks, and for the English settlers. These diverse perspectives and points of view should be studied within a sound multiethnic curriculum.[19]

I am not suggesting that we eliminate or denigrate Anglo-American perspectives on history and society. I am merely suggesting that Anglo-American perspectives should be among many different ethnic viewpoints taught in the schools. Only by teaching in this way will students gain views of America and the world that are consistent with the complex realities of our global society.

MODEL A
Anglo-American Centric Model

MODEL B
Ethnic Additive Model

MODEL C
Multiethnic Model

MODEL D
Multinational Model

Ethnic studies is conceptualized as a process of curriculum reform which can lead from a total Anglo-American perspective on our history and culture (MODEL A), to multiethnic perspectives as additives to the major curriculum thrust (MODEL B), to a completely multiethnic curriculum in which every historical and social event is viewed from the perspectives of different ethnic groups (MODEL C). In MODEL C the Anglo-American perspective is only one of several and is in no way superior or inferior to other ethnic perspectives. MODEL D, which is multinational, is the ultimate curriculum goal. In this curriculum model, students study historical and social events from multinational perspectives and points of view. Many schools that have attempted ethnic modification of the curriculum have implemented MODEL B types of programs. It is suggested here that curriculum reform move directly from MODEL A to MODEL C and ultimately to MODEL D. However, in those districts which have MODEL B types of programs, it is suggested that they move from MODEL B to MODEL C and eventually to MODEL D types of curricular organizations.

FOOTNOTES

[1]Robert E. Park, *Race and Culture* (Glencoe, Ill.: The Free Press, 1950), p. 150.

[2]Milton M. Gordon, "Toward a General Theory of Racial and Ethnic Group Relations," in *Ethnicity: Theory and Experience,* edited by Nathan Glazer and Daniel P. Moynihan (Cambridge: Harvard University Press, 1975), pp. 84-110.

[3]For a cogent statement of this position, see Orlando Patterson, *Ethnic Chauvinism: The Reactionary Impulse* (New York: Stein and Day, 1977).

[4]See, for example, Barbara A. Sizemore, "Social Science and Education for a Black Identity," in *Black Self-Concept: Implications for Education and Social Science,* edited by James A. Banks and Jean D. Grambs (New York: McGraw-Hill, 1972), p. 141-170; Rudy Acuna, *Occupied America: A History of Chicanos,* 2nd ed. (New York: Harper and Row, 1981); and the essays in Amy Tachiki, Eddie Wong, Franklin Odo, with Buck Wong, Eds., *Roots: An Asian American Reader* (Los Angeles: UCLA Asian American Studies Center, 1971).

[5]Nathan Glazer, "Cultural Pluralism: The Social Aspect," in *Pluralism in a Democratic Society,* edited by Melvin M. Tumin and Walter Plotch (New York: Praeger Publishers, 1977).

[6]U.S. Commission on Civil Rights, *Civil Rights Issues of Euro-Ethnic Americans in the United States: Opportunities and Challenges* (Washington, D.C.: The Commission, 3 December 1979).

[7]For a comprehensive treatment of the "new pluralism," see Andrew Greeley, *Ethnicity in the United States: A Preliminary Reconnaissance* (New York: Wiley & Sons, 1974).

[8]David E. Washburn, "Ethnic Studies in the United States," *Educational Leadership* 32 (March 1975): 409-12.

[9]Charles A. Valentine, "Deficit, Difference, and Bicultural Models of Afro-American Behavior," *Harvard Educational Review* 41 (May 1971): 137-157.

[10]For a discussion of the teaching implications of ethnic diversity, see Manuel Ramirez and Alfredo Castaneda, *Cultural Democracy, Bicognitive Development and Education* (New York: Academic Press, 1974); and Judith S. Kleinfeld, *Eskimo School on the Andreafsky: A Study of Effective Bicultural Education* (New York: Praeger Publishers, 1979).

[11]Milton M. Gordon, *Assimilation in American Life: The Role of Race, Religion and National Origins* (New York: Oxford University Press, 1964).

[12]The concept of multiple acculturation and its teaching implications are discussed in James A. Banks, *Multiethnic Education: Theory and Practice* (Boston: Allyn and Bacon, 1981).

[13]See, for example, the descriptions of the socialization of Black youths in Ulf Hannerz, *Soulside: Inquiries into Ghetto Culture and Community* (New York: Columbia University Press, 1969).

[14]David E. Apter, "Political Life and Pluralism," in Tumin and Plotch, *Pluralism in a Democratic Society,* op. cit.

[15]Nathan Glazer, "Cultural Pluralism: The Social Aspect," in Tumin and Plotch, op. cit.

[16]Larry Cuban, "Ethnic Content and 'White' Instruction," *Phi Delta Kappan* 53 (January 1972): 270-273.

[17]James A. Banks, *Teaching Strategies for Ethnic Studies,* 2nd ed. (Boston: Allyn and Bacon, 1979).

[18]Ibid.

[19]This student text presents historical events from diverse ethnic perspectives: James A. Banks, *We Americans: Our History and People,* Vol. 1 and 2 (Boston: Allyn & Bacon, 1982), (with Sam L. Sebesta).

INTERNALIZING THE CONCEPT
OF MULTICULTURALISM

By H. Prentice Baptiste, Jr.
University of Houston

In this paper the writer will further define and elaborate on his typology[1] of multicultural education which will enable educators and others to determine the extent they have conceptualized and operationalized the principles, concepts, and parameters of multiculturalism.

During the last twenty years the defining of the concept multiculturalism along with other concepts such as multiethnic studies, cultural pluralism, and bilingualism have been tossed around in the educational arena falsely purporting clarification. Perhaps more than any other concept — multicultural education — has been blamed for this confusion because of the ambiguity which has characterized its use. To facilitate a clarification of the concept multicultural education, one must examine it from a historical perspective.

HISTORICAL PERSPECTIVE

A definitive clarification of multicultural education lies in a socio-historical look at our society. The national society of our country has been examined and analyzed from a sociological perspective on several occasions. Each of these analyses deal with the various kinds of people, i.e., the diversity of groups which constituted the population of this country. A few sociologists, e.g. Gunnar Myrdal of *American Dilemma* and Talcott Parsons, presented explanations of the interactive relationship among the various cultural, racial, and ethnic groups.

The three sociological concepts which have primarily been utilized to explain the interactive relationship among the various social — racial, cultural, ethnic — groups are Americanization, melting pot, and cultural pluralism. These concepts are dissimilar in their intent for members of various social groups.

THE AMERICANIZATION CONCEPT

The proponents of the Americanization, during the late 1800's and early 1900's were concerned about the influx of more than 20 million eastern and southern European immigrants to the United States. These immigrants were not only viewed as poor, but also of culturally and racially inferior stock. Cubberly, a distinguished educational leader, in his book, *Changing Concepts of Education,* wrote:

> The southern and eastern Europeans are a very different type from the north Europeans, who preceded them. Illiterate, docile, lacking in self-reliance and initiative and possessing none of the Anglo-Teutonic conceptions of law, order and government, their coming has served to dilute tremendously our national stock, and to corrupt our civic life. ...
>
> Our task is to break up their groups or settlements, to assimilate and to amalgamate these people as part of our American race, and to implant in their children, so far as can be done, the Anglo-Saxon conceptions of righteousness, law and order and popular government, and to awaken in them reverence for our democratic institutions and for those things in our national life which we as people hold to be of abiding worth.[2]

Cubberly's stature in the educational community led to an unquestionable acceptance of his ideas and beliefs. Educational systems operationalized his philosophy in an assimilation process of immigrants' children, which debased them of their cultural heritage as they were Americanized.

This process did not leave out their parents. Theodore Roosevelt[3] shared the xenophobic views of Cubberly and utilized his political influence to enhance the Americanization process. He denounced the idea of hyphenated Americans; i.e., Irish-Americans, Polish-Americans, etc. This he considered to be disloyal to the country, because he perceived it as holding allegiance to America and something else. His uncompromising position coerced many immigrants to forsake their heritage, their roots, for the new and "better life." The Americanization phenomenon was an assimilation process of Anglo-Saxon cultural imperialism.

THE MELTING POT

The melting pot theory was not synonymous with the Americanization process. The objective of these two concepts were distinctly different. Promotion of Nordic Anglo-Saxon superiority in all aspects of life along with the inherent inferiority of non-Nordic origins of life was the fundamental essence of the Americanization process. Whereas the melting pot theory proposed that a new "hybrid" group would emerge from the various distinct socio-cultural groups. The sine qua non of this theory was that all groups would contribute on a parity basis to the production of a unique and superior American race. However, the mutual mixing of the diverse groups of this country was not allowed to occur and did not take place. Subsequently, we had the myth of the melting pot. As Pratte stated:

> When a metaphor is no longer believed to be an "as if" vehicle for organizing our thinking and is taken to be a literal statement, a myth has been born.[4]

It was in the early 1900's when this myth received its greatest impetus. The broadway play entitled, *The Melting Pot* by Israel Zangwill transformed the ideal to a myth by implying this amalgamation was a fact of American life, not an ideal by which we might judge our attempts to achieve a very difficult goal.

CULTURAL PLURALISM

The concept cultural pluralism is not new. However, of the three, it is possibly the least understood. One of its most able proponents — Horace Kallen — met with fierce opposition when he presented his theory of cultural pluralism as an ideal sociological model for our society. He believed that the various cultural groups of our society could maintain their *identity* while coexisting in a mutual supportive system. He argued that cultural pluralism did not necessarily lead to disunity. Kallen's conception of cultural pluralism did not mean that our country would become a "mosaic of cultures." He stated in the early 1920's that there was a mainstream American culture that was historically *not* monolithic, but pluralistic. Kallen believed that this pluralism had its roots in the founding of America, its basic political documents (The Declaration of Independence and the Constitution), the frontier tradition, the way in which the American people settled on this continent, and the values they developed. He believed cultural pluralism was intrinsic to what he called "the American Idea."

In his book, *Cultural Pluralism and the American Idea,* Kallen presented his idea of Americanization. Kallen wrote, Americanization means the acceptance by all Americans, native and foreign born of "an over-arching culture based on the 'American Idea.' " This over-arching American culture is pluralistic because it reflects a pluralistic society. Pluralism is the essense of its strength and attraction. Kallen believed that cultures "live and grow in and through the individual, and their vitality is a function of individual diversities of interests and associations. Pluralism is the sine qua non of their persistence and prosperous growth."[5]

A COMPARATIVE ANALYSIS

The previously discussed sociological concepts had their strong proponents and followers during the early part of the 20th century. It is of interest that the real winner (Americanism) was never *publicly attested* to by the masses, and that the alleged winner (melting pot) was a psychological myth and the loser (cultural pluralisms) has since reemerged. Furthermore *each* of the sociological concepts Americanism, Melting Pot, Cultural Pluralism promoted during the early 20th century explicitly or implicitly supported racism. Each concept was politically motivated, and the public school system had a role in the operationalizing or non-operationalizing of the concepts.

The hind sight of contemporary history allows us to realize that the Americanization process as proposed by Cubberly and others became the modus operandi for the socialization of inhabitants of the United States. Our institutions — public schools, government entities, etc. — exuded copiously the values and attitudes of Anglo-Americans to the detriment of any other group's values and attitudes. The Anglicization of non-Anglos names, life styles, family practices, speech patterns, etc. surreptitiously became the order of the times. In spite of the ideal society as presented in Zangwill's play *The Melting Pot* which found strong support in the masses of Americans the real winner as to the accepted values, lifestyles, and social practices was Americanism.

It may come as a surprise to some readers that none of these sociological concepts were devoid of racism. Proponents of the melting pot theory did not intend for the amalgamation or melting process to include people of color or our visible ethnics. Actually Afro-Americans, Asian-Americans, Native-Americans, and Mexican-Americans, although very numerous in these United States during the turn of the century were not included in the theories of Americanization, melting pot, and cultural pluralism. The focus of these conceptual theories were the immigrants from Southern and Eastern Europe. It was not the intent of these conceptual theories to provide any equitable relationship between people of color and white people. Therefore each had a definite racist nature.

This is a political society. The basis of its operation is majority rule within a political democracy. Paramount to this political democracy is the inequitable distribution of goods, values, statuses and power. Because politics is the management of conflict which results when different groups are in dispute over scarce resources, power and statuses, an identification of the opposing groups must be made, and an interpretation of their stakes and stands must be given.[6] The Americanization idea explicitly stated its political position as illustrated by Henry Pratt Fairchild, in 1926, in his book entitled *The Melting Pot Mistake,* he argued ...

> that while the racial makeup of the American people would be hard to define, an American nationality did exist, based on Nordic or Anglo-Saxon cultural values and mores. The American nation, according to Fairchild, was formed principally by immigrants from England, Ireland, Germany, and the Scandanavian countries. But "beginning about 1882," he wrote, "the immigration problem in the United States has become increasingly a racial problem in two distinct ways, first by altering profoundly the Nordic predominance in the American population, and second by introducing various new element which are so different from any of the old ingredients that even small quantities are deeply significant." These "new elements" consisted of Italians, Poles, and Jews, who were coming to the United States in large numbers. "The American People" Fairchild argued, "have since the revolution resisted any threat of dilution by a widely different race and must continue to do so in the case of large-scale immigration. If they fail to do so, the American nation would face the beginning of the process of mongrelization."
>
> The "melting pot" idea, according to Fairchild, was "slowly, insidiously, irresistibly eating away the very heart of the United States. What was being melted in the great Melting Pot, losing all form and symmetry, all beauty and character, all nobility and usefulness, was the American nationality itself."
>
> What the immigrants had to be told, with great kindness and full consideration, according to Fairchild, was that they were welcome to the United States under the condition that they would renounce their respective cultural values and embrace the dominant culture forged by the predominantly Nordic American people since its independence. The American public schools must be made the effective tools of achieving this objective, at least as far as the children of the immigrants were concerned. And this process must be accomplished as fast as possible.[7]

Neither the melting pot or cultural pluralism theorists provided clear explanations for dealing with the political context of our society. Their single minded focus on the "amalgamation" or "unity in diversity" of the various white cultural/ethnic groups blinded them to the reality of the political obstacles which stood in the way of such noble endeavors. As Pratte pointed out "the melting pot ideology made two assumptions: first, that immigrant groups in American society were unwilling to pay the price of Americanization and did not want to 'make it' on WASP terms; second, that the American culture was accepting and tolerant enough of 'foreign ways' to allow for the fusion and emergence of a 'new' American."[8] Basically, each assumption, was faulty. Kallen maintained that the majority culture would benefit from the coexistence and constant inteaction with the various cultural/ethnic groups; whereas, the various cultural/ethnic groups would accept and cherish the 'common' elements of American cultural, political, and social mores as represented by the public schools. However, through their own efforts they would support supplemental education for their children to preserve their ethnic cultural awareness and values. Kallen's theory failed to consider the intolerant attitude of the Americanists and the willingness of the immigrant groups to forsake their cultural and ethnic heritage. Kallen's theory of cultural pluralism ignored to its detriment the political nature of our society.

REDISCOVERY OF CULTURAL PLURALISM

I am sure that scholars writing in 2082 will have a clearer perspective as to what led to a broader acceptance of the ideal of cultural pluralism during the 1980's. Nevertheless, without the benefit of their time lag, I would like to briefly submit my reasons as to the rediscovery of cultural pluralism. It had become obvious to many Americans that Americanization was a denigrating, ethnocentric process which forced many individuals to scoff or reject their heritage. Also, numerous publications had led to the renouncement of the melting pot theory as a myth.[9] These observations paved the way for the acceptance of cultural pluralism via the demise of the Americanization process and the melting pot theory. However, certain proactive actions such as (1) emergence of self determination by minority ethnic groups, (2) Brown vs. Topeka Supreme Court decision, (3) civil rights legislation, (4) emergence of ethnicity, (5) impact of mass media and (6) the sociopolitical climate of our country led to the rediscovery of the cultural pluralism ideal as a viable alternative philosophical goal governing the interrelationship of the various cultural/ethnic groups within our country. It is beyond the scope of this paper to examine the function or role each action has played or continues to play in the acceptance of cultural pluralism by a majority of the public. For a discussion of action #1, 2, 3, I would like to refer the reader to one of my previous publications — *Developing the Multicultural Process in Classroom Instruction.*[10] In his publication The Rise of the Unmeltable Ethnics,[11] Novak presents an eloquent case for white ethnic groups which failed to melt and who also rejected the Americanization process. These groups have maintained their ethnicity. They believed that being a hyphenated American is perfectly allright. Actually, they will argue that being an American is being the composite product of several cultures. The intense resurgence of ethnicity by numerous groups — Afro-Americans, Polish-Americans, Italian-Americans, etc. during the 1970s led several writers to refer to it as the decade of the ethnics.

The mass media, especially television, has been a significant catalyst in the resurgence of cultural pluralism. The consciousness of Americans was raised via the television exposure of Martin Luther King's marches for freedom, segregationists taunting obscenities toward Black students entering Little Rock High School, Jewish Americans being taunted in Cicero, Roots, Holocaust, etc. It is my belief that these and many other televised examples of racism, ethnocentrism, discrimination, and other forms of dehumanization served a significant function in the recognition and acceptance of all groups.

There is no question about the sociopolitical climate of our society being more receptive of cultural pluralism during this time than any other time in our history.

The concept of cultural pluralism which emerged in the sixties was not the same as the one espoused by Kallen in the early 1900's. Nor was the impetus the same. Furthermore, the ambiguity of the sixties concept has been greater. The ambiguity of the concept has been extensively discussed in the writings of Pratte[12], Green[13], and Pacheo[14]. Briefly, I would like to reiterate and comment on some of those discussions. Each of the above writers agreed that cultural pluralism refers to a theory of society, however, the often raised question is, should the theory be viewed as descriptive or prescriptive? My response is that it is both. It has also been stated that there are different conceptual theories of cultural pluralism. Several which have recently appeared in the literature are democratic pluralism, insular pluralism, modified pluralism, and open society.

Democratic pluralism is descriptive. It refers to a concept of cultural pluralism in which there is a balance of power between competing and overlapping religious, cultural, ethnic, economic, and geographical groupings. Pacheco writes: "Each group has some interests which it protects and fosters and each has some say in shaping social decisions which are all binding on all groups that make up the society. Common to all groups is a set of political values and beliefs which serve to maintain the entire social system through accommodation and resolution of conflicts via appropriate channels."[15] This description has largely been accepted as the form of political organization which exists in our society.

Insular Pluralism is descriptive of the relationships among various social groups. The subgroups of the society as much as possible live in isolation from one another. Each group places restrictions on the amount and kind of associations its members may have with outsiders. As Green and Pratte have pointed out in separate writings, the various social groups will allow their members to develop primary and secondary relationships within their respective groups, however, intergroup associations and relationships may exist only at the level of polity. Although this form of cultural pluralism professes a respect and recognition of cultural diversity within society, it is very restrictive of each individual. The individual is confined to the social and cultural confines of his/her cultural group regardless of the wishes of the individual. Thus, insular pluralism allows each group to maintain its community and culture while supporting the social value of freedom of association for groups but not for individuals.

The modified or Halfway Pluralism is not too different from Insular

Pluralism; however, it encourages a high degree of functional contact between members of various cultural groups at the level of secondary associations. Pratte's criticism of this form of cultural pluralism is

> The fundamental difficulty inherent in the dynamics of the model of halfway pluralism is that the increased contact among groups on the secondary level of association may and often does promote cultural assimilation.[16]

Pratte fails to acknowledge the possibility of cultural acculturation. In cultural acculturation the individual retains and maintains his/her primary cultural heritage and experience while acquiring the skills and knowledge of another or other cultures. Thus the individual is able to function effectively in his/her primary culture and other cultures, also. The faultiness of Pratte's reasoning lies in his belief that primary and secondary associations of members from various cultures can only culminate in an assimilation process. His writings implied that an individual can only function in one culture and that in order to function in another cultural setting, one will lose the ability to function in his/her primary culture. Banks' typology model on ethnicity addresses the hypothesis that an individual may function effectively in two or more cultures, however more importantly, Banks' typology opens the door for the exploration of way for facilitating the acculturations process.[17] Some research I have done utilizing Banks' model lends support to the acculturation process.[18]

The concept of cultural pluralism as an open society appears both descriptive and prescriptive. However, there is confusion because some observers believe our society is moving toward an open society and therefore away from cultural pluralism. One such observer, Green[19], believes that an open society is one in which cultural groups and differences are irrelevant and eliminated. This has an apparent similarity to Talcott Parsons' prediction of the disappearance of ethnic groups from American society during the 20th century. Green's assertion that we are moving toward an open society in the United States is highly questionable, where upon examination one realizes his concept of an open society eliminates the significance of cultural groups much less the reality of their present and future existence.

In the ASCD 1974 yearbook[20], we are introduced to another definition of an open society. This definition includes the very essence of cultural pluralism because it is descriptive and prescriptive.

> ... "open society" in which a variety of cultures, value system, and life styles not only coexist but are nurtured ... The major concern of the society at large, and of the schools in particular, would be for full participation of all human beings with rights which are not dependent on race, ethnicity, sex, or social class. Individual and group differences would be prized, not merely accepted or grudgingly tolerated, and every person would have equal access to what they want from and can give to the society.[21]

I consider the ASCD's open society concept of cultural pluralism to be more relevant to the contemporary meaning and philosophical intent of cultural pluralism. This concept of cultural pluralism is both descriptive and prescriptive. Descriptive in that it recognizes the real social structure of this society i.e. the existence of cultural diversity as evident by the various cultural ethic groups, and their relationship to certain national institutions and value systems of this country.

It is prescriptive because it dares to say what ought to be i.e. cultural diversity should not only be recognized but also *valued* at both the group and personal levels; and that not only is equitable treatment received by all, but equitable accessibility provided to all for societal rights and privileges.

MULTICULTURALISM

The concept of cultural pluralism led to the emergence of multiculturalism. Multiculturalism refers to a process of education which affiliates itself not only to the descriptive nature but more importantly to the prescriptive nature of cultural pluralism. This prescriptive nature of cultural pluralism is manifested in numerous statements and definitions of multiculturalism (multicultural education) as illustrated in the following.

> Multiculturalism (multicultural education) rejects the view that schools should seek to melt away cultural differences or the view that schools should merely tolerate cultural pluralism ... recognizes cultural diversity as a fact of life in American society ... affirmed ... cultural diversity is a valuable resource that should be preserved and extended ... teaching of values which support cultural diversity and individual uniqueness.[22]

> a philosophy for education that promotes certain principles — equality, mutual acceptance and understanding, a sense of moral commitment — of positive cross-cultural interactions.

> ... should treat ethnic groups as full contributing members of American society rather than as sources of problems to be solved ... should be cross-cultural in nature instead of being structured upon separate and distinct racial or ethnic groups.[24]

> ... should help students develop a better understanding of their own backgrounds and of other groups that compose our society. Through this process the program should help students to respect and appreciate cultural diversity, overcome ethnocentric and prejudicial attitudes and understand the socio-historical, economic and psychological factors that have produced the contemporary conditions of ethnic polarization, inequality and alienation. It should also foster their ability to critically analyze and make intelligent decisions about real-life problems and issues through a process of democratic, dialogical inquiry. Finally, it should help them conceptualize and aspire toward a vision of a better society and acquire the necessary knowledge, understanding, and skills to enable them to move society toward greater equality and freedom, the eradication of degrading poverty and dehumanizing dependency, and the development of meaningful identity for all people.[25]

Common to definitions and statements of multiculturalism is what should or ought to be and the implicitness of their relationship to the development of an ideal society.

Therefore, education which is truly reflective of cultural pluralism will be guided by the prescriptive statement of multiculturalism.

Thus, the purpose of multiculturalism becomes that of ascertaining the ideal cultural pluralistic society.

TYPOLOGY OF MULTICULTURALISM*

DESCRIPTION

In this section I will describe typology levels of multiculturalism that one may observe in a school, a teacher, a classroom or some other educational entity. These conceptual levels are also reflective of the evolvement of multicultural education during the 1960's and 1970's.[26] However, my typology levels focus on the developmental sequence which an educational entity will undergo as it becomes encouched in the philosophical orientation of multiculturalism. It is my contention that any educational entity involved in multiculturalism can be categorized into one of the ascribed conceptual levels of multiculturalism.

My hypothesis is that educational entities may exemplify three levels of multiculturalism. These levels are distinct with readily identifiable parameters or characteristics. It is my notion that these conceptual levels differ qualitatively and quantitatively in respect to multiculturalism. There is a qualitative variation in the levels as to emphasis on product, process, or philosophy. The extent of this variation (quantity) as to the amount of product, process, and philosophy is also distinctive for each level.

Basically all educational components or entities can be observed to have the same kind of characteristic when at level one. All educational components such as teacher educational programs, school districts or schools, service departments (counseling, library, etc.), academic departments (social studies, language arts, science, etc.), elementary or secondary classrooms, and educators (administrators, teachers, counselors, etc.) will display similar kinds of characteristics. For illustrative purposes as to how these characteristics may manifest themselves I have chosen two educational components — teacher education program and classroom instruction (K-12 setting).

Perhaps my direct involvement in teacher education programs at several universities and two national research studies led to my first observations regarding evolvement of multiculturalism in a teacher education program. It became obvious that the extent of multiculturalism had a distinct qualitative dimension as well as a quantitative one. Quite obviously teacher education programs would differ in the number of cultural/ethnic groups, number of workshops, courses or programs devoted to multiculturalism ethnic/culturally makeup of faculty and students, amount of funds budgeted for multiculturalism, etc. This I consider the quantitative dimension. However a more salient feature appeared missing in most teacher education programs. This feature I refer to as the qualitative dimension. Further exploration of the educational arena reveal the omission or paucity of this dimension (qualitative) in other educational entities or components. The qualitative dimension of multiculturalism may be divided into three conceptual levels. Thus, the typology model which is presented later in this paper is primarily based on this dimension, however not

---

*Typology of Multiculturalism was first described in *Multicultural Teacher Education: preparing educators to provide educational equity.* AACTE, Washington, D.C. 1980.

the omission or paucity of this dimension (qualitative) in other educational entities or components. The qualitative dimension of multiculturalism may be divided into three conceptual levels. Thus, the typology model which is presented later in this paper is primarily based on this dimension, however not completely exclusive of the quantitative dimension. It is also along the qualitative dimension that internalization or multiculturalism must occur if educational equity and the prescriptive aspects of multiculturalism are going to be achieved.

The purpose of the typology is to help facilitate research in multiculturalism and also to aid in the intrinsic operatization (internalization) of multiculturalism in educational entities or components. It is my hypothesis that the internalization of multiculturalism in an educational entity can occur at at least three conceptual levels. Each level has a distinct set of characteristics which may be utilized to identify which conceptual level of the qualitative dimension of multiculturalism the educational entity has reached.

The focus of level one is characterized by a single cultural or ethnic emphasis. This single dimension emphasis may be illustrated by ethnic or cultural specific courses, celebration of cultural or ethnic holidays, fragmented and unrelated topics on various cultural groups in the curriculum, etc. Furthermore, level one is characterized by such tangibles as workshops, seminars, or courses on specific minority or ethnic groups coupled with a lack of clear cut programmatic goals or objectives. The additive notion is usually in vogue. During this period the dominating feature for incorporating multiculturalism is the addition of courses (usually on one of the visible minority ethnic groups) or conferences or workshops. These tangibles are obviously paraded to suggest something more than the real intent of the program. Often these cultural/ethnic emphases are for specific populations and are geographically limited. Perhaps the most salient characteristics of level one are its reaction posture and lack of institutionalization. These tangible cultural/ethnic displays are the result of external pressures brought about for example by interest groups, social pressures or community groups.

In level two, one will find its most sagacious quality as the confluent relationship of both product and process. One will note a seminal qualitative difference between levels one and two. The tangible products are embedded in a matrix of process. In this period there is a theoretical referent link with the practice. Multiculturalism takes on a broader base in its incorporation into the educational entity. Generic components of multicultural education are identified along with strategies for incorporating them into the entire educational entity or program. In addition, steps are taken to institutionalize various facets of multiculturalism. Specific courses and related experiences become a formalized part of the educational program.

This level forms a broad conceptual framework which provides a lucid guidance for amalgamating the elements and principles of multiculturalism with the core components of the educational program.

Attainment of level three represents a highly sophisticated internalization of the process of multiculturalism combined with a philosophical orientation that permeates all components of the educational entity. This pervasiveness quality will cause all facets of the educational entity to be governed by the accepted concepts, principles, and goals of multiculturalism. The attainment of level three by an educational entity surmises that it has emerged from level one (product) and level two (product/processes) to a sophisticated and regenerative conceptual knowledge base for multiculturalism.

These levels are sequential; however, levels two and three must be viewed as eclectic mixtures of those elements from the previous level. (See Diagram A).

Levels of Multiculturalism

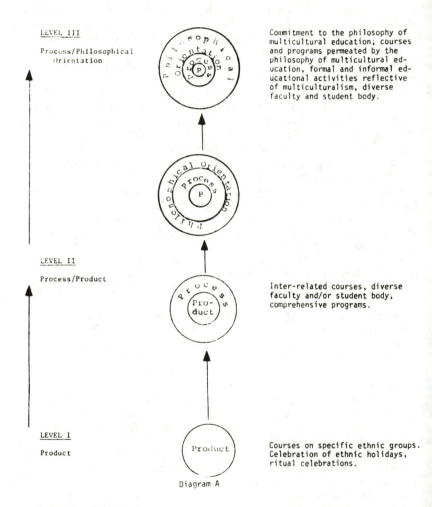

LEVEL III

Process/Philosophical
Orientation

Commitment to the philosophy of
multicultural education; courses
and programs permeated by the
philosophy of multicultural education, formal and informal educational activities reflective
of multiculturalism, diverse
faculty and student body.

LEVEL II

Process/Product

Inter-related courses, diverse
faculty and/or student body,
comprehensive programs.

LEVEL I

Product

Courses on specific ethnic groups.
Celebration of ethnic holidays,
ritual celebrations.

Diagram A

H. Prentice Paptiste, Jr.

RESEARCH

Presently, I am conducting several studies on the internalization of multiculturalism. Utilizing my typology of multiculturalism as a guide, several appropriate instruments have been developed to aid in determining the extent which the internalizing of multiculturalism has occurred in two selected educational entities. At this time I will present preliminary data and results on my research into the internalization of multiculturalism by teacher education programs and public school teachers.

The teacher education program entity was selected as a starting point for my research because of its significant role in the training of our teachers for the public schools. Furthermore AACTE, along with numerous other teacher associations and state departments of education have stressed through position papers, certification requirements, legislative mandates and accreditation standards, the importance of teacher education programs incorporating multiculturalism into all aspects of their programs.

Questionnaires validated against my typology of Multiculturalism model were mailed to one hundred and fifty randomly selected undergraduate teacher education programs. The Dean of the school of education or his/her designate was requested to complete the questionnaire and return it to the researcher. Forty-four percent of the disseminated questionnaires were completed and returned. Preliminary analysis of the data has revealed the following:

1) Eighty-four percent (84%) of the responding institutions scored at the *low end* of Level I. The extent of multiculturalism was the offering of one or two short workshops or seminars and/or one multicultural course during the previous year.

2) Fifty-one percent (51%) of the responding institutions had elected not to offer any multicultural courses.

3) Twenty-nine percent (29%) had not scheduled workshops, seminars or multicultural courses.

4) Approximately eleven percent (10.6%) of the responding institutions were at Level II. This was accomplished through the restructuring of some education courses to reflect multiculturalism and/or to offer a major in multiculturalism. However, a vast majority of multicultural majors were based on just one or two regional multicultural courses.

5) Ten percent (10%) of the responding institutions were at the lower end of Level III. This was ascertained by an institution having included objectives relevant to multiculturalism within their institutional objectives, however, upon closer scrutiny one realized these objectives were not being implemented.

The second study focused on the extent of internalization of multiculturalism within teachers and their opinion as to its extent in their classroom instruction and school. The procedure was the following. The typology of multiculturalism was explained to each teacher. The explanation included a complete description of each level including pertinent characteristics of the levels. Examples of school climates and behavioral contexts, classroom instructional strategies and lessons, and teacher behavioral patterns with students, parents and others were discussed for each level. Then a film of a teacher in demonstrable Levels II and III behavioral patterns was shown to each teacher. Each teacher was then given the typology of multiculturalism matrix to complete. (See appendix A). This matrix allowed each teacher to determine the multiculturalism level for his/ her school, class instruction, himself/ herself, and the film.

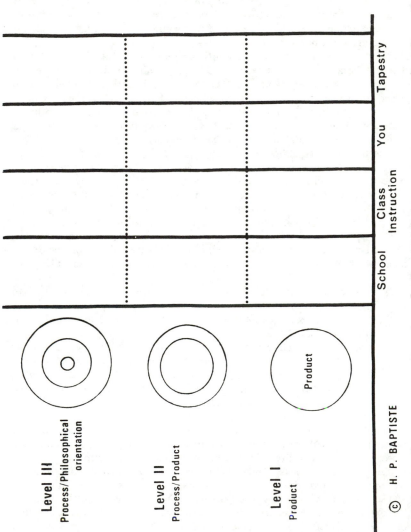

Typology of Multiculturalism Matrix

© H. P. BAPTISTE

Preliminary analysis of the responses of forty teachers indicates the following:

1) All of the teachers stated that the teacher depicted in the film was operating at Level III.

2) Sixty-eight percent (68%) of the teachers believed that their schools were operating at Level I. The five percent (5%) which placed their schools at Level III did so reluctantly.

3) Sixty-six percent (66%) stated that their classroom instruction was at Level II of multiculturalism. Eight percent (8%) felt they were at Level III.

4) Sixty-one percent (61%) believed that their personal behavior and interaction with students were at Level II. Twenty-eight percent (28%) felt they were at Level III.

CONCLUSION

The results cited in the two studies appear to confirm that the internalization of Multiculturalism in education as elsewhere in America is moving at a *snail's* pace. Uhuru, por favor.

REFERENCES

[1]Baptiste, M.L. and Baptiste Jr., H.P. Competencies toward multiculturalism. *Multicultural teacher education* Washington, D.C. AACTE, 1980, pp. 44-72.

[2]Cubberly, Elwood. *Changing conceptions of education* New York: Riverside Educational Mimeographs, 1909.

[3]Roosevelt, Theodore. Americanism. Speech given in 1910.

[4]Pratte, Richard. *Pluralism in Education* Charles C. Thomas publisher: Springfield; 1979, p. 29.

[5]Kallen, Horace. *Cultural pluralism and the American idea.* Philadelphia: University of Philadelphia Press, 1956.

[6]Sizemore, Barbara. The Politics of Multicultural Education. Unpublished manuscript, 1979.

[7]Krug, Mark. *The Melting of the Ethnics.* Bloomington: Phi Delta Kappa, 1976, p. 12-13.

[8]Ibid., Pratte, R. p. 48.

[9]Novak, Michael. *The Rise of the Unmeltable Ethnics.* New York: MacMillan Publishing Co., Inc., 1973.

[10]Baptistle, Jr. H. Prentice et al. *Developing the Multicultural Process in Classroom Instruction* Washington, D.C.: University Press of America, 1979 pp.

[11]Ibid., Novak, M.

[12]Ibid., Pratte, R.

[13]Green, Thomas F. Education and Pluralism: Ideal and Reality. (Twenty-sixth annual J. Richard Street Lecture, Syracuse University School of Education, 1966). p. 25.

[14]Pacheco, Arcturo. Cultural Pluralism: A Philosophical Analysis. *Journal of Teacher Education* May-June, 1977, p. 16-20.

[15]Ibid., Pacheco, Arturo, p. 18.

[16]Ibid., Pratte, R., p. 129.

[17]Banks, James. The Implications of Multicultural Education for Teacher Education. *Pluralism and the American Teacher.* AACTE, Washington, D.C.: 1977, p. 17-26.

[18]Ford, Margaret. The Development of an Instrument for Assessing Levels of Ethnicity in Public School Teachers. Unpublished dissertation. University of Houston. Houston, Texas, 1979.

[19]Ibid., Green, Thomas, p.

[20]Dora-Della, Delmo et al., editors. *Education for an Open Society* 1974 yearbook. ASCD, Washington, D.C., 1974.

[21]Ibid., Dora-Della, Delmo, p. 3.

[22]AACTE Commission on Multicultural Education. No one model American. *Journal of Teacher Education.* Winter, 1973, p. 264-265.

[23]Baptiste, H.P. et al. Multicultural Teacher Education: Preparing Educators to Provide Educational Equity. AACTE, Washington, D.C., 1980, p. 44.

[24]*Planning for Multicultural Education as a Part of School Improvement.* Bureau of Publications, California State Department of Education, Sacramento, CA., 1979, p. 10.

[25]Suzuki, Bob. Multicultural Education: What's it all about? *Integrated Education* January-April, 1979, p. 47-48.

[26]Gay, Geneva. Changing Conceptions of Multicultural Education. *Educational Perspectives,* December, 1977, p. 4-9.

NON-VERBAL
COMMUNICATION SYSTEMS
AND TECHNIQUES FOR THE
CULTURALLY DIVERSE
HANDICAPPED CHILD
By Deborah Goldstein, Ph.D.

INTRODUCTION

Functional language production through traditional channels is not possible for some culturally diverse handicapped children. These non-verbal and motorically impaired children from various cultural groups are incapable of speaking or writing and may produce only undifferentiated gutteral sounds and gross gestures to transmit their thoughts and ideas. Since statewide enactment of Public Law 94-142 mandates that every handicapped child must be provided with a free appropriate public education (Turnbull & Turnbull, 1978), educators are attempting to implement meaningful educational programs for all handicapped children, regardless of the severity of their handicap. In order to design instructional procedures for the non-verbal handicapped child, these children must be furnished with an effective means of a communication channel (Hagen, Porter, & Brink, 1973). Providing an appropriate communication system for children who are handicapped, non-verbal, and who come from culturally diverse backgrounds is a great challenge confronting special educators (Baca, 1980). Not only do we need to devise specialized communication systems for these children, but we must ensure that the communication is conveyed in a language they understand and that is sensitive to cultural patterns (Hilliard, 1980). It is the intent of this paper to examine the issues that comprise the importance and instructional design of communication systems for the culturally diverse non-verbal handicapped child. These issues will deal with: 1) the rationale for early language intervention, 2) the functional uses and considerations in selecting non-verbal communication systems, and 3) vocabulary determination for the non-verbal culturally diverse handicapped child.

RATIONALE FOR EARLY LANGUAGE INTERVENTION

It is imperative for the culturally diverse handicapped child who lacks functional speech to be provided with a non-verbal communication system. Kates and

McNaughton (1975) emphasize the importance of the role of speech in giving the child a good self-concept, the ability to exercise control over his environment, and in making possible a challenging and appropriate educational program. The culturally diverse handicapped child who lacks sufficient speech to fulfill his communication needs is limited in his total development. An effective means of communication is vital for the handicapped child who is deprived of many of the normal exploratory and learning experiences of infancy and childhood. Non-verbal communication aids will enable a motorically impaired child without speech to ask questions about the environment or ask questions when task presentations are unclear and will allow the child to respond to questions from the parent or teacher (Rees, 1973). Furthermore, opportunities to add to the child's experiential background decrease in number as his motor disabilities increase (McNaughton & Kates, 1975). When the inability to question and express ideas is coupled with the child's lack of learning experiences, there is little hope for either adequate assessment or appropriate educational programming.

In the past there has been a reluctance to intervene early with non-verbal infants and children (McDonald, 1977a). There has been a long held conviction that if infants and children were trained with a non-verbal method for communication, the non-verbal system would interfere with eventual speech performance. It is now known that intervention with non-verbal communication methods have not hampered the development of speech and, in many cases, have facilitated speech development by improving intelligibility in children who had limited vocalizations (Grinnel, Detamore, & Lippki, 1976; Harris-Vanderheiden, 1977; Harris-Vanderheiden, Brown, MacKenzie, Reinin, & Scheibel, 1975; MacDonald, 1977b; Vanderheiden, 1977; Vicker, 1974). Until recently, speech therapists have been trained specifically to teach children to speak and they were certain that working on another modality other than the oral mechanism was an admission of their own failure. Currently, speech therapists are being trained to instruct non-verbal children in total communication, language, and speech development in all modalities. These recent advancements posit that non-verbal communication techniques and aids should not be considered alternatives to speech but rather as auxiliary or supplementary modes of communication. These auxiliary modes serve to facilitate and augment language instruction for children who were not able to communicate effectively through speech (Harris-Vanderheiden & Vanderheiden, 1977; Nietupski & Hamre-Nietupski, 1979).

It is recognized that infants and children at risk for the development of speech need early intervention and stimulation which comes from interaction with their environment (Ainsworth & Bell, 1975; Friedlander, 1970). Lloyd (1976) has indicated that although the child under two years of age has limited verbal expression, he is still very linguistic. Furthermore, the first two years are the most critical for language learning (Lloyd, 1976). Butterfield and Cairns (1976) have shown that auditory experience in infancy is a determinant of later language development. In their studies of the infant's response to the auditory environment, they have demonstrated that the infant selectively attends to auditory variations. When given the opportunity, the infant actively works to control his auditory environment (Butterfield & Cairns, 1976). In other studies, speech has been found to be a more stimulating part of the newborn infant's environment than other events such as food, music, or tactile sensation (Butterfield & Siperstein, 1972; Condon & Sander, 1974).

There is evidence that the development of communication skills in the child relates to both the amount and quality of parent stimulation (Horowitz, 1968; Hursh & Sherman, 1973; Simeonsson & Wiegarink, 1974). Baker (1976) stresses the need for early language training for the at risk language infant beginning as soon after birth as possible. Lloyd (1976) suggests that the involvement of the parents as critical change agents has a great impact on the infant and child at risk. The parents are primary language teachers since they interact most with the child and have the greatest opportunity to facilitate positive change (Tharp & Wetzel, 1969; Lloyd, 1976).

In sum, there is a lack of evidence that non-verbal communication systems inhibit the development of oral communication (Wilbur, 1976), but rather that they may result in an improvement in vocalizations (Hopper & Helmick, 1977). However, while some researchers stress the importance of early non-verbal communication training (Guess, Sailor, & Baer, 1977), others suggest that there are cognitive prerequisites for auxiliary communication systems (Chapman & Miller, 1977; Harris-Vanderheiden, 1977; Miller, 1977). Those proposing that certain cognitive prerequisites must be in the child's repertoire before non-verbal communication instruction can begin, suggest that object permanence (Harris-Vanderheiden, 1977) and reaching Piaget's Stage VI of sensorimotor intelligence (Chapman & Miller, 1977; Kahn, 1975) are necessary prerequisites. Nietupski and Hamre-Nietupski (1979) have made the following conclusions regarding the remedial vs. cognitive-developmental positions controversy for non-verbal communication intervention with the handicapped:

> ... The key to the controversy would seem to be whether instructional personnel are concerned with the development of a self-generated representational system or the development of skills necessary to use specific linguistic elements. If the former, it would seem reasonable to hold that students must comprehend their physical environment (prerequisite sensorimotor skills) before dealing with abstract representations of their environment. If the latter, it may not be necessary to teach students all the presumed cognitive prerequisites prior to teaching them to communicate. (p. 110)

It is the viewpoint of this author to provide students with functional non-verbal communication systems at the earliest age and then match the child's cognitive level to the type of non-verbal communication system. By providing the non-verbal culturally diverse handicapped child with a means to communicate, he can begin to acquire the cognitive, social, and emotional skills basic to his development. The experiences that enrich cognitive, social, and emotional development can be provided to the child who lacks functional speech with the use of a non-verbal communication system. This system will enable the child to become an active participant in the many language activities necessary to his total growth and development.

THE FUNCTIONAL USES AND CONSIDERATIONS
IN SELECTION OF NON-VERBAL COMMUNICATION SYSTEMS

Non-verbal communication systems can be grouped in three non-exclusive categories (Nietupski & Hamre-Nietupski, 1979): a) manual systems (e.g., American Sign Language), b) communication aids (e.g., communications boards, display devices), and c) communicative codes (e.g., the use of actions, such as eye movements or foot taps, as communication responses). Presented as a hierarchy, these non-verbal communication systems can be used with children whose physical abilities range from normal motor function to severely impaired motoric involvement. Therefore, the selection of a non-verbal communication system should be directly related to the child's degree of motor functioning. For example, a child with maximum gross and fine motor functioning in the upper extremities may be very capable of acquiring manual communication skills, while a child with weak upper extremity functioning will need instruction in using an aid or communicative code. Through the use of a series of formal and informal evaluation techniques (Alberto, Briggs, Sharpton & Goldstein, in press) motor functioning of the child can be evaluated and communication options can be narrowed to one of the three communication categories. It should be noted that since this paper deals with the non-verbal, motorically impaired, culturally diverse child, manual communication systems will not be reviewed. Manual sign language has been shown to be an impractical non-verbal communication system for the non-verbal motorically impaired child as: a) the child may lack the physical coordination to efficiently use manual signs for communication (Vicker, 1974), b) the culturally diverse child may not comprehend the subtleties that can be expressed through sign language (Cicourel & Boese, 1972), and c), the child's audience may not be familiar with sign language (Vicker, 1974). Thus, a discussion of communication aids and codes will follow.

COMMUNICATION AIDS AND COMMUNICATIVE CODES

According to Nietupski and Hamre-Nietupski (1979), communication aids are "display devices which contain objects, pictures of objects or actions, symbols, or printed words" (p. 111). Communicative codes involve the use of actions such as eye movements or foot taps to respond to communication aids and techniques (Nietupski & Hamre-Nietupski, 1979). Communication aids and communicative codes are used to provide non-verbal children with an immediate and functional augmentative mode of communication. These non-verbal children are unable to communicate effectively through traditional speech due to oral musculature deficiencies and are unable to utilize gestures or manual signing due to fine motor skill impairment (Harris, Lippert, Yoder, & Vanderheiden, 1979). The use of a communication aid or code is based on the results of a communication assessment that has focused on the strengths and weaknesses of the language user, including physical limitations and types of interactions with others. Nietupski and Hamre-Nietupski (1979) have posited that the use of a communication aid with a student is appropriate if the student:

1. Has physical impairments which preclude the control of his or her hand and finger movements;
2. Tends not to attend to the action of others, but prefers to interact with objects;
3. Has access to an audience that is not willing to learn a manual system. (p. 115)

Communicative codes should be utilized "only if physical impairments preclude all but the rudimentary motor movements" (Nietupski & Hamre-Nietupski, 1979, p. 115).

The use of communication aids (display devices) and codes (motor responses) involve the selection of a communication technique that provides the non-verbal child with an effective means of indicating the elements of his message (Vanderheiden, 1977). In attempting to provide the child with a communication technique, it is important that the technique be within the physical and mental capacities of the student as well as having the technique capitalize upon these abilities to facilitate the most efficient mode of communication. Vanderheiden (1977) suggests that it is important to select the technique that allows the non-verbal child the greatest speed and ease of communication. Vanderheiden and Harris-Vanderheiden (1976) have emphasized the importance of selecting the technique that is most effective for the child, considering his environment, communication needs, and cognitive and physical abilities. It should be noted that as a child develops, his needs will change, thereby necessitating a modification in the communication technique.

There are three basic communication techniques to be used with communication aids and codes: a.) direct selection, b.) scanning, and c.) encoding (Harris & Vanderheiden, 1980; Vanderheiden, 1977; Vanderheiden & Harris-Vanderheiden, 1976). Within each technique presented, there is a distinct hierarchy dealing with the equipment used in the communication process and consisting of five levels of implementation: a.) unaided techniques (do not involve any physical communication aid and require the aid of another person), b.) fundamental communication aids (communications aids that have no electronic or moving parts and require the aid of another person), c.) simple electronic and mechanical aids (consist of electronic and mechanical communication aids that require assistance from another person), d.) nonportable fully independent aids (consist of nonportable devices that enable the child to independently print out messages), and e.) portable fully independent aids (portable devices that can be moved to a variety of settings and that enable the child to independently print out messages). Each consecutive level serves as an increase in both function and cost of the associated aids. It also signifies an increase in the independence of communication for the non-verbal child as well as a decrease in the amount of effort on the part of the second person aiding the student (Vanderheiden & Harris-Vanderheiden, 1976). Thus, the three major communication techniques of direct selection, scanning, and encoding will be described according to their various levels of implementation in addition to the advantages and disadvantages for each technique.

Direct selection. Techniques in which the non-verbal child indicates the elements of his message by directly pointing to them in some manner describes the direct selection approach (Harris & Vanderheiden, 1980). Although the child usually points with his finger or fist, any part of the body can be used to indicate the vocabulary items such as toes or elbows or even adaptive devices such as headsticks or mouthpieces.

In the simple unaided level of direct selection, the child points to or looks at an object in his environment in order to convey a message. In the fundamental level of direct selection, the child directly indicates with a particular part of his body or adaptive device which pictures, symbols, letters or words he wants to use on a communication board. Any type of expanded or recessed keyboard that is connected to an electric typewriter exemplifies a fully independent with printed output direct selection device. At the fully independent and portable level of implementation, a direct selection device could include a device such as the Auto-Com, whereby the child uses a magnet to directly select message elements on an electronic communication board and the message is printed onto a TV screen or a strip printer (Harris-Vanderheiden, 1977).

The direct selection technique is easy to implement as the child only needs to point to the desired object, picture, symbol, letter, or word to communicate with another individual. According to Vanderheiden and Harris-Vanderheiden (1976), other advantages of this technique include the use of immediate, direct feedback and that this approach can be used with non-verbal children of low cognitive abilities. The major disadvantage of this technique is that it requires sufficient control of some part of the body to be able to point accurately. If the child is able to develop the physical control necessary for this technique, direct selection is a relatively fast, simple, and "direct" means of communication.

Scanning. A technique is considered scanning if message elements (pictures, symbols, letters, or words) are presented individually so that the child can indicate the message element he wants by providing a response or signal when the desired element is reached (Harris-Vanderheiden & Vanderheiden, 1977). This technique therefore involves a teacher, aide, parent, another student, or any other individual who scans the message elements for a child. The child is passive until the desired item is presented and at that time, the non-verbal student responds.

The types of scanning techniques that the child can utilize form a level of implementation hierarchy. The unaided level of a scanning technique would consist of a yes/no or twenty-questions approach whereby a second person asks the child questions, one at a time, and the child signals by either smiling, looking up, or using some other pre-arranged signal. The fundamental level consists of a second individual manually pointing to a communication board while the non-verbal child signals when the person has pointed to the message element the child desires. The simple electronic scanning level consists of the same technique but rather than a second person scanning, the communication aid automatically scans the material. The non-verbal child can control the pointer by using a switch that is designed to stop the pointer when the child presses on it with some part of his body. The child can start and stop the scanning device by pressing on the switch to indicate the elements of his message. The second person verbally repeats the child's choice but is "relieved of the task of pointing to each element and watching for a response from the child" (Vanderheiden & Harris-

Vanderheiden, 1976). The fully independent with printed output scanning aid consists of an electronic communication display that scans pictures, symbols, letters, or words. When the child responds to the desired message element by pressing a switch, the aid would automatically print it out on a typewriter or other device. The fully independent and portable scanning technique consists of a portable printing communication aid using scanning and a switch that allows the student to respond to desired message elements.

A major advantage of this approach is that it can be used with non-verbal children who have minimal physical control and are unable to use the direct selection approach. In the scanning approach, the motorically impaired child only has to develop a communicative code, such as a movement or signal that can be detected by a second individual or display device. Furthermore, scanning techniques are simple to operate for all children, including low cognitive level children. The major disadvantage of this technique is its slow approach, as the child waits for the scanner to present unwanted as well as desired message elements. The rate of scanning remains slow as the indicator must rest at each message element long enough for the child to respond and make a selection by responding correctly. This slow rate intensifies when additional pictures, symbols, letters, or words are added to the child's communicative aid.

Encoding. Vanderheiden (1977) has defined encoding as "any technique or aid in which the desired choice is indicated by a pattern or code of input signals, where the pattern or code must be memorized or referred to on a chart" (p. 22). Any number of switches or movements (codes) can be utilized including the activation of switches or making movements sequentially, simultaneously, or in a specific pattern as in Morse code (Vanderheiden & Harris-Vanderheiden, 1976).

The unaided encoded technique consists of having the letters of the alphabet (or pictures, symbols, or words) arranged in a 5 x 5 matrix (with the letter z excluded) with the numbers one to five written horizontally and vertically. If a child wanted to indicate the letter B, he would hold up two fingers indicating the second column and then one finger indicating the first letter down. In the fundamental encoding approach, another type of two-movement technique is utilized. Pictures, symbols, letters, or words are arranged on a communication chart as described above. The child indicates the desired message element by pointing to the two numbers on a small chart in front of him that correspond to the desired message. If the non-verbal child was not able to point with his upper extremities or with an adaptive device, an eye gaze chart could be used. With the clear plastic chart, called an ETRAN chart, the child indicates which picture, symbol, or word he wants on a vocabulary chart by using his eye gaze to indicate the numbers that are printed next to the message element (Vanderheiden, 1977). The simple electronic encoding technique consists of the child using the Morse code or some other code on a switch attached to his shoulder or other area. The code is decoded by an aid and displayed on an electronic communication aid. According to Vanderheiden (1977) the message receiver only has to watch the display to see what letters or words appeared to determine what message the child was attempting to communicate. At the fully independent with printed output level of implementation, the code would be interpreted and printed out onto an electronic typewriter or other display.

The encoding technique is more expedient than scanning but requires a higher degree of physical control on the part of the non-verbal child. In addition, this technique requires more complex movements and more responses for each message element than scanning. Therefore, encoding for the physically handicapped non-verbal child with weak, slow or erratic movements may be a less efficient technique than scanning. In addition, the encoding scheme must be learned by the child before the technique can be used, possibly resulting in problems for the lower cognitive ability non-verbal child. It should be noted that encoding does provide access to large vocabularies for a non-verbal child with limited motoric abilities. As Vanderheiden and Harris-Vanderheiden (1976) have indicated, a child can retrieve any one message element from a 700-element vocabulary in a few seconds by only using the numbers 1 to 10 and a three-movement encoding strategy. Thus, encoding techniques require more physical control than scanning techniques and higher cognitive processes than either scanning or direct selection, but encoding provides a faster and more extensive means of communication for the motorically impaired non-verbal child than scanning techniques.

Summary. Any one technique or a combination of the three techniques will assist the non-verbal child in acquiring augmentative communication skills. It has been suggested (Harris & Vanderheiden, 1980; Nietupski & Hamre-Nietupski, 1979; Vanderheiden, 1977) to start with the direct selection approach if the child has the physical abilities since it offers the greatest speed and simplicity. Scanning techniques should be considered with severely physically impaired children who have a limited range of motion. Encoding techniques should be considered with large vocabulary systems for the child with more physical control than needed for scanning. Vanderheiden and Harris-Vanderheiden (1976) have posited that it is important to provide the child with an effective communication system as early as possible; therefore, it may be appropriate to utilize a slower technique for functional communication use with the child while simultaneously building the development of skills necessary to use a more expedient technique.

VOCABULARY DETERMINATION

After the selection of an appropriate communication aid and code, initial vocabulary needs to be determined for the non-verbal child. Communication aids include some type of system to signify the intent of the language user. Typically these systems include either pictures (photographs or drawings), symbols (Blissymbolics, rebuses), letters, or words (Silverman, 1980). Regardless of the type of system used, initial vocabulary selection for a non-verbal child involves the formation of a list of potential vocabulary items through the following procedures: a.) student preference, b.) frequency of occurrence, c.) functional utility across situations, and d.) basic human needs (Nietupski & Hamre-Nietupski, 1979).

STUDENT PREFERENCE

When attempting to determine initial vocabulary based on student preferences for a non-verbal culturally diverse handicapped child, there needs to be a concern for racial and ethnic differences. Alamanza and Mosley (1980) have suggested that the culture, history, values, and learning styles of the individual child should be considered in teaching situations. They posit that by focusing on the processes of learning and the manner in which these processes differ among various culturally diverse groups, teachers will be more successful with these students. Thus, initial vocabulary selection for a non-verbal culturally diverse handicapped child should be based on the objects, actions, places, and persons toward which the child demonstrates a preference in his environment. As mentioned, it is important to be sensitive to the cultural differences between the child and those responsible for determining the initial vocabulary to ensure that the student's preferences are selected as opposed to preferences imposed on the child by others.

FREQUENCY OF OCCURRENCE

A "frequency of occurrence" strategy in which the child is taught vocabulary items comprising frequently engaged activities has been posited (Grinnel et al., 1976; Hamre-Nietupski, Stoll, Holtz, Fullerton, Ryan-Flottum, & Brown, 1977). It has been advocated that rapid skill acquisition of the vocabulary items will be demonstrated since there is a greater opportunity to practice the frequently occurring items. Hamre-Nietupski et al. (1977) have devised recording forms to facilitate systematic notation of frequently demonstrated activities and vocabulary items.

FUNCTIONAL UTILITY ACROSS SITUATIONS

Vocabulary items that are applicable across various settings should be considered initial vocabulary (Scheuerman, Baumgart, Sipsma, & Brown, 1975). Warren, Rogers-Warren, Baer, and Guess (1980) have stressed the importance of generalization of language in communication contexts. They have suggested that vocabulary items be utilized in different settings with different language trainers using various cues before generalization will be achieved. Scheuerman et al. (1976) posit that words such as "no," "stop," "want," and "more" are applicable across a child's various settings (home, school, after-school activities) and situations (during academics, recess, lunch) and therefore promote functional generalization of these vocabulary items.

BASIC HUMAN NEEDS

This strategy involves teaching students to use vocabulary items concerning their basic human needs. According to Nietupski and Hamre-Nietupski (1979), activities of daily living or self-help skills such as toileting, dressing, eating, drinking, grooming, playing are important initial vocabulary items. These items are important to the non-verbal and involve frequently occurring situations.

SUMMARY

Non-verbal communication techniques, congruent with the cognitive and physical capabilities of the communication user, should be initiated early with the non-verbal, motorically impaired, culturally diverse handicapped child. These auxiliary methods facilitate communication instruction and have been found to enhance speech development (MacDonald, 1977b). When providing a child with a non-verbal means of indicating his communication needs, the technique must be within the child's capabilities and should enhance these abilities to permit efficient communication. The three main communication techniques of direct selection, scanning, and encoding were presented to emphasize those factors that are important to consider when selecting appropriate communication aids and codes. Strategies for the determination of initial vocabulary were also described to facilitate the selection process that should occur after the delineation of the appropriate communication system and technique. Future research should focus on specific instructional procedures such as prompting, fading, shaping and chaining and reinforcement procedures such as positive reinforcement and punishment with non-verbal children utilizing communication systems and techniques.

REFERENCES

AINSWORTH. M.D., AND BELL. S.M. Mother-infant interaction and the development of competence. In K. J. Connolly & J. S. Bruner (Eds.), *The growth of competence*. New York: Academic Press, 1975.

ALAMANZA. H.P., AND MOSLEY. W.J. Curriculum adaptations and modifications for culturally diverse handicapped children. *Exceptional Children*, 1980, *46* (8), 608-614.

ALBERTO. P., BRIGGS. T., SHARPTON. W., AND GOLDSTEIN. D. Teaching a non-verbal yes/no response to severely handicapped students. *Journal of Communication Disorders*, in press.

BACA. L. Issues in the education of culturally diverse exceptional children. *Exceptional Children*, 1980, *46* (8), 583.

BAKER. B.L. Parent involvement in programming for developmentally disabled children. In L. Lloyd (Ed.), *Communication assessment and intervention strategies*. Baltimore: University Park Press, 1976.

BUTTERFIELD. E.C., AND CAIRNS. G.F. The infant's auditory environment. In T. D. Tjossem (Ed.), *Intervention strategies for high risk infants and young children*. Baltimore: University Park Press, 1976.

BUTTERFIELD. E.C., AND SIPERSTEIN. G.N. Influence on contingent stimulation upon non-nutritional suckle. In J. Bosma (Ed.) *Oral sensation and perception: The mouth of the infant*. Springfield: Charles C. Thomas, 1972.

CHAPMAN. R.S., AND MILLER. J. *Analyzing language and communication in the child*. Paper presented at the Conference on Nonspeech Language Intervention, Gulf State Park, Alabama, March, 1977.

CICOUREL. A.V., AND BOESE. R.J. Sign language acquisition and the teaching of deaf children, Part I. *American Annals of the Deaf*, 1972, *117*, 27-33.

CONDON. W.S., AND SANDER. L.W. Neonate movement is synchronized with adult speech: Interactional participation and language acquisition. *Science*, 1974, *183*, 99-101.

FRIEDLANDER. B.Z. Receptive language development in infancy: Issues and problems. *Merrill-Palmer Quarterly*, 1970, *16*, 7-51.

GRINNEL. M., DETAMORE. K., AND LIPPKE. B. Sign it successful-manual English encourages expressive communication. *Teaching Exceptional Children*, 1976, *8*, 123-124.

GUESS. D., SAILOR. W., AND BAER. D. A behavioral-remedial approach to language training for the severely handicapped. In E. Sontag, J. Smith, & N. Certo (Eds.), *Educational programming for the severely and profoundly handicapped*. Reston, Va.: The Council for Exceptional Children, 1977.

HAGEN. C., PORTER. W., AND BRINK. J. Nonverbal communication: An alternate mode of communication for the child with severe cerebral palsy. *Journal of Speech and Hearing Disorders*, 1973, *38* (4), 448-455.

HAMRE-NIETUPSKI. S., STOLL. A., HOLTZ. K., FULLERTON. P., RYAN-FLOTTUM. M., AND BROWN. L. Curricular strategies for teaching selected nonverbal communication skills to severely handicapped students. In L. Brown, J. Nietupski, S. Lyon, S. Hamre-Nietupski, T. Crowner, & L. Gruenewald (Eds.), *Curricular strategies for teaching nonverbal communication, functional object use, problem solving and mealtime skills to severely handicapped students*. (Vol. VII, Part I). Madison: University of Wisconsin-Madison and Madison Metropolitan School District, 1977.

HARRIS. D., LIPPERT. J.C., YODER. D.E., AND VANDERHEIDEN. G.C. Blissymbolics: An augmentative symbol communication system for nonvocal severely handicapped children. In R. L. York & E. Edgar (Eds.), *Teaching the severely handicapped* (Vol. IV). Seattle: American Association for the Education of the Severely Profoundly Handicapped, 1979.

HARRIS. D., AND VANDERHEIDEN. G.C. Augmentative communication techniques. In R. L. Schiefelbusch (Ed.), *Nonspeech language and communication: Analysis and intervention*. Baltimore: University Park Press, 1980.

HARRIS-VANDERHEIDEN. D. Blissymbols and the mentally retarded. In G. Vanderheiden & K. Grilley (Eds.), *Non-vocal communication techniques and aids for the severely physically handicapped*. Baltimore: University Park Press, 1977.

HARRIS-VANDERHEIDEN. D., BROWN. W., MacKENZIE. P., REININ. S., AND SCHEIBEL. C. Symbol communication for the mentally handicapped. *Mental Retardation*, 1975, *13*, 34-37.

HARRIS-VANDERHEIDEN. D., AND VANDERHEIDEN. G.C. Basic considerations in the development of communicative and interactive skills for non-vocal severely handicapped children. In E. Sontag, J. Smith, & N. Certo (Eds.), *Educational programming for the severely and profoundly handicapped*. Restor. Virginia: Council for Exceptional Children, 1977.

HARRIS-VANDERHEIDEN, D., AND VANDERHEIDEN, G.C. Basic considerations in the development of communicative and interactive skills for non-vocal severely handicapped children. In E. Sontag, J. Smith, & N. Certo (Eds.), *Educational programming for the severely and profoundly handicapped.* Rester, Virginia: Council for Exceptional Children, 1977.

HILLIARD, A.G. Cultural diversity and special education. *Exceptional Children,* 1980, *46* (8), 584-588.

HOPPER, C., AND HELMICK, R. Nonverbal communication for the severely handicapped: Some considerations. *American Association for the Education of the Severely and Profoundly Handicapped Review,* 1977, *2,* 47-52.

HOROWITZ, F.D. Infant learning and development: Retrospect and prospect. *Merrill-Palmer Quarterly,* 1968, *14,* 101-120.

HURSH, D.E., AND SHERMAN, J.A. The effects of parent-presented models and praise on the vocal behavior of their children. *Journal of Experimental Child Psychology,* 1973, *15,* 328-339.

KAHN, J.V. Relationship of Piaget's sensorimotor period to language acquisition of profoundly retarded children. *American Journal of Mental Deficiency,* 1975, *79,* 640-643.

KATES, B., AND McNAUGHTON, S. *The first application of Blissymbolics as a communication medium for non-speaking children: History and development, 1971-1974.* Toronto: Blissymbolics Communication Foundation, 1975.

LLOYD, L.L. Discussant's comments: Language and communication aspects. In T. D. Tjossem (Ed.) *Intervention strategies for high risk infants and young children.* Baltimore: University Park Press, 1976.

McDONALD, E.T. *Facilitating communication in non-verbal cerebral palsy children.* Paper presented at the Eugene McDonald Symposium on Non-Verbal Communication, St. Petersburg, January, 1977. (a)

McDONALD, E.T. Identification of children at risk. In G. Vanderheiden & K. Grilley (Eds.), *Non-vocal communication techniques and aids for the severely physically handicapped.* Baltimore: University Park Press, 1977. (b)

McNAUGHTON, S., AND KATES, B. *Teaching guidelines.* Toronto: Blissymbolics Communication Foundation, 1975.

MILLER, J.F. On specifying what to teach: The movement from structure, to structure and meaning, to structure and meaning and knowing. In E. Sontag, J. Smith, & N. Certo (Eds.), *Educational programming for the severely and profoundly handicapped.* Reston, Va.: The Council for Exceptional Children, 1977.

NIETUPSKI, J., AND HAMRE-NIETUPSKI, S. Teaching auxiliary communication skills to severely handicapped students. *American Association for the Education of the Severely and Profoundly Handicapped Review,* 1979, *4* (2), 107-124.

REES, C.L. Noncommunicative functions of language in children. *Journal of Speech and Hearing Disorders,* 1973, *38* (1), 98-110.

SCHEUERMAN, N., BAUMGART, D., SIPSMA, K., AND BROWN, L. Toward the development of a curriculum for teaching nonverbal communication skills to severely handicapped students: Teaching basic tracking, scanning, and selection skills. In N. Scheuerman, L. Brown, & T. Crowner (Eds.), *Toward an integrated therapy model for teaching motor, tracking and scanning skills to severely handicapped students.* (Vol. VI, Part 3.), Madison, Wisc.: Madison Metropolitan School District, 1976.

SILVERMAN, F.H. *Communication for the speechless.* Englewood Cliffs, N.J.: Prentice-Hall, 1980.

SIMEONSSON, R.J., AND WIEGERINK, R. Early language intervention: A contingent stimulation model. *Mental Retardation,* 1974, *12* (2), 7-11.

THARP, R.G., AND WETZEL, R.J. *Behavior modification in the natural environment.* New York: Academic Press, 1969.

TURNBULL, H.R., AND TURNBULL, A.P. *Free appropriate public education: Law and implementation.* Denver: Love Publishing Company, 1978.

VANDERHEIDEN, G.C. Providing the child with a means to indicate. In G. C. Vanderheiden and K. Grilley (Eds.), *Non-vocal communication techniques and aids for the severely physically handicapped*. Baltimore: University Park Press, 1977.

VANDERHEIDEN, G.C., AND HARRIS-VANDERHEIDEN, D. Communication techniques and aids for the nonvocal severely handicapped. In L. Lloyd (Ed.), *Communication assessment and intervention strategies*. Baltimore: University Park Press, 1976.

VICKER, B. (ED.) *Nonoral communication system project: 1964-1973*. Iowa: Campus Stores Publishers, 1974.

WARREN, S.F., ROGERS-WARREN, A., BAER, D.M., AND GUESS, D. Assessment and facilitation of language generalization. In W. Sailor, B. Wilcox, & L. Brown (Eds.), *Method of instruction for severely handicapped students*. Baltimore: Paul H. Brookes Publishing Co., 1980.

WILBUR, R.B. The linguistics of manual languages and manual systems. In L. L. Lloyd (Ed.), *Communication, assessment and intervention strategies*. Baltimore: University Park Press, 1976.

ORAL AND VISUAL LITERACY: DEVELOPING COMPREHENSION APART FROM THE PRINTED WORD

By Sharon Kossack
Florida International University

Multi-cultural/lingual students experience significant performance difficulties when asked to interpret materials printed in standard English. Such comprehension difficulties can be avoided if instruction begins *before* the student is required to decode. Comprehension, as a thought process integrated with language meaning, must begin long before a child encounters the written word. It requires the development of oral language and visual literacy. This is especially true when the multi-cultural/lingual child is involved.

Using the diverse populations of children found in Dade County, instructional techniques have been developed and refined which draw the child from understanding oral language to transferring those understandings to visual images and finally the printed word.

ORAL LANGUAGE

Anticipation is a technique which guides children to predict recurring patterns in orally-presented language using rhyming, repeated stanzas, and finally, meaning.

In the *impress* method, the student reading along with whisper-reading adult is supplied unknown words. This impresses unknown words on the child.

Sense and Nonsense presentations encourage students to determine what portions of statements (oral then printed) seem to be inconsistent with customary experiences.

VISUAL LITERACY

Taxonomy. A taxonomic approach to guiding students to understand visual images (T.V., movies, newspaper or magazine pictures, etc.) and transfer comprehension processes learned during normal classroom activities to the task of understanding printed materials has been derived from Bloom's (Barrett's) Taxonomy.

ORAL AND VISUAL LITERACY:
DEVELOPING MULTILEVEL COMPREHENSION SKILLS
APART FROM THE PRINTED WORD

Comprehension difficulties can often be avoided if instruction begins *before* the comprehension processes learned during normal classroom activities to the task of understanding printed materials has been derived from Bloom's (Barrett's) Taxonomy.

ORAL AND VISUAL LITERACY: DEVELOPING MULTILEVEL COMPREHENSION SKILLS APART FROM THE PRINTED WORD

Comprehension difficulties can often be avoided if instruction begins *before* the student is taught to decode. Comprehension, as a thought process, needs to begin long before a child encounters the written word. It requires readiness and background just as any word recognition skill requires the prerequisite skills of auditory and visual discrimination. The rudiments of logic/illogic, cause/effect, sequence must be firmly established prior to reading in order that they be recognized when encountered in a written context. This requires oral and visual instruction prior to encountering written language.

BUILDING THE FUNDAMENTALS OF COMPREHENSION IN ORAL LANGUAGE

First, students must *hear* language. Parents and teachers of young children should budget time to read to their children. This serves two purposes. It motivates and builds language sense. Children learn to love language and come to view books in a positive way. They become acquainted with language patterns and meaning via orally-presented language. They learn to anticipate certain interactions within language. This sense transfers to a greater understanding of printed selections.

Anticipation. Children are guided to predict words and phrases by identifying recurring patterns in language. Poetry with predictable refrains can be used to build this sense. Margaret Wise Brown's *Nibble, Nibble, Nibble* contains such recurring refrains. Children can predict patterns after hearing:

Nibble, nibble, nibble goes the mouse in my heart,
Nibble, nibble, nibble goes the mouse in my heart.
Nibble, nibble, nibble goes the mouse in my heart,
And the mouse in my heart is you.

Rhyming patterns and meaning contrast/comparisons also allow youngsters to effectively predict units. In *Pease Porridge,* a familiar *Mother Goose* rhyme, children can easily predict the underlined units:

Pease porridge hot,	Some like it hot,
Pease porridge *cold,*	*Some like it cold,*
Pease porridge in the pot,	*Some like it in the pot,*
Nine days old	*Nine days old.*

Notice the use of recurring phrases, contrast of meaning, and rhyme elements which students use as clues to upcoming words.

Impress. The above activities involving anticipation can be used as warm up exercises to give students an overview of what to expect in a story. When reading aloud to the child is involved, the youngster should be encouraged to guess at upcoming words. To initiate this, the adult can read standard passages and pause before words that youngsters could predict; the youngster's task involves guessing a probable word. The adult is cautioned always to provide the word, to reinforce the correct guess, and to underscore the continuity of meaning in the written language passage. As an adult reads *Little Bo Peep,* the rhythm of reading might be as follows:

Little Bo Peep has lost her sheep, and can't tell where to find (pause) *them.*

Leave them alone, and (pause) *they'll* come (pause) *home,*

And bring their tails behind (pause) *them.*

The children are operating an oral close awareness as they deal with such oral reading — they become adept at listening to anticipate using language structure and meaning by first using recurring language patterns and rhyme, elements removed from meaning.

Sense and Nonsense. Once stories are read aloud to the students, they can be manipulated to cause students to be aware of nonsense contrary to language and meaning expectations. For example, as the story is reread, the teacher can substitute/omit/insert non-meaningful words. The child's task is to listen carefully to identify such nonsensical changes. An example:

The *red* hippo *flew* to the *purple* tree. The baby hippos lolled about in the river, splashing dirty mud on the reeds.

Children should be able to identify the nonsensical insertions (*red* hippo *flew* and *purple* trees) and substitutions (*flew*) within a realistic context.

BUILDING THE FUNDAMENTALS IN VISUAL LITERACY

When providing students with interaction with visual contexts, a taxonomy of questioning is a useful guide to probing. It aides the parent or teacher in phrasing question types, assures that multiple question types will be accounted for, and guides the questioner to ask questions in a roughly sequenced manner. For the purposes of visual literacy, an adaptation of Barrett's Taxonomy is used (see Table I).

Identifying level/subskill. One purpose of the taxonomy is as a means of identifying level (literal, inferential, critical) and subskill (main idea, sequence, predicting outcome, fact/fantasy). Using the adaptation of the taxonomy, the teacher can determine the level and subskill of the following visual literacy tasks:

During juice break, Johnny's cup was knocked off the table.

Juice spilled all over the floor. The teacher took this opportunity to discuss why the juice spilled and what happened when the table was jostled. What level of comprehension is the teacher developing; what subskill is involved? (Literal, since the youngsters experienced the sequence;

Subskill: Cause-effect.)

The class discussed the latest *Hulk* show. The teacher asked the children to identify which things happened that would not likely happen in real life. What level of comprehension is involved? What subskill is the teacher developing? (Level: Critical; Subskill: fact/fantasy)

Notice the situations in which comprehension is developed. The teacher used real-life experiences and television as the medium for exchange. Visual literacy takes advantage of what is familiar and understood to develop in students the processes of comprehension.

BUILDING COMPREHENSION VIA EVERYDAY SITUATIONS

Teachers can take the opportunity to stress comprehension processes throughout the school day; not using prepared materials, but capitalizing on normal classroom routines. When the logic of children is verbalized in familiar situations, they will find it all the easier to apply the same logic when they encounter similar situations in writing.

Growing Plants. For example, as the primary teacher conducts science projects, like plant growth, she may wish to photograph or illustrate the *sequence* (seed, sprout, plant), *predicting outcome* (seed + water + sun + soil = ?), *cause-effect* ("What would happen if we did not water the plants? What would happen if they had no sun?")

Cleaning the Classroom. After science or art projects, the cleanup time is an excellent opportunity to stress cause-effect ("What caused the table to have paint spills on it? What will happen to the paint spills when we rub them with a wet rag?"), *desirability* ("Is it better to paint carefully to avoid the spills? Why?), *appropriateness* ("Who should be the person to clean up the spills? Why?"), *main idea* ("Stop a minute. Look at the room. What can you say we are doing in here; coloring with crayon, singing, painting? How can you tell?").

Playground. During a hearty activity period, there are many opportunities for the teacher to emphasize comprehension subskills. As children enter the playground, they can be asked to view other classes for identification of *main idea* ("What is this area used for?"), *inferring details* ("What is Mr. Jones' class playing? How can you tell — what were the clues?"), *sequence* ("We will be playing baseball. What do we need to do first?"), and *cause-effect* ("Sue fell down. Why did that happen?").

Fire Drill. This involves critical understanding on the part of the students. *Sequence* ("When we have a fire drill, what do we do first?"), *cause-effect* ("What would happen if we talked during the fire drill?"), *predicting outcome* ("What would happen if we ran in line during the drill?").

Many opportunities in the home lend themselves to comprehension development as well. *Washing dishes and clothes* can provide a means of developing *categorizing* skills ("We put all of the white things in this pile, all of the colored things in this pile"), *cause-effect* ("Why do you suppose these white T-shirts turned pink?"), *predicting outcome* ("We must measure the soap powder carefully. What would happen if we put too much?"). The *supermarket* is a classroom-full of comprehension: *main idea* ("Look at the things on this aisle. What is the big idea here?"), *sequence* ("Now the bagboy puts the food in the bag. What kind of things does he put on the bottom of the bag?"), *predicting outcome* ("What would happen as we shop if we did not have a cart to use?").

BUILDING THE FUNDAMENTALS
OF COMPREHENSION
VIA TELEVISION AND MOVIES

Current studies have shown that youngsters, on the average, tend to watch far more television than they spend time in school. Teachers are not in a position to stop this practice, but they can use the motivation that television provides to help build comprehension. Two of the most popular current shows, *Hulk* and the *Six Million Dollar Man,* provide excellent means of developing the idea of fact/fantasy ("Can a man really outrun a car?"), *cause-effect* ("What caused David Banner to turn green last night on *Hulk*?"), *character traits* ("Hulk is an ugly monster; but is he a bad person? Why?"), *contrast* ("How are the Hulk and the Six Million Dollar Man alike?"), *appropriateness* ("Is it right for the Hulk to destroy all those cars when he was mad at the bad guy?"), *identification with character* ("Who is your favorite character in Hulk? Why?").

BUILDING THE FUNDAMENTALS
OF COMPREHENSION
VIA MAGAZINE AND NEWSPAPER PICTURES

For any given subskill on the taxonomy, pictures can be selected to help students move to more abstract levels of understanding in comprehension processing. When shown a picture of a dog being washed in a tub, children can be asked *cause-effect* questions ("Why do you think the dog was being washed?"), *predicting outcome* questions ("What do you think the dog will look like after his bath?"), *identification with character* ("How do you think the dog feels about being bathed?").

In another picture of young children playing baseball, there are clues that lead us to believe the children are not in the U.S.A. This setting provides an excellent opportunity for children to *infer details* ("What season do you think this might be? What makes you say so?"), *cause-effect* ("Why do you suppose the girl is wearing a band-aid on her leg?"), *identification with character* ("How is the boy who is about to swing at the ball feeling? Why?").

An Adaptation of Barrett's Taxonomy
of Reading Comprehension

1.0 Literal Comprehension. Focuses on ideas and information explicitly stated in selection itself or in exercises which use the explicit ideas and information presented in selection. READING THE LINES

    1.11 Recognition of Details. locates/identifies facts (names of characters, time/place of story)

    1.12 Recognition of Main Ideas. locates/identifies stated main idea of a selection.

    1.13 Recognition of Sequence. locates/identifies order of actions stated in selection.

    1.14 Recognition of a Comparison. locates/identifies likenesses and differences in characters, times, places stated in selection.

    1.15 Recognition of Cause and Effect Relationships. locates/identifies stated reasons for happenings or actions.

    1.16 Recognition of Character Traits. locates/identifies statements about a character which point to type of person character is.

    1.20 Classifying. Places, people, things, places, events into categories

    1.21 Outlining. organizes selection into outline from using direct statements or paraphrased statements from the selection.

    1.22 Summarizing. condenses selection using direct/paraphrased statements

    1.23 Synthesizing. consolidates explicit ideas/information from more than one source.

2.0 Inferential Comprehension. Student uses ideas/information states in selection, his intuition, and his personal experience as a basis for conjectures/hypotheses. Student is required to use thinking which goes beyond the printed page. READING BETWEEN THE LINES

    2.11 Inferring Supporting Details. conjectures about additonal facts the author might have included in the selection which would have made it more informative, interesting, appealing.

    2.12 Inferring Main Ideas. Provides the main idea, general significance, theme, or moral which is not explicitly stated in selection.

    2.13 Inferring Sequence. Conjectures as to what action/incident might have taken place between two explicitly states actions/incidents, may be asked to hypothesize what would happen next, venture an ending to unfinished story.

    2.14 Inferring Comparisons. Infers likenesses and differences in characters, times, places; can revolve around ideas like: "here and there", "then and now", "he and she", and "she and she", etc.

    2.15 Inferring Cause and Effect Relationships. Hypothesize about motivations of characters and their interactions with time and place; what caused the author to include certain ideas, words, characterizations, actions.

    2.16 Inferring Character Traits. hypothesize on nature of characters and their interactions on the basis of explicit clues presented.

    2.17 Predicting Outcomes. after reading an initial portion of selection, required to conjecture about the outcome of the selection.

    2.18 Interpreting Figurative Language. Infers literal meanings from author's use of figurative language.

3.0. Applications/Evaluation/Appreciation. Evaluative judgment has been made by
     comparing ideas presented in the selection with external criteria provided
     by the teacher, other authorities, other written sources, or with internal
     criteria provided by the reader's experiences, knowledges, values.
     Deals with judgments, focuses on qualities of accuracy, acceptability,
     desirability, worth, probability of occurrence, psychological and aesthetic
     impact of selection. READING BEYOND THE LINES
     3.11 Judgments of Reality or Fantasy. Could this really happen? (based on
          experience)
     3.12 Judgments of Fact/Opinion. Does author provide adequate support for
          his conclusions? Is author attempting to sway your thinking? Questions
          like these require student to analyze and evaluate and writing on the
          basis of the knowledge he has on the subject as well as to analyze and
          evaluate on the intent of the author.
     3.13 Judgments of Adequacy/Validity. Is information presented in keeping with
          what you have read on the subject? Reader compares written sources
          of information, with an eye toward agreement and disagreement, complete-
          ness, incompleteness.
     3.14 Judgments of Appropriateness. What part of the story best describes the
          main character? Require the reader to make judgment about the relative
          adequacy of different parts of the selection.
     3.15 Judgments of Worth, Desirability, Acceptability. Was the character
          right or wrong in what he did? Was his behavior good/bad? Judgments
          based on reader's moral code/value system.

     3.21 Emotional Response to the Content. Express feelings about the selection
          in terms of interest, excitement, boredom, fear, hate, amusement, etc.
          Emotional impact of total work on the reader.
     3.22 Identification with Characters or Incidents. Reader must be sensitive
          to, have sympathy for, and empathy with characters/happenings.
     3.23 Reactions to the Author's Use of Language. Responds to author's
          craftsmanship in terms of sematic dimension of the selection, namely,
          connotations, denotations of words.
     3.24 Imagery. Verbalize feelings with regard to author's artistic ability
          to paint word pictures causing the reader to visualize, smell, taste,
          hear, feel.

     3.31 Application. Given a similar situation, student can outline what
          character, author would do/say. Given a similar problem student can
          apply solution to arrive at end to situation.

BIBLIOGRAPHY

DEBES, JOHN, "The Loom of Visual Literacy — An Overview," *Proceedings of the First National Conference on Visual Literacy,* (Williams and Debes, editors), Pitman Publishing Company: New York, 1969.

GROPPER, GEORGE L., "Who is Visually Illiterate: The Student or the Teacher?" *Proceedings of the First National Conference on Visual Literacy,* (Williams and Debes, editors), New York: Pitman Pub. Co., 1969, p. 223.

KACHUCK, BEATRICE AND ALBERT MARCUS, "Thinking Strategies and Reading," *Reading Teacher,* Vol. 30, No. 2, November, 1976, pp. 157-161.

LAPOLT, RUTH, "A New Approach to Visual and Written Sequencing," *Audio-visual Instruction,* 13, May, 1968, pp. 477-479.

NEVIUS, JOHN R., "Teaching for Logical Thinking is a Prereading Activity," *Reading Teacher,* Vol. 30, No. 6, March, 1977, pp. 641-3.

WENDT, PAUL R., "The Language of Pictures," in S. I. Hayakawa edition, *The Use and Misuse of Language,* Fawcett Pub., Inc., 1962, pp. 175-8.

WILLIAMS, CLARENCE, "Nine Visual Literacy Propositions and Some Related Research," *Proceedings of the First National Conference on Visual Literacy,* (Williams and Debes, editors), New York: Pitman Publishing Corp., 1969, p. 60.

BILINGUAL CURRICULUM DEVELOPMENT FOR HISPANICS: A PRIMER FOR THE PROSPECTIVE PRODUCER

By Ralph F. Robinett
Dade County Public Schools
Miami, Florida

This "primer" on bilingual curriculum development for Hispanics is not a scholarly effort, for bilingual curriculum development for Hispanics (and for many ethnic minorities) has been less influenced by scholarly activity than it has by a wide variety of practical and political issues requiring pragmatic resolutions. The focus here, therefore, is on the identification of some of these issues and the implications of the alternatives available to the producer of bilingual curriculum materials.

THE ISSUE OF TERMINOLOGY

The very title of this area of concern is fraught with terms which must be defined before any meaningful consideration can be given to the nature of the curriculum to be developed. The word *bilingual,* for example, conjures up a host of stereotypes reflecting the full range of Office for Civil Rights categories:

A: Monolingual speaker of a language other than English
B: Predominantly speaks a language other than English
"Bilingual"C: Bilingual; speaks English and another language equally well
D: Predominantly speaks English
E: Monolingual speaker of English

Dictionary definitions have relatively little value in discussions on *bilingual.* What is important is that in any given context everyone concerned has a common understanding of how the word is being used.

Similar ambiguities arise with *bilingual curriculum.* Does it refer to materials written in two languages? Are the materials directed toward Spanish language origin students who are in the process of learning English? Does the term encompass materials for the teaching of English as a second language, or is it limited to instruction in and through the home language? Does the term encompass materials for teaching of Spanish to English language origin peer groups, or to Spanish language origin students who are English dominant, or monolingual English speakers?

The term *Hispanic* is equally innocent. But is it generic in its intent in a given curriculum development effort? Or on a practical level does it refer primarily to Mexican-American, Puerto Rican, or Cuban variations of the language? Again, theoretical definitions are irrelevant. The meanings of these code words are derived from the contexts in which the code words are being used, and it behooves the curriculum developer to establish clearly from the outset the

The term *Hispanic* is equally innocent. But is it generic in its intent in a given curriculum development effort? Or on a practical level does it refer primarily to Mexican-American, Puerto Rican, or Cuban variations of the language? Again, theoretical definitions are irrelevant. The meanings of these code words are derived from the contexts in which the code words are being used, and it behooves the curriculum developer to establish clearly from the outset the ethnolinguistic frame of reference for which the materials are intended.

THE ISSUE OF GRADE LEVEL

Given the assumption that an adequate search has been made for existing material which may satisfy an identified need, the question of extent of need plays a major role in prioritizing the expenditure of limited available funds. Materials development is both expensive and time consuming, and the projected continuation of need plays a major role in targeting certain grade levels for production of materials.

In many communities, the large majority of participants in bilingual education programs are in the primary grades and thus constitute the major target population for bilingual curriculum materials. Further, since most students in bilingual education programs are of limited English proficiency and are involved in transitional-type programs as a result of Civil Rights requirements, Federal pressure at the elementary level is greater than at the secondary level, where more options are available in program offerings.

Although the distribution of Cuban and Haitian entrant students by grade level in 1980-81 is significantly different from the normal limited English proficient membership by grade level for the community recorded above (Dade County, Florida), it is projected that within two years the distribution of the former entrant students will approximate that of the normal "ESOL" membership and that no long term effect in grade level distribution will result from the entrant influx.

It should be noted that the problems posed by the massive influx of Cuban and Haitian students into the Dade County Public Schools during the 1980 "boatlift" were unique in proportion but not entirely in nature. Prior to the "boatlift" period, Dade County had a persistent growth of Cuban and Haitian students as well as others from a variety of countries. This influx is summarized below.

MONTHLY AVERAGE OF "PRE-BOATLIFT" CUBAN/HAITIAN ENTRIES 1974-1980

	1974-75 School Year	1975-76 School Year	1976-77 School Year	1977-78 School Year	1978-79 School Year	1979-80 Pre-May Period
Cubans	309	155	105	106	133	290
Haitians	10	14	24	24	35	35

During the period 1974-75 through 1978-79, a total of 11,463 students were processed through the Foreign Student Registration Center of the Dade County Public Schools. These students represented more than twenty-three different countries or points of origin. By the end of April, 1980, this number had increased to 15,741. This represents an annual average of + 2,700 new "pre-boatlift" students, or a monthly average of 225 such students. These students are of all ages, and tend to distribute themselves over all grade levels of the elementary and secondary schools. "Peaking" at grades 5 and 10 appears to be the result of local administrative decision rather than a peculiarity of refugee populations.

The entry of "post-boatlift" Cuban and Haitian students has followed a reduced but parallel pattern, as noted below.

MONTHLY AVERAGE OF "POST-BOATLIFT" CUBAN/HAITIAN ENTRIES

	Oct. 1980	Nov. 1980	Dec. 1980	Jan. 1981	Feb. 1981	Mar. 1981	Apr. 1981	May 1981	June 1981	July 1981	Aug. 1981
Cubans	268	69	62*	69	55	40	53	82	83	45	49
Haitians	41	18	15*	50	18	11	17	17	16	12	17

*Average based on three weeks

Based on the November 1980-August 1981 data and barring some unusual event, it may be projected that + 725 new Cuban students will enter the Dade County Public Schools through the Foreign Student Registration Center within the 1981-82 school year; and based on October 1980-August 1981 data and barring some unusual event, it may be projected that + 250 new Haitian students will enter the school system through the same process during 1981-82. These projections do not include other new entries, such as Nicaraguans, whose number approximated that of new Haitians during the 1980-81 school year. Again, these students tend to distribute themselves over all grade levels.

From the above data, which are paralleled in many other points of entry, curriculum producers within a transitional-type bilingual education setting should recognize that the development of materials for the secondary level is aimed primarily at students entering the school system from other countries, as opposed to the local "ESOL" population, which represents the resident population. Curriculum producers should also recognize that these students bring with them (1) a repertory of linguistic skills in their home language which is superior to the home language of the local "ESOL" population, and (2) educational experiences which are substantially different from those of the local "ESOL" population, both qualitatively and quantitatively by local standards.

THE ISSUE OF SUBJECT AREA

Inasmuch as the function of the home language in a transitional-type bilingual education program is to help ensure maintenance of academic achievement while the students are learning English, subject area selection for areas where no suitable materials are available is commonly limited to basic communication skills, social studies, science, and/or mathematics.

To make major curriculum development efforts beyond the "hard core" subjects of the school curriculum may respond to legitimate psychological and other needs of limited English proficient students; however, in light of the intense competition for time within an already crowded curriculum, the probability that such materials will actually be utilized in a transitional setting is relatively low unless the materials correspond to objectives which also occur in the "hard core" subject areas. This limitation is further compounded by desegregation requirements of the Office for Civil Rights, and the regulations underlying some funding sources, which require that certain subjects, such as music and art, be provided in an integrated setting.

At the secondary level, development efforts most practically focus on discrete subject areas, and correspond to commonly taught semester courses. Even then, it must be recognized that unless the materials are developed for a specific school system at a specific point in time, they will remain supplementary rather than basic. Crudely put, the tail does not wag the dog.

At the elementary level, development efforts may be subject area discrete, or they may be interdisciplinary in nature, focusing on support materials for high priority objectives corresponding to systemwide and state minimum standards.

Uniqueness in bilingual curriculum materials properly and practically lies in alternative approaches stemming from the cultural and socio-economic background of the students and possible differences in learning styles. Uniqueness in basic course content generally contributes little to accelerating the students' successful entry into the academic mainstream. The question of how to rectify historical injustice and distortion of national history as it relates to minority groups, including Hispanics, presents a fine line which bilingual curriculum developers must be prepared to walk within their sense of professional integrity and social consciousness with respect to the past, present, and future.

For the producer of bilingual curriculum, the issue of subject area selection and the substance of that curriculum poses a problem of balance between the probable time available for instruction in diverse subject areas in the home language, and the relative importance of the home language in the acquisition of basic concepts and skills in a given subject area, as for example, the difference between the role of the home language in the study of social studies and the study of mathematics. Both time and language-significance are prime considerations for school administrators when scheduling instruction in and through the home language.

THE ISSUE OF CURRICULAR INTEGRATION

The extent to which bilingual curriculum products are self-contained inherently poses the problem of "regular curriculum" versus "bilingual curriculum" on the one hand and the problem of a "total curriculum" on the other. Development of a self-contained bilingual curriculum based on the objectives of a given school system, or broader base, has the advantage of potential for continuous progress of students within a pre-determined curricular framework; thus development of concepts and skills can best be delivered on a unit basis extending over several weeks rather than on a basis of daily lessons adjusted on short notice as may be determined by the plans of diverse teachers delivering the instructional program in English, often without adequate joint planning time. On the other hand, this very advantage tends to isolate instruction in and through the home language and puts it out of synchronization with learning which is occurring during the rest of the school day.

Attempts to build a "total curriculum" involving instruction in both the home language and in English, in spite of their obvious advantages, are frequently, even generally, abortive. Curriculum revision is basically an on-going process, progressing on a broken front. Bilingual curriculum development initiated at a given point in time, is based on the best subject area information available, may actually be in advance of the curriculum being implemented by the school system serving as host to the curriculum project, and thus embody inherent incompatibilities regardless of the merit of the bilingual materials. In a similar manner, incompatibility also arises when major changes are made in the English curriculum subsequent to the initiation of curriculum development in the home language.

Should the bilingual curriculum developer overtly support the outdated curriculum in English for the goal of an integrated curriculum? Can bilingual curriculum developers, commonly subsidized through external grants, meet requirements of their grants within established time frames if they attempt to initiate major program design changes in mid-stream? Such dilemmas pose problems of pedagogical and fiscal responsibility which every bilingual curriculum developer will be likely to face if the funding period extends beyond two or three years and if the curriculum development effort is not optimally integrated with the current curriculum programs of the potential "customers". A product without customers serves little purpose beyond ego satisfaction for the developer.

THE ISSUE OF INSTITUTIONALIZATION

Closely linked to the issue of curricular integration is the issue of institutionalization — how it comes about, and the conditions conducive to its accomplishment, and the conditions which inhibit its accomplishment.

Some people, both inside and outside the educational establishment, labor under the innocent illusion that activities carried out under the heading of research in bilingual education have a major impact in reaching decisions with respect to curriculum offerings and curriculum content. By and large, however, any impact of research in bilingual education has been coincidental rather than causal in the decision making process. Other factors tend to have significantly greater impact on curriculum development and implementation, including but not limited to:

1) The Federal posture with respect to civil rights requirements for limited English proficient students
2) The Federal posture with respect to funding of national and/or regional support projects, or awarding of contracts for similar purposes
3) The State posture with respect to requirements for limited English proficient students
4) The State posture with respect to funding diverse components of bilingual education.

One of the above factors or some combinations thereof is commonly the source of the felt/imposed need for bilingual curriculum development, while the Federal level directly, or working through the State, is commonly the source of the funds necessary to carry out such activities. The linkage between the administrative unit within the local education agency which solicits funds and the administrative units which are responsible for the day-to-day district level management varies greatly from school system to school system. In some districts, the "fund seekers" represent what is in effect a "mini-system" with little practical interaction with the "major system". In other school systems the linkage is strong and active, and the priorities in fund seeking are established by the "major system".

The net result from curriculum development under these two types of linkage tends to lead in the first instance to self-contained projects whose products have but little perceived relevance by the subject area consultant/supervisor, who may have been the person responsible for the installation of the existing program and who may feel threatened by potential change. In many such cases, the merits of the product are outweighed by the vested interests in place.

In the second instance, the prospects for institutionalization are far greater, for the relevance of the product, perceived or otherwise, has been established by an on-going involvement of the person(s) most influential in opening doors for continued or expanded use of the product. The bilingual curriculum producer who prefers independence to facilitate product development or to maintain the integrity of the product may discover when the project closes that the whole effort has been little more than an academic exercise. This same concept of involvement-during-production has become a standard procedure between commercial publishers and authors of textbooks, and is as critical in the field testing of materials, where revision is generated and credibility is established.

THE ISSUE OF ORIGINALITY

At the heart of the issue of originality is the question of translation versus adaptation versus original writing. Interwoven with this issue are two related sub-issues, dealing with cost-effectiveness and ownership. Over the past ten years in the field of bilingual curriculum development, considerably collective experience has been gained with respect to these problems as a result of heavy subsidies for curriculum development through Title VII of the Elementary and Secondary Education Act. This major investment in bilingual materials came about primarily for two reasons:

1) Curriculum materials in Spanish from abroad were by and large incompatible, both in terms of language and in terms of the socio-political content, with the needs of students participating in bilingual education programs, and

2) Early efforts to incorporate a modest curriculum component in each of the Title VII demonstration projects had proved disappointing in terms of residual products which could be shared with the blossoming number of new bilingual education projects.

In more recent years, Title VII materials development support has been regionalized to some extent in a dual effort which is designed on the one hand to accelerate curriculum development to fill critical gaps in materials, and which on the other hand aims to find a responsive medium between the inefficiency of purely local product development and the remoteness of national product development.

In each of these stages of Federal involvement in the development of bilingual curriculum development, program designers have had to face the pitfalls and advantages of each approach.

Translation.   At the outset, translation seemed to be the most expeditious means of acquiring a bilingual curriculum. Textbooks in English had the advantage of being readily available, and reflected both the established curricular programs and a level of sophistication in textbook production which took years and substantial sums of money to develop. But this approach, despite its surface cost-effectiveness, embodied two major problems.

One, available materials in English, which had been developed for a market of the power structure, tended to be highly limited or devoid in treatment of the socio-cultural experience of the limited English proficient students to be served.

Their content and treatment of the content tended to focus on the "Anglo" culture and expectations. A simple translation to make brown-faced Dick's and Jane's was to be less successful than earlier attempts to make black-faced Dick's and Jane's.

Two, the questions surrounding ownership, copyright, and securing permissions were involved and lengthy in resolution. Pre-funding efforts related to these questions were costly in time and money, which many local education agencies were reluctant to put forth at local expense under uncertain funding circumstances and no reimbursement. Further, at that point in time commercial publishers were attempting to get a feel for the market potential of Spanish editions, and were reluctant to give away what might be a profitable venture. Both the local education agencies and the funding sources tended to look with reservation on attempts at prior commitments with respect to residual rights on materials developed with public funds. Curriculum developers who made such efforts were often suspected of having vested interests. New bilingual curriculum developers who opt to use the translation approach must be prepared to respond to the kinds of problems and pressures identified above. Outside of technical areas, such as the sciences at the secondary level, translation is the least effective approach.

Original writing. Partly as a result of inadequacies of translation and partly in response to a complete lack of appropriate materials in certain areas, considerable Federal resources have been expended on original writing, particularly in but not limited to the social sciences, where available materials have tended to reflect dominant culture biases and where ethnic studies materials were lacking.

This approach has the obvious advantage of freedom from copyright/ permissions complications inherent in translations. At the same time, it has the built in potential for wide variability in quality of products, depending on the length of funding period and the availability of highly skilled and knowledgeable curriculum technicians and consultants as may be necessary. As more commercial publishers have entered the bilingual curriculum market, and as national and regional curriculum project have filled gaps in curriculum inventories, the need for original writing has been sharply reduced, particularly with respect to students of Spanish language origin at the elementary level.

Adaptations. Although adaptation of materials already existing in English and in Spanish has the same types of copyright/ permissions complications as the simple translation, there is a growing trend with both commercial publishers and publicly subsidized projects toward this approach to bilingual curriculum development. Adaptation rather than simple translation offers the potential to meet the special needs of limited English proficient students while maintaining the technical quality of the original product. An awareness of the merit of this approach has emerged within funding sources, which now tend to encourage project involvement with commercial publishers at an early stage in development.

Earlier attitudes favoring publishing in the public domain created a backlog of materials which were ready for dissemination which, for lack of commercial interest in risking the marketing of public domain materials, forced the funding sources into the distribution business on a major scale. Thus, the use of limited copyright has also gained acceptance beyond what was possible ten years ago.

THE ISSUE OF VALUE SYSTEMS

In the development of bilingual curriculum materials, as noted earlier, a major concern has been for the incorporation within the scope and sequence of the cultural heritage of the students and the contributions of the students' ethnic group to the overall development of the United States. The justification of this thrust lies (1) in the need to better bridge the gap between the students' world and the world of the educational establishment, and (2) in the need to rectify a distortion of historical facts with respect to the development of the nation.

Bilingual curriculum producers involved in responding to these needs are at times faced with the problem faithfully representing the home culture and traditions on the one hand, and the problem of responding to changes in the overall social structure on the other hand. The glorification of a particular historical role model, for example, may at the same time present in a positive light outdated concepts of interpersonal relationships. At the same time students must learn to put their cultural past into perspective, they must also learn to live in the future, in which the roles of male/female, parent/child may be markedly different from their traditions.

THE ISSUE OF LANGUAGE VARIATION

As noted earlier, the role of the home language in most bilingual education programs is one of helping the students to maintain academic achievement while they are learning English. The viability of the home language, in this case Spanish, as a tool for learning depends in no small measure on the intelligibility of the variation of the language used by the school when delivering instruction in or through the home language. Although this may seem axiomatic, a sensitivity to language variation among ethnic groups such as Mexican-Americans, Puerto Ricans, and Cubans, and within such groups, is critical if the home language is to play its legitimate role in the educational process.

Depending on the number of years that the home language is used as a component of bilingual instruction, the home language may assume a different role, becoming both an object of instruction as well as a medium of instruction. If the bilingual curriculum developers anticipate a continued social usefulness of the home language, as is the case of Spanish in many communities, such as Dade County, they must from the outset initiate a planned introduction of the "standard" language which the student will find in printed instructional support materials. To deny the value of the home language variation is to deny the students the opportunity to use what they bring to school as a tool for learning. To fail to introduce the "standard" language in a timely manner is to deny the student the opportunity to extend the use of that tool.

The issue of language variation does not present an either-or situation, but rather a situation in which the respective role of each variation is adequately defined through the curriculum program being developed, each with a legitimate function derived from the instructional objectives and the usefulness of each in achieving those objectives at a given point in time.

SUMMARY

The eight issues here discussed (terminology, grade level, subject area, curricular integration, institutionalization, originality, value systems, and language variation) reflect major considerations which must be taken into account early in planning if the development process is to lead to a successful conclusion. It is evident that production *per se* is not a set of activities isolated from the philosophical/pedagogical framework and political climate in which they are carried out.

INFORMATION RESOURCES IN THE EDUCATION OF ETHNIC IMMIGRANTS: SOME LESSONS FROM THE PAST

By Erwin Flaxman, Ph.D.
Director, ERIC Clearinghouse
on Urban Education
Teachers College,
Columbia University
New York, New York 10027

Over the past twenty years the conduct of education in America has been aided by an elaborate formal system of information dissemination. We have assumed that the formal flow of organized information will make it possible to develop better educational policies, make better administrative decisions, design and implement better programs, and finally, carry out better research to support educational policies, decisions, and practices. Educational information has been formally disseminated through a variety of information systems, usually designed and managed by the Federal government. How much this information has been used and has had an ameliorative or detrimental effect on education is not clear. Common sense tells us the more information we have at critical times in our educational planning, the more confident we will feel abut our decisions and the better our actions will likely be. We are at such a critical time now in determining how we can successfully provide equal and quality education for newly-arrived immigrant minorities that considers their educational needs and the social situation in which they currently live. It would be useful now to pause for a moment to consider the existing educational information resources and networks that can support this effort, particularly to understand how their current structure and organization can be used or revised to deal with the distinct educational needs of ethnic immigrants.

I propose to do this in several ways in this paper. First, I will trace the history of the development of educational information dissemination in the United States as a way of indicating what resources currently exist, particularly for educating ethnic minorities — blacks, Hispanics, Asian Americans, American Indians. Second, as an outgrowth I will examine the state of information and existing information networks for planning programs for ethnic immigrants. Here I want to make some suggestions for documentation, analysis, and networks. And third, I will examine another dimension of information dissemination, not to professionals who serve this group, but to the immigrant minorities themselves. In collecting and disseminating information we must have two concerns: to collect and disseminate the best information available for educational social planning but at the same time to increase the opportunity for appropriate information about life in the United States to reach the group itself in forms and through systems and networks that make it meaningful to the lives of members of this group. Along with other disadvantages, members of ethnic minority groups, particularly immigrants and refugees, are information poor, and in our society information is a distinct premium.

INFORMATION DISSEMINATION IN THE UNITED STATES

HISTORICAL DEVELOPMENT

The story of the growth and maintenance of information networks in the United States is a tale of increased Federal involvement in education. At almost the same time that Congress passed the Elementary and Secondary Education Act in 1965, the most substantial Federal investment and intervention in schooling, the U.S. Office of Education created the ERIC system, the largest and most sustained effort to identify, collect, analyze, and disseminate educational information currently undertaken. The U.S. Government became involved in education and education dissemination, traditionally the domain of the states, for a number of reasons, but a few are particularly relevant to the education of ethnic minorities and other special populations.

In the late 1950s the Soviet Union appeared to be more scientifically and technologically advanced than the United States. The Sputnik crisis stimulated the passage of the National Defense Education Act, which supported basic and applied research of all kinds and, importantly, provided funds for the model of all subsequent Federally-funded inservice education programs, the NDEA teacher institutes for science and mathematics and foreign language teachers. We assumed that Soviet success was due to the national control of education, including identification of scientifically talented youth who were given special educational support. We followed suit. To make sure that we would have a generation of scientists and internationalists, the government intervened directly to upgrade the skills of science, math, and foreign language teachers. At the same time it increased its investment in science and technology. It developed what we now know as the R and D paradigm: funds would be available for research that can be readily applied to the development of technological products in the service of establishing our scientific and military superiority. Remember the social fervor of the 1960s was accompanied by a race to the moon. Science and technology have never been constrained by geographical or legal entities; scientists and engineers have never had to be licensed by any state or municipality. Just so with the transfer of scientific and technical information, which was carried out by Federal information systems and national professional associations.

At this same time the Federal government assumed a second educational responsibility. Following the 1954 *Brown* decision in the U.S. Supreme Court, the nation recognized that a portion of the U.S. population was not receiving equal educational opportunities because they were being educated in segregated schools. *De jure* and *de facto* school segregation was a violation of the Fourteenth Amendment of the U.S. Constitution and thus support for state and local remedies could come from the Federal government. By the early 1960s at almost the same time that the space program was initiated, the nation saw the first summer Head Start programs, which followed the scientific and technical R and D model for designing educational services for disadvantaged preschool children. And by 1966, with the passage of the Civil Rights Act, we began the first Title IV programs for assisting schools in educating minority or disadvantaged youth in desegregated schools. Here too the Federal government assumed a role in education of poor, minority, and segregated youth, and in doing so transcended traditional state and local prerogatives and boundaries in educational jurisdiction and control. It developed a national information system, first through ERIC and later through complementary networks, to support these interventions.

The Federal involvement in education in the early 1960s established the character of a great deal of later educational research, service, and dissemination. First, following the lead of science and technology, research would follow the R and D model in which nationally-determined educational problems would be studied so that a variety of educational products, mostly curriculums but also tests, desegregation models, training programs, and so forth, could be developed and disseminated to the states and local school districts. (Consider the long history of the contributions of the regional educational laboratories and the R and D centers to educational practice and their current role in dissemination.) Second, formal information dissemination through systems that transcend local, state, and regional districts was a legitimate Federal role. And third, the educational issue of greatest concern was the education of special populations, the gifted and talented and the poor, minority, and segregated.

What followed, the current structure for the collection and dissemination of educational resources and information, is the concern of the next section of this paper.

CURRENT STATE OF INFORMATION DISSEMINATION

Information is currently being disseminated through various Federal, state, regional and local networks, and by the individual systems of a variety of special educational interests.

National dissemination networks. National networks are characteristically more comprehensive than other dissemination networks. The subject of the information rather than the user determines what is collected and disseminated. Just as the coverage of a particular field is comprehensive, so too the dissemination is broad and scattered in an attempt to reach anyone who might use the information stored in the system. The user of the information only rarely or superficially defines the kind of information being collected or disseminated.

Some cases in point. ERIC, the Educational Resources Information Center, is made up on sixteen clearinghouses, each with a subject domain, which identifies, collects, and processes mostly unpublished reports and journals into central agencies that create *Resources in Education,* an abstract journal of mostly unpublished educational reports; *Current Index to Journals in Education,* an index to the published journal literature; ERIC microfiche, filmed reproductions of most of the actual documents available through ERIC (these are announced in *Resources in Education* and *Current Index to Journals in Education.* In well over 3,000 libraries or information centers in the United States any educator or lay person can use one or all of these abstract journals or microfiche or conduct a search of ERIC documents or journal articles. Because the system is national (even international now) the Clearinghouses collect every type of information that has national relevance; if it appears too parochial or specific to a local situation it will not be made part of the data base. Currently no ERIC-related service or product is out of the geographic or professional reach of any educator in the United States. What is more, each ERIC Clearinghouse serves a constituency directly (foreign language teachers, special educators, early childhood educators, educational administrators, for example) through a variety of reference services or publications. Here too a service or product is available in some form to anyone for the asking.

There are a large number of other national but less comprehensive information data bases or clearinghouses in education currently. All of them in one way or another collect, store, analyze, and disseminate information on a specialized subject to a subset of a national audience. Some of them are:

1. The National Diffusion Network (NDN) provides information and services to help education agencies improve their programs by adopting or adapting validated exemplary programs described in a number of publications, catalogs, and brochures distributed nationally.

2. The National Clearinghouse for Bilingual Education, modeled after the ERIC structure, collects and disseminates a variety of products internally developed and distributed to a specialized audience of workers in bilingual education. It also offers direct reference services to a network of regional Title VII centers.

3. The National Clearinghouse on Drug Abuse Information provides information services and a variety of publications to a broad range of users, from scientists and technicians to parents and children in communities throughout the United States.

Finally, a very different information dissemination system. Since the late 1960s the Federal government has been delivering educational information directly through television. First with *Sesame Street* and *Electric Company,* developed by Children's Television Workshop with funds made available by the U.S. Office of Education, and then through television programming developed by the National Institute of Education, educational information has been provided directly to a client population, who, even here, however, have been passive recipients.

Regional and state dissemination programs and networks. Our of a realization of the distance of users of a national system from the products and means of dissemination, the Federal government has helped to develop several regional and state networks which would increase the utilization of R and D information by school system and teachers.

One of these networks is the R and D Utilization Program of the National Institute of Education. In this program a number of project sites, mainly state departments of education, were given awards to develop special networks consisting of (1) an organization to develop R and D products to provide information on new educational practices, (2) a linkage network involving intermediary service agencies to help communicate the new practices developed by the R and D organization to and between the state departments of education and the local school systems, and (3) practitioners in local school systems, who would carry out needs assessments and implement new classroom practices. The service area in each of these networks has been at least one and up to twelve sites. State and local officials, including school practitioners, participate actively in the design and implementation of the program through considerable participation in decisions about the organization of the overall project site and the educational practices implemented in the classroom, although the program is coordinated by a Federal agency and the R and D products are usually developed by Federally-funded R and D centers with national perspectives.

There have been other regional and state dissemination programs that have some of the features of the RDU model:

1. The Network of Child Service Demonstration Centers, which are funded to develop and disseminate model programs serving learning disabled students. The Network consists of 53 Child Service Demonstration Centers in 33 states and Puerto Rico and the National Learning Disabilities Assistance Project which provides technical assistance to the Centers.

2. The Research and Development Exchange, which provides a variety of information services, including information exchange and the targeting of information services to meet local needs to state educational agencies, intermediate service agencies, and local educational agencies, preschool through postsecondary. The primary participants of the Exchange are the regional educational laboratories, service contractors located at the laboratories, and the 33 participating states.

In almost all of these programs, the partitioner more actively participates in the dissemination system by choosing and adopting only those products and practices that satisfy local needs, yet there is still a "trickle down" effect. For the most part local officials adopt only what is made available to them, and, importantly, they have not initiated and managed these programs but have been "invited" to participate. Significantly, most of the schools involved have been in suburban, small urban, and rural areas; most dissemination programs have not been designed to consider the peculiar ways schooling takes place in big cities.

Another kind of regional and state educational dissemination system should be considered here: the Federal technical assistance centers created to provide consultative and other services to assist school districts and schools to bring about race, sex, and national origin desegregation and the Title VII resource centers to deal more specifically with supporting schools in developing ESL and bilingual education programs for linguistic minorities. Here technical assistance and information provision would seem to be joined. The providers of this assistance are free to combine teacher training, materials development and assessment, information packaging, and direct consultation and advice to help the schools provide special services to ethnic minority children and youth. Here too, however, the extent and nature of these services are regulated by the Federal government, although the local schools and the technical assistance agency jointly determine the educational needs to be addressed and the remedies to be used in solving any problems.

Local School initiatives. In the past few years schools and school districts have increasingly identified and determined their various information needs and drawn on existing available resources and networks. As the evaluations of the planned national educational programs showed striking variations in local settings and research begin to suggest that education can most effectively be carried and managed by controlling local school and classroom factors, school personnel have begun to form local collaborations to increase school effectiveness. Since the midseventies the National Institute of Education has been funding local problem solving projects precisely to determine the outcomes of school initiatives in analyzing local problems and drawing on existing resources or developing new resources to solve them. Even with a continuing Federal role in the dissemination of educational information, as the government removes itself from the provision of direct educational services, state and local educational agencies will have to consider more individual and local ways to obtain information.

One such local dissemination source is cable television. The cable provides an opportunity for the addition of numerous channels beyond the six or seven typically available. Cable capabilities allow for the reception of twenty or more channels in which the picture reception is much better than UHF broadcasts over-the-air. This provides an opportunity for new programs oriented toward specific communities, including discrete educational communities, who can be served by dedicated cable systems. There can be local program production to meet local educational needs. Very important, existing technology makes it possible for cable systems to carry signals in two directions — they are interactive; thus, viewers as learners in a educational or training mode can actively participate in a two-way program.

Special educational interests. A number of private organizations and associations, maintained by membership, special project, and often philanthropic income, provide information, usually in the form of publication, but occasionally information sources and technical assistance. Most of them are not devoted to ethnic minority or immigrant educational concerns, however.

INFORMATION DISSEMINATION AND THE EDUCATION OF ETHNIC MINORITY GROUPS

The organized formal information dissemination system in the United States has helped the progress to improve the education of ethnic minority groups. For at least the last fifteen years there have been regular channels for systematically disseminating research information and descriptions of innovative practices to any educator at any professional level. What is more, as the history of information dissemination in education shows, the Federal designers and managers of the system have developed some ways for the local user to initiate demands for information that alters the flow of information to the local school district of building. Arguably, the system works too well. Because of their wide availability ambiguous research or descriptions of questionable or untested innovations have been applied or adopted before they have been adequately scrutinized. The pressure to disseminate information forces us to provide it prematurely. Rapid information transfer encourages rapid decisionmaking and policymaking. For example, there is a considerable amount of information about bilingual education circulating despite the short history of bilingual education in the United States. Under pressure to justify the value of bilingual education we may have overdocumented its early results, some of which do not support its promised success in educating Hispanics, Asian Americans, and other groups, in part because a system exists for disseminating them. Unless those who use dissemination systems to transfer critical information regulate their input they will contribute to the misuse of their own work. Notwithstanding this problem, the easy flow of educational information to educators has stimulated better research, policy, and practice in the education of the minority and poor. Because there has been an open and systematic flow of information about Head Start, for example, we have good information about the comparable value of a number of curriculums and instructional strategies, better materials in several mediums, more sensitive and tested techniques for parent involvement in the education of young children, and so forth.

The dissemination of information about the minority and poor has also been troubled by another problem: within the structure of large dissemination systems information cannot easily flow laterally or upwards. Thus a substantial amount of the work of individuals or organizations outside the educational mainstream can be left out or lost. It is not surprising that ver recently a number of the larger equal opportunity agencies and associations or groups such as the Urban League, NAACP, Aspira, the National Council for La Raza, and others, either have developed their own R and D dissemination capabilities or have allied themselves with existing organizations which are part of the R and D mainstream and dissemination network. The smaller, less well organized, special interest equity groups, however, still bemoan that most existing information resources do not satisfy their needs, nor are dissemination channels and networks structured meaningfully or fully open to them. Smaller minority colleges, parent and community groups, and other concerned with influencing policymakers and administrators who allocate, organize, and use educational resources (human, technical, and economic) recognize that it is vital for them to have appropriate dissemination channels to make their needs known and satisfied. Ethnic immigrant advocacy and education groups who require educational resources and information and in turn want these requirements felt will have to consider this problem.

The most pressing issue in the education of ethnic immigrant groups has been their resettlement and absorption into American society first, and then schooling and training for life here. There is a considerable amount of information about the resettlement experience, particularly its social and psychological effects. We know that the immigrants' loss of status, identity confusion, generational conflict, language difficulties, poverty, prejudice and hostility in the United States work as alien pressures on the immigrant refugees' state of mind, already beset by the problems of war, hunger, chaos, danger of escape, and separation from family that they brought to the United States. There is a growing literature on the development of cross-cultural mental health counseling models and such community agencies on mutual assistance associations, and soon we will hear of programs in criminal justice (Lopate, 1981). We have less information about the occupational training of these adults, and more critically, about the education of ethnic immigrant children.

Since 1975 at the time of the earliest immigration of refugees, a number of agencies have developed bilingual orientation materials for refugees and their sponsors dealing with such problems as community services, consumer education, employment, family planning and child care, health, housing, and so forth (Center for Applied Linguistics, 1981). A number of local school districts and such national organizations as the Center for Applied Linguistics developed bilingual teaching materials, phrase books, study and orientation guides to school behavior to meet the immediate and pressing needs of educating these new school groups. And there is a growing descriptive literature on Title VII bilingual education programs. Yet we know scarcely nothing about how these children and youth are being educated or their parents or families being trained for jobs. And with the possible limiting of Federal and other funds for the documentation and evaluation of special programs, we not easily get this information in the future, even about mental health and adjustment programs which have been better documented.

There are several kinds of information resources and methods for disseminating them we should consider. First, for educators, the literature on the social stress of resettlement will be more useful to us when we are able to distinguish the differential effect of the resettlement experience on children and youth at different ages or ethnic or social class. Also we must have cross-cultural perspectives in counseling these youth and understand that behavior disorders may be responses to an immediate situation rather than endemic to the child or culturally-determined. We must increase the incentives for conducting educational research into these questions and for developing programs and materials. The channels for making this information available are in place, through professional meetings and formal dissemination systems.

Second, we must document out-of-classroom and within-classroom programs for educating ethnic immigrant youth. It will not be enough to compile, the traditional data for a progress report on a bilingual education or ESL program. These program reports do not adequately convey the complex interaction between the child's culture and cognitive and language ability and his or her academic progress. Also, they never tell us enough about the teacher's methods, the quality of particular materials, and the local school situation to help us continue to improve program design. Here I question whether there is enough incentive to provide this kind of formal documentation. This is likely local information that can be exchanged through interpersonal communication. To disseminate it local authorities must institute workshops and seminars for local educators to exchange this kind of information.

Finally, the problem of ethnic immigrant advocacy groups to make their concerns felt. Many such groups readily consider themselves peripheral to the educational and social mainstream. Sometimes this can strengthen their capacity and legitimacy in working for the good of the group they represent. Nevertheless, they share a concern for maintaining a flow of variety of economic, intellectual, and technical resources to their special group with every other ethnic advocacy group. We now know that making the education of the ethnic and minority poor part of the national education agenda will do more for these groups than any other strategy. Immigrant ethnic advocacy groups should form collaborations and associations with a number of research, policy, and dissemination agencies to seek their help in articulating their information and other needs in ways that they can gain and hold local, regional, or national attention. The networks for making these needs known or for delivering the required information and resources are in place. Local cable and on-the-air television is a good starting point both for increasing public awareness of ethnic immigrant social life and for providing education and training to the groups themselves.

PROVIDING INFORMATION TO ETHNIC IMMIGRANT GROUPS

It is very important that we become conscious of the ways of providing information to ethnic minority groups to allow them to function successfully in American society. To be without information or access to information sources is to be without resources for social betterment. We must realize that neither increased dissemination through existing channels nor new opportunities created by further growth in social and educational information is going to improve the lives of ethnic immigrants until we address the distinct problems of information poverty characteristic of ethnic minorities in our society.

Information poverty is a lack of information, a lack of access to information, and a lack of appropriate information to meet social goals. It is usually a consequence of being part of a low status cultural group, who by virtue of race, ethnicity, socioeconomic status, geographic location, language or dialect, or age is less well served socially or even is disenfranchised. The information poor, particularly low status racial and ethnic groups but others as well, share some of the following characteristics:

1. Little literacy and few number or memorization skills.

2. Little ability or inclination to seek and use formal or literate information and to value it in any way, possibly because of previous failures to have needs met or suspicious about the source of the information.

3. An inclination to value oral over written sources of information.

4. A tendency to interact with people essentially like oneself; a mistrust of outsiders, including so-called experts or informed professionals as sources of help, information, or advice.

5. A strong habit of spending a long media day (in some cases up to half a waking day) watching or listening to high entertainment and low information television or radio.

6. A dependency on social agencies for information and service which are beset by problems of inefficiency, red tape, ambivalence toward clients, which are barriers to effective delivery of help or information. (Childers and Post 1975; Dervin 1977).

As in many interventions with low status cultural or social groups to bring about information equity we must adopt a multicultural perspective. This means recognizing that attitudes toward information are functions of the idiosyncratic values and beliefs of a particular cultural heritage and usually come from cultural affiliations rather than individual experiences. Since we know that information tends to be transmitted through social relationships for these groups rather than through formal, impersonal information channels, we must determine the roles that oral channels, the media, schools, adult centers, libraries and social agencies can play in the cultural lives of these groups. (Cochrane and Atherton 1980). Very important we must consider the relevance and value of the information to the group, and not be confused by our estimate of the worth of the information:

> Most people seek access only to information that they value. Most individuals disseminate information that is seen as useful to others. A mismatch of values between information seekers and information disseminators may account for information inequity. ... Often information is not valued unless it is produced by a certain source and thus given legitimacy. Officially produced information which comes from a source that is not known to have done anything for the information constituency is not likely to be regarded with a great deal of redibility. (Cochrane and Atherton 1980:290)

There is a clear connection here between culture and the value of information which is rarely considered in our society. Information specialists usually do not actively design information and communication networks to consider cultural behavior. The result is that the number of information poor increase as our society becomes more complex and the control of information flow continues to rest in the same hands.

There are obvious ways that we can reduce the information poverty of ethnic immigrant groups. First we must adopt a multicultural perspective that recognizes the importance of cultural behavior. More specifically, we should determine the appropriate medium of interaction or communication (print, film, video, interpersonal, and so forth). Then we can assign the best personnel to teach or communicate knowledge or information (member of the cultural group or outsider, paraprofessional or professional) and the setting (school, community setting, home). These are not radical suggestions; common sense would dictate that we follow them.

CONCLUSION

No piece of information can change a situation unless conditions allow it. The best designed program with validated curriculum and instructional strategies will fail if local school or school district factors inhibit effective schooling. So with any piece of information. Even more, if the policy of the U.S. government or any state or local agency is ambivalent about educating ethnic minority immigrants they will not be properly educated, no matter how much we know about appropriate educational practices or how we disseminate this information to these who need it. Information like everything else exists in a social and political world.

Yet we do know something about increasing the chance that information will be used effectively if the conditions are right. I want to conclude by pointing out one or two fundamental truths. Resistance to the change that information makes possible is firmly entrenched and lies at both national and emotional levels. People change only because the change is rewarding to them personally, to their group, or to their institutions. People also want to be successful; educators, especially those working with populations difficult to educate, need to feel that they are effective professionals. The information we disseminate must show them that it is possible to educate ethnic immigrant groups and that it is in their best professional, social, and moral interests to do so. This means that information systems have to do more than collect, store, and disseminate information. They have to provide ways for the client or consumer, whether educational professional working in a minority school or community or a member of the ethnic minority group itself, to make sense of the information being provided. For those working with minorities, this means that the information cannot just be facts, but also must clarify issues, offer a sense of control and motivate the client to use the information, and finally must provide some kind of resolution, even only a temporary one. Information must increase the possibility of success, not make it harder to achieve it.

REFERENCES

Center for Applied Linguistics, Washington, D.C. Orientation Resource Center. *A Guide to Orientation Materials for Indochinese Refugees and Their Sponsors.* April, 1981.

CHILDERS, THOMAS, AND JOYCE A. POST. *The Information Poor in America.* Metuchen, N.J. Scarecrow Press, 1975.

COCHRANE, GLYNN, AND PAULINE ATHERTON. "The Cultural Appraisal of Efforts to Alleviate Information Inequity," *Journal of the American Society for Information Science,* 31)4):283-92, July, 1980.

DERVIN, BRENDA. *Communicating With, Not to, the Urban Poor.* ERIC/CUE Urban Diversity Series, No. 50. New York: ERIC Clearinghouse on Urban Education, Teachers College, Columbia University, 1977. ED 150240.

LOPATE, CAROL. *The United States' New Refugees: A Review of the Research on the Resettlement of Indochinese, Cubans, and Haitians.* ERIC/CUE Urban Diversity Series, No. 75. New York: ERIC Clearinghouse on Urban Education, Teachers College, Colombia University, 1981.

EDUCATIONAL PROGRAMS FOR IMMIGRANT GROUPS IN DADE COUNTY PUBLIC SCHOOLS

By Sylvia H. Rothfarb, Ph.D.
Title VII Elementary Project BASICS
Miami Springs, Florida

The Dade County Public School system has been experiencing massive changes in the composition of its student population during the past decade and a half. In the period of 1968-78 alone, the Hispanic population of Dade County grew from 16.93% to 32.3% (Robinett, 1979). Miami, one of the twenty-seven municipalities in Dade County, is currently 55% Latin (Simms, 1981). In addition to the rapidly increasing Hispanic population, numerous other groups have grown, such as Chinese, Russian, Arabic, Hebrew and particularly Haitian. Between April 28, 1980 and April 17, 1981, some 16,336 refugee students entered Dade County Public Schools, mainly through the well-known Mariel boatlift from Cuba, and the almost daily arrival of boats bringing refugees from Haiti. The average weekly entry rate of entrant students currently ranges between 60 and 65. These changes in and additions to Miami's population have had significant impact on the school system's instructional programs. Long a pioneer in bilingual education, Dade County Public Schools have had to rapidly expand the delivery of bilingual programs to 1) facilitate the linguistic, academic and cultural integration of first limited English proficiency students and later new entrant students into the mainstream and 2) to meet Civil Rights requirements for equal educational opportunities for minority language students. At the same time, the School District was planning a viable range of programs for the 80's and beyond, that would enable all students to become functionally bilingual and bicultural, and to successfully participate in a multicultural society.

In this brief paper, I will describe several key programs that have been designed and implemented for immigrant groups in Dade County Public Schools. I will try to answer these questions: *What are the key instructional programs provided for immigrant students? What are some of the major cultural, adjustment and programmatic problems encountered? What steps have been taken by Dade County Public Schools, toward their solution? What additional steps can Dade County Public Schools and other institutions take toward solving the problems identified?*

1. *What are the key instructional programs for immigrant groups in Dade County Public Schools?*

Bilingual education was defined by the United States Office of Education (1971) as the use of two languages, one of which is English, as mediums of instruction in a well-organized program which encompasses all or part of the curriculum and includes the study of the history and culture associated with the mother tongue. Transitional bilingual education is the use of the student's home language in instruction until such time as the student becomes proficient in English. An attendant goal in both types of programs is to develop and maintain the student's self-esteem and a legitimate pride in both cultures (Blanco, 1977).

Fishman and Lovas (1970) identify four different types of bilingual programs: traditional bilingualism (teaching the national (origin) language just long enough to permit its use as a medium of instruction), monoliterate bilingualism (where both languages are used orally but only one in writing), partial bilingualism (literacy in both languages, with one language limited to certain subjects), and full bilingualism (with all school subjects taught in both languages). One can find each of these types with slight variations, operant in Dade County Public Schools.

These programs; described in official   1-C, 1978), are summarized below:

ENGLISH FOR SPEAKERS OF OTHER LANGUAGES (ESOL)

Students whose native language is other than English and who are classified as less than independent in English are enrolled in ESOL. This is a full language arts and culture program which includes listening comprehension, oral expression, pronunciation, reading and writing. It supports the skills and concepts presented in the regular English curriculum, the Early Childhood and Basic Skills Plans, and State and local minimum standards. When feasible, it is based on a contrastive linguistic and cultural analysis of the English and the student's home language systems, and of the culture(s) each language reflects.

SPANISH FOR SPANISH SPEAKERS (SPANISH-S)

Spanish-S is a language and culture program designed to teach Spanish Language Arts skills to Spanish language origin students and to other students with proficiency in Spanish. It is comparable to the English Language Arts program.

BILINGUAL CURRICULUM CONTENT (BCC)

Selected basic skills and concepts which are generally offered only in English are provided in other languages through the Bilingual Curriculum Content component. The same instructional objectives are taught in each curriculum area, such as Science, Mathematics or Social Studies, as are taught in the regular curriculum in English. This program is offered where there are limited English-speaking students and in Bilingual School Organizations. The proportion of time in which the language other than English is used as a medium of instruction depends on the student's growth in English proficiency.

BILINGUAL SCHOOL ORGANIZATION (BISO)

Bilingual School Organization refers to a curriculum construct offered at the elementary level which, in addition to the regular instructional program in the English language, provides for instruction in English for Speakers of Other Languages, Spanish for Spanish Speakers, Spanish as a Second Language, and Bilingual Curriculum Content. It also introduces basic concepts and skills in the student's native language and reinforces them in the second language. Because of the intensity in terms of time and scope with which Spanish is offered to English language origin students in this situation, a major objective pursued is to make Spanish a second language for these children.

TRANSITIONAL BILINGUAL BASIC SKILLS (TBBS)

TBBS is a program at the elementary school level which enables students of limited English-speaking ability to progress academically by acquiring basic skills in the home language as well as in English while they are learning English. The Office for Civil Rights of the U.S. Department of Education requires that students at this level who are not yet proficient in English be offered the opportunity to study such subjects as Science, Social Studies, and Mathematics in their home language. The intent of this requirement is to ensure that students are not deprived of equal educational opportunities because of a language barrier. The use of the student's home language is phased out as a medium of instruction as competencies are developed in and through the use of English.

ENTRANT PROGRAM

A special program for nearly 13,000 Cuban and Haitian entrants was established in 1980-81, in order to provide (them) the best instructional program possible within the constraints of limited resources and housing facilities confronting Dade County Public Schools (Bell, 1980). For the purpose of identifying students for the Entrant Program, any Cuban student who entered the United States after April 21, 1980 and who registered in a school after that same date was included; as were all Haitian students who had been processed through the Foreign Student Registration Center since November 5, 1979.

Special Entrant Program resources included: auxiliary personnel (full-time bi-lingual teachers and teacher aides or assistants), supplementary monies for bilingual allocations, entrant facilities and centers, instruction in and through the home language as well as ESOL instruction, student services, transportation and food services. During the summer of 1980, a Summer Entrant Program was provided. This program offered orientation, intensive English and home language instruction to the new entrants.

Other special resources were: instructional materials produced and/or duplicated in a very short time, guidelines for organizing instruction, inservice education, bilingual counselors, visiting teachers and psychologists, relocatable classrooms and operational support.

By the end of the school year, 16,615 entrant students had thus been served (Robinett, 1981). The success in meeting these entrant students' learning and cultural integration needs within the transitional bilingual program was evidenced by the advancement of many students to higher levels of English proficiency. The 1981-82 program projects ESOL instruction for 13,313 students K-12 and home language instruction for 10,800 students at the elementary school level. The *total* number of limited English proficient students projected for 1981-82, including entrants, is 29,500.

PROGRAMS AND SERVICES FOR HAITIAN ORIGIN STUDENTS

Approximately 8,200 Haitian origin students are enrolled in 72 Dade County Public Schools (Dade County Public Schools, 1981). Some 3,000 of these students are in grades K-12, including 965 new Haitian refugees as of March 20, 1981. The remaining + 5,200 Haitian students have been served in adult education programs.

Haitian origin students are provided the same types of programs as other students. If they are independent in English, they are placed in regular classes and participate in the mainstream English curricular program. In grades K-12, if the students are limited in English, they are assigned to the transitional bilingual basic skills program. In the adult program, the main thrust has been in the area of English for Speakers of Other Languages.

In grades K-12, the transitional bilingual basic skills program uses the home language of the student as well as English to help students maintain their academic achievement while they are learning English. In this case, Haitian-Creole is used for part of the time in Social Studies, Science, and Mathematics as necessary to ensure comprehension of the concepts being presented. As the students gain proficiency in English, use of Creole is reduced and finally phased out so the students have a full program in English. Home language components in TBBS are taught by specially allocated teachers. The schools that have high concentrations of limited English proficient students generate full-time teachers or teacher aides/assistants. In the schools with low concentrations, the students are served by itinerant personnel. In the adult education program, enrollments have been absorbed by State of Florida and local funds, which provide for building use and teacher costs.

The following federal and state projects provide special services to Haitian origin students:

Southeast Curricula Development Center. This center, an ESEA Title VII project, is in the process of adapting and/or developing materials in Haitian Creole in the areas of social studies and language arts.

Elementary Project BASICS. The purpose of this ESEA, Title VII project is to improve the transitional bilingual program. Edison Park Elementary School, with an enrollment of approximately 200 limited English proficient Haitian students, is one of the project's demonstration centers. Services provided Haitian origin students are: instruction in home language arts, parent training sessions, adult education classes for parents of program students (English and literacy in Creole), and identification/adaptation of instructional materials and tests in Haitian-Creole.

Secondary Project BASICS. Secondary Project BASICS, an ESEA, Title VII project, provides services similar to those of Elementary Project BASICS, but at the junior high and middle school levels. The project uses Miami Edison Middle School as the demonstration center where Haitian origin students of limited English proficiency are provided special instruction.

Bilingual Desegregation Assistance Project. This ESEA, Title VII project, supplements the services provided by the Dade County Public Schools to Haitian origin students of limited English proficiency in the area of Bilingual Curriculum Content.

Multilingual/Cultural Alternative for Secondary Education. The Multilingual/Cultural Alternative for Secondary Education Project, an ESEA, Title IV-C project, has as one of its purposes the development of materials to assist with the acculturation problems of junior high and middle school students of Haitian background. The materials are designed to:

(1) Help students understand the school system.
(2) Train guidance counselors/school administrators to deal more effectively with problem students and their families.
(3) Provide parents with a better understanding of the United States and American education.

Project Haitien. Project Haitien was an ESEA, Title IX, Ethnic Heritage Studies project during 1978-79 school year. The project developed cultural resource materials reflecting unique contributions of Haitian Americans and the integration of Haitian Americans into an American community. These materials are currently used in the Dade County Public Schools.

These and other federally-funded projects support the system's total bilingual program. For example, Elementary Project BASICS provides resource teachers to six schools. The overall goal of this project is to improve the design and implementation of the TBBS program in the Dade County Public Schools. The project staff therefore conducts numerous workshops in demonstration and satellite schools, adapts materials into Haitian-Creole, and provides personnel and parent training and immersion programs in Spanish, English and Haitian-Creole.

2. *What are some of the major cultural, adjustment and programmatic problems encountered?*

Three major problems have been encountered in trying to provide a comprehensive instructional program for limited English proficient students of Haitian origin:

(1) Difficulty in seeking federal assistance to provide programs and services, even when commitments have been made for such assistance.

(2) Lack of qualified instructional personnel who are native speakers of Haitian Creole to provide quality education in and through the home language.

(3) Lack of instructional materials in Haitian-Creole, both in the United States and Haiti, due to the fact that until recently Haitian Creole was primarily a spoken language, not a written one.

Other problems are:

(4) A need for school personnel to understand and be sensitive to the Haitian culture.

(5) More flexible licensing policies for Haitian teachers.

(6) Strategies for dealing with a wide range of literacy skills among Haitian students.

Cultural differences between the educational systems of Haiti and the United States were recently identified by Auguste (1981):

> In Haiti, students start with cursive writing. They have limited study skills due to few libraries. Students take an elementary exam in French. Peer tutoring is not common, nor is grouping: instruction is basically lecture-type. Students are very respectful. Tests are usually essay. Children are ranked in their class according to achievement, teachers publicize good and bad students, parents are used to this. Grades are numerical, not letter; the average is 50. There are no standardized tests on the grade level equivalences. In Math, the decimal system is used, with commas, not periods.
>
> In the U.S., Parent Information Booklets have been found useful, e.g., on vaccinations. In New York, children are often kept home because parents are afraid of immigration authorities. At home, there frequently are broken families, as children come here later than their parents. Children have to adapt to cold weather clothing, and frequently wear garlic, pins and herbs when sick.
>
> In general, many Haitians are deprived of extensive formal education, although they value it highly. In rural areas, resources such as textbooks are scarce and widely shared.

Problems related to the language, and characteristics of Haitian-Creole summarized by Dejean (1981) are:

> Many people confuse *Patois* with Haitian-Creole. *Patois,* spoken in some Caribbean Islands, is a variety of the French language, akin to Haitian Creole. It has inferior connotations, lacks rules of grammar and organization, is spoken by older, less-educated people and will tend to disappear. Because a dialect is a local variety of a language, it doesn't impede communication. There are several dialects of Haitian-Creole, spoken in different parts of Haiti. A monolingual speaker of Haitian-Creole cannot communicate with a monolingual speaker of French.
>
> There is a need to create Haitian-Creole materials — French materials cannot simply be translated or parrotted, as the technicality of words and concepts is involved. There is a lack of people prepared to develop materials.
>
> Can parents read Haitian-Creole? Yes, if they can read in French. However, higher educated Haitians would feel insulted, and possibly claim that they can't read Haitian-Creole.
>
> The illiteracy problem is high among Haitian students. Using an ESOL approach and teaching students reading and writing in Haitian-Creole would give

them a feeling of success, as they have been traumatized and deprived of education. Haiti is an illiterate society but where education is highly valued. The entry level of Haitian students reflects a wide range of literacy-illiteracy through high academic achievement.

Local institutions of higher education should teach Haitian-Creole, and re-validate training obtained in Haiti.

CULTURAL ADJUSTMENT PROBLEMS OF NEW ENTRANT CUBANS

The following information is extrapolated from the Report *El Sistema Escolar de Buca (The School System in Cuba),* written by two recently arrived educators, Rita and Omelio Vilardell (1980). The report was funded by Elementary Project BASICS.

HIGHLIGHTS OF THE SCHOOL SYSTEM IN CUBA

EDUCATIONAL PROGRAMS

The educational programs that exist today in Cuba's educational system reflect the type of socialist government that the country has. They pursue the idea of turning out a new man based on Marx' and Lenin's ideals.

EDUCATIONAL OBJECTIVES

These objectives are solely used to form and mold the behavior patterns of the student as well as his/her political ideology. Some of these objectives are:

1. To point out all the help that Cuba receives from socialist countries.
2. To appreciate the advantages of living under a socialistic type of government.
3. To determine the types of crimes that American imperialism has committed in different parts of the world.
4. To infer the many advantages of socialism over capitalism.
5. To point out all the laws that have been passed since Castro took power and that benefit the people of Cuba.
6. To analyze the speeches that were made by different Revolutionary leaders.
7. To point out and emphasize the economical growth and the increase in production since the revolution.
8. To awaken a love for work among the students.
9. To recognize other people's struggle against imperialism around the world.
10. To try to convince the students that what is being taught to them is right and unquestionable.

TYPES OF EDUCATIONAL PROGRAMS

The educational programs are:
1. Pre-school program
2. Primary Elementary Program (Grades 1-6)
3. Basic Secondary Program (Grades 7-9)
4. Middle School Program (Grades 10-12)
5. University Program
6. Special Education Program (For students with learning disabilities)
7. Rural School Program
8. Secondary Night School Program for Adults

PRE-SCHOOL

It is mandatory by law that every child who is 4 years and 9 months old attend school. If the child's parents fail to register him/ her for school at that age, they are reported to the police and they could be sent to jail.

CRITERIA USED FOR PLACING STUDENTS AT DIFFERENT LEVELS

The decision as to where the child should be placed depends on different factors, but the main one is how much involved is he or she, and his or her parents with the government. A very smart child has been known to have been taken ut of school because his/her parents do not belong to any communist organization.

DISCIPLINE

Teachers have no control over discipline in their classrooms. Discipline is controlled and enforced by a group called the *Pionner Detachment.* Each classroom has a chief that comes out of this detachment and he/she is usually chosen for being the most revolutionary and pro-communist.

MORNING EXERCISES

All students remain standing when they enter the classroom. Then, the Detachment Chief will lead them into singing revolutionary songs and reciting governmental poems.

PARENT PARTICIPATION

There is very little participation from the parents in the schools. This is mainly due to the fact that most of them have to work very hard and for many long hours. At many times they are required to attend propaganda meetings and perform work on a voluntary basis. In most schools, there is always a group of mothers that help the teachers on Sunday with the cleaning and the maintenance of the classroom.

LANGUAGES OFFERED AT DIFFERENT LEVELS

The Spanish language is mandatory at all levels. English is taught in grades 7-9 and is offered in Grades 10-12. In some important cities, night school offers classes in English, Russian, French and German.

SCHOOL DAYS

In Grades 1-6, students attend school five days a week (Monday-Friday). In Grades 7-12, students attend school six days a week (Monday-Saturday).

PUNISHMENT

Corporal punishment is forbidden.

Problems encountered by teachers of Cuban entrants in Dade County Schools include:
1. Children are severely traumatized by the boat trip from Mariel.
2. Discipline problems.
3. Lack of skills in the home language (Spanish).
4. Adjustment to the new culture.

3. *What steps have been taken by Dade County Public Schools toward solution of the problems identified?*

Some of the major steps taken by Dade County Public Schools toward solving these problems are:
1. The development of instructional materials and tests in Haitian-Creole by the Southeast Curricula Development Center and Elementary Project BASICS; and the production, acquisition and dissemination of appropriate bilingual materials for Hispanic and other language groups by the Department of Bilingual Education/Foreign Languages.
2. The provision of inservice training for teachers and paraprofessionals working with entrant students.
3. The provision of immersions in Haitian-Creole, Spanish, and English.
4. The provision of immersion and other parent training programs.
5. The provision of psychgological services and working with community agencies for counseling and other needs.
6. The delivery of services on an ongoing basis, in spite of fiscal cutbacks.

4. *What additional steps can Dade County Public Schools and other institutions take toward solving these problems?*

The following recommendations are offered toward the solution of the problems identified:

1. Increase training and recruitment efforts, thereby providing needed certified professionals, particularly Haitian origin teachers.
2. Continue the cooperative effort in the production of instructional materials and tests, and parent information books.
3. Increase entrant parents' involvement in the education of their children.
4. Establish a climate of mutual cooperation and support in designing, implementing and evaluating educational programs for refugee students.
5. Become familiar with, knowledgeable in and sensitive to the diverse cultures and languages of students, including these as feasible as part of the curriculum for English language origin students (Rothfarb, 1970).

Dade County Public Schools have made many inroads in providing educational programs for immigrant students. Many problems remain to be solved. Through continued effort, and forums such as these, we will improve education for students entering our city from other countries, escaping economic hardships and political oppression.

REFERENCES

AUGUSTE, MICHAELLE. "The Haitian Culture and Educational System." Presentation at the Workshop for Educators of Haitian Children, Ft. Lauderdale, Florida: May, 1981.

BELL, PAUL W. "Procedures for Providing Educational Services to Cuban-Entrant Students." Memorandum, Dade County Public Schools, Miami, Florida: August 15, 1980.

BLANCO, GEORGE. "The Education Perspective." In *Bilingual Education: Current Perspectives, Volume 4.* Arlington, Virginia: Center for Applied Linguistics, 1977.

Dade County Public Schools. *Procedures Manual, Bilingual Education/Foreign Languages, Bulletin 1-C Revised.* Dade County Public Schools, Miami, Florida: 1978.

––––––– . "Report on Programs and Services for Haitian Origin Students in the Dade County Public Schools." Bureau of Education, Dade County Public Schools, Miami, Florida: March 26, 1981.

DEJEAN, IVES. "Language Characteristics and Survival Skills." Presentation at the Haitian Workshop for Educators of Haitian Children, Ft. Lauderdale, Florida: May, 1981.

FISHMAN, JOSHUA AND J. LOVAS. "Bilingual Education in Sociolinguistic Perspective." *TESOL Quarterly* 4:3, pp. 215-222, 1970.

ROBINETT, RALPH. Demographic data quoted in Title VII Elementary Project BASICS Proposal Application. Dade County Public Schools, Miami, Florida: 1979.

––––––– . "Supplemental Analysis of Cuban Haitian Program Excess Cost Projection." Report, Bureau of Education, Dade County Public Schools, Miami, Florida: April 27, 1981.

ROTHFARB, SYLVIA H. "Second Language Learning in Bilingual Communities." ERIC ED 031-690: December, 1970.

SIMMS, ROBERT H. Demographic data included in *Community Relations Board Annual Report for Metropolitan Dade County,* 1978-79; Memoranda for Mobile Seminar Participants: May 7, 1981.

U.S. Office of Education. "Bilingual Education Proposed Regulations." *Federal Register* 41:69: April 8, 1976.

VILARDELL, OMELIO AND R. VILARDELL. *Sistema Escolar de Cuba.* Elementary Project BASICS, Dade County Public Schools, Miami, Florida: 1980.

BIOGRAPHICAL SKETCH

Sylvia H. Rothfarb is the Project Manager for ESEA Title VII Elementary Project BASICS, Dade County Public Schools. She received the Bachelor and Master of Arts degree in Hispano-American Languages and Literature from the University of the Americas (Mexico); and the Ph.D. in Educational Administration from the University of Miami. She has been an administrator for bilingual and foreign language education in the Dade County School System for thirteen years, and was Associate Director of the Bilingual Education Teacher Training Program at the University of Miami. She has published articles on second language learning in bilingual communities, and on teacher-pupil interaction in foreign language classes. Dr. Rothfarb has presented numerous papers on the administration and evaluation of bilingual programs at national conferences.

THE MIAMI EXPERIENCE:
A MULTICULTURAL CURRICULUM

By George S. Morrison, Ed.D.,
Professor of Education
and Director
The Center for
Parent and Family Studies
and Mislady A. Velez
Program Assistant
Florida International University

The recent influx of Mariel entrants and Haitian refugees into Florida and the growing number of tourists and immigrants from many countries, has generated an ideal climate for the teaching of multicultural awareness in our schools. The multicultural nature of our community can be a positive resource in the educational system. Saville-Troike, (1978), refers to man as a cultural animal: "all of us in one way or another are products of our culture, and many of our behaviors, values, and goals are culturally determined." Our responsibility, therefore, as suggested by Saville-Troike, should be to explore how the positive and humanistic aspects of this force can be maximized in our schools. This task may be accomplished by first seeking an honest appraisal and understanding of what multicultural awareness is and then familiarizing ourselves with the goals of a multicultural curriculum.

MULTICULTURAL AWARENESS DEFINED

There are numerous definitions of what multicultural awareness is, some of which may confuse the general public and alienate the possibility of realizing a multicultural curriculum in our schools. In its simplest form, multicultural awareness may be defined as an appreciation, understanding of and esteem for other people and their cultures, as well as one's own culture. This definition supports and promotes the skills, attitudes and abilities of children, as well as adults, to interact in a positive and meaningful manner with others in varied cultural situations and circumstances as a way of life.

It is unfortunate though that society in general does not consistently promote cultural awareness. However, the writers believe that this absence of a conscious attempt to promote cultural awareness is often circumstantial rather than intentional. Hence, the task of promoting multicultural awareness is delegated by default to educational institutions so they can develop a *lifetime* awareness of the richness that other cultures add to all societies.

EMBARKING ON A MULTICULTURAL CURRICULUM

A multicultural awareness program must have realistic goals. Additionally, inherent problems and issues must be addressed if a successful program is to be realized. Critical issues which are related to and which influence the development of multicultural programs include: societal attitudes; misconceptions on behalf of the public; existing rules and regulations; justification; development, and most importantly, the implementation of the curriculum itself.

JUSTIFICATION OF A MULTICULTURAL AWARENESS PROGRAM

Reasons for the importance of offering a multicultural awareness program must be examined and clearly understood by educators before they endeavor to incorporate it in their curricula. By doing so, the institution will be able to support and form a firm commitment to the program, which will later enable the school to better meet the goals of a multicultural awareness curriculum.

The United States has always been multi-ethnic in its composition. However, never before have we been more aware of this than the present times. Because of its demographic location, Miami is known as the "gateway to the Americas." Indeed, if we were to carefully examine all of the ethnic groups which constitute our community, a more appropriate term might be "gateway to the world." Oftentimes, in an area such as Miami where there is such a diverse ethnic population, people withdraw to themselves and form pockets of culture. In such a situation, the concept of multicultural awareness is more important than ever because of the need to break out of our ethnic encapsulations, and because ethnic harmony should be realized in our communities.

It is important to recognize that simply because Miami is a multi-ethnic community, it is still not reason enough in and of itself to justify promoting multicultural awareness. With our advanced technology, we need only to depress a few digits on a telephone, flick the knob of a television or radio, pick up the daily newspaper, or open a letter in order to communicate with people in the farthest places imaginable on the globe.

Leon Panetta, congressman of California, stated to his constituents (1979), that "we live in a world that is rapidly shrinking as the technologies of communication and transportation grow more advanced, and as the role of international economics in our everyday lives becomes increasingly important." He further stated that "unless this nation finds ways of improving its knowledge and understanding of ... foreign cultures, we will be placing a severe handicap on our ability to understand, influence, and react to world events." Obviously, it is certainly a time when we need *global* ethnic harmony and awareness in our society.

When dealing with culture, we may discover things that will fascinate us, intrigue us, perplex us and even things that will appall us. Additionally, some things we may *never* understand about a culture, even when that culture is our own. However, ethnic content is in fact legitimate knowledge which *should* be explored in the classroom if both children and adults are to dispel the fears which often are associated with dealing with themselves and with others. Elementary children and "adults" frequently have many misconceptions about their own cultures and the cultures of others (Morrison, 1981): a multicultural awareness curriculum can help clear these misunderstandings.

It is important to realize that norms need to be established in our society which respect and accept cultural and ethnic differences. Children need to learn about, love and respect each other. They in turn can influence the attitudes of their parents who may have unknowingly encouraged them to be ethnocentric in their beliefs and actions.

GOALS OF A MULTICULTURAL AWARENESS PROGRAM

The terms and concepts used to depic multicultural awareness are not as important as the methods, procedures and activities used to *develop* a meaningful program. Educators and the public are often under the assumption that they are promoting multicultural awareness in various situations, when in fact they are only presenting a fragment of the concept.

An example is bilingual education in which people are learning in two languages; not *about* two languages. Learning about a culture enhances and makes more interesting the acquisition of a second language. However, many of us have learned languages without discovering much about the culture associated with that language. Educators who teach a language often mistakenly labor under the good intention that their classroom is multicultural.

Likewise, an ornately decorated classroom with travel posters left to fade on the walls without expanding or elaborating on the purpose of why they were put up in the first place is *not* multicultural education. Such a situation may actually promote a negative attitude toward others through misconceptions and inaccuracies.

Similarly, a travel-log approach to the study of other countries and people often promotes a feeling that students are tourists and the differences they experience in another culture might not be "as good" as habits and customs in their own. Frequently, these "tourists" will judge another country's worth by comparing such things as technological advancement, commodities, or living facilities. Intermingling with people of another country as a tourist is quite different from the experiences acquired when living with them.

Most importantly, multicultural awareness in the classroom is not the presentation of other cultures and an exclusion of the cultures represented by children in the class. Rather, a multicultural awareness program should focus on other cultures, while at the same time making children aware of the content, nature and richness of their own. The learning of other cultures concurrently with their own will enable children to integrate commonalities and appreciate differences without undertones of inferiority or superiority of one or the other.

The goals for an exemplary multicultural awareness program should be guided by efforts which focus on the nature of its content and the selection of meaningful activities using appropriate materials. The following suggestions will help serve such a purpose:

1. *Provide multicultural awareness training for teachers, administrators and parents.*

Teachers are the most important variable in a multi-ethnic curriculum. The pedagogical manner of the teacher's presentation about a culture has the most impact on students. If teachers portray negative attitudes toward others in their teaching, they are less likely to encourage the learning process, (Fisher, 1977). Teachers must show that they value individual differences as they draw upon the students' experiences with respect for their feelings and beliefs. If teachers are first able to level with their own attitudes toward other cultures and have an accurate knowledge of what is to be presented, they may refrain their teaching from being stereotypical. Administrators are often excluded from in-service training, under the assumption that their task is only to administrate. However, if a multicultural awareness program is to be implemented in any school, the catalyst for change will in fact be the administrator. It will be up to this key person to restructure the curriculum in order to implement goals which promote and enhance multicultural awareness in educational institutions.

Furthermore, if educators are to extend and perpetuate multicultural awareness beyond the school setting, parental training must be provided. Additionally, if parents are made aware of what transpires in the schools and why, they will be better able to take part in their child's educational process, thereby enhancing the multicultural awareness program. We cannot expect school programs to have the continued and lasting impact we desire unless families and communities support what schools teach.

2. *Use the local school and community to teach multicultural awareness.*

Just as each culture varies and differs *within* itself, so does each school and community. Both the school and its community offer unique resources which should be incorporated in the implementation of a multicultural awareness program. By doing this, maximized communication, which is essential in such a program, will occur. The learning of a culture begins with children's experiences in the environment in which they live.

3. *Use the most available and special resources: children and parents.*

Children and their parents can personalize and make cultures come alive, thereby avoiding multicultural awareness as an abstract theory. Children are better able to understand concepts when they are allowed to become actively and meaningfully involved in the learning process. It is the child's own discoveries which will lead to retention: "for they will forget what [the teacher says] but not what they themselves bring forth from the inmost recess of their beings," (Nine Curt, 1976). This approach will yield a much better understanding of *themselves* which will in turn allow them to be ready for the lifetime process of multicultural awareness. Hence, human interaction is an integral process of multicultural awareness; the concept should be presented as a human process.

4. *Minimize Stereotypes and Prejudice*

In the implementation of a multicultural curricula, it is imperative that we do so in an honest, just and accurate manner; failing to do so, any program is doomed for failure. Educators have an obligation and responsibility to "reflect the dignity and worth of *ALL* human beings," (Williams, 1975) by erradicating existing stereotypes and prejudices which have no place in a multicultural awareness program. Educators must strive to promote a positive atmosphere of respect for all members of our society. People are culturally different, but "loaded with virtues and some defects, and definitely worth a lot," (Nine Curt, 1976).

5. *Provide Variance in the Program.*

Students are best motivated when they are presented with diversified opportunities for learning. Children should have access to properly assessed multicultural elements, including: artifacts; activities which help sensitize them; resources (including people); and appropriate textbooks which provide visual and supplemental enrichment activities. Such stimuli will serve to broaden the students' choice for cultural experiences. Each child has a unique learning style, whatever her/his cultural background is. We must therefore, never assume that there is one best way to teach a particular culture.

6. *Making a Commitment.*

Teaching multicultural awareness must be viewed as an integral, meaningful and important process of our educational institutions. We must abide by the rights of all children to realize universal brotherhood and understanding. We need global/intercultural communication and comprehension, not alienation or miscommunication. A multicultural "movement" must therefore involve the alliance and perseverance of everyone who faces the classroom. If the school is to be a disseminator of multicultural awareness, it must embark upon its task as a lifetime process. Multicultural awareness will permeate society only when a firm commitment is undertaken by all to see that it becomes a reality.

REFERENCES

FISHER, L. *To Live In Two Worlds.* Oklahoma: State Department of Education, Oklahoma. (National Clearinghouse for Bilingual Education, Rosslyn, Virginia: 1977).

MORRISON, G.S. "Kids Say the Darndest Things About Their World" paper presented at National Council for the Social Studies Meeting, Detroit, Michigan, November, 1981.

NINE CURT, C.J. *Teacher Training Pack for a Course on Cultural Awareness.* (National Assessment and Dissemination Center for Bilingual/Bicultural Education, Cambridge, Massachusetts: 1976).

SAVILLE-TROIKE, M. *A Guide to Culture in the Classroom.* (National Clearinghouse for Bilingual Education, Rosslyn, Virginia: 1978).

WILLIAMS, C.T. "The Curriculum Leader as a Change Agent in Institutionalizing Cultural Pluralism," Michigan Education Association, East Lansing, Michigan: 1975.

SCHOOL AND COMMUNITY INVOLVEMENT FOR MINORITY LANGUAGE PARENTS: AN UNTAPPED RESOURCE

By George S. Morrison, Ed.D.
Professor of Education
and Director
The Center for
Family and Parent Studies
Florida International University
Miami, Florida

ABSTRACT

Parent involvement is a process of actualizing the potential of parents; of helping parents discover their strengths, potentialities and talents, and using them for the benefit of themselves, the family, the school and community (Morrison, 1978). Implicative in this comprehensive concept is the view that parent development and involvement are reciprocal processes. A parent involvement model can no longer emphasize the utilization of parents solely as sources of help. An effective approach must also make provisions to meet the special developmental needs of parents.

The concept and attitude that individuals possess of parent involvement will ultimately affect the manner in which these programs will be conceived, designed and implemented. Teachers, administrators and persons involved in parent involvement processes must develop clear definitions, and realistic objectives regarding parent involvement.

Involving minority language parents in the school and community has recently received the needed support from social, legislative and public mandates and forces. Bilingual education programs (Title VII), the Civil Rights movement, consumerism, and the new surge of back to basics, have provided impetus to the parent involvement movement. The minority language parent must be included as a willing and able partner in this process.

When considering a parent involvement program a number of factors mut be taken into consideration: the requirements of specific legislation, attitudes of administrators, teachers and parents, the needs of the program and the community. In addition, the specific needs of minority language parents such as language spoken, decision-making skills, and understanding of the American and local educational system will dictate many of the constructs of a particular program.

Strategies for involving the language minority parent must be developed in the context of a philosophy and attitude toward parent involvement. Procedures should also be based on the goals of the program and the needs and characteristics of the minority language parents for whom the program is designed.

Strategies for involving the language minority parent must be developed in the context of a philosophy and attitude toward parent involvement. Procedures should also be based on the goals of the program and the needs and characteristics of the minority language parents for whom the program is designed.

RENEWED INTEREST IN PARENTS

Parents have finally been rediscovered. This rediscovery, during the last decade, has resulted in the recognition that parents are a potent force in the lives of their children and play as important a role as do schools, teachers and administrators in the educational process. Educators are now more interested than ever in devising ways to involve parents in their programs and in defining the nature, kind and extent of the relationships that should exist between parents and schools. At the same time, colleges and universities are gradually beginning to assume more responsibility for training preservice teachers in parent involvement procedures.

However, even with this renewed interest, there is a sector of the parent population which is frequently ignored and consequently does not play as significant a role as it should in the educational process. This sector is the language minority parent. These parents, which comprise a majority in certain localities of our country, have traditionally been excluded from participating tyo the fullest by teachers and administrators. In an era where the link between home and school has been identified as a significant determinant in a child's social and academic achievement, the need to include and actively involve all parents, regardless of race, culture or language becomes of eminent importance.

This state of affairs gives rise to a number of critical questions: Can we continue to disregard the language minority parent as an equal partner in the educational process? Are we effectively utilizing the skills and contributions these parents can make? How can we facilitate the involvement of these parents in our children's schools? Have we truly examined our parental involvement programs, to see that they meet the special needs of language minority parents?

The identification and answers to these questions must be the concern of all who have chosen to upgrade the quality and state of parental involvement. Addressing these issues represents the beginning of a renewed and effective partnership between home, school and community.

REASONS FOR PARENTAL INTEREST

Reasons for the rediscovery of relationship between parents and schools can be found in political and societal forces and specific legislation. The Consumer Movement of the last decade has convinced parents that they should no longer be accepting of products and processes which are not in the best interest of them or their children. This same attitude of accountability also applies to programs parents support such as the public schools. Parents believe that if they have a right to demand more accountability from industries and government agencies, they can also demand from schools effective instruction in the basic skills. The Consumer Movement has encouraged parents to be more militant in their demand for quality education. Schools have responded by seeking ways to involve parents in their renewed quest for quality.

Specific federal legislation has also been responsible for encouraging and accelerating the rate of parent involvement. Title VII, Bilingual Education of the Elementary and Secondary Education Act (ESEA) of 1965, allocates funds to develop and operate bilingual programs for children of limited English proficiency. This legislation mandates parental involvement in the development and implementation of these special programs through School Advisory Council's and the formation of special parent groups. In these ways, parents have a direct voice in the manner in which these programs serve their children. Parents are encouraged to actively participate in classroom instruction, and observation, as well as in the review process of any proposal requiring federal funding. In essence, the Title VII, provides a basis for involving the language minority parent in the decision-making realm.

Another important legislative measure that encourages parental participation is Public Law 94-142, The Education for All Handicapped Children Act of 1975. This law extends to parents and their handicapped children, specific rights and ways they must be involved in the educational process.

Educators have also been gradually recognizing that their teaching and classroom efforts can be more effectively achieved by encouraging parent assistance. Teachers are turning to parents for help with increasing frequency for the solution of school problems. Parents in turn, who believe discipline is the number one problem of the schools, (Gallup, 1981, p. 34) are more inclined to effect linkages which will improve the teaching learning process. Parent involvement has become an essential reality.

WHAT IS PARENT INVOLVEMENT?

While a certain relationship between parents and schools has existed through such entities as parent-teacher groups, parent involvement by teachers and administrators has been somewhat reluctant, tentative and self serving. Parent involvement has often been viewed as a process which occurs only when necessary, on certain stated meeting nights, when money raising projects are essential or when local school tax levies are in danger of failing. School authorities and teachers have often been hesitant to give parent access to school and classroom activities and decision making processes.

Classroom teachers and administrators must have clear ideas and conceptions of what they want to accomplish in a parent involvement program, if they want to achieve success. Too often, teacher's conceptions of parent involvement can be classified as narrow and one-dimensional. This interpretation consists of viewing parents mainly as source of help, e.g., what parents can do for them, without any extra concern for establishing mutual developmental relationships.

From this perspective teachers consider parents to be another person in the classroom, e.g., an aide; a possible solver of childrens' disruptive classroom behavior; a helper on field trips; and a means of furnishing needed items, such as daily classroom snacks. Certainly, parents are capable of doing all of these kinds of things but they are also capable of much more. Parent involvement should be a comprehensive and developmental process in which parents discover and develop their strengths, potentialities and talents and use them for the benefit of themselves, their families, the school and the community (Morrison, 1978, p. 22). Such a concept dignifies parents as people with needs and recognizes that involvement is a reciprocal process of parents helping educators and educators helping parents.

Another important change that must be taken into consideration when we conceptualize parent involvement is the fact that the term "parent" no longer only connotate "mother". A parent is ... "any individual who provides the child with basic care, direction, support, protection, and guidance (Morrison, 1978, p. 28). Therefore, many families are now headed by single males, grandparents and guardians. Realistically then, an effective parent involvement program must involve whoever is considered to be the child's parent or guardian. Furthermore, the more family members we can successfully involve in a parent involvement program, the greater the positive effects this interaction will yield.

LANGUAGE MINORITY PARENTS

The developmental concept of parent involvement is particularly important when working with language minority parents. Any program designed to promote parental involvement must possess a clear definition of this target group. Language minority parents are individuals whose dominant language proficiency is minimal, and who lack a comprehensive knowledge of the dominant culture's norms and social system including basic school philosophy, practice and structure.

Analyzing this definition, we can conclude that these parents possess specific needs that must be taken into consideration if we want to effectively establish a partnership between teachers/administrators and language minority parents. For example, language minority parents are often plagued by language and cultural barriers which greatly hamper their ability to get actively involved. Nevertheless, the majority possess a great desire and willingness to participate in the educational process. They must be given opportunities to do so.

The benefits minority language parents can provide our educational system is unmeasurable. A number of studies have concluded that, in the case of minority students, parental involvement facilitates the children's adjustment to the integrated school setting and that this, in turn, significantly improves the students' academic progress. (Arisso and Garcia, 1981, p. 3).

Teachers and administrators must bear in mind that minority language parents possess one important skill, and this is knowledge of their own culture. The nature of a specific culture determines to a great extent, the behavior of a particular child in a classroom. Creating an authentic relationship with these parents will facilitate the teachers' task of educating that child and promote his development. Methods and techniques to create this interaction between parent/teacher and administrators must be created in order to effectively tap parent's unused resources.

NEEDS OF LANGUAGE MINORITY PARENTS

The language minority parent has needs which are common to parents in general and specific needs inherent to their cultural and linguistic characteristics. Among the general needs that these parents have are: the desire to be treated in a fair, courteous and human way; the desire to obtain knowledge of the characteristics and procedures of the school; access to available support services; and, meaningful school involvement activities.

In addition, non or limited English speaking parents face a problem of communication (with the school system in general; and with school officials in particular) which often leads to fear, feeling sof inadequacy, powerlessness, or incompetence. (Arisso and Garcia, 1981, p. 2). Unfortunately, these limitations only help curtail the abilities of these parents to become adequately involved in the educational process of their children. The consensus of opinions found in professional journals is that when provided with the needed skills training programs, parents significantly influence the overall performance and adjustment period of their children. The key to the success of these programs lies in the strength of the parent training design. An effective parent involvement program must make provisions for both the general and specific needs of language minority parents.

Because the culture of language minority parents is different from that of the dominant American culture, those who seek a truly collaborative community, home and school involvement must take into account cultural features which would tend to negate that involvement. Traditional styles of child rearing, family organization, attitudes toward schooling, organizations around which families center their lives, e.g., churches, life goals and values, political influences, and methods of communication within the cultural group, all have implications for parent participation.

Minority language parents often lack information about the American educational system, resulting in misconceptions, fear, and a general reluctance to respond to invitations for involvement. Furthermore, what the American educational system is like may be quite different to what minority language parents are used to in a former school system. Many language minority parents may have been taught to refrain from becoming actively involved in the school process resulting in an attitude of leaving all decisions concerning childrens' education to teachers and administrators.

The American ideal of a community controlled and supported educational system must be explained to parents from cultures where this concept is not highly valued. Traditional roles of children, teachers and administrators likewise have to be explained. Many parents and especially non-language minority parents are quite willing to relinquish to teachers any rights and responsibilities they have for their children's education. Parents have to be educated to their roles and obligations toward schooling and the education of their children.

In essence, addressing the specific needs of language minority parents constitutes a crucial objective in the development of a parent involvement program. These parents have unique skills and contributions which they can offer to children and schools. Our responsibility as educators is to facilitate this process. Focusing on the existing strengths of parents, rather than stressing their dissimilarities or inadequacies will facilitate the task of creating greater parental participation.

OBJECTIVES OF A MINORITY LANGUAGE PARENT INVOLVEMENT PROGRAM

The general and specific needs of minority language parents, should serve as a guide and provide a basis for an effective parent involvement program. Consequently, an effective parent involvement program should:

1. Make provisions for the special needs of parents in order to effectively increase their participation.
2. Have clear and defined goals and objectives regarding program results.
3. Provide parents with opportunities for assuming an active role in the planning and decision-making process of the school.
4. Provide for the self-development of parents and school personnel.
5. Incorporate parents in the conceptualization, planning, decision-making, and operation of the parent involvement program.

Parent participation is more easily sought than achieved. More is required than merely inviting parents to take part. Parent involvement requires a true commitment on the part of teachers and administrators, and includes patience, hard work, and a strong belief in what the program can achieve. An effective program also requires being sensitive to parents' needs. No longer can we expect to have parent participation when we ignore parent's dominant language, i.e., giving parents an invitation to an open house in a language they cannot read; scheduling meetings at inconvenient hours; or not providing special services for parents to facilitate their coming i.e., child care and transportation services.

Teachers and administrators must also view a developmental role for themselves. They must change their attitudes and conceptions about what parent involvement is and what it should accomplish. Teachers who believe that parents have no place in the classroom and administrators who believe that parents are unable to participate in planning and decision-making will unlikely develop successful parent involvement programs.

STRATEGIES FOR INVOLVING LANGUAGE MINORITY PARENTS

Ways educators can effectively involve minority language parents in educational processes are suggested below.

Schoolwide Activities:
1. Workshops for parents which introduce them to the policies, procedures and programs of the school. These workshops and orientations should be reality-based and undertaken in a spirit of wanting to sincerely bring about a cooperative interaction. Most parents want to know and would do a better job of parenting and educating if they knew how.
2. Family nights, cultural dinners, carnivals and festivities, covered dish dinners, and other activities serve to bring parents and the community to the school in non-threatening, entertaining and informative ways.
3. Adult education classes which provide the community with opportunities to learn about a wide range of subjects including language courses. Many school districts have designated certain schools as community schools which seek to provide such programs.
4. Training programs for parents which give them skills as classroom aides and participants in school activities such as clubs and activity sponsors.
5. Support services such as car pools, babysitting, and other means of making attendance and involvement possible.

Teacher Activities:
1. Training sessions for parents conducted by teachers. Quite often parents are reluctant to be involved in the activities of their children, simply because they are not knowledgeable about the curriculum. Teachers can conduct workshops for parents who want to know how to help their children in certain subject areas, e.g., reading. Determination of specific workshop content can be based on a survey of parent needs and desires.
2. Increasing communication between teacher and parent through letters and notes, phone calls, and newsletters (available in the parents' native language).
3. Visiting children's homes so that meaningful and mutually beneficial information can be exchanged by all parties involved. Additionally, such visits serve to create greater cultural understanding.
4. Training and orienting parents to help in individual classrooms.
5. Sponsoring activities which encourage parent-child interaction in school-related activities.
6. Using the talents of parents to extend, enrich, and make practical everyday school life and work. Parents have career skills and hobbies which can compliment school and classroom curricula.

Parent Activities:
1. Volunteering time and services in classrooms and schools as aides, monitors, clerks, media coordinators and tutors.
2. Sharing hobbies and career talents in classrooms.
3. Becoming participants in advisory groups, task forces, and other programs of the school designed to encourage community/ school/ parent interaction.
4. Helping organize and operate the school's volunteer program.

Special Services

1. Providing child care services to facilitate parents attendance at school functions and participation in special programs. These child care services can be operated and staffed by parents.

2. Providing a parent resource room in the school where parents can meet, talk about their concerns and feel at home while at school. The parent resource room should be comfortably furnished and have books, newsletters and curriculum materials in the parents native language.

While there is literally no end to the type and kind of parent involvement activities that are possible, the coordinated efforts of everyone is required to build an effective and meaningful program for language minority parent involvement. Such a meaningful relationship can bring about a change in the state of education and provide mutual benefits for all concerned: parents, children, teachers and the community. The challenge and the choice is ours. We can continue to give all the old excuses for not involving parents, or we can begin now to develop genuine linkages with parents and the community. Parents *can make a difference* in their children's education. With our assistance, the language minority parent is willing and able to join teachers in a productive partnership.

REFERENCES

ARISSO,M. AND GARCIA, D., "Adjustment, Development and Parent Training Program" paper presented at the *10th Annual International Bilingual Bicultural Education Conference* (NABE), Boston, May 23-30. Unpublished Manuscript, 1981. (Available from [author's address]).

GALLUP, G.H. The 13th Annual Gallup Poll of the Attitudes Toward the Public Schools. Phi Delta Kapan 1981, *63* (1), 34.

MORRISON, G.S. *Parent Involvement in the Home, School and Community.* Columbus, Ohio: Charles E. Merrill Publishing Co., 1978.